New Canadian Readings

OUT OF THE BACKGROUND

Readings on Canadian Native History

New Canadian Readings

OUT OF THE BACKGROUND

Readings on Canadian Native History

Edited by
Robin Fisher and Kenneth Coates

Copp Clark Pitman Ltd.
A Longman Company
Toronto

ISBN 0-7730-4767-0

Editing: Camilla Jenkins
Design: Kathy Cloutier and Susan Coull
Cover: Detail of a totem pole. Courtesy of the Royal Ontario Museum,
    Toronto, Canada
Typesetting: Compeer Typographic Services Limited
Printing and Binding: Alger Press Limited

Canadian Cataloguing in Publication Data

Main entry under title:

Out of the background : readings on Canadian
   native history

(New Canadian readings)
Bibliography: p.
ISBN 0-7730-4767-0

1. Indians of North America — Canada — History.
I. Fisher, Robin, 1946–   . II. Coates, Kenneth,
1956–   . III. Series.

E78.C2088 1988   971'.00497   C87-095111-4

Copp Clark Pitman
2775 Matheson Blvd. East
Mississauga, Ontario
L4W 4P7

Associated companies:
   Longman Group Ltd., London
   Longman Inc., New York
   Longman Cheshire Pty., Melbourne
   Longman Paul Pty., Auckland

Printed and bound in Canada

FOREWORD

New Canadian Readings is an on-going series of inexpensive books intended to bring some of the best recent work by this country's scholars to the attention of students in Canada. Each volume consists of ten or more articles or book sections, carefully selected to present a fully-formed thesis about some critical aspect of Canadian development. Where useful, public documents or even private letters and statistical materials may be used as well to convey a different and fresh perspective.

The authors of the readings selected for inclusion in this volume (and all the others in the series) are all first-rank scholars, those who are doing the hard research that is rapidly changing our understanding of this country. Quite deliberately, the references for each selection have been retained, thus making additional research as easy as possible.

Like the authors of the individual articles, the editors of each volume are also scholars of note, completely up-to-date in their areas of specialization and, as the introductions demonstrate, fully aware of the changing nature of the debates within their professions and genres of research. The list of additional readings provided by the editor of each volume will steer readers to materials that could not be included because of space limitations.

This series will continue into the foreseeable future, and the General Editor is pleased to invite suggestions for additional topics.

J.L. Granatstein
General Editor

CONTENTS

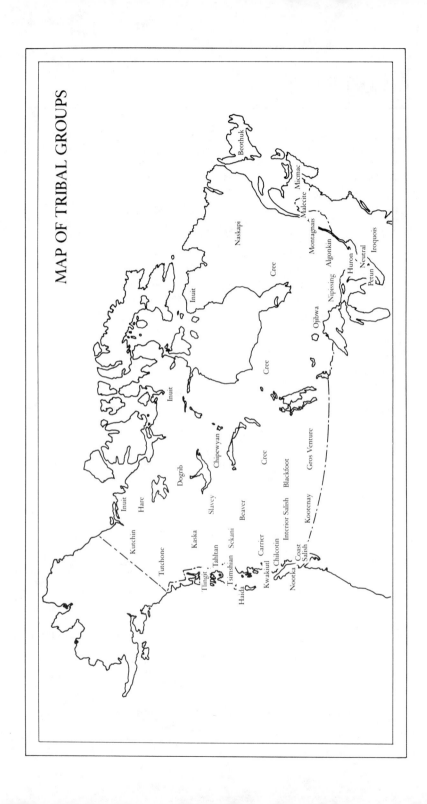

MAP OF TRIBAL GROUPS

INTRODUCTION

This collection of essays demonstrates the vigor and diversity of recent historical writing on Canada's native peoples. As Bruce Trigger points out in the first article, historians have been writing about the first Canadians for generations, and yet it is only recently that native people have stepped forward to become important players in the pageant of the past. Earlier in this century writers were fond of describing "the Indian background to Canadian history" and even as late as 1971 James Walker deplored the fact that the native people of Canada had either been completely ignored by historians or treated in terms of negative stereotypes.[1] Since the early 1970s, however, there has been a great deal of exciting new writing on the history of native people in Canada. This development is closely related to the upsurge of interest in social history, as Canadian historians have become less preoccupied with the self-proclaimed winners of the past and more interested in the disadvantaged and the dispossessed. The new literature partly results from the techniques of history and anthropology being brought together to form the hybrid discipline of ethnohistory.[2] And, since the past cannot be separated from the present, the recent interest in Indian history has also been associated with the growing assertiveness of native people themselves.

The increasing recognition of the role of native people in Canada's past does not mean that they have been fully integrated into the pages of the nation's history books. Although Indians may now play a larger role in regional histories, new writing on native people has not yet forced a major reinterpretation of mainstream Canadian history as, say, the American historian Francis Jennings did when he wrote *The Invasion of America*.[3] Thus James Walker noted again in 1983 that Indians were still largely absent from the general histories of Canada.[4] Nor do native people fare any better in popular histories. As the controversy over Peter Newman's *Company of Adventurers* shows, academics who write about Indian history are often distressed about the way in which the so-called popular writers use, or misuse, their work.[5] And there is still very little history, as distinct from polemics about the past, written by Indians.[6] Clearly much remains to be done, and yet this collection of essays is now possible because there is a substantial and stimulating body of historical literature on Canada's native peoples.

We have brought together some of the best of this new writing in order to indicate the various directions that it has taken. Each one of these articles has something unique and important to say about native history and many of them present new methodological approaches to the subject. Naturally this collection is not exhaustive, and there are significant topics that are not covered. There is still much more work and more energetic debate on the early contact and fur trading period than there is on the later phase of settlement and dispossession. There is very little good historical writing on the twentieth century, and the work that has been done tends to focus on government policy and native education, often from the perspective of administrators rather than Indians.[7] There are comparatively few scholars working on the North and the Inuit are virtually excluded from the historical literature. While a little less than one third of Canada's Indian population lives in British Columbia, that province does not have anything like one third of the nation's historians of native people.

The unevenness of the regional coverage is particularly significant since one of the most obvious points to emerge from the new writing is that Canada's native peoples represent a great diversity of cultures and their historical experience has been vastly different from place to place and from time to time. Because historians are dealing with many distinct native histories, common patterns are elusive and general rules always seem to have an exception to prove them. This book, then, reflects both the strengths and the weaknesses of the recent historical writing.

Within the limitations imposed by the historical literature, we have for the most part included work that focusses on the native people themselves. Many of these articles deal with Indians rather than with Europeans. Obviously, since their arrival in North America, the new-comers have been a major and increasingly important factor in native history. Because they cannot be ignored, at least one essay deals with European attitudes towards Indians, one examines government policy, and the European as a component in Indian history is recognized by all the authors. But most of the articles in this collection emphasize what some historians like to call "the Indian side of the story." Since views of the past are not determined by race, there are not, in fact, two exclusive sides to this story. The Indians and Inuit did, however, play an important role in the past. Perhaps the clearest and most consistent point to emerge from the recent writing is that, throughout their history, Canada's native people have not merely been standing on the stage, they have had active and decisive roles. In the long run the European may have brought significant changes to their way of life, but native people have not just been bit players responding and reacting to the European presence. Rather they have influenced the development of the plot by acting out of their own self-interest and according to their own norms and priorities. In many instances they have caused the Europeans to change their ways. If this collection of essays has a central point, it is that native people have been a determining factor in Canadian history.

Some scholars have argued that, because history is an intellectual tool of European culture, it cannot be used to fashion a valid understanding of the past as native people experienced it.[8] Or, to put it more crudely, Europeans cannot write Indian history. Obviously this book is a denial of that argument and it need not detain us long here. It is, however, important to remember the extent to which our view of the past is determined by our cultural background. Bruce Trigger makes this point in his article, "The Historians' Indian: Native Americans in Canadian Historical Writing from Charlevoix to the Present." Trigger observes that historical writing on native people in Canada has a long tradition and he reminds us that historians have not always seen native people in negative terms. When the Indians were a significant component of the population and were useful as allies, they were treated seriously and respectfully by historians. Much more derogatory views of native people developed in the nineteenth century as the Indians ceased to be needed as allies and both French and English Canadian historians were influenced by evolutionary and racist ideas. Views of the past are thus partly determined by the present. One historian, who writes about the indigenous people of the south Pacific, has pointed out that, because history is what we choose to see, "the past has no independent existence."[9] Indeed, it might well be argued that history has some of the same functions in western cultures as mythology does in Indian cultures: it validates the past in terms that are meaningful for the present.

That is not to say, of course, that the historians of one particular age will have uniform views about the past. The second part of Bruce Trigger's article introduces some of the issues that are being debated, often with great enthusiasm, by the current generation of ethnohistorians. The nature of the new ethnohistory, the need for historians to use a wide variety of sources while recognizing all of their limitations, the economics of the fur trade relationship, the impact of disease, the influence of missionaries and Christianity, the nature of native beliefs, and the notions of dependency, coercion, and domination, are all matters touched on by Trigger and covered more fully by subsequent essays in this volume.

The first group of native people to make contact with Europeans was one that never became part of Canada. The Beothuck disappeared from the scene long before Newfoundland became a province and their unhappy story is discussed by L.F.S. Upton in "The Extermination of the Beothucks of Newfoundland." There is, perhaps, something about islands that makes possible the complete elimination of the indigenous population for, as Upton notes, in the Caribbean Islands and in Tasmania the aborigines were also completely destroyed. But obviously not all islands were depopulated. On Vancouver Island, for example, the Indian population was too large and the cultures too resilient to be destroyed. And therein seems to lie the nub of the problem. By all accounts the Beothuck were a small and scattered population and they tended, obviously with good reason, to withdraw from sustained relations with Europeans. Thus Upton concludes his article with the startling suggestion that the Beothuck disappeared because they experienced too little, rather than too much, contact with Europeans. The implication is that the presence of newcomers from Europe may have been a mixed blessing, but was not always a complete disaster for native people. While the Beothuck were decimated, Micmac groups from Cape Breton came to Newfoundland and, having closer contacts with the Europeans, managed to survive.[10] The Beothuck were neither the first nor the last group of indigenous people to be destroyed by European expansion around the world. Fortunately in the Canadian context their fate, while not unique, was extreme, and so the notion that European contact was not always destructive for native people is frequently expressed in work on the subject.

This view is not, however, shared by Calvin Martin, who sees European contact in very negative terms. Martin has made a considerable contribution to Indian history by establishing a new way of looking at the early contact period. Not all historians agree with his conclusions, but he has prompted many scholars to go back to their research and to think again about their own ideas. In his article, "The European Impact on the Culture of a Northeastern Algonquian Tribe: An Ecological Interpretation," he begins by making the point that it is very important to understand that for native people culture and environment were closely intertwined. He calls his approach "cultural ecology." He then goes on to describe in some detail how, for the Micmac Indians, the bond with nature was forged and maintained by their spiritual beliefs. Given the undoubtedly close relationship that existed between Indian people and the natural environment, Calvin Martin sets out to explain why, with the development of the fur trade, the Indians proceeded to kill vast numbers of animals. What, he asks, were the reasons for overkill? He rejects the perhaps obvious explanation that the Indians were encouraged to destroy the animal population simply by the economic incentive of the fur trade, and he suggests instead that the causes were much more complex. His argument is that Indian spirituality, the traditional bond with the ecosystem, was destroyed by European contact. Introduced diseases, missionary Christianity, and the demands of fur traders formed an "unholy" trinity of influences that had a destructive impact on the Indians. According to Martin, disease depleted their numbers, Christianity eroded their spiritual beliefs, and the fur trade provided the economic incentive and the technology that made overkill possible. Europeans, in short, corrupted the Indians' traditional relationship with the environment.

While few would quarrel with his general points about the need to see traditional Indian cultures within their environmental context and to understand the nature of Indian spirituality, the details of Calvin Martin's specific argument have been very controversial. He has developed his case more fully and applied it more widely in his book entitled *Keepers of the Game*.[11] A number of scholars have, however, questioned his thesis. Some insist that he does not provide enough evidence to substantiate the links between disease, despiritualization, and destruction of game, even among the Algonkian tribes for whom he makes the case most strongly. Others argue that, whether or not his interpretation works for the Algonkian it definitely cannot be applied to other Indian groups and therefore does not have the more general explanatory value that Martin seems to want to attribute to it.[12] At the end of the article reprinted here, as in *Keepers of the Game*, he asserts that "this grim tale was to be repeated many times along the moving Indian–white frontier."[13] Because of the great diversity of the historical experience of Canada's native people, such generalizations are, at best, of limited value.

Calvin Martin's work also raises, although it certainly does not resolve, the difficult problem of the impact of European disease on native people. There is considerable debate about both the demographic and the psychological effect of disease. Along with many other scholars, Martin believes that new diseases had a catastrophic impact on susceptible Indian populations. Some groups were completely wiped out and most were decimated. While this is the generally held view, and no one doubts that the Indian population did decline, a few historians have urged the need for more caution. They draw attention to the difficulties involved in estimating the precontact population and therefore the exact rate of decline once the epidemics struck, and they remind us that there was great regional variation in the impact of disease.[14] There is even less unanimity about Martin's supposition that the Indians' response to the onslaught of disease was to reject their indigenous beliefs because they no longer seemed to be efficacious. There was a range of native responses to disease, and among some groups the threat led to a reassertion, rather than a denial, of traditional spirituality.

Bruce Trigger presents a much more subtle interpretation of the impact of early European contact than Calvin Martin does, and one that is firmly grounded in detailed evidence. His conclusions are also more satisfactory because he clearly focusses his attention on one Indian group: the Huron. Trigger is the most successful exponent of ethnohistory in Canada and his masterwork on the Huron, *The Children of Aataentsic*, is a model of what can be achieved by putting together historical and anthropological sources.[15] In his article included here, "The Road to Affluence: A Reassessment of Early Huron Responses to European Contact," he emphasizes the crucial role that archaeological evidence can play in getting at the historical problem of change over time. In particular, archaeology can take us back into the period prior to direct European contact that is virtually inaccessible to the historian who relies solely on written documents.

On the basis of the archaeological evidence, Trigger argues that there had been major changes in Huron culture before the first contact and recorded observations by Europeans. All cultures are constantly changing and therefore the first Europeans to describe a particular Indian group were not writing about a pristine culture that was frozen in time and awaiting the arrival of outsiders before change could begin.[16] Furthermore, partly because Indian cultures were already changing, not all change that came as a result of direct contact was destructive. In the case of the Huron, Trigger shows that the indirect trade of the protohistoric phase immediately prior to contact was more disruptive than the trade that developed after direct contact was established with Europeans in 1609. There were major cultural adjustments in the years before 1609, followed by a period of renewed stability and affluence after the establishment of direct trading contact. This relative tranquillity lasted for perhaps thirty years before the Huron faced a new set of crises. When the Jesuit missionaries convinced French government officials to interfere in Huron culture in an effort to convert them to Christianity, the strain was too much. The Huron became vulnerable and divided, and eventually they were dispersed by the Iroquois in 1649. But the years of direct trade immediately after 1609 had been a time of cultural florescence for the Huron. It has been similarly argued that, two hundred years later on the northwest coast, the fur trade stimulated Indian cultures.[17] In his important recent book, *Natives and Newcomers*, Bruce Trigger develops the idea that it was the fur traders who made a real effort to understand the Indians and who played an important role in establishing good relations with them, and so he suggests that they should replace the missionaries and government officials as the heroes of the "heroic age" of New France.[18]

Among other things, Trigger's conclusion implies that we should not generalize about Europeans any more than we should about Indians. Different groups of Europeans had distinctive attitudes towards native people that were, in large part, a consequence of their various intentions as they came to the new world. Several historians have studied European perceptions of native people in Canada.[19] Cornelius Jaenen, on the other hand, has tackled the much more tenuous task of describing Indian attitudes towards Europeans. He recognizes the problem that is faced by every historian who writes about native people: that it is very difficult to understand what is going on in the minds of the people of one culture on the basis of documents produced by individuals from another culture. The written record left by Europeans is the major source on Indian attitudes. Archaeological evidence, for example, does not tell us as much about what the Indians were thinking as it does about what they were making or what they were doing. So the intellectual historian must rely largely on written records which, of course, means European records. This issue is not confined to the history of indigenous peoples. European historians encounter the same problem when they write the history of inarticulate peasant movements. In the case of the Indians of Canada there is a larger cultural gap between the people being studied and those producing the written record, but Jaenen's article is predicated on the assumption that, however biased they may be, the written records left by Europeans are not completely worthless. Even the letters and journals of missionaries, who are often said to have had the most limited vision of any European observers, provide the historian with valuable and valid information.

Having acknowledged the limitations of his sources, Jaenen goes on to describe "Amerindian Views of French Culture in the Seventeenth Century." It is perhaps surprising to find that Indian opinions about the French were very mixed. There were some aspects of the French way of life that Indians may have admired. Apparently they were impressed with the Europeans' technology and some of their material goods, shared the French regard for ceremonial, and respected some aspects of their treatment of the sick. But Jaenen also provides a long catalogue of French traits that the Indians disliked. Among other things, the Indians were unimpressed with the physical appearance and stamina of the French, suspected them of being carriers of disease and death, distrusted the missionaries as sorcerers, accused the French of having low standards of morality and personal hygiene, criticized their attitudes towards children, disapproved of their system of law and government, and held a low opinion of French methods of warfare. In short, the Indians had many of the same negative attitudes towards the French as the French, or the English for that matter, had towards them. It is clear from the historical literature that Europeans invariably believed in the pre-eminence of their own culture. Jaenen makes the less obvious point that the whites frequently failed to convince the Indians of the self-evident superiority of European culture. During the early contact phase the Indians did not simply cave in to European ideas, but often remained confident in their own world view and continued to think that in many ways they were superior to the newcomers. In contrast to Calvin Martin, who argues that the Indian belief system collapsed soon after the arrival of the European, Jaenen implies that the Indians were much more resilient.

The effort to establish the nature of Indian attitudes has also been fundamental to the debate among historians about the Indians' role in the fur trade. Much of this argument turns on the question of whether Indian involvement in the fur trade can be understood in the same terms as one would use to describe European economic behaviour. The issue goes back at least as far as Harold Innis' pioneering work, first published in the 1930s, *The Fur Trade in Canada*.[20] While Innis acknowledged that the Indians were participants in the fur trade, he was too preoccupied with the Europeans to deal with the native fur traders in any detail. It was the historian of the Hudson's Bay Company, E.E. Rich, who opened up discussion of Indian motives for participating in the fur trade. In an article published in 1960, he argued that the Indians clearly had economic reasons for trading furs, but at the same time they did not respond like

Europeans to the price mechanism. According to Rich, when company traders raised the price paid to the Indians, they responded, not by bringing in more furs, but by offering fewer. The Indians had a finite demand for material necessities, so when the price they received for furs went up they did not have to produce as many pelts to meet their limited requirements.[21] Having taken this middle line, Rich is cited favourably by both sides in the ensuing debate.[22]

Some historians have pushed Rich's point much further and argued that Indian fur traders were not really motivated by economics at all. Calvin Martin, as we have already seen, claims that Indian involvement in the fur trade had little to do with economic factors and a great deal to do with the breakdown of indigenous spiritual beliefs. Abraham Rotstein rejects the economic argument altogether. He insists that the fur trade should not be seen as a supermarket in the wilderness and that the Indians did not behave like consumers. Rotstein suggests instead that the Indians saw the fur trade in terms of non-economic factors such as traditional politics and ritualized gift exchange.[23]

Arthur Ray, on the other hand, argues that Indian traders behaved most economically. In "Indians as Consumers in the Eighteenth Century," he shows that Indians not only responded to price, but also exercised a great deal of control over it. The Indians were shrewd bargainers who were quite able to take advantage of economic opportunities and were, in this respect, the equal of the European traders who came to deal with them. They were able to manipulate competition between fur trading companies and they were keen judges of the quality of the goods that they took in trade. They either rejected or clearly expressed their dissatisfaction with those items that were not up to standard. Because the Hudson's Bay Company had to meet Indian demands, it had to adjust its trading methods and modify the goods that it sold no matter how reluctant the remote London Committee may have been to make changes in policy. The Indians were not, according to Ray, simple minded savages who were cheated by greedy traders. Arthur Ray has elaborated the argument that he outlines here in much greater detail in his book written with Donald Freeman entitled *"Give Us Good Measure,"* in which he examines the economic interaction, during the early years of contact, between the Indians around Hudson Bay and the Hudson's Bay Company.[24] Whereas "Indians As Consumers" offers impressionistic evidence, *"Give Us Good Measure"* presents similar findings based on a computer analysis of statistical data taken from the Company's account books. In both this article and his book, Ray takes the story up to 1763, leaving the implication that one cannot necessarily generalize about the entire fur trading period. Arthur Ray is not, however, alone in his views about the nature of the trade. Other historians, who have examined other areas during different periods, have come to similar conclusions about the astuteness of fur trading Indians.[25]

The debate between those who emphasize economic factors and those who advocate non-economic reasons for Indian involvement in the fur trade sometimes seems to degenerate into an either/or controversy between the so-called formalists and substantivists. As is usually the case in human history, motives were probably mixed and cannot always be separated. Just as in European society, the fact that people engaged in trade for economic reasons does not exclude the possibility that they also sought to enhance their prestige. In many Indian cultures wealth and authority were closely associated and so Indian traders presumably added to both when they struck good deals with European traders. Above all, this new work on the fur trade emphasizes the need to be aware of the complexities of both groups involved in cultural contact.

The same general point, that there are two sides to everything, is made by the work of those historians who have examined the role of native women in the fur trade. These scholars have concentrated on the fur trade as a social, rather than an economic system, but they too show that the Indians played a crucial and active part. In " 'Women in Between': Indian Women in Fur Trade Society in Western Canada," Sylvia Van Kirk begins by recognizing that historians writing about Indian women face a double problem with their sources. Because the original accounts of fur trade marriages were written by European males there is both a cultural and a gender gap between the observer and the observed. Yet here too, although the documentary sources have limitations, they are not worthless. Van Kirk is able to tease out a great deal of information on the nature of fur trade marriages. Indian women took the initiative in establishing relationships with fur traders and, no less than the European males, had their own good reasons for establishing marriage alliances. For the Indians there were economic advantages in establishing kinship connections with company men, and native women could achieve positions of considerable influence through these marriages. In some ways they may also have lived easier lives as the wives of fur traders, but it was by no means a bed of roses. Indian women who married fur traders often bore more children than they would have in native marriages, were more susceptible to European disease, and probably were more subject to the will of men. Generally, however, these marriages were lasting relationships and not just casual liaisons, although Van Kirk does suggest that during periods of intense competition between fur trading companies Indian women were sometimes treated as chattels.

The pattern of fur trade marriages did not remain constant. At the end of her article Sylvia Van Kirk briefly alludes to a point that she develops much more fully in her book on fur trade society called "*Many Tender Ties*."[26] In the later years of the fur trade in western Canada Indian women were replaced by mixed-blood girls, who were often the daughters of the first marriages, as the potential wives of fur traders. Then in the nineteenth century these country marriages and the racially mixed society that they produced were disrupted by the arrival of white women. Another historian of fur trade society, Jennifer Brown, has emphasized the differences between the marriage patterns and kinship relations of North West Company and Hudson's Bay Company traders.[27] These scholars then, also point out that monolithic interpretations of the fur trade will not do. Along with Arthur Ray, they show that the fur trade went through a number of distinct phases during the two hundred years during which it dominated western Canada. The historians writing about fur trade society have nevertheless clearly established the point that, in order to work as an economic system, the trade required the marriage of two cultures.

One of the most important ideas to emerge out of recent historical writing on the fur trade is that, far from being a disaster for native peoples, it was a mutually beneficial economic activity in which the Indians played a determining part.[28] Arthur Ray's call to consider the positive role of the Indians in the fur trade has now been answered by historians.[29] But, for most Indians, the fur trade did not last forever. In some parts of Canada, particularly the North, native people continue to hunt and trade furs to the present day, but wherever the land was suitable for agriculture the fur trader was eventually superseded by the farming settler. The timing was different in different parts of the country and the shift was more abrupt in some areas than others, but the arrival of settlers would always mark the beginning of the end of the fur trade. Settlers were, of course, much more numerous than fur traders, their economic intentions were very different, they brought more rapid and thorough-going change, they saw little need either to understand or to accommodate Indian ways, and they had greater power to force change. Whereas the fur trade involved the interplay of two cultures, settlement led to the domination and dispossession of the Indians by Europeans.

The transition from fur trade to settlement also brought a fundamental shift in European attitudes towards native peoples. As we have already seen, Bruce Trigger has argued that in eastern Canada in the seventeenth century the fur traders made more effort to understand the Indian way of life than did either the missionaries or government officials. He is describing a situation in which all three groups were present and influential at the same time. Robin Fisher looks at the changes in the "The Image of the Indian" on the west coast where, in the mid-nineteenth century, there was a sharp break between fur trade and settlement. He notes the complex relationship between attitudes and actions and the fact that people often act more on the basis of perceived image than actual reality. To the extent that one can generalize about the racial views of groups of people, he argues that fur traders who lived among the Indians for long periods had a greater understanding of, and sympathy for, native people than had the settlers who began arriving in the 1850s.

Settlers were much more prone to look at Indians through the lens of their own culture, and they dogmatically clung to their derogatory views about native people. In short, settlers were more prejudiced than fur traders, both in the sense that they prejudged native people, and in the sense that their attitudes towards them were more negative. Although the change from fur trade to settlement was more gradual than on the west coast, other historians have shown that there was a similar shift in the climate of opinion with the growth of the non-fur trading population at the Red River settlement.[30]

In his book, *Contact and Conflict*, Fisher's chapter on the image of the Indian is a prelude to a discussion of the wider effects of the shift from fur trade to settlement in British Columbia. In the far West, as elsewhere in Canada, hardening European attitudes were only one indication of the changed tenor of race relations after the coming of settlers. Native people also ceased to play an integral part in the economy as the fur trade declined. With the arrival of settlers, Indians were often seen as an obstacle in the way of new development and they were quickly shunted to the margins of the settler economy, where out of sight would be out of mind. Thus the argument that native people played an active role in Canadian society seems more difficult to sustain for areas affected by the advance of the settlement frontier.

There can be no doubt that settler domination had a drastic impact on native people. As the native population continued to decline, as Indian groups were deprived of most of their land and their livelihood, and as the pace of cultural change quickened beyond their control, it seemed that Canada's original peoples would become an irrelevant minority. Certainly Indian groups from the Maritimes to the west coast had less room to manoeuvre as the pressures of the settlement frontier closed in around them.[31] And yet native people did not simply passively succumb to this onslaught. Although their freedom of action was more and more tightly constrained, they still retained the ability, and often the will, to respond adaptively to the new situation. One historian has claimed that Indians provided a significant labour force for the development of the resource-based economy of British Columbia, and another has shown that, when they had the opportunity, northwest coast Indians could still be astute traders.[32]

But the fundamental conflict between native and non-native Canadians during the settlement phase was over land. The survival of both groups depended on land. Their traditional territory was crucial to the survival of native people, whether they were to maintain the old way of life or adapt to the new. Farming settlers needed to acquire land in order to establish and improve themselves and to create a new society. The conflict was one that was repeated in colonial situations all over the world, and at one level it was very simple. While the native people owned the land, the newcomers wanted it, and they had the power to take it. The details of the process of the dispossession of indigenous peoples in settlement colonies may have varied somewhat, but the outcome was always the same: the Europeans took what they wanted. Even on the Canadian Prairies, where it might seem that there was enough for everybody, the Indians were deprived of the land that was their life during the treaty-making and reservation period of the 1870s and 1880s.

In his article on "Canada's Subjugation of the Plains Cree, 1879–1885," John Tobias makes two major points about the manner in which the Indians were removed from the path of settlement. First he dismisses the notion that Canadian Indian policy was honourable and just.[33] He shows instead that the representatives of the federal government doggedly pursued the Prairie Indians until they were confined to tiny reserves and largely deprived of their independence. His second point is that, in spite of this pressure, the Indians did not passively acquiesce to every government demand. On the contrary, they were active and flexible in promoting their own self-interest. The capacity to adapt creatively to the European presence that had characterized the Indian response to the fur trade persisted into the settlement period. Indian leaders on the Prairies initiated the treaty-making process and, bargaining initially from a position of some strength, made every effort to modify the proposals that government officials laid before them. Some Cree groups saw the need for change, and made every effort to adopt an agricultural way of life. But they were never given a chance. Their efforts were systematically subverted by the parsimony and narrowness of federal officials.[34] The coercive pressure mounted until finally the government representatives of settler society took the opportunity provided by the turmoil of the Louis Riel uprising of 1885 to arrest Cree leaders and force their followers onto small reserves. Having been subjugated, the Cree became an administered people as the Department of Indian Affairs worked to reorganize their culture. On the face of it at least, they were now subject to the will and interference of the government in nearly every aspect of their daily lives.

Along with government officials, missionaries have also been seen as particularly aggressive agents of cultural change, who strove mightily to convert native people to Christianity and to turn them into red-skinned replicas of Europeans. Like the bureaucrats, they have also tended to dominate historical interpretation, even among historians determined not to be influenced by their views, because of the sheer volume of the written record that they have left.[35] Recently, however, scholars have become more concerned to separate missionary objectives and rhetoric from the evidence of what they actually achieved among specific groups of native people. Clarence Bolt's "The Conversion of the Port Simpson Tsimshian: Indian Control or Missionary Manipulation?" is an example of this approach. He shows that the Indians were not necessarily passive followers of missionary dogma. The Port Simpson Tsimshian invited the Methodist missionary Thomas Crosby to their community for their own reasons and they followed his teaching only as long as it seemed to be bringing the results that they wanted. Even then, Bolt suggests that the Tsimshian adoption of missionary culture may have been a veneer under which many traditional ways continued as before. When Crosby failed to deliver, particularly in negotiations with governments on the land issue, his influence soon declined. Even the religious life of the village developed outside of his control. This article makes the important point that the Indians' response to Christianity and social change was often very different from what the missionaries advocated and expected. And it is the Indian perspective that demands more attention from historians.

Obviously not all native people were subjugated, in spite of the often combined efforts of government officials and missionaries. Some Indian groups were given the latitude to maintain much of their traditional way of life until well into the twentieth century. In "Best Left as Indians: The Federal Government and the Indians of the Yukon, 1894–1950," Ken Coates presents an argument that is, in part at least, similar to Bolt's view of the missionaries. Coates draws our attention to the gap that often existed between the formulation of Indian policy in Ottawa and its application on the ground, particularly in remote areas. The Indian Act was not always used to sweep every native group into the ash can of assimilation. In the Yukon, central policy was modified to suit local conditions and most Indians in the territory remained hunters and trappers long after the Klondike gold rush first opened up the area. While agents of the federal government provided limited welfare and medical assistance, education, which in other parts of Canada was a major means of acculturating native people, was given a low priority in the Yukon. The federal government intervened more vigorously in the lives of Yukon Indians, as it did in the lives of all Canadians, after 1945, but until then the impact of Indian policy was limited in this northern territory. It is, of course, true that the non-Indian population of the Yukon was also small and concentrated and so there was less pressure on the federal government to bring Indians under its control than there was in the South. Nevertheless Coates does suggest that his approach might well be applied to other parts of Canada. Obviously Indian policy was not applied as rigorously in the North as it was in more settled areas, but historians looking at southern Canada should also pay more attention to the detail of how policy was worked out at the local level rather than merely describing the broad concepts that were developed in Ottawa.

Distance may have protected the native people of the North from the full impact of government policy, but the economy of resource development knows no limits and it posed a serious threat to the livelihood of even the most isolated groups of hunters. And yet, as Hugh Brody shows in his beautiful and evocative book *Maps and Dreams*, at least some of the condemned have escaped execution.[36] His book is based on the eighteen months that he spent living among the Beaver Indians of the Peace River country of northeast British Columbia. One of Canada's last frontiers, the Peace River is an area where, in comparatively recent times, new dreams of wealth from exploiting the resources of the land have been superimposed on the traditional dreams of a hunting way of life. Maps with straight lines and square sections have been drawn to replace the circuitous routes of the hunt. But although it has rearranged the landscape, the advance of the new frontier of exploitation has not completely eliminated the old ways of the hunter. Brody's chapter, "Maps of Dreams," affirms the native people's enduring presence on the land. By withdrawing to the bush the Beaver Indians can escape free and clean to a world where old skills and old dreams still persist, and where the connections with the past continue, even if tenuously. His chapter is also, perhaps, a comment on Calvin Martin's view that the advent of the European always destroyed the Indians' close relationship with the natural environment.

Brody does not, however, simply paint a romantic picture of native people withdrawing to the natural world. The Beaver Indians also have had to deal with the newcomers to the area. While the odd numbered chapters of *Maps and Dreams* depict the Indian way of life, the even numbered chapters are about the new forces that are impinging upon them. Like the sections of Brody's book, the two societies remain separated but at the same time interrelated. The Indians have developed various strategies for accommodating the new order represented by resource towns such as Fort St. John. As others have also shown for other areas, self-images based on a degree of mutual ignorance have facilitated limited interaction between the distinct communities of town and reserve.[37] After centuries of interaction in Canada, native and non-native are still separated, which is a testament to both native survival and European intransigence.

Whatever the barriers that separate them from the rest of the population, most native people in Canada no longer have the option of withdrawal as a way of coping with non-native society. They have to accommodate the wider Canadian community and come to terms with it from day to day. Increasingly in recent years, they must also deal with that community on a political level. Noel Dyck's piece on "Negotiating the Indian 'Problem' " shows that native people are still doing what they have been doing since the first Europeans arrived in their midst: working out ways to communicate with the rest of Canadian society. They are still trying to break through the layers of misunderstanding and presumed knowledge. This article also takes us back to one of the points with which we began by showing how the recollection of the past has become entangled in the issues of today. Past problems are now current issues and so remembering, or writing history, "can be an act with an ethical purpose."[38] As the past has become a major factor in the assertion of native claims, native and non-native historians alike are being called upon as interpreters in both the legal and the political arenas. History has, in short, become relevant. Since the past is what we see, and we usually see what we are looking for, it has become very important that historians see clearly.

In his book *The Fourth World*, George Manuel, a Shuswap leader from British Columbia, presents his view of the native past and present.[39] Published in 1974 before aboriginal rights were unsatisfactorily written into the patriated Canadian constitution of 1982, Manuel's book also emphasizes the survival of native people in Canada. Yet he likens their position not to that of either of the two "founding" races or to subsequent immigrant groups, but rather to the dispossessed indigenous people in other parts of the world. Unlike those in the Third World, the peoples of Manuel's Fourth World cannot identify themselves in terms of national boundaries even though they have a claim to lands that is equally longstanding. Other historians have pointed out the "colonial parallel" between Canada's native people and those in other parts of the world.[40] Manuel also draws on Canada's colonial past to compare the earlier demands of colonists for responsible government within the British Empire to the current insistence by native people for a say in their own affairs within Canada. Just as Canada evolved into a nation that is separate and equal within the British Commonwealth, her original inhabitants now want a similar status within the Canadian collective. Manuel argues that native ways have persisted and still have validity. Having survived the past, Canada's native people now want a place in the present that, among other things, recognizes their role in the nation's history.

Interpretations of the native past and present within Canada will no doubt change with time, but history will continue to be the link between the two. Societies, like individuals, without memories tend to be aimless, and so the understanding of the past will always be important both for its own sake and as a guide to the present. The role of native people in both the past and the present may well increase in the future: it surely cannot be diminished and it certainly cannot be ignored. But, while historians may provide insight into the present, it is not their function to predict the future. In this volume we have presented a view of the Canadian past as seen by those now writing the history of native people. It is a view of our history in which the native people have equal billing with other Canadians.

Notes

1. See Diamond Jenness, *The Indian Background of Canadian History*, Department of Mines and Resources Bulletin no. 86 (Ottawa: J.O. Patenaude, 1937); George F.G. Stanley, "The Indian Background of Canadian History," Canadian Historical Association, *Report* (1952): 14–21; and James W. St. G. Walker, "The Indian in Canadian Historical Writing," Canadian Historical Association, *Historical Papers* (1971): 21–47.

2. On the nature of ethnohistory see James Axtell, "Ethnohistory: An Historian's Viewpoint," *Ethnohistory* 26 (Winter 1979): 1–13; and Calvin Martin, "Ethnohistory: A Better Way to Write Indian History," *Western Historical Quarterly* 9 (January 1978): 41–56.

3. In his recent history of the Prairies, Gerald Friesen deals with native people in some detail, at least in the early years. See Gerald Friesen, *The Canadian Prairies: A History* (Toronto: University of Toronto Press, 1984), 10–44 and 129–61. Francis Jennings, *The Invasion of America: Indians, Colonialism, and the Cant of Conquest* (Chapel Hill: University of North Carolina Press, 1975). See Bruce Trigger's comments on this book below on 36.

4. James W. St. G. Walker, "The Indian in Canadian Historical Writing, 1972–1982," in *As Long as the Sun Shines and Water Flows: A Reader in Canadian Native Studies*, ed. Ian A.L. Getty and Antoine S. Lussier (Vancouver: University of British Columbia Press, 1983), 349–51.

5. Peter Newman, *The Company of Adventurers* (Toronto: Penguin Books, 1985); Jennifer Brown, "Newman's *Company of Adventurers* in Two Solitudes: A Look at Reviews and Responses," *Canadian Historical Review* 67 (December 1986):562–71.

6. A notable exception is Chief John Snow, *These Mountains are our Sacred Places: The Story of the Stoney Indians* (Toronto: Samuel Stevens, 1977). The best known example of the more polemical writing is Harold Cardinal, *The Unjust Society: The Tragedy of Canadian Indians* (Edmonton: Hurtig, 1969), which was written in response to the 1969 federal government white paper on Indian affairs. Cardinal is not unmindful of the past, but neither his primary concern nor his approach is historical.

7. For an introduction to this writing see Robert J. Surtees, *Canadian Indian Policy: A Selected Bibliography* (Bloomington: Indiana University Press, 1982); Jean Barman, Yvonne Herbert, and Don McCaskill, eds., *Indian Education in Canada*, vol. 1, *The Legacy* (Vancouver: University of British Columbia Press, 1986), and *Indian Education in Canada*, vol. 2, *The Challenge* (Vancouver: University of British Columbia Press, 1986). A recent example of this focus on policy and policy makers is E. Brian Titley, *A Narrow Vision: Duncan Campbell Scott and the Administration of Indian Affairs in Canada* (Vancouver: University of British Columbia Press, 1986).

8. Peter Munz, "The Purity of the Historical Method: Some Sceptical Reflections on the Current Enthusiasm for the History of Non-European Societies," *The New Zealand Journal of History* 5 (April 1971):1–17. The question is also raised in the introduction to Calvin Martin, ed., *The American Indian and the Problem of History* (New York: Oxford University Press, 1987), 16.

9. K.R. Howe, *Where the Waves Fall: A New South Sea Islands History from First Settlement to Colonial Rule* (Sydney: George Allen and Unwin, 1984), xii and 312.

10. For an account of Micmac history see L.F.S. Upton's *Micmacs and Colonists: Indian–White Relations in the Maritimes, 1713–1867* (Vancouver: University of British Columbia Press, 1979).

11. Calvin Martin, *Keepers of the Game: Indian–Animal Relationships and the Fur Trade* (Berkeley and Los Angeles: University of California Press, 1978).

12. For the various criticisms of Calvin Martin's argument see Shepard Krech III, ed., *Indians, Animals and the Fur Trade: A Critique of Keepers of the Game* (Athens, Georgia: University of Georgia Press, 1981).

13. See below, 82; and Martin, *Keepers of the Game*, 65.

14. See, for example, Bruce G. Trigger, *Natives and Newcomers: Canada's "Heroic Age" Reconsidered* (Kingston: McGill-Queen's University Press, 1985), 231–51; and Robin Fisher, *Contact and Conflict: Indian–European Relations in British Columbia, 1774–1890* (Vancouver: University of British Columbia Press, 1977), 21–23 and 44–45.

15. Bruce G. Trigger, *The Children of Aataentsic: A History of the Huron People to 1660* (Montreal: McGill-Queen's University Press, 1976). In the introduction Trigger clearly outlines his methodology and discusses some of the issues involved in writing ethnohistory, 1–26.

16. The same general point is made about the Prairies by Olive Patricia Dickason, "A Historical Reconstruction for the Northwestern Plains," *Prairie Forum* 5 (Spring 1980):19–37.

17. See for example, Wilson Duff, *The Indian History of British Columbia*, vol. 1, *The Impact of the White Man*, Anthropology in British Columbia Memoir no. 5 (Victoria: Provincial Museum, 1964), 53–59.

18. Trigger, *Natives and Newcomers*, 298–343.

19. See, for example, Robin Fisher, "The Image of the Indian," below 167–189. Olive Patricia Dickason, *The Myth of the Savage and the Beginnings of French Colonialism in the Americas* (Edmonton: University of Alberta Press, 1984); and Cornelius J. Jaenen himself in "French Attitudes towards Native Society," *Old Trails and New Directions: Papers of the Third North American Fur Trade Conference*, ed. Carol M. Judd and Arthur J. Ray (Toronto: University of Toronto Press, 1980), 59–72, and also *Friend and Foe: Aspects of French–Amerindian Cultural Contact in the Sixteenth and Seventeenth Centuries* (Toronto: McClelland and Stewart, 1976).

20. Harold A. Innis, *The Fur Trade in Canada: An Introduction to Canadian Economic History* (Toronto: University of Toronto Press, 1956).

21. E.E. Rich, "Trade Habits and Economic Motivation Among the Indians of North America," *Canadian Journal of Economics and Political Science* 26 (1960):35–53.

22. Martin, *Keepers of the Game*, 10; and Arthur J. Ray and Donald B. Freeman, *"Give Us Good Measure": An Economic Analysis of Relations between the Indians and the Hudson's Bay Company before 1763* (Toronto: University of Toronto Press, 1978), 5.

23. A. Rotstein, "Trade and Politics: An Institutional Approach," *Western Canadian Journal of Anthroplogy* 3 (1972):1–28.

24. Ray and Freeman, *"Give Us Good Measure."* Ray also discusses the economics of the fur trade more generally on the Prairies in Arthur J. Ray, *Indians and the Fur Trade: Their Role as Trappers, Hunters, and Middlemen in the Lands Southwest of Hudson's Bay 1660–1870* (Toronto: University of Toronto Press, 1974), 125–65.

25. See, for example, Fisher, *Contact and Conflict*, 1–48; Paul C. Thistle, *Indian–European Trade Relations in the Lower Saskatchewan River Region* (Winnipeg: University of Manitoba Press, 1986); and Daniel Francis and Toby Morantz, *Partners in Furs: A History of the Fur Trade in Eastern James Bay, 1600–1870* (Kingston and Montreal: McGill-Queen's University Press, 1983), 167–71.

26. Sylvia Van Kirk, *"Many Tender Ties": Women in Fur Trade Society in Western Canada, 1670–1870* (Winnipeg: Watson and Dwyer, 1980).

27. Jennifer S.H. Brown, *Strangers in Blood: Fur Trade Company Families in Indian Country* (Vancouver: University of British Columbia Press, 1980).

28. Not all historians agree with this interpretation. Calvin Martin still argues that the fur trade was a disaster, but he is wrong when he says that all scholars agree with him. See Martin, *Keepers of the Game*, 2.

29. Arthur Ray, "Fur Trade History as an Aspect of Native History," in *One Century Later: Western Canadian Reserve Indians Since Treaty 7*, ed. Ian A.L. Getty and Donald B. Smith (Vancouver: University of British Columbia Press, 1978), 7.

30. Van Kirk, *"Many Tender Ties,"* 201–42; Frits Pannekoek, "The Anglican Church and the Disintegration of Red River Society, 1818–1870," *The West and the Nation: Essays in Honour of W. L. Morton*, ed. Carl Berger and Ramsay Cook (Toronto: McClelland and Stewart, 1976):72–90.

31. Upton, *Micmacs and Colonists*, 127–81; Fisher, *Contact and Conflict*, 95–211. L.F.S. Upton makes the same general point when he compares the two coasts in "Contact and Conflict on the Atlantic and Pacific Coasts of Canada," *BC Studies*, no. 45 (Spring 1980):109–15.

32. Rolf Knight, *Indians at Work: An Informal History of Native Indian Labour in British Columbia, 1858–1930* (Vancouver: New Star Books, 1978); Douglas Cole, "Tricks of the Trade: Northwest Coast Artifact Collecting, 1875–1925," *Canadian Historical Review* 63 (December 1982):439–60.

33. It often used to be argued that Canadian Indian policy was superior to that of the United States. See, for example, below, 23–24; George F.G. Stanley, "Western Canada and the Frontier Thesis," *Canadian Historical Association Report* (1940):111; and Paul F. Sharp, "Three Frontiers: Some Comparative Studies of Canadian, American, and Australian Settlement," *Pacific Historical Review* 24 (1955):373. More recently historians have emphasized the point that, whatever the differences in the detail of Indian policy and in the process of settlement, the eventual outcome for the Indians on both sides of the border was pretty much the same. See Desmond Morton, "Cavalry or Police: Keeping the Peace on Two Adjacent Frontiers, 1870–1900," *Journal of Canadian Studies* 12 (Spring 1977):27; and Robin Fisher, "Indian Warfare and Two Frontiers: A Comparison of British Columbia and Washington Territory during the Early Years of Settlement," *Pacific Historical Review* 50 (February 1981):31–51.

34. This argument is developed in some detail by Noel Dyck, "An Opportunity Lost: The Initiative of the Reserve Agricultural Programme in the Prairie West," *1885 and After: Native Society in Transition*, ed. F. Laurie Barron and James B. Waldram (Regina: Canadian Plains Research Center, 1986), 121–37; and Sarah Carter, "Agriculture and Agitation on the Oak River Reserve, 1875–1895," *Manitoba History* 6 (Fall 1983):2–9.

35. For a general history of missions to the Indians of Canada see John Webster Grant, *Moon of Wintertime: Missionaries and the Indians of Canada in Encounter Since 1534* (Toronto: University of Toronto Press, 1984).

36. Hugh Brody, *Maps and Dreams: Indians and the British Columbia Frontier* (Vancouver: Douglas and McIntyre, 1981), xii.

37. Niels Winther Braroe, *Indian and White: Self-Image and Interaction in a Canadian Plains Community* (Stanford: Stanford University Press, 1975).

38. Below, 267.

39. George Manuel and Michael Posluns, *The Fourth World: An Indian Reality* (Don Mills: Collier Macmillan Canada, 1974).

40. The only attempt to write a general history of Indians in Canada has been couched in these terms. See E. Palmer Patterson II, *The Canadian Indian: A History Since 1500* (Don Mills: Collier Macmillan Canada, 1972). See also Robin Fisher, "The Impact of European Settlement on the Indigenous Peoples of Australia, New Zealand, and British Columbia: Some Comparative Dimensions," *Canadian Ethnic Studies* 12 (1980):1–14.

THE HISTORIANS' INDIAN: NATIVE AMERICANS IN CANADIAN HISTORICAL WRITING FROM CHARLEVOIX TO THE PRESENT†

BRUCE G. TRIGGER

Since 1971 several important studies have chronicled the treatment of native peoples in Canadian historical writing.[1] During the same period there has been a growing interest in the history of native peoples as their descendants begin once more to play a greater role in national life. The range of topics being investigated and the understanding of the general outlines of native history have increased as historians, anthropologists, archaeologists, geographers, and economists have combined their professional skills in the pursuit of ethnohistorical research. There is also evidence of a new concern to integrate the findings of ethnohistorians into the broader framework of national history. Now is an opportune time to survey current trends in the study of native history. In chapter one of *Natives and Newcomers* I sought to broaden the discussion of these trends by relating successive fashions in the historical portrayal of native peoples to changing anthropological understanding and the actual position of Indians in Canadian society at the time when these accounts were written.[2] In this paper I will attempt to consolidate some of the main themes of these earlier studies and to evaluate significant trends in more recent work.

Indians as Allies

In histories of Canada written prior to the 1840s Indians played a prominent role and were treated respectfully. This reflected the actual

† *Canadian Historical Review* 67, no. 3 (September 1986): 315–42. This paper is a revised version of the first of two Seagram Lectures delivered to the Department of History, University of Toronto, 3 February 1986. The author thanks those attending for their comments and Nobuhiro Kishigami for his discussions of ethnohistory.

significance of native people, who as trappers and traders were important to the Canadian economy and who, with the exception of the Iroquois prior to 1701 and the Micmac in the late eighteenth century, were allies of successive French and British governments in their struggles against the English colonists and later the Americans to the south. The model for these early histories was the *Histoire et description générale de la Nouvelle France*, published by the French Jesuit priest Pierre-François-Xavier de Charlevoix in 1744.[3] This work must be regarded as the first serious study of Canadian history, earlier self-styled histories being either chronicles of contemporary events, to which summaries of previous happenings were sometimes added, or later compilations and digests of these accounts.[4] Charlevoix provided a systematic treatment of French colonization, mission work, and conflict with the English in the New World. Although a strong Jesuit bias coloured his interpretations, his careful evaluation of alternative sources and provision of bibliographies and footnotes marked a significant advance in the writing of Canadian history.

Charlevoix knew native peoples at first hand. He had come to Quebec in 1705, where he taught grammar at the seminary until 1709. In 1720 he returned to Canada charged by the French government with evaluating various proposals concerning the least expensive way to reach the Pacific Ocean. Between 1721 and 1722 he travelled slowly, by way of Michilimackinac and the Mississippi River, to New Orleans, visiting French trading posts along the way.[5] In the course of these two visits, he had the opportunity to meet Indians from many different groups and to hear what French in different places and occupying various positions had to say about them. In his history he expounded a view of native peoples that embodied concepts that have remained important until the present. Like some other Jesuit scholars of his day, he subscribed to certain beliefs about human beings that characterized the new thinking of the Enlightenment and these beliefs are reflected in his interpretations of native behaviour.

He believed that nations, like individuals, possess characters or temperaments that they cannot lay aside at will.[6] The specific characteristics that he ascribed to different native peoples were, however, based on little more than the various stereotypes that the French had developed in the course of their relations with these groups. Yet he did not restrict negative stereotypes to native people, but argued, for example, that the French were presumptuous and perfidious to the point that it impeded their relations with native groups.[7] He regarded temperament as being physically innate in human beings, but did not interpret it, as many nineteenth-century scholars were to do, as being racial in character and therefore fixed over innumerable generations. Instead, he attributed it largely to the influence of the environment.[8] He therefore concluded that temperament was alterable as environmental circumstances changed.

Like most Enlightenment scholars, Charlevoix viewed native peoples as being as inherently rational as Europeans. He also believed that the conduct of all human beings was determined by similar calculations of honour and self-interest. The main difference between French and Indian was the extent of their knowledge; the Indians' lack of education made them more superstitious and violent. Yet he believed that even the most savage peoples could be improved intellectually and morally by associating with more educated groups.[9] He also thought that in uncultivated nations exceptionally gifted individuals would spontaneously rise above their fellows. As a result, some Indians were equal in ability to the most carefully educated Europeans and entitled to the latter's respect.[10] Because of this talent, even Indians who had become dependent on Europeans were repeatedly able to outwit them; and this was never easier to do than when they were dealing with Europeans who regarded them as stupid. These insights led Charlevoix to observe that the Iroquois had always stopped attacking the French at the point where they could have done them the most harm. He maintained that they did this because they wished to protect their independence by continuing to play French and English against one another.[11]

Charlevoix influenced in content and viewpoint the earliest histories of Canada that were published in English by George Heriot[12] in 1804 and William Smith[13] in 1815, and belatedly he influenced Michel Bibaud's *Histoire du Canada*,[14] which appeared in 1837. Each of these writers relied heavily on Charlevoix as a source of information about early times and, like him, they paid considerable attention to native peoples and presented relatively rational interpretations of their behaviour. Heriot's and Smith's views of native peoples were also clearly influenced by their appreciation of the role that Indians continued to play as allies of the British against the Americans. This treatment was very different from the image of native people in contemporary French-Canadian folklore, which primarily kept alive the memory of Iroquois attacks against missionaries and European settlers during the seventeenth century.[15]

The Antiquated Indian

After the War of 1812–14 the usefulness of Indians as military allies against the Americans declined rapidly. Few native people lived in southern Ontario and Quebec and those that did were increasingly isolated on reserves. Indians thus ceased to be a living presence in the lives of most Euro-Canadians, including those who wrote accounts of Canadian history. This new reality is evident in François-Xavier Garneau's *Histoire du Canada*.[16] This book was written explicitly to be a history of the

French-Canadian nation and sought to glorify the struggle of a people to survive and maintain their cultural identity in the face of the British threat. Because of this, native peoples were accorded a more restricted and negative role than they had been previously.

Garneau, like the French-Canadian folklore of the early nineteenth century, sought to glorify the achievements of French settlers by showing the extent to which their lives had been threatened and the dangers they had overcome. Unlike Charlevoix, he had little, if any, personal contact with native people. Hence, nothing inhibited him from developing his main theme by contrasting the moral and physical courage and Christian virtues of the French not only with the alleged cruelty and fiendishness of the Iroquois but also with the primitiveness of all native peoples. While not totally uninfluenced by Charlevoix, he portrayed Indians as more savage and backward than they had been described in previous histories of Canada. Scalping, torture, and massacres, which had been elements in earlier accounts, were now given greater emphasis. Indians were belaboured with general charges of sexual promiscuity, enslaving their womenfolk, and mistreating their children.[17] He also claimed that before the coming of the Europeans all of them had been hunter-gatherers. Astonishingly, despite abundant evidence to the contrary, he implied that the Huron had learned to practise agriculture from the French after they had sought refuge at Quebec in 1650.[18]

Garneau's portrayal of the American Indian was clearly influenced by the Gothic romanticism that had become fashionable in European literature in the nineteenth century and was already evident in Dainville's *Beautés de l'histoire du Canada*.[19] Garneau also read contemporary American ethnologists and historians and from them learned about the derogatory evolutionary and racist views that American anthropologists had come to hold concerning native peoples by the middle of the nineteenth century.[20] These views, as well as the negative stereotypes about native Americans that abounded in popular literature in the United States at that time, reflected the continuing struggle that European settlers were waging for control of what was to become the continental United States.

Garneau's work clearly influenced the orientation of later Quebec historians, such as Jean-Baptiste Ferland, Etienne-Michel Faillon, and Henri-Raymond Casgrain. As priests, these men tended to emphasize the role of the church in implanting French civilization in North America and uplifting the Indians more than Garneau had done. This gave them an additional motive to stress the vices of native people, whom they generally portrayed as dirty, immoral, cruel, and animal-like prior to their conversion to Christianity.[21] Towards the end of the nineteenth century, in the writings of Benjamin Sulte[22] and Lionel-Adolphe Groulx,[23] the alleged biological superiority of the French over the Indians and Métis was made explicit in a way that had not been done before.

Because the Indians were said to be a "less evolved race," they were maintained to be incapable of developing a more civilized style of life as Europeans had done. Despite their disapproval of the Boston historian Francis Parkman's portrayal of French Canadians as a backward people, Quebec historians were attracted by his romantic approach to historiography and spiritedly reproduced his even more negative stereotypes of American Indians, as individuals, tribes, and a so-called race.[24] They also began to share the American conviction that the Indians were inexorably doomed to extinction. Beginning in the 1860s, Parkman became the principal channel through which American racism and evolutionary anthropology tainted French-Canadian historiography.[25] Yet we must conclude that his negative portrayals of American Indians only intensified similar views that had already become ingrained in French-Canadian historiography.

English-Canadian writers began to produce their own patriotic versions of Canadian history, beginning with John McMullen's *The History of Canada* in 1855.[26] In these books the French regime was described in detail as a heroic prologue to the development of a British nation. In contrast, Indians were viewed as marginal to the history of European settlement and were accorded even less attention than in nationalistic French-Canadian histories. They were generally portrayed as primitive and animal-like. Particular emphasis was placed on their cruelty, dirtiness, laziness, and lack of religion, while their love of freedom, which Heriot and Smith had praised, was now dismissed as being wild and primeval in nature.[27] Indians were frequently asserted to be incapable of becoming civilized and hence doomed to perish with the spread of European civilization. Leaders, such as Joseph Brant and Tecumseh, who had fought alongside the British, were portrayed as heroic figures, but also as being exceptional.[28] Parkman's influence on the portrayal of native people became increasingly strong after the publication of *The Jesuits in North America in the Seventeenth Century* in 1867.[29] This book was widely read in Ontario and accepted as an authentic portrayal of regional history.

Yet there was considerable inconsistency in the way that English-Canadian historians treated native people. They frequently castigated their American colleagues for exaggerating the cruelty and treacherousness of Indians.[30] Canadian historians also relished comparing the brutal treatment of native people by the Americans with the "generous" treatment they had received from Euro-Canadians. John Castell Hopkins informed the readers of his popular *Story of the Dominion* that in Canada, Indians had never suffered from racial antagonism, treaty breaking, removal from their reserves, abuse by greedy Europeans, or failure to receive legal justice. He also asserted that there was no prouder page in Canada's history than its treatment of its "native wards."[31] Yet these same historians expressed gratitude that Providence had sent epidemics and intertribal wars to sweep away the native peoples of southern Ontario and Quebec. Hence these regions were left to be occupied by French and English settlers who, unlike their American neighbours, had no wrongs against native people for which to atone.[32]

These interpretations of Canadian history required great self-deception, or hypocrisy, on the part of writers whose governments were treating their former allies with much the same mixture of repression and economic neglect as American governments were treating defeated enemies. Their analyses of relations between Indians and Europeans were far less well-informed than those of Charlevoix or other historians working before the 1840s had been. In the absence of significant personal contact with native people, English-Canadian historians had allowed themselves to be influenced by their sense of ethnic self-righteousness as well as by popular American stereotypes and by Parkman's racist portrayals of Indians. These views were only slightly ameliorated by the arguments of three distinguished Canadian scholars who were interested in native peoples: Daniel Wilson, John William Dawson, and Horatio Hale.[33] All of these amateur anthropologists were older men who had become familiar with Enlightenment views of humanity prior to the development of the evolutionary racism of the nineteenth century. Each in his own way argued that the triumph of Europeans over other races was due far less to their physical constitution than to learned patterns of behaviour, and they rejected the view that native peoples could not successfully be integrated into the new society that was emerging in North America. Negative stereotypes were also modified by some of Charlevoix's more favourable interpretations of native behaviour, which Canadian historians continued to recycle in piecemeal fashion, often without being aware of their origins.

After 1900 the attention paid to native people declined still further as English-Canadian historians, who were now increasingly professional academics, abandoned a romantic concern with the French regime and began to pay more attention to constitutional history.[34] At the same time French-Canadian historical writing continued in its accustomed vein. Indians were assigned an ever smaller role even in general histories, where they were normally confined to introductory chapters describing the natural environment and early European settlement. To the extent that they were mentioned at all, their negative image as being a primitive and static people who were doomed to disappear tended to persist.[35] Canadian history, like that of the United States, had as its theme the achievements of Europeans; native people, who were seen as possessing no history of their own, remained the concern of anthropologists. The increasing remoteness of native people from the daily lives of most Canadians made it easier for historians to ignore the role that they had played in Canada's past.

Although the more obviously pejorative stereotypes have largely been excised from historical works written in the last twenty years, the neglect of native peoples has persisted in mainstream Canadian historical studies, French and English.[36] In most works, it has become fashionable to point out that European settlers learned how to use canoes, snowshoes, local foods, and herbal medicines from the Indians and that the Indians had a religion adequate to their needs and were often better nourished than were European settlers.[37] Such observations, for all their good intentions, leave native people far from centre stage; indeed, they continue to treat them more like props than like actors. In both Canada and the United States the main impulses for the serious study of native history have come initially from anthropology, and to a lesser degree from economic history and geography.

The Origins of Ethnohistory

Beginning late in the nineteenth century, anthropology in the United States was transformed by the young German ethnologist Franz Boas.[38] Strongly influenced by German romanticism and by his association with Horatio Hale,[39] Boas rejected as being unacceptably ethnocentric the invidious distinctions that unilinear evolutionary anthropologists had drawn between cultures at different levels of technological development. He sought instead to document the many and often unpredictable ways in which different economic, social, and religious practices might combine in specific cultures. He also rejected racist interpretations of behavioural differences among human groups. In their place he expounded the doctrine of cultural relativism, which interprets each culture as having developed to satisfy the collective needs and wishes of its people. The worth of any culture can therefore be judged only in terms of its own ethical and aesthetic principles, not by any universal standard. Yet Boasian anthropology tended to regard native cultures as being largely static and attributed change in prehistoric times mostly to external influences. Boasians also viewed change since the beginning of European contact as a process of disintegration. This made the prime duty of ethnologists to determine what traditional cultures had been like before they disappeared completely. In these latter respects, the Boasian view of native peoples was not so different from the evolutionary one that it sought to replace.

Only in the 1930s, when it became evident that native people were not going to die out or disappear through total assimilation, did growing numbers of American anthropologists become interested in studying changes in native cultures since European contact.[40] Yet they continued ethnocentrically to conceptualize these changes as a process of acculturation, which implied that over time native peoples naturally came to behave more like Euro-Americans. Not until the 1950s did these studies acquire sufficiently particularistic and historical features to emerge as a new branch of anthropology called ethnohistory.[41] By that time anthropologists had ceased to study only factors bringing about acculturation and had begun to investigate the ways by which many native Americans had also resisted acculturation and struggled to preserve their cultures over the centuries.[42]

Native American history became popular among historians as well as anthropologists in the United States during the 1960s. At that time the traditional study of American political history gave way to a radical and centrifugal social and cultural history that was focused on specific classes, genders, and racial and ethnic groups.[43] Studies of American Indian history and of changing Euro-American perceptions of native people took their place alongside those of immigrants, workers, blacks, and women, and history and the generalizing social sciences drew closer together. Yet the study of native history in Canada is not merely a belated reflection of academic trends to the south.[44] Canadians have made distinctive and important contributions to the study of ethnohistory. Moreover, serious investigations of native history began with the social sciences earlier in Canada than in the United States.

In Canada the first social scientist to pay significant attention to the historical role of native people was Harold Innis, in his book *The Fur Trade in Canada*.[45] For this and for many other innovative contributions to the understanding of Canadian history and the historical significance of technology, Innis still deserves respect and admiration. Partly inspired by studies of the Indians' role as middlemen by the American historian Charles H. McIlwain,[46] Innis stressed the importance of native Americans in the fur trade. He assumed that they quickly became dependent on European technology and were locked into a network in which they served as the primary collectors of a staple for a world economy. Yet he elaborated his interpretations in terms of purely economic arguments and without significant reference to anthropological studies or trying to understand the fur trade from a native point of view. Native peoples remained economic stereotypes "only minimally disguised in feathers."[47] Innis was an economic formalist who believed that the same rules could be used to explain the economic behaviour of both Indians and Europeans. Yet in his works, for the first time since the 1840s, native peoples were assigned a significant and prolonged role in the history of Canada after European discovery.

Innis's work inspired the American economist George T. Hunt to write *The Wars of the Iroquois*,[48] in which he argued that the economic implications of the fur trade quickly rendered former relations among native peoples obsolete and created new patterns of alliances and warfare. Both Innis and Hunt played a significant role in Léo-Paul Desrosiers's *Iroquoisie*,[49] which was the first book written in modern times to examine in detail the important role played by the Iroquois in shaping the development of New France. Desrosiers's work was flawed, however, by an old-fashioned evolutionary view of Indians as possessors of a primitive Stone Age culture. Like French-Canadian historians going back to the nineteenth century, Desrosiers stereotyped Indians as cruel, unstable, capricious, incapable of feeding themselves except when living in the midst of natural abundance, and unable to develop beyond the Palaeolithic stage. His views of native people had much in common with the racist pronouncements of Lionel Groulx, although the biologist and amateur ethnologist Jacques Rousseau had already vigorously refuted Groulx's arguments in his book *L'Hérédité et l'homme.*[50] As a result of these attitudes, Desrosiers tended to underestimate the sagacity of native politicians and failed to note their astuteness in dealing with the French to the same extent that Charlevoix had done two hundred years before. Yet the value of his pioneering work should not be overlooked. That only the first of his two volumes was actually published is a striking testimony to the general lack of interest in the role played by native people in Canadian history among the Quebeckers of the 1940s.

A striking contrast to both Innis and Desrosiers is Alfred G. Bailey's *The Conflict of European and Eastern Algonkian Cultures, 1504–1700.*[51] Bailey studied history at the University of Toronto but was also influenced by two other scholars at the university: the economist Harold Innis and the anthropologist Thomas McIlwraith, who was Cambridge-trained but Boasian in outlook.[52] Bailey's principal accomplishment was his analysis in terms of cultural relativism of the changing responses of native people to early European encroachment in eastern Canada. His book is remarkable for its explicit awareness of the many cultural as well as economic factors that influenced relations between native peoples and Europeans. For example, it stressed the need to examine tools from a native viewpoint and therefore to take account of their symbolic as well as technological significance. Thus Bailey sought to understand the introduction of European technology not simply in economic terms, as Innis had done, but in relation to the totality of native cultural patterns. He likewise tried to ascertain how exposure to European societies and religious beliefs altered or failed to alter specific native customs. Bailey's research thus contrasted with and complemented that of Innis. His study of relations between native peoples and Europeans in eastern Canada was the most innovative ethnohistorical study prior to *Cycles of Conquest* published by the American anthropologist Edward Spicer in 1953. Unfortunately, Bailey's book was published in an obscure Canadian series, went unreviewed in United States journals such as the *American Anthropologist*, and its major importance was not recognized until it was reprinted by the University of Toronto Press in 1969. By that time Bailey's accomplishments had been outflanked, to the detriment of Canadian scholarship.

Canadian Ethnohistory and the Fur Trade

Since the 1950s Innis's work has stimulated a rich, if inconclusive series of studies of the fur trade and the relationship of native peoples to it. Many of these studies are based on the voluminous records of the Hudson's Bay Company. Edwin E. Rich followed Innis in recognizing that many Cree and Assiniboine functioned as professional traders, in the sense that they obtained the European products they needed by charging tribes who lived inland more for these goods than they themselves had paid for them. He also noted that, if rival European traders were present, the Indians would charge higher prices for their furs. Yet he concluded that their aim in doing this was not to obtain more European goods but to satisfy their relatively fixed needs with less effort. In general, Indians traded goods with a particular neighbouring group at a price that remained fixed regardless of annual variations in supply. Rich also believed that native peoples had succeeded in imposing their traditional customs on European traders.[53] Inasmuch as he rejected the notion that native people were seeking to maximize their profits in the style of European entrepreneurs, he can be described as a modified formalist. The economist Abraham Rotstein adopted an explicitly substantivist or anti-formalist position. Substantivism, as formulated by Karl Polanyi,[54] maintains that the rules of economic behaviour change as the overall complexity of a society increases. Rotstein argued that in prehistoric times the rates of exchange were determined by political factors, such as maintaining intertribal alliances, rather than by economic considerations, and that in order to participate in the fur trade Europeans were compelled to enter into such alliances and abide by their terms.[55]

In their book *"Give Us Good Measure,"* the geographers Arthur Ray and Donald Freeman presented detailed statistical analyses of Hudson's Bay Company records that are relevant for understanding the nature of European trade with the native peoples of the Subarctic prior to 1763.[56] These analyses called into question the degree to which trade was governed by political alliances and also the notion of a de facto fixed exchange rate between Indians and the Hudson's Bay Company. They also concluded that Indians took account of marginal costs, such as the different times required to carry their furs to rival European traders, and sought to manipulate prices by bargaining for more than the standard measure of European goods in return for their furs. European traders for their part tried to increase profits by giving short measures or supplying goods of inferior quality. Ray and Freeman nevertheless accepted Rotstein's view of what a traditional native economy was like and interpreted the situation recorded in the Hudson's Bay Company records as a "transitional" economy, already considerably modified by European influences. The latter conclusion may be erroneous. French descriptions of trade in the St. Lawrence Valley at the beginning of the seventeenth century indicate that traditional trade resembled the patterns Ray and Freeman describe more than it did those that Rotstein has proposed.[57]

In *Indians in the Fur Trade*, Arthur Ray traced the impact of the fur trade on native patterns of ecological adaptation, including intertribal relations, in the region southwest of Hudson Bay from 1660 to 1870.[58] For the first time, the skills of a professional geographer were brought to bear on the study of regional native responses to the fur trade. Robin Fisher's *Contact and Conflict* contrasted the generally accommodative relations between Indians and fur traders in coastal British Columbia with the suppression of native peoples that followed large-scale European settlement in the region beginning in the late nineteenth century.[59] Daniel Francis and Toby Morantz's *Partners in Furs* stressed the slowness of the Cree who wintered far from any European trading posts in the region east of James Bay to become dependent on European goods. Because European ammunition might run out or guns not be in working order at a critical time, these Indians continued to trust their lives to their traditional technology until trading posts were established in the interior in the nineteenth century.[60]

All of these books carry on debates about the role played by Indians in the fur trade that were started by Harold Innis. Although considerable progress has been made in eliminating erroneous and overly simplistic assumptions, much remains to be learned and many issues have still to be resolved. These books also largely share a common orientation. Each of them contains more detailed examinations of how Indian cultures have shaped the fur trade than are found in Innis's work; yet culturally specific analyses remain muted. Many of the arguments are phrased in terms of the general debate between substantivists and formalists about the nature of economic systems; the economic logic of relations between traders, settlers, and Indians; and changing ecological adaptations. While allowing that the economic behaviour of tribal peoples, viewed as a general stage of development, may differ in fundamental ways from that of capitalist societies, these studies stress the rationale of intergroup competition to control resources rather than the inner values of specific native cultures as the main factor structuring native behaviour. This sort of approach also characterized Conrad Heidenreich's *Huronia*, which combined modern agricultural data, archaeological information, and palaeo-environmental reconstructions, as well as historical sources, to produce a quantified reconstruction of seventeenth-century Huron subsistence and settlement patterns.[61] This is an approach that appeals to many anthropologists and historians because it greatly simplifies what has to be known about human behaviour in order to explain the course of history. Some anthropologists and historians would further argue that it provides a fully satisfactory account of why events happen, at least in the long run. For example, the historian Robert Berkhofer, Jr., has affirmed that variations in natural resources and in the level of the native societies available for exploitation by Europeans were much more important factors in determining how Europeans treated native peoples than were the specific cultural characteristics of individual native groups or the differing racial prejudices and missionary zeal of various European nations.[62]

Culturally Specific Studies

Other ethnohistorians, whose orientations more closely resemble that of Alfred Bailey, have emphasized the need to know much more about changing native beliefs and how Indians perceived Europeans, if they are to understand Indian reactions to European behaviour. Some of these positions have been specifically anti-economic and most of them have a strong tendency to concentrate on religious beliefs. Yet not all studies that stress religious beliefs are based on a detailed understanding of native cultures. The American ethnohistorian Calvin Martin has attracted much attention by arguing that the fur trade was made possible not so much by the growing reliance of native people on European goods as by a continent-wide war of extermination that the Indians unleashed against fur-bearing animals to retaliate for unprecedentedly destructive epidemics of newly introduced European diseases for which they held animal spirits to be responsible.[63] Yet he does not demonstrate that there was any widespread native belief that animal spirits would punish human beings with diseases or that the way to respond to angry ones was to slaughter animals indiscriminately rather than to try to appease these spirits.[64] He also does not explain how close relations have survived between Indian hunters and animal spirits in areas such as Nouveau Québec where he claims that epidemics led native people to sever these supernatural links in the seventeenth century.[65] Nor does he account for why the animals that were hunted to extinction were those species whose pelts were valued for the fur trade rather than the main ones hunted for subsistence, even though the latter were probably of greatest interest in terms of traditional religion. Martin's view of native religions, despite his claims to the contrary, is no more culturally specific than are the economic explanations that we have been examining. Instead, he makes assertions that lack either specific ethnographic documentation or the status of universal generalizations.

Canadian ethnohistorians have followed Calvin Martin and W.H. McNeill[66] before him by claiming that early epidemics undermined native religions and made conversion to Christianity easier. Denys Delâge argues that Indians embraced Christianity during these epidemics because it promised them a better life after death than their own religions, although he also correlates conversion with the destabilization of native life as a result of wars, the fur trade, and growing reliance on Europeans, as well as with the accompanying erosion of economic egalitarianism that native religious systems had reinforced.[67] Lucien Campeau maintains that already in the early seventeenth century conversions were based on a genuine understanding of Christianity that had been conveyed to native peoples by Jesuit missionaries.[68] Yet it is difficult to understand how certain key Christian concepts, such as that of obedience to God, could so quickly have been conveyed to members of egalitarian societies in which the general concept of obedience was unknown. The anthropologist David Blanchard concludes that early converts perceived Christianity more in terms of their traditional religious and social concepts than in terms of European ones and that syncretistic versions of Christianity persisted among groups such as the Iroquois of Caughnawaga into the nineteenth century.[69] Similarly, Jacques Rousseau noted that the Cree of northern Quebec have dualistically maintained knowledge and belief in Christian teachings and their traditional religion alongside one another into modern times.[70]

There is little solid evidence that early epidemics seriously undermined native religious beliefs or that Indians turned to Christianity during these epidemics because it promised them a more attractive form of immortality. The Jesuit missionaries among the Huron were scandalized when they discovered that most Indians sought baptism because they believed it was a curing ritual like their own or, alternatively, because they feared that the epidemics were caused by European witchcraft and hoped that baptism would forge a personal bond with the French that would induce the newcomers to spare them.[71] A few deviant individuals, such as the young Huron "convert" Joseph Chihwatenha, appear to have embraced Christianity because they hoped by doing so to acquire the Jesuits' powers of witchcraft.[72] Yet most Indians abandoned any further pretence of obeying the Jesuits when it became clear that baptism neither prevented nor cured disease. Among the Huron the search for appropriate curing rituals through communication with the spirit world resulted in an intensification of traditional native religious practices during outbreaks of disease. It also ensured that specific rituals were discredited when they failed to work rather than the Huron religion as a whole. Those rituals that were in vogue when the epidemics ceased were credited with being valid cures, thus reinforcing the general credibility of native beliefs.[73] The fragility that Martin and others attribute to native religions is more reminiscent of the condescending views of nineteenth-century cultural evolutionists than in accord with the evidence.

It is generally accepted, however, that as native peoples grew economically and militarily subordinate to Europeans, their confidence in their own value systems was undermined and they became increasingly susceptible to Christian indoctrination and conversion.[74] With the Huron this process was underway by the 1640s, but among the Iroquois who remained living in New York State it did not begin in earnest for almost another fifty years. This leaves the nature of earlier, often spectacular conversions unresolved. It appears that as native people became more dependent on Europeans it was those individuals who had to interact most closely with Europeans who first sought to be regarded as Christians. The French in particular encouraged this development by offering higher prices to converts for their furs, selling guns only to them, and according them greater honour in ritual situations.[75] Yet it is by no means certain to what extent individuals who conformed outwardly to Christianity understood or believed Christian teachings. In 1671 a Huron who had been considered a believing Christian for over twenty-five years, while being interrogated on a charge of kidnapping, claimed that he had only feigned to be one in order to gratify the Jesuits. He then requested to be rebaptized and began to live what appeared to be a life of exemplary piety.[76] We are left wondering what this man believed at any time.

This raises an important methodological problem. How much can ethnohistorians learn about what native people understood or believed about Christianity from descriptions that were mostly recorded by missionaries? Sometimes missionaries confessed that they had been too optimistic about how easily conversions could be accomplished and acknowledged that mission work they had once thought to be successful had in fact been a failure.[77] In other cases, comparisons of year-by-year accounts of missions reveal that initial impressions of success were not justified.[78] In general, the Jesuits worked on the principle that if a native could be persuaded to talk and behave like a Christian, eventually he might think like one.[79] This policy by its very nature left missionaries uncertain about what their "converts" actually believed.

Furthermore, most of what we know about missions was written for publication in tracts designed to encourage European donors to support this work; hence, few failures are discussed at length. The accounts of missionaries do not open the "windows in men's souls" that an accurate evaluation of success in conversion requires. More attention should be paid to statements made by contemporary critics of various missionary efforts than has been done in the past. These critics include administrators and members of rival religious orders. Yet their comments are generally limited and quite as biased as those offered by the advocates of particular missions. Historians must be very careful about any claims that they make concerning the effectiveness of conversion in the absence of independent sources of information about the views of so-called converts. It appears that what historians and ethnohistorians have concluded about missionary successes in early New France is largely a reflection of the hopes and fears of the missionary chroniclers and of what modern scholars wish to have been the case.

Multi-disciplinary Approaches

I agree wholeheartedly that it is vital to understand the behaviour of native people in terms of their own beliefs and perceptions, if progress is to be made in comprehending their history from the inside. The standard ethnohistorical technique is to interpret historical sources in the light of ethnographic knowledge about specific peoples, but this method has its limitations, especially where historical records contain little information about native people. In recent years Canadian ethnohistorians have played a significant role in broadening the scope of their discipline by seeking additional sources of information about native behaviour in the past.

Oral traditions constitute one such source, although the tendency for this lore to be refashioned as circumstances change tends to make it unreliable for all but the recent past, when the personal recollections of known individuals can be checked against one another.[80] Yet when oral traditions can be verified using other kinds of information, they may be a valuable source of historical data. Peter Schmalz and L.V. Eid have independently used Ojibwa traditions together with seventeenth-century documents to reconstruct the details of how the Ojibwa wrested southern Ontario from the control of the Iroquois in the 1690s.[81] Their work has not only revealed how the Ojibwa came into possession of this region but also corrected an historical account that for various political reasons was hitherto biased in favour of Iroquois claims.

Ethnologists agree that in order to understand a culture completely, a thorough knowledge of its language is essential. Only in this way can the categories in terms of which a people perceives and evaluates reality be comprehended. It is clear that a vast amount of ethnographic information that is not found in European descriptions of native cultures is contained in old grammars and dictionaries of native languages, often preserved only in manuscript form.[82] Studying Christian religious texts prepared in these languages also reveals the degree to which missionaries understood native languages at successive phases in their work and how over time native categories of religious thought, such as their concepts about souls, were modified by European contact.[83] The ethnosemantic approach, which seeks to understand how native peoples perceived reality by systematically analysing the meanings of the words they used and the contexts in which they used them, provides a chink through which their changing ideas and values may be perceived, albeit often in a dim and imperfect fashion. Yet it is an approach that few ethnohistorians have so far applied systematically in either Canada or the United States. Using it requires the acquisition of major new skills in the highly technical field of linguistics. Finally, it must be cautioned that a better understanding of how native peoples perceived reality does not by itself explain why they behaved as they did. It merely helps to make clear the knowledge on which they acted.

Understanding the written sources used by ethnohistorians has been greatly aided in recent years by studies of how Europeans perceived native peoples at different periods. In the United States and Europe this branch of intellectual history has proliferated since the 1960s. In my opinion the best general study of changing perceptions of native peoples by Euro-Americans is Robert F. Berkhofer's *The White Man's Indian*, although many other studies offer more detailed insights into specific periods and issues. These studies help to reveal the cultural stereotypes, biases, and precedents that shaped the understanding that Europeans had of the native peoples with whom they interacted. In Canada Cornelius Jaenen, Olive Dickason, and François-Marc Gagnon have studied how European verbal and visual stereotypes influenced French views of native people and how actual experiences with native people modified these views.[84] Their work, although technically not ethnohistorical, aids ethnohistorians to perceive the biases and assess the objectivity of written accounts so that descriptions of the behaviour of native people can be interpreted more objectively. These studies are therefore an important contribution to the critical analysis of the source material used by ethnohistorians.

In North America ethnohistory has generally been viewed as a combination of historical and ethnographical data and methods, with only a minor role being assigned to archaeology. Yet Canadian archaeologists and ethnohistorians have recognized that native cultures were altered as a result of European activities in North America long before the earliest recorded contacts or the first significant written descriptions of most Indian groups.[85] It now appears likely that in many parts of the continent major population declines occurred prior to the earliest substantial historical records as a result of the introduction of European diseases which spread quickly and against which native people had little immunity.[86] It is also probable that in at least some of these areas major population declines disrupted and simplified native social and political organization. Therefore, the earliest historical records do not necessarily provide descriptions of native cultures prior to any changes resulting from European contact. Archaeologists are now devoting increasing amounts of time to studying the protohistorical period, which lasts from the earliest archaeological evidence of European goods or diseases in native sites to the first substantial written accounts of particular groups.[87] Only by employing archaeological data concerning the late prehistoric and protohistoric periods can the extent to which new patterns of behaviour emerged as a result of the early presence of Europeans be objectively determined. Archaeologists are investigating questions such as whether intertribal trade increased significantly in the protohistorical period; whether genocidal intertribal warfare arose as a result of the fur trade;

and whether scalping was introduced into North America by Europeans, as some popular writers maintain.[88] Without archaeological data most matters such as these would be topics for endless speculation, with the positions defended being largely reflections of personal opinion and stereotypes of native people. The answers that archaeology supplies are often not the ones that are anticipated. For example, while the volume of intertribal trade did increase in northeastern North America following earliest European contact,[89] it appears that some native groups had already been shattered by intertribal warfare in late prehistoric times.[90] There is also evidence that the Iroquoians were practising scalping, as well as ritual torture and cannibalism, for centuries prior to European contact.[91] This sort of information is important for understanding native cultures and evaluating the impact that European contact had on them.

Little detailed attention has so far been paid to the role of women in Canadian native history, apart from Jennifer Brown's and Sylvia Van Kirk's studies of the position of native women in the fur trade.[92] Yet there is evidence of growing interest in this topic as part of a broader concern with women's studies. Even less has been done to integrate what native people write about their past with academic studies of native history. It is, however, clearly wrong to dismiss such work as only polemical or of ethnological interest. On the contrary, what native people currently believe about their history may provide valuable insights into the significance of that history.

The preceding discussion indicates that ethnohistory can become better history only by becoming better anthropology. Specifically, this requires broadening the range of anthropological knowledge that is employed. Ethnohistorians must learn to combine the study of written documents more effectively with data provided by ethnology, historical linguistics, ethnosemantics, archaeology, and oral traditions, as well as with the analytical perspectives of economics and ecology. No one scholar can be expected to become equally proficient in all of these fields and the combinations mastered by individuals will vary according to personal preferences and the nature of the problems being investigated. Yet, if ethnohistory is to expand as a methodology for understanding the history of native peoples, all ethnohistorians must display growing sensitivity and openness to the methods that are collectively available to help them in their work.

Native History as Canadian History

We must next ask to what degree ethnohistory, which has largely developed outside the mainstream of Canadian and United States historiography, has become an integral part of the latter studies. The most direct way to answer this question is to enquire to what extent the study of native history has influenced the way in which Euro-Canadians and

Euro-Americans view the history of their own ethnic groups. The trail-blazing book that defined a significant relationship between these two histories was Francis Jennings's startling and in some quarters most unwelcome *The Invasion of America*.[93] In it he made use of an anthropological understanding of how native peoples could be expected to have behaved to challenge the traditional version of political relations between the various Puritan colonies and the Indians of southern New England during the seventeenth century. Jennings was not the first American historian to adopt a sympathetic view towards the Indians of that region, but he was the first to claim that English colonists systematically disguised intercolonial rivalries by accusing Indians of plotting against them. Jennings's documentation forced American historians to recognize that those settlers who initially recorded relations between native people and Europeans often either did not understand why Indians acted as they did or else had vested interests in misrepresenting their behaviour in order to portray self-seeking and exploitation by Europeans in a benevolent or at least an innocent fashion. Historians since the seventeenth century, especially those who were naturally predisposed to idealize Euro-American history, have tended to accept these accounts at face value. One role of ethnohistory is therefore to free mainstream North American history from its legacy as a colonial ideology.

In Canada John Tobias used ethnohistorical methodology in this fashion in his analysis of how events surrounding the Rebellion of 1885 were exploited by the federal government to defeat the aspirations of the Plains Cree for a consolidated reserve in the Cypress Hills of Saskatchewan and Alberta.[94] In *Natives and Newcomers*, I argued that Canadian historians have ignored the role of fur traders in forging good relations with native peoples and hence creating conditions favourable for early French colonization and instead have laid undue emphasis on the positive contributions of missionaries and government officials. This happened because their own biases led them to accept the writings of these missionaries and officials at face value and they did not assess from a native point of view how indigenous peoples would have responded to the European actions described in these accounts.[95]

This renewed interest in the role of native people in North American history corresponded with their growing importance in modern society. After World War II native populations, which had continued to decline into the 1920s, began to increase rapidly both on reserves and in the cities. In the 1960s native groups became politically active and started to demand the right once more to control the resources necessary to shape their own lives. Their struggle against poverty and government tutelage was accompanied by a cultural renaissance that witnessed native painters, singers, and actors gain worldwide recognition. At the same time a rapidly increasing native population confronted governments with escalating problems of health care, poverty, unemployment, inadequate education, and alienated youth. All of these trends created a growing awareness of native people that encouraged an interest in their history among some North Americans of European origin. The latter sought through historical studies to understand how native peoples related to the larger society that had grown up in North America.

The concepts that are most important for understanding the unequal relations that have prevailed since soon after contact between native Americans and European settlers are those of dependency, coercion, and domination. The notion of coercion already played a major role in the early acculturative studies by the American anthropologist Ralph Linton, especially in connection with his distinction between non-directed and directed contact situations.[96] That distinction, which depended on the degree to which European settlers could and did use coercion to control native behaviour, was later popularized by Edward Spicer in his pioneering ethnohistorical studies.[97] It is now recognized that coercion is only one element in the development of dependency by Indians on Europeans. The latter is a complex process involving economic, military, and ideological factors that in varied ways bring about the encapsulation of one originally self-sustaining society within another.[98] Only in this way can we understand how native people have become the most deprived groups in Canadian society; seven times more likely to go to prison than non-natives, six times more prone to suicide, four times more likely to die in infancy, and only one-quarter as likely to graduate from high school.[99]

Dependency is a subject that has attracted much attention in recent ethnohistorical writing in the United States. In Canada a number of important studies have also been published in recent years. The most ambitious of these is Denys Delâge's *Le Pays renversé*, which employs a world-systems approach to understand European colonization in northeastern North America between 1600 and 1664. Delâge argues that the incorporation of this region into the European world system, economically dominated first by Holland and then by England, reduced native peoples to a state of permanent dependence on Europeans, undermined their egalitarian social structures, compelled native men and women to work harder than ever before, depleted the natural environment, and gave rise to unprecedented intergroup conflicts. While Delâge tends to idealize traditional native cultures to an unwarranted degree and underestimates their capacity to cope with European disruptions, his worldsystem analysis is a useful provisional model for an integrated understanding of the result of growing native American dependence on Europeans during the seventeenth century.

Leslie Upton, in his *Micmacs and Colonists*, explicitly confronted the issues of coercion and dominance in a splendid study of relations between the Micmac and the British in the Maritime provinces between 1713 and 1867.[100] He portrayed British settlers as wresting control of that region from the Micmac, leaving them an impoverished and powerless minority in their own country. Once established, British society confronted the Micmac at many levels and sought, albeit at minimum expense and effort, to substitute its norms for theirs. Roman Catholicism persisted among the Micmac as a bond that could not be severed by provincial administrations and became an integral part of Micmac tribal identity. Likewise, the traditional authority of band chiefs survived because the Micmac, although deprived of most of their land, were largely left to settle their own affairs.

Finally, John W. Grant's *Moon of Wintertime* is an impressive survey of relations between missionaries and native people in Canada from the sixteenth century to the present.[101] To a considerable degree these relations centred around a struggle for power and control between native people and European settlers. Of particular interest is Grant's documentation of the refusal by missionaries to allow native people to control the practice and dissemination of Christianity, especially when the emergence of native preachers made this possible in the nineteenth century. So pervasive were the stereotypes of native inferiority and fickleness that Euro-Canadian missionaries felt justified in continuing to regulate the religious lives of their native parishioners.

Yet, despite these excellent studies, the examination of dependency and coercion is only beginning. We require many further detailed investigations of the economic, social, and political history of native peoples under European control as well as more systematic historical studies of the policies that colonial, provincial, and federal governments formulated for dealing with these peoples and how these policies were administered. The latter studies would be historical equivalents of such important contemporary analyses as Sally Weaver's *Making Canadian Indian Policy* and Michael Asch's *Home and Native Land*.[102]

Ethnohistorians have yet to resolve basic questions concerning how and when native peoples became dependent on an expanding Euro-Canadian society and how they were alienated from the resources of half a continent and prevented from making major decisions concerning their own lives. For example, little systematic attention has been paid to the exploitation of concepts of native racial inferiority as a justification for Euro-Canadian paternalism and the abridgment of native freedoms. Ethnohistorians must also learn more about how native peoples have responded to such deprivation, successfully resisting European claims sometimes and succumbing to them on other occasions. Finally, they must study the responses of both native peoples and Euro-Canadians to the recent demographic increase of native people. These studies will result in a better understanding not only of native people as a minority group but also of the growth of Canadian society as a whole since earliest European encounters with the New World.

Conclusions

In *The Children of Aataentsic* I sought to demonstrate that it was possible to write the history of a native group primarily using written documentation that was of European origin. In doing so, I tried in part to answer the concerns of ethnohistorians, such as Edward Spicer, who feared that in using such data it might never be possible to understand native history from the inside.[103] I believe that I succeeded in writing a history that is specifically centred on a single native group — the Huron — rather than the French, Dutch, or English colonists, or even on the theme of relations between Europeans and Indians that was ethnohistory's heritage from earlier studies of acculturation. I did this by relying more heavily than most ethnohistorical studies previously had done on archaeology as a secondary source of information that is not biased by European transmission as well as by using the concept of "interest group" to overcome the lack of detailed information about individual Huron and to secure comparable treatment of the internal diversity of Indian and French behaviour. Although I dealt mainly with the Huron prior to 1660, I am convinced that it is worthwhile to trace the history of specific native groups from prehistoric times to the present. Such studies not only are interesting as ends in themselves to native and Euro-Canadian readers but also provide the building blocks from which a detailed picture of native history can be constructed on a national and continental scale. To date, broader treatments of the history of the native peoples of Canada remain impressionistic or confined to specific topics.[104]

Yet I do not suggest that native history since the sixteenth century should be studied as if it occurred in isolation. On the contrary, treating native people as members of autonomous groups denies the realities of life for most Indians over the last several centuries. If many of them have valiantly resisted European domination and fought to preserve what they could of their freedom and way of life, they have all been forced into increasingly narrow spheres of action and had to adapt to these straitened conditions. It is no less important to understand what has happened to native people who live in cities, who have been denied Indian status by federal laws, and who have sought to escape from domination through assimilation into Euro-Canadian society than it is to study what has happened to those who continue to inhabit reserves or band territories. Only in this fashion can the full meaning of dependency and coercion and their effects on the lives of native people be understood.

Finally, it must be recognized that the study of native history is no less an evaluation of Euro-Canadian treatment of native people and how that behaviour was often misrepresented as altruistic than it is an account of native life. Ethnohistory, as Jennings brilliantly demonstrated, is the basis for a new beginning in the understanding of what Europeans did in the past.[105] Only as these studies progress will we be able to distinguish systematically between the manner in which previous generations of Euro-Canadians treated native peoples and the false consciousness that justified their actions and coloured the historical records they produced. This in turn is a necessary preliminary to a deeper and more genuine understanding of native history. In spite of the progress that has been made so far, there are strong reasons to believe that entrenched European stereotypes continue to distort our understanding of native peoples and their history.

Notes

1. J.W. St. G. Walker, "The Indian in Canadian Historical Writing," Canadian Historical Association, *Historical Papers* (1971):21–47; D.B. Smith, *Le Sauvage: The Native People in Quebec Historical Writing on the Heroic Period (1534–1663) of New France* (Ottawa, 1974); Walker, "The Indian in Canadian Historical Writing, 1972–1982," in *As Long as the Sun Shines and Water Flows: A Reader in Canadian Native Studies*, ed. I.A.L. Getty and A.S. Lussier (Vancouver, 1983), 340–57.

2. B.G. Trigger, *Natives and Newcomers: Canada's "Heroic Age" Reconsidered* (Montreal, 1985), 3–49.

3. P.F.X. Charlevoix, *Histoire et description générale de la Nouvelle France avec le journal historique d'un voyage fait par ordre du roi dans l'Amérique septentrionale*, 3 vols. (Paris, 1744); later references are to Charlevoix, *History and General Description of New France*, ed. J.G. Shea, 6 vols. (New York, 1866–72).

4. The most important of these are Marc Lescarbot, *Histoire de la Nouvelle-France* (Paris, 1609, rev. ed. 1617); Samuel de Champlain, *Les Voyages de la Nouvelle France occidentale . . . depuis l'an 1603 jusques en l'an 1629* (Paris, 1632); Gabriel Sagard, *Histoire du Canada . . . ,* 4 vols. (Paris, 1636); François Du Creux, *Historiae Canadensis* (Paris, 1664); Chrestien Le Clercq, *Premier Etablissement de la foy dans la Nouvelle-France*, 2 vols. (Paris, 1691).

5. D.M. Hayne, "Charlevoix, Pierre-François-Xavier de," *Dictionary of Canadian Biography* (Toronto, 1974), 3:103–10.

6. Charlevoix, *History*, 5:23.

7. Ibid., 3:275–76.

8. Ibid., 2:190.

9. Ibid., 3:30.

10. Ibid., 1:270; 2:136; 3:41.

11. Ibid., 4:247–48.

12. George Heriot, *The History of Canada, from Its First Discovery . . .* (London, 1804).

13. William Smith, *History of Canada: From Its First Discovery, to the Peace of 1763* (Quebec, 1815).

14. Michel Bibaud, *Histoire du Canada, sous la domination française* (Montreal, 1837).

15. Smith, *Le Sauvage*, 18–20.

16. François-Xavier Garneau, *Histoire du Canada depuis sa découverte jusqu'à nos jours*, 3 vols. (Quebec, 1845–48); later references are to Andrew Bell's translation, Garneau, *History of Canada from the Time of Its Discovery to the Union Years (1840–1)*, 3 vols. (Montreal, 1860).

17. Garneau, *Histoire du Garneau*, 1:98–116.

18. Ibid., 153; for earlier native subsistence patterns see 102, and for an oblique reference to Iroquois agriculture, 141.

19. D. Dainville [Adolphe Bossange?], *Beautés de l'histoire du Canada* (Paris, 1821), especially ii.

20. William Stanton, *The Leopard's Spots: Scientific Attitudes toward Race in America, 1815–59* (Chicago, 1960); Reginald Horsman, "Scientific Racism and the American Indian in the Mid-Nineteenth Century," *American Quarterly* 27 (1975):152–68; Horsman, *Race and Manifest Destiny: The Origins of American Racial Anglo-Saxonism* (Cambridge, Mass., 1981); C.M. Hinsley, Jr., *Savages and Scientists: The Smithsonian Institution and the Development of American Anthropology, 1846–1910* (Washington, 1981).

21. D.B. Smith, *Le Sauvage*, 34–45.

22. Serge Gagnon, *Quebec and Its Historians, 1840 to 1920* (Montreal, 1982), 90–91.

23. Lionel-Adolphe Groulx, *La Naissance d'une race* (Montreal, 1919).

24. On Parkman's views of native people see Francis Jennings, "Francis Parkman: A Brahmin among Untouchables," *William and Mary Quarterly* 42 (1985):305–28.

25. Mason Wade, *Francis Parkman: Heroic Historian* (New York, 1942), 380–424.

26. J.M. McMullen, *The History of Canada from Its First Discovery to the Present Time* (Brockville, 1855).

27. J.C. Hopkins, *The Story of the Dominion* (Toronto, 1901), 44.

28. Walker, "The Indian in Canadian Historical Writing," 26–27.

29. Francis Parkman, *The Jesuits in North America in the Seventeenth Century* (Boston, 1867).

30. Hopkins, *Story of the Dominion*, 43.

31. Ibid., 65.

32. McMullen, *History of Canada*, xiv.

33. Daniel Wilson, *Prehistoric Man: Researches into the Origin of Civilization in the Old and the New World* (London, 1862); John William Dawson, *Fossil Men and Their Modern Representatives* (London, 1880); Horatio Hale, *The Iroquois Book of Rites* (Philadelphia, 1883).

34. Carl Berger, *The Writing of Canadian History: Aspects of English-Canadian Historical Writing, 1900–1970* (Toronto, 1976), 183.

35. Walker, "The Indian in Canadian Historical Writing."

36. Walker, "The Indian in Canadian Historical Writing, 1972–1982."

37. See, for example, Marcel Trudel, *Histoire de la Nouvelle-France*, vol. 2, *Le Comptoir, 1604–1627* (Montreal, 1966), 376–84; W.J. Eccles, *France in America* (Vancouver, 1973), 25.

38. M.J. Herskovits, *Franz Boas: The Science of Man in the Making* (New York, 1953); Marvin Harris, *The Rise of Anthropological Theory* (New York, 1968), 250–421; G.W. Stocking, Jr., *A Franz Boas Reader: The Shaping of American Anthropology, 1883–1911* (New York, 1974).

39. J.W. Gruber, "Horatio Hale and the Development of American Anthropology," *Proceedings of the American Philosophical Society* 111 (1967): 5–37.

40. Robert Redfield, Ralph Linton, and M.J. Herskovits, "Outline for the Study of Acculturation," *American Anthropologist* 38 (1936):149–52; Linton, ed., *Acculturation in Seven American Indian Tribes* (New York, 1940).

41. E.H. Spicer, ed., *Perspectives in American Indian Culture Change* (Chicago, 1961); Spicer, *Cycles of Conquest: The Impact of Spain, Mexico, and the United States on the Indians of the Southwest, 1533–1960* (Tucson, 1962).

42. R.F. Berkhofer, Jr., *The White Man's Indian: Images of the American Indian*

from Columbus to the Present (New York, 1978; Vintage Book edition 1979), 67–68.

43. Thomas Bender, "Making History Whole Again," *New York Times Book Review*, 6 October 1985, 1, 42–43.

44. Cf. W.J. Eccles, "Forty Years Back," *William and Mary Quarterly* 41 (1984): 410–21, especially 420.

45. Harold Innis, *The Fur Trade in Canada* (New Haven, 1930); 2nd ed. (Toronto, 1956).

46. C.H. McIlwain, ed., *An Abridgement of the Indian Affairs . . . Transacted in the Colony of New York, from the Year 1678 to the Year 1751, by Peter Wraxall* (Cambridge, Mass., 1915).

47. Trigger, *Natives and Newcomers*, 184.

48. G.T. Hunt, *The Wars of the Iroquois: A Study in Intertribal Trade Relations* (Madison, 1940).

49. Léo-Paul Desrosiers, *Iroquoisie*, vol. 1 (Montreal, 1947).

50. Jacques Rousseau, *L'Hérédité et l'homme* (Montreal, 1945).

51. A.G. Bailey, *The Conflict of European and Eastern Algonkian Cultures, 1504–1700: A Study in Canadian Civilization* (St. John, N.B., 1937; reprinted Toronto, 1969).

52. Bailey, "Retrospective Thoughts of an Ethnohistorian," Canadian Historical Association, *Historical Papers* (1977): 15–29.

53. E.E. Rich, "Trade Habits and Economic Motivation among the Indians of North America," *Canadian Journal of Economics and Political Science* 26 (1960): 35–53; Rich, *Hudson's Bay Company, 1670–1870*, 3 vols. (Toronto, 1960).

54. Karl Polanyi, *The Great Transformation* (New York, 1944).

55. Abraham Rotstein, "Fur Trade and Empire: An Institutional Analysis" (PhD dissertation, University of Toronto, 1970); Rotstein, "Trade and Politics: An Institutional Approach," *Western Canadian Journal of Anthropology* 3, no. 1 (1972): 1–28.

56. A.J. Ray and D.B. Freeman, *"Give Us Good Measure": An Economic Analysis of Relations Between the Indians and the Hudson's Bay Company Before 1763* (Toronto, 1978).

57. Trigger, *Natives and Newcomers*, 183–94.

58. A.J. Ray, *Indians in the Fur Trade: Their Role as Trappers, Hunters, and Middlemen in the Lands Southwest of Hudson Bay, 1660–1870* (Toronto, 1974).

59. Robin Fisher, *Contact and Conflict: Indian–European Relations in British Columbia, 1774–1890* (Vancouver, 1977).

60. Daniel Francis and Toby Morantz, *Partners in Furs: A History of the Fur Trade in Eastern James Bay, 1600–1870* (Montreal, 1983).

61. C.E. Heidenreich, *Huronia: A History and Geography of the Huron Indians, 1600–1650* (Toronto, 1971).

62. Berkhofer, *The White Man's Indian*, 116.

63. Calvin Martin, *Keepers of the Game: Indian–Animal Relationships and the Fur Trade* (Berkeley, 1978).

64. Shepard Krech, III, ed., *Indians, Animals, and the Fur Trade: A Critique of Keepers of the Game* (Athens, Georgia, 1981).

65. Adrian Tanner, *Bringing Home Animals: Religious Ideology and Mode of Production of the Mistassini Cree Hunters* (St. John's, 1979).

66. W.H. McNeill, *Plagues and Peoples* (Garden City, 1976), 183–84.

67. Denys Delâge, *Le Pays renversé, Amérindiens et Européens en Amérique du nord-est, 1600–1664* (Montreal, 1985), 195.

68. Lucien Campeau, *Etablissement à Québec (1616–1634)* (Quebec, 1979), cxxviii–cxxxi.

69. David Blanchard, "Patterns of Tradition and Change: The Re-creation of Iroquois Culture at Kahnawake" (PhD dissertation, University of Chicago, 1982).

70. Jacques Rousseau, "Dualisme religieux des indiens forestiers," *La Patrie*, 12 August 1951, 31.

71. B.G. Trigger, *The Children of Aataentsic: A History of the Huron People to 1660* (Montreal, 1976), 505–7, 529–32, 546–50, 563–70, 589–98.

72. Ibid., 550–51, 598–601.

73. Ibid., 533–34. For similar evidence of the durability of traditional religious beliefs among the Narragansett people of New England see P.A. Robinson et al., "Preliminary Biocultural Interpretations from a Seventeenth-Century Narragansett Cemetery in Rhode Island," in *Cultures in Contact*, ed. W.M. Fitzhugh (Washington, 1985), 107–30.

74. A.W. Trelease, *Indian Affairs in Colonial New York: The Seventeenth Century* (Ithaca, 1960), 172.

75. Trigger, *Children of Aataentsic*, 699–702.

76. R.G. Thwaites, *The Jesuit Relations and Allied Documents*, 73 vols. (Cleveland, 1896–1901), 55:289–99.

77. Ibid., 26:213; 17:229.

78. Cf. ibid., 47:113, and 58:229.

79. Trigger, *Children of Aataentsic*, 701.

80. Jan Vansina, *Oral Tradition as History* (Madison, 1985).

81. P.S. Schmalz, *The History of the Saugeen Indians* (Toronto, 1977); L.V. Eid, "The Ojibwa–Iroquois War: The War the Five Nations Did Not Win," *Ethnohistory* 26 (1979):297–324; Schmalz, "The Role of the Ojibwa in the Conquest of Southern Ontario, 1650–1751," *Ontario History* 76 (1984):326–52.

82. See, for example, John Steckley, "The Clans and Phratries of the Huron," *Ontario Archaeology* 37 (1982): 29–34.

83. Steckley, "The Soul Concepts of the Hurons" (MA thesis, Memorial University of Newfoundland, 1978).

84. Cornelius Jaenen, *Friend and Foe: Aspects of French–Amerindian Cultural Contact in the Sixteenth and Seventeenth Centuries* (Toronto, 1976); O.P. Dickason, *The Myth of the Savage and the Beginnings of French Colonialism in the Americas* (Edmonton, 1984); F.-M. Gagnon, *Ces Hommes dits sauvages* (Montreal, 1984).

85. Trigger, *Children of Aataentsic*; P.G. Ramsden, *A Refinement of Some Aspects of Huron Ceramic Analysis* (Ottawa, 1977); Trigger, "Ethnohistory and Archaeology," *Ontario Archaeology* 30 (1978):17–24.

86. H.F. Dobyns, *Their Number Become Thinned: Native American Population Dynamics in Eastern North America* (Knoxville, 1983); cf. D.R. Snow, "The Mohawk Valley Project," *De Nieu Nederlanse Marcurius*, 1: 3, 3–4.

87. See, for example, D.R. Wilcox and W.B. Masse, eds., *The Protohistoric Period in the North American Southwest, A.D. 1450–1700* (Tempe, Arizona, 1981).

88. For a critique of these claims see James Axtell and W.C. Sturtevant, "The Unkindest Cut, or Who Invented Scalping?" *William and Mary Quarterly* 37 (1980): 451–72.

89. W.R. Fitzgerald, *Lest the Beaver Run Loose: The Early 17th Century Christianson Site and Trends in Historic Neutral Archaeology* (Ottawa, 1982).

90. Trigger, *Natives and Newcomers*, 144–48.

91. J.B. Jamieson, "An Examination of Prisoner-Sacrifice and Cannibalism at the St. Lawrence Iroquoian Roebuck Site," *Canadian Journal of Archaeology* 7 (1983): 159–75.

92. Jennifer Brown, *Strangers in Blood: Fur Trade Company Families in Indian Country* (Vancouver, 1980); Sylvia Van Kirk, *Many Tender Ties: Women in Fur-Trade*

Society in Western Canada, 1670–1870 (Winnipeg, 1980).

93. Francis Jennings, *The Invasion of America: Indians, Colonialism, and the Cant of Conquest* (Chapel Hill, N.C., 1975); for a similar approach in the field of historical biography see B.G. Trigger, "Champlain Judged by his Indian Policy: A Different View of Early Canadian History," *Anthropologica* 13 (1971): 85–114.

94. J.L. Tobias, "Canada's Subjugation of the Plains Cree, 1879–1885," *Canadian Historical Review* 64 (1983): 519–48.

95. Trigger, *Natives and Newcomers*, 298–343.

96. Linton, ed., *Acculturation in Seven American Indian Tribes*, 501.

97. Spicer, ed., *Perspectives in American Indian Culture Change*, 519–28.

98. Eric Wolf, *Europe and the People Without History* (Berkeley, 1982); Richard White, *The Roots of Dependency: Subsistence, Environment, and Social Change Among the Choctaws, Pawnees, and Navajos* (Lincoln, 1983).

99. Tony Hall, *1784–1984, Celebrating Together? Native People and Ontario's Bicentennial* (Manitoulin Island, 1984), 45–46.

100. L.F.S. Upton, *Micmacs and Colonists: White–Indian Relations in the Maritimes, 1713–1867* (Vancouver, 1979).

101. J.W. Grant, *Moon of Wintertime: Missionaries and the Indians of Canada in Encounter since 1534* (Toronto, 1984).

102. S.M. Weaver, *Making Canadian Indian Policy: The Hidden Agenda 1968–1970* (Toronto, 1981); Michael Asch, *Home and Native Land: Aboriginal Rights and the Canadian Constitution* (Toronto, 1984).

103. Spicer, *Cycles of Conquest*, 289.

104. E.P. Patterson, II, *The Canadian Indian: A History since 1500* (Don Mills, 1972); Grant, *Moon of Wintertime*.

105. Jennings, *Invasion of America*.

THE EXTERMINATION OF THE BEOTHUCKS OF NEWFOUNDLAND†

L.F.S. UPTON

The extermination of native people as the result of white contact was a recurrent feature of European expansion. Certain well-defined causes are offered to explain the process: the first informal contacts spread disease; missionaries arrive to challenge tribal customs and disrupt traditional lines of authority; settlers come to farm on the lands of people already decimated by epidemics, and kill those who resist; the surviving natives move on to be absorbed by other indigenous groups on the fringes of white settlement. Where there is no hinterland to serve as a refuge, as in the Caribbean Islands or Tasmania, the aborigines are destroyed completely.

The natives of Newfoundland were exterminated, but events there do not follow this pattern. The whites who made the first contact were fishermen, as was usual for the area, but no missionaries followed to challenge and disrupt tribal society. No farmers settled in Newfoundland, so the usual reason for dispossessing the natives did not operate; nor, consequently, did the customary rationale for wars of extermination. The insular situation of Newfoundland meant that there was no retreat for the natives, yet, while they were being annihilated, another Amerindian people, the Micmacs, successfully established themselves there in the face of the white presence.

The natives of Newfoundland were the first North Americans to come into contact with Europeans, who called them Red Indians because of their liberal use of ochre on bodies, clothing, food, and weapons. The Beothucks were equipped for life in a taiga economy, in common with the other peoples of the northeastern boreal forest. They used the full range of equipment to be found in the region: bark canoes, snowshoes, moccasins; they wore skin clothing, lived in bark or skin covered shelters, ate out of bark dishes and containers. Their diet was almost entirely animal, caribou from late fall to early spring, fish, shellfish, waterfowl,

† *Canadian Historical Review* 58, no. 2 (June 1977): 133–53.

and berries in the relaxed months of summer. Their ability to preserve food was superior to that of the mainland Indians, for they had storehouses fifty feet long, covered with deerskins and birch bark, with a ridge pole and gable ends. These stores may have been a late development, inspired by the sheds of the white fishermen; and the elaborate deer fences that stretched for miles to control the caribou during the hunt may also be of post-contact origin.[1]

It is impossible to know what the population of any part of northeastern America may have been at the time of first contact; before the first written estimates were made, in the seventeenth century, there had already been a hundred years of exposure to new European diseases. Estimates of the Beothuck population in 1500 range anywhere from 500 to 20 000. The ability of the northeastern forest to support hunters and gatherers has been calculated by Eggan as being one person per hundred square kilometres. Kroeber suggests that the resources of one mile of coastline, in association with interior land, could support the same number of persons as one hundred square kilometres.[2] These criteria would give Newfoundland a pre-contact population somewhere between 1 123 and 3 050 persons. Given that the ability of the northeastern forest to support life decreased as man moved north, the lower figure would seem more reasonable; but as Newfoundland had a climate mild by comparison with the mainland in the same latitude, I would place the pre-contact population at 2 000.

The relationship between whites and Beothucks passed through three well-defined stages. The first lasted from 1500 to 1612 and was marked by occasional kidnapping, casual trade, sporadic pillage, and mutual retaliation. This period saw the introduction of European goods and, presumably, European disease. The second stage began when the Beothucks withdrew into the interior to live beyond the restricted range of the European fishermen who visited the coast. This strategy of withdrawal has no parallel elsewhere in the region, and its cause cannot be known: epidemic disease may have been the catalyst that prompted the decision. The third and final stage began in the middle of the eighteenth century when whites moved in from the north coast to use the resources of the interior along the line of the Exploits River, the very area to which the Beothucks had withdrawn. The resulting competition saw the extermination of the Beothucks despite attempts by British officials and a few belated humanitarians to stop the process.

The first description of the Beothucks was written in 1500 by Alberto Cantino; fifty-seven of them had been brought to Lisbon for display:

> I have seen, touched, and examined these people . . . they are somewhat taller than our average, with members corresponding and well-formed. The hair of the men is long, just as we wear ours, and they wear it in curls, and have their faces marked with great signs. . . . Their eyes are greenish and when they look at one, this

gives an air of great boldness to their whole countenance. Their speech is unintelligible, but nevertheless is not harsh but rather human. Their manners and gestures are most gentle; they laugh considerably and manifest the greatest pleasure. So much for the men. The women have small breasts and most beautiful bodies and rather pleasant faces. The colour of these women may be said to be more white than otherwise, but the men are considerably darker.[3]

Other Beothucks were reported to have been brought to England as early as 1502, but it is not always possible to tell at this distance who the marauding Europeans actually brought home with them. In 1509 a French ship landed six or seven natives at Rouen, together with their clothes, weapons, and canoes. These men were described as being "of the colour of soot . . . tattooed on the face with a small blue vein from the ear to the middle of the chin, across the jaws."[4] By the middle of the century an uncomplimentary note had crept into the scattered references accorded the Beothucks. "The people are large & somewhat dark. They have no more God than beasts, & are evil folk," noted Jean Alphonse de Saintonge in 1559. André Thevet heard that they were "extremely inhuman and intractable: according to the experiences of those who have gone there [Newfoundland] to fish for cod."[5]

The difference between the laughing captives in Lisbon in 1500 and the intractable natives of mid-century was precisely the result of their exposure to those who came to fish for cod. The explorer with his quest for human souvenirs was an occasional invader, but from 1500 on European fishermen were a permanent feature of the summer landscape. Their contacts with the Beothucks have gone unrecorded, but they must have included the occasional trade and pillage that took place elsewhere on the northeast coast of America. But there was an aggravating circumstance peculiar to Newfoundland: the cod-fishery required that the catch be dried and cured before carrying it back across the Atlantic, and this meant that some rudimentary works had to be erected on the shoreline in the form of fish-flakes (drying racks), cabins (tilts), sheds, and landing stages. These buildings were used for only a few weeks in the year, and it saved considerable time, labour, and expense if they were all to be found standing when the next fishing season came around. These abandoned structures were a natural attraction to natives eager to acquire European goods by salvaging what had been left behind; and such salvage would be regarded as theft by the Europeans on their return. From salvaging during the off-season it was a short step to theft during the fishing season itself.[6] This situation did not prevent the growth of a casual fur trade, but it did not make for mutual trust. Cartier stopped at Quirpon in 1534 and exchanged goods with some Red Indians, but two years later came the first report of the natives fleeing at the sight of white men.

Fighting must have taken place, as implied in Thevet's comment of 1557 that the Beothucks "are little prone to warfare if their enemies do not search them out. Then they defend themselves completely in the fashion and manner of the Canadians."[7] It would seem that the cycle of Indian provocation and white revenge began early.

Whether by trade or salvage or theft, the Beothucks acquired European goods in the sixteenth century. When John Guy established contact with a band in 1612 he noted that they had a brass kettle, sailcloth, and a fishing reel; the sail was being used as covering for a tepee. In the last friendly contact ever recorded, Guy sent one of his men ahead to meet two Indians who were waving a white skin as a sign that they wished to parley. Small gifts were exchanged, "a chaine of leather full of small periwinkles shels [sic], a splitting knife, and a feather," a linen cap and a knife; then, "hand in hand they all three did sing and dance." The whites made further small gifts, for they did not carry a trading stock with them: a shirt, two table napkins, a hand towel, bread, butter, raisins, beer and brandy. Two days later, the Red Indians left "twelve furres of beauers most, a fox skin, a sable skin, a bird skin, and an old mitten, set euery one upon a seuerale pole" in exchange. Obviously they were familiar with trade and the items most favoured by the whites.

Guy's success was not to be repeated. In the following year another ship arrived at the same place, and the captain, knowing nothing of the earlier peaceful trade, opened fire on the Beothucks as they assembled.[8] Never again did the Beothucks attempt to trade with the white man. They withdrew from all voluntary contact and remained hidden to the end. Presumably the first phase of contact had had the same results in Newfoundland as elsewhere in the northeastern coastal region. European disease had been introduced there by casual trade, and there is no reason why the Beothucks should have been exempt. Estimates of the impact of these diseases have been made for seventeenth-century New England, where some population figures are available. Cook states that the effect of new endemic diseases, quite apart from epidemic or warfare, was to reduce a northeastern population by 80 percent in one hundred years.[9] If the Beothucks suffered loss on this scale, their numbers would have been about 400 when Guy made contact with them, even less if epidemic or warfare had ravaged them to any significant extent.

The Beothucks do not re-emerge into the written record until Sir Joseph Banks made a few notes on them in his journal for 1766.[10] The obscurity that surrounds them is part of the greater obscurity that surrounds Newfoundland itself. Development was stifled by a deliberate British policy to keep the island an unpopulated fishing station; settlement was officially forbidden and the bulk of the white population were summer transients. From ten to twelve thousand men made the return crossing of the Atlantic every year. Not until 1785 did the resident population overtake the transient, growing quickly to 20 000 by 1804 and 60 000 by 1832. The exercise of authority was proportioned to the needs of the fishery. Ordinary fishermen, styled fishing admirals, maintained a seasonal control harbour by harbour. In 1729 the British government appointed the naval officer commanding the North Atlantic squadron as governor, with the power to appoint justices of the peace throughout the island. His jurisdiction was seasonal, ebbing when the year's fishing and the need for a naval presence ended. Between 1764 and 1830 there were twenty-one such governors, few of whom stayed more than one season. They chose to live for a few weeks at St. John's, but their choice did not make the town into a capital city. There was no person or place of authority in Newfoundland.[11]

As long as the resident population remained small and totally oriented towards the needs of the Atlantic fishery the whites made no demands on the native peoples except to be left alone. However, as the number of residents increased, some began to seek profit within Newfoundland

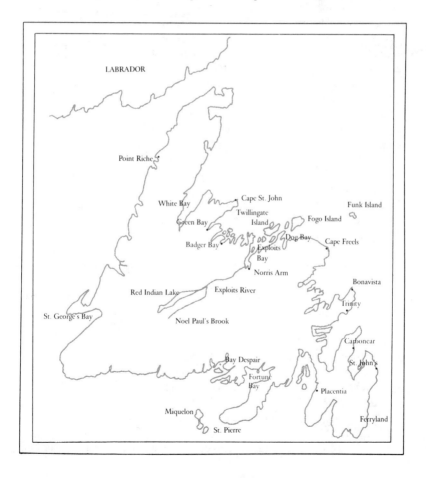

itself, and at that point it became obvious that the lack of government created an anarchic vacuum. English settlers first appeared in the north at Fogo Island in 1729 and Twillingate in 1732; by the 1740s they were well established in the Exploits Bay area. By mid-century there were some four hundred settlers in tiny communities scattered along the north coast. These whites were salmon fishers, and from this base they began to enter into direct competition with the Red Indians for the resources of the land. On their annual migrations down the Exploits River the Beothucks took salmon; so did the whites, and in the same season. The whites sold the feathers of sea birds slaughtered on Funk Island, the very place to which the Indians went for their seasonal diet of wild fowl and eggs. Even more valuable to the whites was the fur trade, which led them inland along the same routes that the Indians used along the Exploits River and its tributaries.

Thus the period of withdrawal ended and the final phase of the Beothucks' existence began. Their refuge had become a source of profit. The diversity of interests available in the north meant that this was the only part of Newfoundland where year-round employment in extractive industry was available as a basis for permanent settlement. Salmon-catchers in the summer became furriers (fur-trappers) in the winter. They laid their trap-lines across the Beothucks' deer runs, thus disrupting the caribou hunt. They destroyed campsites and stores of food, and stole the Red Indians' stocks of fur. They made no attempt to open a trade, and the Beothucks, true to their strategy of withdrawal, made no known overtures to open one. Travelling through and living off the land, the furriers became wise in its ways: they learned how to identify Indian trails and campsites, to calculate the age of a track or the length of time a fire had been abandoned. This knowledge made them dangerous enemies, as much at home in the interior as the Beothucks themselves. The salmon-feathers-fur industry threatened the natives where they lived at all seasons — in their hunting grounds, on their migrations to the bays and river mouths, even on their voyage over open water to Funk Island. The Beothucks resisted as best they could by taking the traps and converting the iron to their own uses, by stealing from the tilts and cottages and boats, and by the occasional ambush. But their main defence was to remain invisible, and it became increasingly difficult to hide from the furriers. This was a hard country in which to make a living. The profit of one group left little room for the survival of the other. It made sound business sense to shoot an Indian.

The most graphic description of the relationship between whites and Beothucks was recorded in a series of interviews conducted by Lt. Pulling, RN, in 1792. He heard tales of Indian ambush: eight men in a punt struck by thirty arrows; Thomas Rousell shot from a blind and beheaded; Thomas Frith, a clerk, similarly dispatched while picking berries; a boy about to have his throat cut and saved at the last moment by his father.

These attacks and the pilfering of sails, nets, traps, and other durables led to punitive raids. Eight whites revenged the death of Rousell, travelling eighty miles before finding an encampment. According to their account, they let the Indians run away, all except two women. They found a tin tea kettle, an iron pot, traps, and nets. They ate the Indians' food, burned three canoes and three of the four wigwams covered with stolen sails. That was in February, with months of winter yet to come. Several veterans of that expedition went looking for stolen nets in the following year, 1791; they found an empty punt and assumed its crew had been killed. Discovering a wigwam, they let two women run away but shot down a man who emerged carrying a child. Both were left to die. This deed, so the murderer explained, was in revenge for the death of his father. That same summer one of the principal employers of the area, John Peyton, led a group whose members were most reluctant to talk about what happened. Three days' travel up Main Brook brought them to their quarry; they fired into the midst of the Beothucks—Peyton had thirty-six pistol balls in his gun—but did not report their kill. They found a wounded Indian lying in a wigwam; the man tried to defend himself and Peyton beat his brains out with a stolen trap.[12] These stories covered a period of only two years.

Governor Hugh Palliser was the first British official to comment on these practices. In 1766 he informed the secretary of state that the "barbarous system of killing prevails amongst our People towards the native Indians . . . whom our People always kill, when they can meet them."[13] He hoped to find a way of making contact with these hidden people and offered a reward for any taken alive. He proposed to welcome the captive with liberal presents and return him to his band overwhelmed at the benevolence of the whites and ready to open trade with them. But the furriers had no wish to see government officials interfering with their trading practices or sharing their knowledge of the interior. One small boy was brought to the governor, and he was obtained by the simple expedient of shooting his mother; the child was of no use, Palliser wrote, "not even to get a word of their language out of it." As a result of this failure, Palliser commissioned two brothers, George and John Cartwright, army and navy officers respectively, to lead an expedition with the object of capturing some natives "in hopes of effecting thereby a friendly intercourse with them, in order to promote their civilization, to afford them the means of conversion to christianity, and to render them in the end useful subjects to his majesty." The Cartwrights travelled sixty miles along the Exploits River, finding numerous wigwams, abandoned canoes, and deer fences; what they saw suggested that the Beothucks numbered between 400 and 500.[14] Following their return, a proclamation was issued enjoining friendship with the natives and directing magistrates to seize those guilty of murder and send them for trial in England.[15]

Official policy towards the Beothucks was now set. Their right to live had been recognized by proclamation but, since they would not show themselves voluntarily, they would have to be kidnapped into civilization either by individuals acting for a reward or through officially sponsored search parties. Neither plan was followed with any energy or consistency, and it was not until 1803 that a Beothuck woman was actually captured and brought to St. John's. Governor James Gambier introduced her to a large gathering at a party, where she showed some interest in the music but none in the dancing. "She squatted on the floor, holding fast a bundle, in which were her fur clothes, which she would not suffer to be taken away from her." Still clutching the bundle, she went shopping, and was allowed to take whatever she liked. And then, as had been proposed long ago, she was returned to her people together with the tokens of white generosity. William Cull of Fogo, who had brought her in, received £50 for his trouble.[16]

The Beothucks were not to be drawn out of hiding. A painting that depicted Indians and whites exchanging furs for blankets and hatchets was left off by a naval expedition, together with some trade goods. Surely the Beothucks would understand?[17] The British government agreed to a full-scale search. William Cull was hired to reconnoitre and reported finding large storage sheds on each bank about sixty miles up the Exploits River.[18] Lt. David Buchan, RN, was ordered to winter at the mouth of the river, find the Beothucks, and "induce them to hold a communication."[19] He set out on 12 January 1811 with twenty-four marines, two guides — one of them the ubiquitous William Cull, and twelve sledges of provisions and presents. After ten days he divided his party: half were to stay with the sledges and half were to accompany him with supplies for four days. At 6:30 on the morning of 24 January Buchan's party sighted three wigwams and achieved complete surprise; they opened the flaps and found dozens of frightened Beothucks, thirty-five adults and as many children. Speech was useless; Buchan made friendly gestures, shook hands; the Indians offered food and the whites exchanged a few personal items for furs. After three-and-a-half hours Buchan decided to go and fetch the trade goods on the sledges twelve miles back; four Indians agreed to accompany him and two of his own men volunteered to stay behind unarmed. Only one of the four Beothucks stayed with Buchan until he reached the sledges, and when the expedition returned to the camp on the following day they found it deserted. All spent a restless night there and in the morning placed blankets, tin pots, and shirts in each wigwam before leaving. After two-thirds of a mile on the return journey the lone Beothuck ran off, and Buchan discovered the naked headless corpses of his two men stretched out on the ice. The expedition beat a fearful retreat, conscious of their small size and the unknown hundreds of Indians that might be all around them. They reached the *Adonis* on 30 January, rested for a month, and went off on a second search. They retraced their route but this time found no Beothucks.[20]

The Red Indians resumed their hidden ways and the evidence for their continued existence lay in the continuing loss of traps, fishing nets, sails, and tackle from the settlements. There were, presumably, more reprisals. Following a particularly daring raid on John Peyton's establishment in 1818 a punitive party overtook some fifteen Indians, captured one woman, and killed her husband when he tried to rescue her.[21] The captive's name was Demasduit but she was dubbed Mary March to commemorate the month of her capture. She was placed in the care of the Rev. John Leigh, minister of the Society for the Propagation of the Gospel, at Twillingate. Leigh, hoping for help from the society, took her to St. John's to be trained as an interpreter.[22] The governor, however, decided that "every feeling of humanity" required her immedite return to her family.[23] There were delays, and it was not until late in 1819 that Buchan, fortuitously back in Newfoundland waters, was able to make the return journey. Demasduit's health had been failing fast, and she died aboard the sloop *Grasshopper* on 8 January 1820, "seized with a sort of suffocation." Buchan set out with fifty men, supplies for forty days, presents, and Mary March in a coffin "handsomely covered with red cloth ornamented with copper trimmings and breastplate." Their approach was obviously watched, for they found signs of hasty retreat in their path. When Buchan reached a spot close to his earlier discovery of the Beothuck camp he left the coffin suspended six feet high in a special tent containing presents and displaying the Union Jack.[24]

Public reaction to the capture of Mary March showed that for the first time "feelings of humanity" were no longer confined to visiting British officers. This new concern reflected the fact that by 1819 Newfoundland was becoming a community in its own right and no longer a mere appendage of the cod-fishery: what happened on the island was beginning to be perceived as the responsibility of those who lived there. For the first time in an Indian killing, judicial process was followed. Leigh, who was a justice of the peace, had the murder of Demasduit's husband, Nonosabuit, presented to the Grand Jury. They found that the act had been committed in self-defence, but at the same time asked for more information; Chief Justice Forbes suggested that new evidence be laid before the next assizes. It was not, but an important gesture had been made.[25] Another innovation was the holding of a town meeting at St. John's that resolved to undertake "the opening of a friendly communication with the Native Indians." There was also a real effort to learn something of the Red Indians and their language; it was from Demasduit that whites first heard the name "Beothuck." Leigh compiled a vocabulary and taught Mary March some English, so that she was able to consult with those who tried to return her home.[26] The mere fact that she was referred to by her own name showed that some at least realized she was a person and not just a curiosity. All this is in marked contrast with the attitude towards the woman brought in by William Cull: then there had been no judicial enquiry into the circumstances of her capture, nobody had tried to learn her tongue, no one had bothered to give her a name let alone think of establishing a society to reach her people.

Feelings of humanity had come too late to save the Beothucks, for the last scenes of their life were about to be played out. In June 1823 the Grand Jury of St. John's returned a true bill against the furriers James Carey and Stephen Adams for the murder of two Red Indians at Badger Bay. Only Carey stood trial; he was the sole witness to the events and pleaded self-defence. Forbes, in his charge to the jury, "pointed out particularly that it is Murder to Kill an Indian" unless there were mitigating circumstances. Was the act necessary for the accused's safety? He claimed to have fired out of fear, and his guilt "could not *exceed Manslaughter*." The jury returned a verdict of not guilty.[27]

Within a week of this trial John Peyton, Jr., brought three Beothuck women to St. John's. They had been seized by Carey and Adams, William Cull, and other furriers.[28] One of the women, the youngest, the only one accorded a name, was in perfectly good health: Shanawdithit was to be the last of the Beothucks. The Rev. William Wilson saw all three of them in the street: "The ladies had dressed them in English garb, but over their dresses they all had on their indispensable deer-skin shawls; and Shanawdithit thinking the long front of her bonnet an unnecessary appendage had torn it off and in its place had decorated her forehead and her arms with tinsel and coloured paper." She enjoyed herself chasing the onlookers, laughing as they fled. Wilson showed her his watch, and, in approved savage fashion, she was amused at its tick; "but when a black lead pencil was put into her hand and a piece of white paper laid upon the table, she was in raptures . . . in one flourish she drew a deer perfectly."[29] After two weeks' lodging at the court house, the women were sent back with presents under the care of Peyton. He left them off at Charles Brook on 12 July.[30] They wandered back to the settlement at Exploits Bay and Peyton built them a tilt on his property. Shortly thereafter the two older women died, and Shanawdithit, renamed Nancy, was taken into the Peyton household. If the Rev. John Leigh had still been alive she might have gone to live under his roof, as had Demasduit, and Leigh's enquiring intelligence would have elicited a great deal of useful information. Peyton was not interested. What little information did leak out was startling enough: Shanawdithit claimed that there were no more than fifteen of her people alive in the early winter of 1823; three had since perished, three had been captured, leaving nine Beothucks all told.[31]

After the natives of Newfoundland had passed over the edge into extinction a determined effort was made to rescue them. John Inglis, bishop of Nova Scotia, made a tour of the furthest corners of his diocese in 1827 and met Shanawdithit at Peyton's home. She told him some very interesting stories: that she had been in the camp surprised by Buchan in 1811, as were all her people; that the marines had been killed when one of them refused to give up his jacket and both ran away. Inglis realized that Shanawdithit was too important to be left a mere servant. He thought a new attempt should be made to reach the surviving Red Indians, with Shanawdithit as an interpreter. Money for this venture could be sought by subscription both in England and Newfoundland.[32]

Bishop Inglis sent his ideas to William Epps Cormack, a man who had already established himself as an authority on Newfoundland. Born in St. John's, Cormack had received a thoroughly modern education at Edinburgh University in botany, geology, and mineralogy; and, further, he had access to the outside world through the *Edinburgh Philosophical Journal* edited by his old tutor, Professor Jameson. The journal had published Cormack's account of his crossing Newfoundland by land in 1822, the first such exploration by a white; he had recorded the topography, climate, minerals, flora and fauna, but had found none of the elusive native Indians. His educated mind could not accept that a whole race might have been exterminated, and he was convinced that Shanawdithit came from but one band of a still numerous tribe.[33]

Spurred by Inglis's suggestions, Cormack decided to do something to prove his theory. He established the Beothuck Institution at Twillingate in October 1827, for the purpose of "opening a communication with, and promoting the civilization of the Red Indians of Newfoundland."[34] The first task was to discover some Beothucks with whom to communicate, and by the end of the month Cormack was off on the search. He travelled as far as Red Indian Lake, finding many traces of the Beothucks, including the grave of Mary March. He passed through a dead land and spent "several melancholy days . . . surveying the remains of what we now contemplated to have been an unoffending and cruelly extirpated race." Even so, he continued to hope, surmising that a few survivors might have moved south of White Bay or down to the southwest of the island. But it was not to be, and two further search parties failed to find any survivors.[35]

The institution's other main purpose was to train Shanawdithit to act as an interpreter. Resolution 15 of the inaugural meeting stated that she should be placed under the institution's "paternal care" and be educated at its expense. The institution having moved to St. John's, its January 1828 meeting resolved to bring her there too. She arrived on 20 September, stayed a few days with Cormack, and was then lodged with Charles Simms, member of the institution and acting attorney general. Cormack found her command of the English language to be very poor, but as she improved and gained confidence in her new surroundings he was able to compile a vocabulary of Beothuck words. However, Cormack realized that there was no longer any point in training her as an

interpreter and concentrated on her artistic talents. The result was a
series of drawings, five of them basically sketch maps and the rest depic-
tions of wigwams, storehouses, tools, and various kinds of preserved
food. The maps told the story of Buchan's expedition of 1811, of the
capture of Mary March, Buchan's return with the body, Shanawdithit's
own capture, and one hitherto unknown double murder about the year
1816. Cormack was able to follow the demise of the Beothucks, from
seventy-two in two camps in 1811 to thirty-one in one camp in 1819;
in that year their numbers were reduced to twenty-seven and by the
spring of 1823 only thirteen were left. At that point Shanawdithit's
knowledge of her people, all knowledge of the Beothucks, ceased. She
herself died of consumption on 6 June 1829 at the age of twenty-three.[36]

Cormack's inaugural address to the Beothuck Institution identified
two villains responsible for the extermination of the Red Indians: not
the English, but the French and Micmacs. "About a century and a half
ago," he said, without offering any proof, the French put a bounty on
Beothuck heads; some Beothucks found two severed heads in a Micmac
canoe and, pretending to know nothing of the crime, invited the Micmacs
to a feast and there killed them all. From then on there was open war,
and since the French supplied the Micmacs with guns, the Beothucks
with their bows and arrows were doomed. It was only after this warfare
had shattered the Beothucks that the English started shooting them. This
was a very comforting explanation, as it relegated the English to the
minor role of finishing off what others had begun. Moreover, the French
were still present in Newfoundland, much to the disgust of the English
residents. France had acknowledged British sovereignty in 1714, but she
kept the exclusive use of long stretches of coast for her fisheries until
1904. Any story that involved her in evil doings would be very acceptable
to Cormack's audience. The tale was sedulously repeated to such diverse
people as the bishop of Nova Scotia and a visiting Cambridge don.[37]
The story received wide currency when *Ottawah: Last Chief of the Red
Indians of Newfoundland* appeared in twenty double-columned penny
issues in Roscoe's Series in London in 1848. The work was reprinted in
Philadelphia and even translated into German. In spite of the title's
reference to "last" the story dealt with the early seventeenth century
and the destruction of the Beothucks by the Micmacs. Tales of Micmac
hostility have been repeated ever since.[38]

The English of Newfoundland had suffered much more from the
French and Micmacs than they ever had from the Beothucks, and Cormack's accusation has that measure of poetic justice about it. The Micmacs had survived the first phase of white contact and learned to
accommodate themselves to the newcomers' trade goods, firearms, and
brandy. They had made their peace with the French missionaries and
amalgamated Christian rituals with their own. They had learned to live
with white settlers, the Acadian French scattered in small numbers across

Nova Scotia. There had been much intermarriage in the seventeenth century and there was an awareness of close blood ties; an "almost symbiotic relationship of mutual tolerance and support grew up between the two cultures."[39] This strength was to serve the Micmacs well as they established themselves in Newfoundland; it was a strength the Beothucks never knew.

The Micmacs had been occasional visitors to Newfoundland, along with Mountaineer Indians and Eskimos from Labrador, for hundreds of years. The French first employed them against white settlers in 1705: "Je les ay Envoyé deux fois sur les Costes Angloises," Governor Subercase informed his minister; "Ils ont donnés aux Ennemis une terreur qu'il n'est pas jamais de croire." The Micmacs were so indiscriminate in their slaughter that Subercase's successor, Costebelle, tried to rein them in, threatening to deny them brandy unless they fought "alafrançaise." They promised they would do so, but the attempt to introduce humane warfare was unsuccessful, and so were Costebelle's subsequent efforts to ship the Micmacs back to Cape Breton. Only the collapse of the French position at Placentia and Port Royal put an end to the scourge.[40]

In 1720 a few Micmacs settled at St. George's Bay on the southwest coast of Newfoundland. They kept in touch with the Catholic priests and French traders of Cape Breton. The situation changed in 1763 with the final expulsion of France from Acadia, the return to her of the islands of St. Pierre and Miquelon, and a shift in the limits of the French fishing shore so that St. George's Bay lay within its bounds. In 1765 some Micmacs landed on the Newfoundland coast near St. Pierre, and Governor Palliser was outraged to learn that they carried passports from the British commander at Louisburg who had been, apparently, only too glad to get rid of them. The next year it was the turn of Lieutenant-Governor Francklin of Nova Scotia to write Palliser; alarmed at the pagan-Christian mix of the St. Anne's Day festivities, he reported that Micmacs were assembling in large numbers with "Holy Water Relicts, Books & other Articles" of the Roman faith and requested Palliser to prevent them communicating with the missionaries at St. Pierre.[41] But there was no stopping the Micmacs; there were 175 of them on the coast in the Bay of Despair area, and there they remained, trading with French merchants.[42] From then on there was a circuit from Cape Breton to St. George's Bay to Bay of Despair and thence to St. Pierre. When the British reoccupied that island in 1793 they found that the Indians from St. George's Bay were coming there regularly to have their children baptized; further, wrote the British commander, the "Political humanity" of the French had paid handsome dividends in ensuring that the Micmacs brought the produce of their winter hunt to them for sale.[43]

English officials regarded the Micmacs with grave suspicion because of these contacts with the French. The Micmacs, having lost their accustomed market with the French for the duration of the war, were forced to trade with the English; they thus became more visible. They were apparently accepted by the furriers on an equal footing, for there is not one story of a white firing on a Micmac encampment, possibly because it was well known that the Micmacs would shoot back. Officials took a sterner line: in 1808 Governor Hamilton tried to stop the Micmacs from crossing Newfoundland, not only because they took fur "at improper Seasons" but also because of their presumed hostility to the Beothucks. The same alarm was sounded by Governor Keats in 1815 when he wrote that the "thriving and populous" Micmac settlements at St. George's Bay "would prove fatal to the Native Indians of the Island."[44] These charges probably derived from George Cartwright's unsupported assertion, published in 1792, that the Micmacs were the implacable enemies of the Red Indians.[45] Officials included that accusation as one in a long list of complaints against the Micmacs and on that basis the notion that Micmacs destroyed Beothucks became the conventional wisdom of the day.

Micmac folklore does speak of hostility towards the Beothucks; once upon a time both peoples lived in harmony, and then two boys quarreled over the killing of a squirrel; the Red Indian boy was killed, his tribe tried to revenge his death and was defeated. This story is so similar to the one explaining Micmac hostility with the Iroquois that it may simply be one variant of a general hostility legend told to satisfy a persistent white.[46] But there can be no doubt that the Micmacs regarded the Beothucks as an inferior people. One communicative Micmac, who stopped a river boat by firing his musket into the air, was asked if the Red Indians, like himself, looked up to God? "No; *no lookee up* GOD: Killee all men dat dem see. Red Indians no good." "Do you understand the talk of the *Red Indians?" "Oh, no; me not talkee likee dem: dem talkee all same dog, 'Bow, wow, wow!'* " The Micmac "appeared so much offended at our last question, that we did not think it prudent to renew the dialogue."[47] Some of this contempt came out in identifying with the whites' bravado: "I see Red Indian I shoot him all the same as one dog."[48] The Micmac, Noel Boss, was reputed to have killed ninety-nine Red Indians, and Shanawdithit had the scars to show that he narrowly missed making her his hundredth victim; but a Micmac long after recalled that Boss had always been ready to give a helping hand to the Beothucks. There were several stories of the kindness shown by Micmacs to those who were, indisputably, their inferiors. The Rev. Silas Rand of the Micmac Mission in Nova Scotia recorded a legend showing how the Micmacs had long tried to prove their friendship to the timorous Beothucks but had only been able to convince one woman and save her from starvation.[49]

It is highly unlikely that the Micmacs played any significant part in the destruction of the Beothucks, either at the bidding of the French or on their own account. The French did not use that part of their fishing shore contiguous with Red Indian territory and would not have suffered from the pilfering and other annoyances that might have led them to offer a bounty for dead Beothucks. Nor did the Beothucks challenge the Micmacs' self-interest. Their point of arrival in Newfoundland was distant from Beothuck territory, their hunting grounds were in the south, their whole orientation was towards the French of Cape Breton or, later, St. Pierre and Miquelon. Moreover, the natural flow of the rivers in the Micmacs' area is southerly, and it would require considerable portaging to journey north to the centre of the island. Some Micmacs were to be found in the north: William Cull took two with him on his expedition from Exploits Bay in 1810. But there are no reports of families or hunting parties of Micmacs in that area. Cormack met numerous Micmacs on his traverse of the island in 1822, but he was following a southerly route. He found the remains of a Micmac canoe on the shore of Serpentine Lake, surmised that it had been brought up from the Bay of Despair along the Cod Roy River, and that this was a route to the centre of the island. John Peyton, Jr., knew of an access: he claimed that the Red Indians used to point out a tributary of the Exploits River by which the Micmacs came north. Since the Beothucks, he said, called the Micmacs "Shannock" — bad Indians — he named it Shannock Brook (now Noel Paul's Brook).[50] There is no doubt that the Micmacs could have gone north had they wished to do so, but the fact remains that there was no reason why they should. And if by chance they had gone, they would not have found Beothucks enough to kill in any quantity.

In reviewing the reasons for the destruction of the Beothucks, Cormack did admit that "the terror of the ignorant European has [sometimes] goaded him on to murder the innocent."[51] The misdeeds of the whites were linked with the greater culpability of the Micmacs from the first, but at the present day the responsibility for exterminating the Beothucks has been laid squarely on the settlers. This interpretation is exemplified by an article titled "The people who were murdered for fun," which cites as evidence reports that 400 Beothucks were massacred at Bloody Lake, another 100 at Red Indian Lake, and so on.[52] These assertions were offered without support, and it goes against all probability that there were ever enough Beothucks in one place at one time to be slaughtered on this scale, or, indeed, enough whites to perpetrate the deed.

Indian killing occurred as part of the whites' drive to use the resources of the Exploits River area and as a defence against intrusions on their isolated and scattered setlements. The Rev. Leigh testified to the universal fear of the natives and the fact that the whites habitually went armed; in the twenty years before 1823, he said, only three Red Indians had been killed by whites, yet eight settlers had been murdered and three badly wounded in the same period. Leigh was as sober and impartial a witness as could be desired.[53] Yet killing an Indian was definitely a source of pride. The man who "has shot an Indian values himself upon the feat, and fails not to speak of it in the mad hours of drunkenness," noted John Cartwight.[54] As the rum flowed, so the stories must have grown by competitive exaggeration from isolated encounters to wholesale mass-acres. The stories collected by J.P. Howley in the 1880s show that a common fate for the first settler in any given locality was to be killed by the Red Indians, sometimes under the guise of friendship. Indian killing was usually presented in the context of revenge, with the avenger seeking out the guilty party.[55]

Folklore concerning the Beothucks is still being gathered in the out-ports. It is still bloody in content. Sandy Cove has the story of Michael Turpin, who was out swimming with William Murray when attacked by Red Indians in a canoe. Turpin was killed and beheaded on a rock that bears his name to this day; Murray escaped thanks to a woman working in a garden who pointed a spade at his pursuers as though it were a musket.[56] An old man living near St. Philips recalled that the brother of one of the Buchan's murdered marines told his grandfather that in the year following the expedition he and his five brothers loaded a boat with artillery and grape shot, sailed up the Exploits River, and massacred the Red Indians they found. Comfort Cove remembers its first resident, John (William?) Cull, who shot many Indians: his grand-father and uncle had been killed at Comfort Island, and Cull himself had been one of the few men in the party to escape with his life. One day Cull and some friends left a loaded musket on the ground, primed to fire. After a while some Beothucks came along; they picked up the gun and it went off. Terrified they ran away, only to be shot down by Cull and his men from ambush. A resident of Brown's Arm heard about the Indians from his aunt, who lived to be 112: she used to keep a chain which she rattled to scare them off, for they thought the noise was gunfire. He told of an ambush by whites at Charles Brook: "dey opened fire, and dey levelled, nothing alive, nothing got ashore, men, women and children, twas barbarous you know. And dey sunk everything right where twas too. Dey cleared away all, dats all was dere see in Charleses Brook at dat time. . . . So dere was no Injuns heared talk of dereafter."[57]

Despite these tales of slaughter, common to all North American fron-tiers, the decrease in the Beothuck population over a period of three hundred years was unspectacular. From 2 000 in 1500 to seventy-two in 1811 is an annual rate of decline of 1.01 percent, far less than the 1.5 percent that Cook found to be the norm for the New England Indians wasted by endemic diseases alone.[58] We may assume a rapid loss of population as a result of first contact diseases followed by a period of recovery and stabilization, with the Beothuck people adapting to new, smaller, hunting grounds. Renewed contacts with the whites in the mid-eighteenth century brought not only death by gunfire but also fresh exposure to disease. Epidemics were spread amongst the populations of neighbouring Greenland and Labrador in this period as a result of white contact.[59] Endemic disease was taking its toll amongst the Beothucks, for all the captive women had tuberculosis at the time they were taken, except Shanawdithit, and she died of it at an early age. Buchan's visit in 1811 may have been the final calamity for her weakened people. She told Cormack that in the second winter following, twenty-two out of seventy-two died, "and the third year also numbers died of hardship and want." The fact that she thought it worthy of note that Demasduit was married four years before bearing any children may point to an unprecedented decline in fertility.[60]

The strategy of withdrawal may have prolonged the life of the Beothuck people, but the success of the Micmacs raises some question about its validity as a response to the white presence. Could it be that the Beothucks died because they did not have enough contact with the whites? There was no missionary to plead for their souls, no trader anxious to barter for their furs, no soldier to arm and use them as auxiliaries in his wars, no government to restrain the settlers. The presence of all these white intruders served to strengthen the Micmacs. Perhaps those same intruders could have saved the Beothucks from extinction.

Notes

1. For the general conditions of life in the area see John M. Hooper "The Culture of the Northeastern Indian Hunters: A Reconstructive Interpretation," in *Man in Northeastern North America*, ed. Frederick Johnson (Andover, Mass., 1946), 272–305. The standard work on the Beothucks is James P. Howley, ed., *The Beothucks or Red Indians* (Cambridge, Mass., 1915), reprinted for Coles Canadiana Collection (Toronto, 1974). This book is a compilation of forty years' search for material concerning the Beothucks and has been the source of everything written about them since 1915. The best brief review of the subject is to be found in W.H. Oswalt, *This Land Was Theirs*, 1st ed. (New York, 1966), 65–80. A "Bibliography of the Beothuck Culture of Newfoundland" has been prepared by Francoy Raynauld and published in typescript by the Ethnology Division, National Museum of Man, Ottawa, 1974.

2. Diamond Jenness, *The Indians of Canada*, 3rd ed. (Ottawa, 1955), 266, asserts without explanation that they "could hardly have numbered much more than five hundred" when Cabot arrived. Much higher estimates, equally without foundation, are more common — for example, Leo F. English, "Some Aspects of Beothuck Culture" *Newfoundland Quarterly* 58, no. 4 and 59, no. 2 (December 1959, Summer 1960), who places them in the 15 000–20 000 range. See also Barbara Whitby, "The Beothucks," ibid. (Summer 1963); James Mooney, *The Aboriginal Population of America North of Mexico* (Washington, 1928), places the Beothuck population in 1600 as "500(?)." This figure is repeated without question and transposed to the year 1500 in A.L. Kroeber, *Cultural and Natural Areas of Native North America* (Berkeley and Los Angeles, 1939), 171. Fred Eggan puts the land support capacity of the area at one person per 100 sq. kms. in "Indians, North America," *International Encyclopedia of the Social Sciences*, 7: 180–200. Kroeber suggests the relationship between capacity and

coastline (169). Archaeology is no help in determining numbers, as no "pure Beothuck occupation site has been excavated" and the burials found are post-contact, containing European items; see Elmer Harp, Jr., *The Cultural Affinities of the Newfoundland Dorset Eskimo* (Ottawa, 1964), 153.

3. Quoted in Bernard G. Hoffman, *Cabot to Cartier* (Toronto, 1961), 29.

4. Howley, ed., *Beothucks*, 7–8; Hoffman, *Cabot to Cartier*, 31–32.

5. Hoffman, *Cabot to Cartier*, 168–69, 177–78. Alphonse noted that the people were named Tabios, the only known reference to this term.

6. Recalling the situation in 1582, Captain Richard Whitbourne, *A Discourse and Discovery of the Newe-found-lannde* (London, 1622), wrote: "many of them come secretly every yeare, into Trinity Bay and Harbour, in the night time, purposely to steale sailes, lines, hatchets, knives and such like" (quoted by Howley, ed., *Beothucks*, 20).

7. Howley, ed., *Beothucks*, 10, 11; Hoffman, *Cabot to Cartier*, 177–78.

8. John Guy's narrative is in Howley, ed., *Beothucks*, 15–18. Gillian T. Cell, *English Enterprise in Newfoundland* (Toronto, 1969), 68, considers that the offer of furs shows that "the Beothucks were more accustomed to the fur trade, presumably with the French, than were the English."

9. Sherburn F. Cook, "The Significance of Disease in the Extinction of the New England Indians," *Human Biology* 45 (1973): 485–508.

10. A.M. Lysaght, ed., *Joseph Banks in Newfoundland and Labrador, 1766* (Berkeley and Los Angeles, 1971), 132–33.

11. See Keith Matthews, *Lectures on the History of Newfoundland* (St. John's, 1973), for a review of the situation in the eighteenth century.

12. John Bland to J.P. Rance, 1 September 1797, with enclosure, CO 194/39, ff. 219–29, Public Records Office, London (microfilm, Public Archives of Canada (hereafter PAC), Ottawa). A slightly different version, entitled "The Liverpool Manuscript" is in the Centre for Newfoundland Studies, Memorial University, St. John's, in photostat. Another copy of Pulling's report was submitted in G.C. Jenner to Gov. William Waldegrave, 28 September 1797, but the document was too lengthy for the clerk to transcribe into the Colonial Secretary's Letter Books, GN 2/1/13, 298–99, Public Archives of Newfoundland and Labrador (hereafter PANL), St. John's.

13. Palliser to Grafton, 31 March 1766, CO 194/27, ff. 178–80.

14. Palliser to Hillsborough, 20 October 1768, CO 194/28, ff. 25–26; Lt. John Cartwright to Dartmouth, 13 January 1773, with "Remarks on the Situation of the Red Indians," William Legge Dartmouth Papers, MG 23, A1, series 1, vol. 16, PAC, printed with variations in *Life and Correspondence of Major Cartwright*, ed. F.D. Cartwright, 2 vols. (London, 1826), 2: 307–25, and in *Beothucks*, ed. Howley, 29–45. A second expedition met with no greater success; see George Cartwright, *A Journal of Transactions and Events* . . . , 3 vols. (Newark, 1792), 1: 3–5; Howley, ed., *Beothucks* 46–49.

15. Review of Instructions for Gov. John Byron, CO 195/10, at ff. 4, 76–78.

16. Gambier to Hobart, 23 November 1803, CO 194/43, ff. 169–70; Rev. Lewis A. Anspach, *A History of the Island of Newfoundland* (London, 1819), 245–46; Howley, ed., *Beothucks*, 63–64.

17. Gov. John Holloway to Castlereagh, 20 May 1808, CO 194/47, ff. 33–35; Howley, ed., *Beothucks*, 66–67. A "Reproduction from description of the picture painted for Governor Holloway" is the frontispiece of Howley's book.

18. "Substance of the Narrative of Wm. Cull of Fogo," CO 194/49, ff. 116–17; Howley, ed., *Beothucks*, 69–70.

19. Eleventh Instruction to Sir J.T. Duckworth, CO 194/49 at ff. 87–90; Duckworth to Castlereagh, 24 July 1810, ibid., ff. 24–25; proclamations, 24 July, 1 August 1810, ibid., ff. 26–27, 113–14; Howley, ed., *Beothucks*, 71; Duckworth to Buchan, 26 July 1810, GN 2/1/21, 29–30, PANL; Duckworth to Buchan, 1 October 1810, CO 194/49, ff. 115–16.

20. Buchan's narrative, 12–30 January, 4–19 March 1811, paper endorsed "Mr. Buchan's Notes," CO 194/50, ff. 153–88; *The Times*, London, 27 November 1811; Howley, ed., *Beothucks*, 72–91, 104; Buchan's sketch map of River Exploits, CO 194/50, map G859.

21. Howley, ed., *Beothucks*, 91–129, has a very extensive account of this event.

22. Letter of Rev. John Leigh, 12 July 1819, before Committee of the SPG, SPGFP (Society for the Propagation of the Gospel in Foreign Parts), vol. 32, 140–44, microfilm, PAC. The society was appalled at Leigh's tangential involvement in an act of violence: Leigh to Rev. Anthony Hamilton, n.d. [1820], before Committee of SPG, ibid., 342f–342g.

23. Orders to Captain Glascock, RN, 3 June 1819, GN 2/1/30, 156–59, PANL; Howley, ed., *Beothucks*, 110–11, 112 List 1.

24. Instructions to Buchan, 8 August, 22 September 1819, GN 2/1/30, 260–62, 299–302, PANL; Howley, ed., *Beothucks*, 116–18, 121–26; Buchan to Hamilton, 10 March 1820, CO 194/63, ff. 64–78; 4 June 1820, ibid., ff. 79–80.

25. "Result of the Enquiry into Peyton's affair with the native Indians," 25 May 1819, GN 2/1/30, 125–26, PANL; Hamilton to Glascock, 3 June 1819, ibid., 156–59; Howley, ed., *Beothucks*, 105, 111. Hamilton to Forbes, 26 June 1819, Forbes to Hamilton, 29 June 1819, GN 2/1/30, 180–81, PANL.

26. Howley, ed., *Beothucks*, 108; Hercules Robinson, "Private Journal kept on board H.M.S. Favourite, 1820," Royal Geographical Society, *Journal* (1834): 207–20, portions in *Beothucks*, ed. Howley, 127–29.

27. *The King v. James Carey*, in the Supreme Court, St. John's, 20–23 June 1823, CO 194/66, ff. 73–77.

28. Ibid.; other accounts in Howley, ed., *Beothucks*, 169–70, 179–81; Buchan to Hamilton, 10 June 1823, CO 194/66, ff. 63–4; Peyton to Buchan, 18 June 1823, ibid., ff. 68–69; Buchan to Peyton, 18 June 1823, ibid., ff. 69–70.

29. Rev. William Wilson, *Newfoundland and its Missionaries* (Cambridge, Mass., 1866), 312–14; Howley, ed., *Beothucks*, 171–72. Buchan was also impressed, sending two of her drawings to Wilmot Horton at the Colonial Office, 24 November 1824, CO 194/68, ff. 249–50.

30. Buchan to Peyton, 28 June 1823, CO 194/66, ff. 70–72; Peyton to Buchan, 23 July 1823, GN 2/1/33, 200–1, PANL; Howley, ed., *Beothucks*, 173. Peyton received £51.15.4 for his troubles, CO 194/66, f. 143.

31. R.A. Tucker to R.W. Horton, 29 June 1825, CO 194/71, ff. 395–98; Howley, ed., *Beothucks*, 174–75.

32. Journal, 2, 4 July 1827, John Inglis Papers, Public Archives of Nova Scotia (hereafter PANS), Halifax; Inglis to Cormack, 10 August 1827 in *Beothucks*, ed. Howley, 205–6.

33. W.E. Cormack, *Narrative of a Journey across the Island of Newfoundland in 1822* (St. John's, 1856); Howley, ed., *Beothucks*, 130–68, 232–37; Cormack to John Barrow, 22 July 1823, CO 194/66, f. 313; Cormack to Bathurst, 22 July 1823, ibid. f. 315.

34. *Royal Gazette*, St. John's, 13 November 1827; Howley, ed., *Beothucks*, 182–87.

35. "Mr. Cormack's Journey in search of the Red Indians," *Edinburgh New Philosophical Journal* (January 1828): 408–10; "Report of Mr. W.E. Cormack's

64 L.F.S. Upton

Journey," ibid. (March 1829): 318–29; Howley, ed., *Beothucks*, 188–97, 216–19; Cormack to Peyton, 28 October 1828, Provincial Reference Section, Public Library, St. John's.

36. W.E. Cormack, "History of the Red Indians of Newfoundland," in *Beothucks*, ed. Howley, 222–29, 231–32, 238–49; Cormack to Inglis, 10 January 1829, ibid., 210; see also 186, 197. Her obituary appeared in the *Public Ledger*, St. John's, 12 June 1829; *Newfoundlander*, St. John's, 11 June 1829; *The Times*, London, 14 September 1829.

37. Howley, ed., *Beothucks*, 182–84; Journal, 2 July 1827, John Inglis Papers, PANS; J.B. Juke, *Excursions in and about Newfoundland in the Years 1839 and 1840*, 2 vols. (London, 1842), 2: 128. The fact that Bishop Inglis heard the story from Peyton a year before Cormack's address indicates that the idea may have originated with Peyton.

38. E.J. Devereux "The Beothuck Indians of Newfoundland in Fact and Fiction," *Dalhousie Review* 50, no. 3 (1970): 350–62. Stories of Micmac hostility received a form of official sanction when they were repeated in the Geographic Board, Canada, *Handbook of Indians of Canada* (Ottawa, 1912), 61–62.

39. Andrew H. Clark, *Acadia* (Madison, 1968), 361. For a survey of the effect of initial contact on the Micmacs see Calvin Martin, "The European Impact on the Culture of a Northeastern Algonquian Tribe," *William & Mary Quarterly* 31 (January 1974): 3–26.

40. Subercase to minister of marine, 22 October 1705; Costebelle to minister, 8 November 1706, 10 November 1707, Archives des Colonies, Paris, Amerique du Nord, c^{11}c, IV, ff. 195–226, V, ff. 30–70, 118–55 (microfilm MG 1, PAC).

41. Palliser to Lt. Col. Pringle, 22 October 1765, GN 2/1/3, 345, PANL; Francklin to Palliser, 11 September 1766, GN 2/1/4, 40, PANL.

42. Palliser to Lords of Trade, 21 October 1766, CO 194/27, ff. 287–92; Palliser to Shelburne, 5 December 1767, ibid., ff. 320–21.

43. Enclosure in Major P.F. Thorne to John Sullivan, 25 June 1793, CO 194/43, ff. 261–64; Thorne to Dundas, 26 May 1794, CO 194/41, ff. 80–82; "Facts respecting the Fishery at the Islands of St. Pierre and Miquelon," in W. H. Miles to Addington, 10 October 1802, CO 194/43, ff. 239–42. There were about 100 Micmacs living at St. George's Bay in 1797, Ambrose Crofton to Waldegrave, 10 January 1798, CO 194/40, ff. 17–34.

44. Hamilton to Castlereagh, 8 November 1808, CO 194/47, ff. 61–69; Keats to Bathurst, 10 November 1815, CO 194/56, ff. 105–14.

45. George Cartwright, *Journal*, 1: 12–13.

46. Compare the stories in Frank G. Speck, *Beothuck and Micmac* (New York, 1922), 27–29, and in W.D. and R.S. Wallis, *The Micmac Indians of Eastern Canada* (Minneapolis, 1955), 449.

47. Lt. Edward Chappell, *Voyage of His Majesty's Ship Rosamond to Newfoundland and the Southern Coast of Labrador* (London, 1818), 71; Howley, ed., *Beothucks*, 288. Chappell may not be the most reliable of reporters, but it is unlikely that this exchange is simply a figment of his imagination; the next quotation corroborates his account.

48. Quoted in James Dobie to Sir G. Cockburn, 10 September 1823, CO 194/66, ff. 324–29.

49. Howley, ed., *Beothucks*, 181, 279, 284–86.

50. Ibid., 69–70, 146, 270. The names Cormack used and the natural features he depicted in no way tally with those on present-day maps, so that it is impossible to

evaluate his surmise. Cormack's map is among the end papers of *The Edinburgh Philosophical Journal* (1824).

51. Howley, ed., *Beothucks,* 183.

52. Harold Horwood in *Maclean's Magazine,* 10 October 1959; see also his *Newfoundland* (New York, 1969), 72–78. The Bloody Bay story is based on three lines in Howley, ed., *Beothucks,* 269.

53. Testimony in *King v. James Carey,* St. John's, 20–23 June 1823, CO 194/66, ff. 73–77.

54. G. Cartwright, "Remarks," *Journal,* vol. 1.

55. Howley, ed., *Beothucks,* 265–81, passim.

56. MS C–77/64–13, 15–16; also 70–24, 23, Memorial University of Newfoundland Folklore Archives (hereafter MUNFLA). MS 69–19, 80 has it that a little girl was beheaded on the rock, which is still stained with her blood. Evidently the stories were invented to explain an unusually reddish rock. The Turpin legend is the only one at MUNFLA to be recorded in Howley, ed., *Beothucks,* 268.

57. MS 72–69, 5–6; MS 75–207, 20–2; MS C–320/66–25, 3, MUNFLA. The only legend that has been checked out referred to three brothers named Pardy, killed by the Red Indians; a visit to the local graveyard revealed a headstone recording that the three died in a blizzard on 27 February 1791. "A Burin Legend about Beothucks," *Evening Telegram,* St. John's, 16 April 1969.

58. Cook, "Significance of Disease," 502, prints a formula for establishing the rate of decline. My figure was reached by correcting that equation to read $\log p_1 = \log p_0 - tk$, where p_0 is the population in the base year, p_1 population in the ith year, t is time elapsed and k the rate of population decline. I am indebted to my colleague Richard Unger for advice on this point.

59. Robert Fortuine "The Health of the Eskimos at the time of first contact," *Bulletin of the History of Medicine* 45 (1971): 97–114.

60. Howley, ed., *Beothucks,* 227.

THE EUROPEAN IMPACT ON THE CULTURE OF A NORTHEASTERN ALGONQUIAN TRIBE: AN ECOLOGICAL INTERPRETATION†

CALVIN MARTIN

As the drive for furs, known prosaically as the fur trade, expanded and became more intense in seventeenth-century Canada, complaints of beaver extermination became more frequent and alarming. By 1635, for example, the Huron had reduced their stock of beaver to the point where the Jesuit Father Paul Le Jeune could declare that they had none.[1] In 1684 Baron Lahontan recorded a speech made before the French governor-general by an Iroquois spokesman, who explained that his people had made war on the Illinois and Miami because these Algonquians had trespassed on Iroquois territory and overkilled their beaver, "and contrary to the Custom of all the Savages, have carried off whole Stocks, both Male and Female."[2] This exploitation of beaver and other furbearers seems to have been most intense in the vicinity of major trading posts and among the native tribes most affected by the trade (the Montagnais, Huron, League Iroquois, Micmac, and others[3]), while those tribes which remained beyond European influence and the trade, such as the Bersimis of northeastern Quebec, enjoyed an abundance of beaver in their territories.[4]

Even before the establishment of trading posts, the Micmac of the extreme eastern tip of Canada were engaged in lively trade with European fishermen. Thus areas that were important in the fishing industry, such as Prince Edward Island, the Gaspé Peninsula, and Cape Breton Island, were cleaned out of moose and other furbearers by the mid-seventeenth century.[5] Reviewing this grim situation, Nicolas Denys observed that game was less abundant in his time than formerly; as for the beaver,

† *William and Mary Quarterly*, 3d ser., 31 (1974): 3–26. The author would like to thank Professors Wilbur R. Jacobs, Roderick Nash, and Albert C. Spaulding for their helpful comments and criticisms of this article.

"few in a house are saved; they [the Micmac] would take all. The disposition of the Indians is not to spare the little ones any more than the big ones. They killed all of each kind of animal that there was when they could capture it."[6]

In short the game which by all accounts had been so plentiful was now being systematically overkilled by the Indians themselves. A traditional explanation for this ecological catastrophe is neatly summarized by Peter Farb, who conceives of it in mechanistic terms:

> If the Northeastern Athabaskan and Northern Algonkian Indians husbanded the land and its wildlife in primeval times, it was only because they lacked both the technology to kill very many animals and the market for so many furs. But once white traders entered the picture, supplying the Indians with efficient guns and an apparently limitless market for furs beyond the seas, the Indians went on an orgy of destruction.

The Indian, in other words, was "economically seduced" to exploit the wildlife requisite to the fur trade.[7]

Such a cavalier dismissal of northeastern Algonquian culture, especially its spiritual component, renders this explanation superficial and inadequate. One can argue that economic determinism was crucial to the course of Algonquian cultural development (including religious perception) over a long period of time. Yet from this perspective European contact was but a moment in the cultural history of the Indians, and it is difficult to imagine that ideals and a life-style that had taken centuries to evolve would have been so easily and quickly discarded merely for the sake of improved technological convenience. As we shall see, the entire Indian–land relationship was suffused with religious considerations which profoundly influenced the economic (subsistence) activities and beliefs of these people. The subsistence cycle was regulated by centuries of spiritual tradition which, if it had been in a healthy state, would have countered the revolutionizing impact of European influence. Tradition would doubtless have succumbed eventually, but why did the end come so soon? Why did the traditional safeguards of the northeastern Algonquian economic system offer such weak resistance to its replacement by the exploitive European-induced regime?

When the problem is posed in these more comprehensive terms, the usual economic explanation seems misdirected, for which reason the present article will seek to offer an alternative interpretation. The methodology of cultural ecology will be brought to bear on the protohistoric and early contact phases of Micmac cultural history in order to examine the Indian–land relationship under aboriginal and postcontact conditions and to probe for an explanation to the problem of wildlife overkill.[8]

Cultural ecology seeks to explain the interaction of environment and culture, taking the ecosystem and the local human population as the basic units of analysis.[9] An ecosystem is a discrete community of plants and animals, together with the nonliving environment, occupying a certain space and time, having a flow-through of energy and raw materials in its operation, and composed of subsystems.[10] For convenience of analysis, an ecosystem can be separated into its physical and biological components, although one should bear in mind that in nature the two are completely intermeshed in complex interactions. And from the standpoint of cultural ecology, there is a third component: the metaphysical or spiritual.

The ecosystem model of plant and animal ecologists is somewhat strained when applied to a human population, although, as Roy A. Rappaport has demonstrated in his *Pigs for the Ancestors*, the attempt can be very useful.[11] The difficulties encountered include the assignment of definite territorial limits to the area under consideration (resulting in a fairly arbitrary delimitation of an ecosystem), the quantification of the system's energy budget and the carrying capacity of the land, and the identification of subsystem interrelations. Assigning values to variables becomes, in many instances, quite impossible.

The transposition of the ecosystem approach from cultural anthropology to historical inquiry complicates these problems even further, for the relationships between a human population and its environment are seldom amenable to rigorous quantitative analysis using historical documents as sources. Yet this is certainly not always so. In the case of the fur trade, for example, one may in fact be able to measure some of its effects on the environment from merchants' records—showing numbers of pelts obtained from a region over a certain time period — and also from lists of goods given to the Indians at trading posts and by treaties. Even when available, such records are too incomplete to satisfy the rigorous demands of the ecologists, but to say that they are of limited value is not to say that they are useless.

Few historians have used the ecological model in their work.[12] Recognizing the need for the environmental perspective in historiography, Wilbur R. Jacobs recently observed that

> those who hope to write about such significant historical events [as the despoiling of the American west] . . . will need a sort of knowledge not ordinarily possessed by historians. To study the impact of the fur trade upon America and her native people, for instance, there must be more than a beginning acquaintance with ethnology, plant and animal ecology, paleoecology, and indeed much of the physical sciences.[13]

In the case of the northeastern Algonquian, and the Micmac in particular, the fur trade was but one factor — albeit an important one — in the process of acculturation. Long before they felt the lure of European technology, these littoral Indians must have been infected with Old

World diseases carried by European fishermen, with catastrophic effects. Later, the Christian missionaries exerted a disintegrative influence on the Indians' view of and relation to their environment. All three of these factors — disease, Christianity, and technology — which may be labeled "trigger" factors, must be assessed in terms of their impact on the Indians' ecosystem.[14]

Among the first North American Indians to be encountered by Europeans were the Micmacs who occupied present-day Nova Scotia, northern New Brunswick and the Gaspé Peninsula, Prince Edward Island, and Cape Breton Island. According to the Sieur de Dièreville, they also lived along the lower St. John River with the Malecites, who outnumbered them.[15] For our present purposes, the Micmac territory will be considered an ecosystem, and the Micmac occupying it will be regarded as a local population. These designations are not entirely arbitrary, for the Micmac occupied and exploited the area in a systematic way; they had a certain psychological unity or similarity in their ideas about the cosmos; they spoke a language distinct from those of their neighbors; and they generally married within their own population. There were, as might be expected, many external factors impinging on the ecosystem which should also be evaluated, although space permits them only to be mentioned here. Some of these "supralocal" relations involved trade and hostilities with other tribes; the exchange of genetic material and personnel with neighboring tribes through intermarriage and adoption; the exchange of folklore and customs; and the movements of such migratory game as moose and woodland caribou. The Micmac ecosystem thus participated in a regional system, and the Micmac population was part of a regional population.[16]

The hunting, gathering, and fishing Micmac who lived within this Acadian forest, especially along its rivers and by the sea, were omnivores (so to speak) in the trophic system of the community. At the first trophic level, the plants eaten were wild potato tubers, wild fruits and berries, acorns and nuts and the like. Trees and shrubs provided a wealth of materials used in the fashioning of tools, utensils and other equipment.[17] At the time of contact, none of the Indians living north of the Saco River cultivated food crops. Although legend credits the Micmac with having grown maize and tobacco "for the space of several years,"[18] these cultigens, as well as beans, pumpkins, and wampum (which they greatly prized), were obtained from the New England Algonquians of the Saco River area (Abnakis) and perhaps from other tribes to the south.[19]

Herbivores and carnivores occupy the second and third trophic levels respectively, with top carnivores in the fourth level. The Micmac hunter tapped all three levels in his seasonal hunting and fishing activities, and these sources of food were "to them like fixed rations assigned to every moon."[20] In January, seals were hunted when they bred on islands off the coast; the fat was reduced to oil for food and body grease, and the women made clothing from the fur.[21] The principal hunting season lasted from February till mid-March, since there were enough marine resources, especially fish and mollusks, available during the other three seasons to satisfy most of the Micmac's dietary needs. For a month and a half, then, the Indians withdrew from the seashore to the banks of rivers and lakes and into the woods to hunt the caribou, moose, black bear, and small furbearers. At no other time of the year were they so dependent on the caprice of the weather: a feast was as likely as a famine. A heavy rain could ruin the beaver and caribou hunt, and a deep, crustless snow would doom the moose hunt.[22]

Since beaver were easier to hunt on the ice than in the water, and since their fur was better during the winter, this was the chief season for taking them.[23] Hunters would work in teams or groups, demolishing the lodge or cutting the dam with stone axes. Dogs were sometimes used to track the beaver which took refuge in air pockets along the edge of the pond, or the beaver might be harpooned at air holes. In the summer hunt, beaver were shot with the bow or trapped in deadfalls using poplar as bait, but the commonest way to take them was to cut the dam in the middle and drain the pond, killing the animals with bows and spears.[24]

Next to fish, moose was the most important item in the Micmac diet, and it was their staple during the winter months when these large mammals were hunted with dogs on the hard-crusted snow. In the summer and spring, moose were tracked, stalked and shot with the bow; in the fall, during the rutting season, the bull was enticed by a clever imitation of the sound of a female urinating. Another technique was to ensnare the animal with a noose.[25]

Moose was the Micmacs' favorite meat. The entrails, which were considered a great delicacy, and the "most delicious fat" were carried by the triumphant hunter to the campsite, and the women were sent after the carcass. The mistress of the wigwam decided what was to be done with each portion of the body, every part of which was used. Grease was boiled out of the bones and either drunk pure (with "much gusto") or stored as loaves of moose-butter;[26] the leg and thigh bones were crushed and the marrow eaten; the hides were used for robes, leggings, moccasins, and tent coverings;[27] tools, ornaments, and game pieces were made from antlers, teeth and toe bones, respectively.[28] According to contemporary French observers, the Micmac usually consumed the moose meat immediately, without storing any, although the fact that some of the meat was preserved rather effectively by smoking it on racks, so that it would even last the year, demonstrates that Micmac existence was not as hand-to-mouth as is commonly believed of the northeastern Algonquian.[29] Black bear were also taken during the season from February till mid-March, but such hunting was merely coincidental. If a hunter stumbled upon a hibernating bear, he could count himself lucky.[30]

As the lean months of winter passed into the abundance of spring, the fish began to spawn, swimming up rivers and streams in such numbers that "everything swarms with them."[31] In mid-March came the smelt, and at the end of April the herring. Soon there were sturgeon and salmon, and numerous waterfowl made nests out on the islands—which meant there were eggs to be gathered. Mute evidence from seashore middens and early written testimony reveal that these Indians also relied heavily on various mollusks, which they harvested in great quantity.[32] Fish was a staple for the Micmac, who knew the spawning habits of each type of fish and where it was to be found. Weirs were erected across streams to trap the fish on their way downstream on a falling tide, while larger fish, such as sturgeon and salmon, might be speared or trapped.[33]

The salmon run marked the beginning of summer, when the wild geese shed their plumage. Most wildfowl were hunted at their island rookeries; waterfowl were often hunted by canoe and struck down as they took to flight; others, such as the Canadian geese which grazed in the meadows, were shot with the bow.[34]

In autumn, when the waterfowl migrated southward, the eels spawned up the many small rivers along the coast. From mid-September to October the Micmac left the ocean and followed the eels, "of which they lay in a supply; they are good and fat." Caribou and beaver were hunted during October and November, and with December came the "tom cod" (which were said to have spawned under the ice) and turtles bearing their young.[35] In January the subsistence cycle began again with the seal hunt.

As he surveyed the seasonal cycle of these Indians, Father Pierre Biard was impressed by nature's bounty and Micmac resourcefulness: "These then, but in a still greater number, are the revenues and incomes of our Savages; such, their table and living, all prepared and assigned, everything to its proper place and quarter."[36] Although we have omitted mention of many other types of forest, marine and aquatic life which were also exploited by the Micmac, those listed above were certainly the most significant in the Micmacs' food quest and ecosystem.[37]

Frank G. Speck, perhaps the foremost student of northeastern Algonquian culture, has emphasized that hunting to the Micmacs was not a "war upon the animals, not a slaughter for food or profit."[38] Denys's observations confirm Speck's point: "Their greatest task was to feed well and to go a-hunting. They did not lack animals, which they killed only in proportion as they had need of them."[39] From this, and the above description of their effective hunting techniques, it would appear that the Micmac were not limited by their hunting technology in the taking of game. As Denys pointed out,

> the hunting by the Indians in old times was easy for them. . . .
> When they were tired of eating one sort, they killed some of
> another. If they did not wish longer to eat meat, they caught some

fish. They never made an accumulation of skins of Moose, Beaver, Otter, or others, but only so far as they needed them for personal use. They left the remainder [of the carcass] where the animals had been killed, not taking the trouble to bring them to their camps.[40]

Need, not technology, was the ruling factor, and need was determined by the great primal necessities of life and regulated by spiritual considerations. Hunting, as Speck remarks, was "a *holy occupation*";[41] it was conducted and controlled by spiritual rules.

The bond which united these physical and biological components of the Micmac ecosystem, and indeed gave them definition and comprehensibility, was the world view of the Indian. The foregoing discussion has dealt mainly with the empirical, objective, physical ("operational") environmental model of the observer; what it lacks is the "cognized" model of the Micmac.[42]

Anthropologists regard the pre-Columbian North American Indian as a sensitive member of his environment, who merged sympathetically with its living and nonliving components.[43] The Indian's world was filled with superhuman and magical powers which controlled man's destiny and nature's course of events.[44] Murray Wax explains:

> To those who inhabit it, the magical world is a "society," not a "mechanism," that is, it is composed of "beings" rather than "objects." Whether human or nonhuman, these beings are associated with and related to one another socially and sociably, that is, in the same ways as human beings to one another. These patterns of association and relationship may be structured in terms of kinship, empathy, sympathy, reciprocity, sexuality, dependency, or any other of the ways that human beings interact with and affect or afflict one another. Plants, animals, rocks, and stars are thus seen not as "objects" governed by laws of nature, but as "fellows" with whom the individual or band may have a more or less advantageous relationship.[45]

For the Micmac, together with all the other eastern subarctic Algonquians, the power of these mysterious forces was apprehended as "manitou" — translated "magic power" — much in the same way that we might use the slang word "vibrations" to register the emotional feelings emanating (so we say) from an object, person, or situation.[46]

The world of the Micmac was thus filled with superhuman forces and beings (such as dwarfs, giants, and magicians), and animals that could talk to man and had spirits akin to his own, and the magic of mystical and medicinal herbs — a world where even inanimate objects possessed spirits.[47] Micmac subsistence activities were inextricably bound up within this spiritual matrix, which, we are suggesting, acted as a kind of control mechanism on Micmac land-use, maintaining the environment within an optimum range of conditions.

In order to understand the role of the Micmac in the fur trading enterprise of the colonial period, it is useful to investigate the role of the Micmac hunter in the spiritual world of precontact times. Hunting was governed by spiritual rules and considerations which were manifest to the early French observers in the form of seemingly innumerable taboos. These taboos connoted a sense of cautious reverence for a conscious fellow-member of the same ecosystem who, in the view of the Indian, allowed itself to be taken for food and clothing. The Indian felt that "both he and his victim understood the roles which they played in the hunt; the animal was resigned to its fate."[48]

That such a resignation on the part of the game was not to be interpreted as an unlimited license to kill should be evident from an examination of some of the more prominent taboos. Beaver for example, were greatly admired by the Micmac for their industry and "abounding genius"; for them, the beaver had "sense" and formed a "separate nation."[49] Hence there were various regulations associated with the disposal of their remains: trapped beaver were drawn in public and made into soup, extreme care being taken to prevent the soup from spilling into the fire; beaver bones were carefully preserved, never being given to the dogs—lest they lose their sense of smell for the animal—or thrown into the fire—lest misfortune come upon "all the nation"—or thrown into rivers—"because the Indians fear lest the spirit of the bones . . . would promptly carry the news to the other beavers, which would desert the country in order to escape the same misfortune." Likewise, menstruating women were forbidden to eat beaver, "for the Indians are convinced, they say, that the beaver, which has sense, would no longer allow itself to be taken by the Indians if it had been eaten by their unclean daughters." The fetus of the beaver, as well as that of the bear, moose, otter, and porcupine was reserved for the old men, since it was believed that a youth who ate such food would experience intense foot pains while hunting.[50]

Taboos similarly governed the disposal of the remains of the moose— what few there were. The bones of a moose fawn (and of the marten) were never given to the dogs nor were they burned, "for they [the Micmac] would not be able any longer to capture any of these animals in hunting if the spirits of the martens and of the fawns of the moose were to inform their own kind of the bad treatment they had received among the Indians."[51] Fear of such reprisal also prohibited menstruating women from drinking out of the common kettles or bark dishes.[52] Such regulations imply cautious respect for the animal hunted. The moose not only provided food and clothing, but was firmly tied up with the Micmac spirit-world—as were the other game animals.

Bear ceremonialism was also practised by the Micmac. Esteem for the bear is in fact common among boreal hunting peoples of northern Eurasia and North America, and has the following characteristics: the beast is typically hunted in the early spring, while still in hibernation. It is addressed, when either dead or alive, with honorific names; a conciliatory speech is made to the animal, either before or after killing it, by which the hunter apologizes for his act and perhaps explains why it is necessary; and the carcass is respectfully treated, those parts not used (especially the skull) being ceremonially disposed of and the flesh consumed in accordance with taboos. Such rituals are intended to propitiate the spiritual controller of the bears so that he will continue to furnish game to the hunter.[53] Among the Micmac the bear's heart was not eaten by young men lest they get out of breath while traveling and lose courage in danger. The bear carcass could be brought into the wigwam only through a special door made specifically for that purpose, either in the left or right side of the structure. This ritual was based on the Micmac belief that . . . women did not "deserve" to enter the wigwam through the same door as the animal. In fact, we are told that childless women actually left the wigwam at the approach of the body and did not return until it had been entirely consumed.[54] By means of such rituals the hunter satisfied the soul-spirit of the slain animal. Of the present-day Mistassini (Montagnais) hunter, Speck writes that "should he fail to observe these formalities an unfavorable reaction would also ensue with his own soul spirit, his 'great man' . . . as it is called. In such a case the 'great man' would fail to advise him when and where he would find his game. Incidentally the hunter resorts to drinking bear's grease to nourish his 'great man.' "[55] Perhaps it was for a similar reason that the Micmac customarily forced newborn infants to swallow bear or seal oil before eating anything else.[56]

If taboo was associated with fishing, we have little record of it; the only explicit evidence is a prohibition against the roasting of eels, which if violated, would prevent the Indians from catching others. From this and from the fact that the Restigouche division of the Micmac wore the figure of a salmon as a totem around their neck, we may surmise that fish, too, shared in the sacred and symbolic world of the Indian.[57]

Control over these supernatural forces and communication with them were the principal functions of the shaman, who served in Micmac society as an intermediary between the spirit realm and the physical. The lives and destinies of the natives were profoundly affected by the ability of the shaman to supplicate, cajole, and otherwise manipulate the magical beings and powers. The seventeenth-century French, who typically labeled shamans (or *buowin*) frauds and jugglers in league with the devil, were repeatedly amazed at the respect accorded them by the natives.[58] By working himself into a dreamlike state, the shaman would invoke the manitou of his animal helper and so predict future events.[59] He also healed by means of conjuring. The Micmac availed themselves of a rather large pharmacopeia of roots and herbs and other plant parts, but when these failed they would summon the healing arts of the most noted shaman in the district. The illness was often diagnosed by the *buowin* as a failure on the patient's part to perform a prescribed ritual; hence an offended supernatural power had visited the offender with sickness. At such times the shaman functioned as a psychotherapist, diagnosing the illness and symbolically (at least) removing its immediate cause from the patient's body.[60]

It is important to understand that an ecosystem is holocoenotic in nature: there are no "walls" between the components of the system, for "the ecosystem reacts as a whole."[61] Such was the case in the Micmac ecosystem of precontact times, where the spiritual served as a link connecting man with all the various subsystems of the environment. Largely through the mediation of the shaman, these spiritual obligations and restrictions acted as a kind of control device to maintain the ecosystem in a well-balanced condition.[62] Under these circumstances the exploitation of game for subsistence appears to have been regulated by the hunter's respect for the continued welfare of his prey — both living and dead — as is evident from the numerous taboos associated with the proper disposal of animal remains. Violation of taboo desecrated the remains of the slain animal and offended its soul-spirit. The offended spirit would then retaliate in any of several ways, depending on the nature of the broken taboo: it could render the guilty hunter's (or the entire band's) means of hunting ineffective, or it could encourage its living fellows to remove themselves from the vicinity. In both cases the end result was the same — the hunt was rendered unsuccessful — and in both it was mediated by the same power — the spirit of the slain animal. Either of these catastrophes could usually be reversed through the magical arts of the shaman. In the Micmac cosmology, the overkill of wildlife would have been resented by the animal kingdom as an act comparable to genocide, and would have been resisted by means of the sanctions outlined above. The threat of retaliation thus had the effect of placing an upper limit on the number of animals slain, while the practical result was the conservation of wildlife.

The injection of European civilization into this balanced system initiated a series of chain reactions which, within a little over a century, resulted in the replacement of the aboriginal ecosystem by another. From at least the beginning of the sixteenth century, and perhaps well before that date, fishing fleets from England, France, and Portugal visited the Grand Banks off Newfoundland every spring for the cod, and hunted whale and walrus in the Gulf of St. Lawrence.[63] Year after year, while other, more flamboyant men were advancing the geopolitical ambitions of their emerging dynastic states as they searched for precious minerals or a passage to the Orient, these unassuming fishermen visited Canada's east coast and made the first effective European contact with the Indians there. For the natives' furs they bartered knives, beads, brass kettles, assorted ship fittings, and the like,[64] thus initiating the subversion and replacement of Micmac material culture by European technology. Far more important, the fishermen unwittingly infected the Indians with European diseases, against which the natives had no immunity. Commenting on what may be called the microbial phase of European conquest, John Witthoft has written:

> All of the microscopic parasites of humans, which had been col-
> lected together from all parts of the known world into Europe,
> were brought to these [American] shores, and new diseases stalked
> faster than man could walk into the interior of the continent.
> Typhoid, diphtheria, colds, influenza, measles, chicken pox,
> whooping cough, tuberculosis, yellow fever, scarlet fever, and other
> strep infections, gonorrhea, pox (syphilis), and smallpox were dis-
> eases that had never been in the New World before. They were
> new among populations which had no immunity to them. . . .
> Great epidemics and pandemics of these diseases are believed to
> have destroyed whole communities, depopulated whole regions,
> and vastly decreased the native population everywhere in the yet
> unexplored interior of the continent. The early pandemics are
> believed to have run their course prior to 1600 A.D.[65]

Disease did more than decimate the native population; it effectively prepared the way for subsequent phases of European contact by breaking native morale and, perhaps even more significantly, by cracking their spiritual edifice. It is reasonable to suggest that European disease rendered the Indian's (particularly the shaman's) ability to control and otherwise influence the supernatural realm dysfunctional — because his magic and other traditional cures were now ineffective — thereby causing the Indian to apostatize (in effect), which in turn subverted the "retaliation" prin-ciple of taboo and opened the way to a corruption of the Indian–land relationship under the influence of the fur trade.

Much of this microbial phase was of course protohistoric, although it continued well into and no doubt beyond the seventeenth century — the time period covered by the earliest French sources. Recognizing the limitations of tradition as it conveys historical fact, it may nevertheless be instructive to examine a myth concerning the Cross-bearing Micmac of the Miramichi River which, as recorded by Father Chrestien Le Clercq, seems to illustrate the demoralizing effect of disease. According to tradition, there was once a time when these Indians were gravely threatened by a severe sickness; as was their custom, they looked to the sun for help. In their extreme need a "beautiful" man, holding a cross, appeared before several of them in a dream. He instructed them to make similar crosses, for, as he told them, in this symbol lay their protection.

For a time thereafter these Indians, who believed in dreams "even to the extent of superstition," were very religious and devoted in their veneration of this symbol. Later, however, they apostatized:

> Since the Gaspesian [Micmac] nation of the Cross-bearers has been almost wholly destroyed, as much by the war which they have waged with the Iroquois as by the maladies which have infected this land, and which, in three or four visitations, have caused the deaths of a very great number, these Indians have gradually relapsed from this first devotion of their ancestors. So true is it, that even the holiest and most religious practices, by a certain fatality attending human affairs, suffer always much alteration if they are not animated and conserved by the same spirit which gave them birth. In brief, when I went into their country to commence my mission, I found some persons who had preserved only the shadow of the customs of their ancestors.[66]

Their rituals had failed to save these Indians when threatened by European diseases and intergroup hostilities; hence their old religious practices were abandoned, no doubt because of their ineffectiveness.

Several other observers also commented on the new diseases that afflicted the Micmac. In precontact times, declared Denys, "they were not subject to diseases, and knew nothing of fevers."[67] By about 1700, however, Dièreville noted that the Micmac population was in sharp decline.[68] The Indians themselves frequently complained to Father Biard and other Frenchmen that, since contact with the French, they had been dying off in great numbers. "For they assert that, before this association and intercourse [with the French], all their countries were very populous, and they tell how one by one the different coasts, according as they have begun to traffic with us, have been more reduced by disease." The Indians accused the French of trying to poison them or charged that the food supplied by the French was somehow adulterated. Whatever the reasons for the catastrophe, warned Biard, the Indians were very angry about it and "upon the point of breaking with us, and making war upon us."[69]

To the Jesuit fathers, the solution to this sorry state of affairs lay in the civilizing power of the Gospel. To Biard, his mission was clear:

> For, if our Souriquois [Micmac] are few, they may become numerous; if they are savages, it is to domesticate and civilize them that we have come here; if they are rude, that is no reason that we should be idle; if they have until now profited little, it is no wonder, for it would be too much to expect fruit from this grafting, and to demand reason and maturity from a child.
>
> In conclusion, we hope in time to make them susceptible of receiving the doctrines of the faith and of the christian and catholic religion, and later, to penetrate further into the regions beyond.[70]

The message was simple and straightforward: the black-robes would enlighten the Indians by ridiculing their animism and related taboos, discrediting their shamans, and urging them to accept the Christian gospel. But to their chagrin the Indians proved stubborn in their ancient ways, no matter how unsuited to changing circumstances.[71]

Since the advent of European diseases and the consequent disillusionment with native spiritual beliefs and customs, some Indians appear to have repudiated their traditional world view altogether, while others clung desperately to what had become a moribund body of ritual. We would suppose that the Christian message was more readily accepted by the former, while the latter group, which included the shamans and those too old to change, would have fought bitterly against the missionary teachings.[72] But they resisted in vain for, with time, old people died and shamans whose magic was less potent than that of the missionaries were discredited.[73] The missionary was successful only to the degree that his power exceeded that of the shaman. The nonliterate Indian, for example, was awed by the magic of handwriting as a means of communication.[74] Even more significant was the fact that Christianity was the religion of the white man, who, with his superior technology and greater success at manipulating life to his advantage, was believed to have recourse to a greater power (manitou) than did the Indian. Material goods, such as the trading articles offered the Indians by the French were believed by the native to have a spirit within, in accord with their belief that all animate and inanimate objects housed such a spirit or power.[75] Furthermore, there were degrees of power in such objects, which were determined and calibrated in the Indian mind by the degree of functionalism associated with a particular object.[76] For example, the Micmac believed that there was a spirit of his canoe, of his snowshoes, of his bow, and so on. It was for this reason that a man's material goods were either buried with him or burned, so that their spirits would accompany his to the spirit world, where he would have need of them. Just as he had hunted in this physical world, so his spirit would again hunt the game spirits with the spirits of his weapons in the land of the dead.[77] Denys described an incident which emphasized the fact that even European trading goods had spirits, when he related how the brass kettle was known to have lost its spirit (or died) when it no longer rang when tapped.[78] Thus Christianity, which to the Indians was the ritual harnessing all of this power, was a potent force among them. Nevertheless, the priests who worked among the Indians frequently complained of their relapsing into paganism, largely because the Micmac came to associate Christianity and civilization in general with their numerous misfortunes, together with the fact that they never clearly understood the Christian message anyway, but always saw it in terms of their own cosmology.[79]

As all religious systems reflect their cultural milieux, so did seventeenth-century Christianity. Polygamy was condemned by the French missionaries as immoral, the consultation of shamans was discouraged, the custom of interring material goods was criticized, eat-all feasts were denounced as gluttonous and shortsighted, and the Indians were disabused of many of their so-called superstitions (taboos).[80] The priests attacked the Micmac culture with a marvellous fervor and some success.[81] Although they could not have appreciated it, they were aided in this endeavor by an obsolescent system of taboo and spiritual awareness; Christianity merely delivered the coup de grace.

The result of this Christian onslaught on a decaying Micmac cosmology was, of course, the despiritualization of the material world. Commenting on the process of despiritualization, Denys (who was a spectator to this transformation in the mid-seventeenth century) remarked that it was accomplished with "much difficulty"; for some of the Indians it was achieved by religious means, while others were influenced by the French customs, but nearly all were affected

> by the need for the things which come from us, the use of which has become to them an indispensable necessity. They have abandoned all their own utensils, whether because of the trouble they had as well to make as to use them, or because of the facility of obtaining from us, in exchange for skins which cost them almost nothing, the things which seemed to them invaluable, not so much for their novelty as for the convenience they derived therefrom.[82]

In the early years of the fur trade, before the establishment of permanent posts among the natives, trading was done with the coast-wise fishermen from May to early fall.[83] In return for skins of beaver, otter, marten, moose, and other furbearers, the Indians received a variety of fairly cheap commodities, principally tobacco, liquor, powder and shot (in later years), biscuit, peas, flour, assorted clothing, wampum, kettles and hunting tools.[84] The success of this trade in economic terms must be attributed to pressure exerted on a relatively simple society by a complex civilization and, perhaps even more importantly, by the tremendous pull of this simple social organization on the resources of Europe.[85] To the Micmac, who like other Indians measured the worth of a tool or object by the ease of its construction and use, the technology of Europe became indispensable. But as has already been shown, this was not simply an economic issue for the Indian; the Indian was more than just "economically seduced" by the European's trading goods.[86] One must also consider the metaphysical implications of Indian acceptance of the European material culture.

European technology of the sixteenth and seventeenth centuries was largely incompatible with the spiritual beliefs of the eastern woodland Indians, despite the observation made above that the Micmacs readily invested trading goods with spiritual power akin to that possessed by their own implements. As Denys pointed out, the trade goods which the Micmac so eagerly accepted were accompanied by Christian religious teachings and French custom, both of which gave definition to these alien objects. In accepting the European material culture, the natives were impelled to accept the European abstract culture, especially religion, and so, in effect, their own spiritual beliefs were subverted as they abandoned their implements for those of the white man. Native religion lost not only its practical effectiveness, in part owing to the replacement of the traditional magical and animistic view of nature by the exploitive European view, but it was no longer necessary as a source of definition and theoretical support for the new Europe-derived material culture. Western technology made more "sense" if it was accompanied by Western religion.

Under these circumstances in the early contact period, the Micmac's role within his ecosystem changed radically. No longer was he the sensitive fellow-member of a symbolic world; under pressure from disease, European trade, and Christianity, he had apostatized—he had repudiated his role within the ecosystem. Former attitudes were replaced by a kind of mongrel outlook which combined some native traditions and beliefs with a European rationale and motivation. Our concern here is less to document this transformation than to assess its impact on the Indian–land relationship. In these terms, then, what effect did the trade have on the Micmac ecosystem?

The most obvious change was the unrestrained slaughter of certain game. Lured by European commodities, equipped with European technology, urged by European traders,[87] deprived of a sense of responsibility and accountability for the land, and no longer inhibited by taboo, the Micmac began to overkill systematically those very wildlife which had now become so profitable and even indispensable to his new way of life. The pathos of this transformation of attitude and behavior is illustrated by an incident recorded by Le Clercq. The Indians, who still believed that the beaver had "sense" and formed a "separate nation," maintained that they "would cease to make war upon these animals if these would speak, howsoever little, in order that they might learn whether the Beavers are among their friends or their enemies."[88] Unfortunately for the beaver, they never communicated their friendliness. The natural world of the Indian was becoming inarticulate.

It is interesting to note that Dièreville, who observed the Micmac culture at the beginning of the eighteenth century, was the only witness to record the native superstition which compelled them to tear out the eyes of all slain animals. Somehow, perhaps by some sort of symbolic transference, the spirits of surviving animals of the same species were thereby blinded to the irreverent treatment accorded to the victim; otherwise, through the mediation of the outraged spirits, the living would no longer have allowed themselves to be taken by the Indians.[89] The failure of the earlier writers to mention this particular superstition sug-

gests that it was of fairly recent origin, a result of the overexploitation of game for the trade. To the Micmac mind, haunted by memories of a former time, the practice may have been intended to hide his guilt and ensure his continued success.

Together with this depletion of wildlife went a reduction of dependency on the resources of the local ecosystem. The use of improved hunting equipment, such as fishing line and hooks, axes, knives, muskets, and iron-tipped arrows, spears, and harpoons,[90] exerted heavier pressure on the resources of the area, while the availability of French foodstuffs shifted the position of the Micmac in the trophic system, somewhat reducing his dependency on local food sources as it placed him partly outside of the system. To be sure, a decreasing native population relieved this pressure to a degree, but, according to evidence cited above, not enough to prevent the abuse of the land.

Other less obvious results of the fur trade were the increased incidence of feuding and the modification of the Micmac settlement patterns to meet the demands of the trade. Liquor, in particular brandy, was a favorite item of the trade—one for which the Indians "would go a long way."[91] Its effects were devastating. Both Jean Saint-Vallier (François Laval's successor as bishop of Quebec) and Biard blamed liquor as a cause for the increased death rate of the natives. Moreover, it was observed that drunkenness resulted in social disintegration as the Indians became debauched and violent among themselves, and, at times, spilled over into the French community which they would rob, ravage, and burn. Drunkenness also provided a legitimate excuse to commit crimes, such as murdering their enemies, for which they would otherwise be held accountable.[92]

European contact should thus be viewed as a trigger factor, that is, something which was not present in the Micmac ecosystem before and which initiated a concatenation of reactions leading to the replacement of the aboriginal ecosystem by another.[93] European disease, Christianity, and the fur trade with its accompanying technology — the three often intermeshed — were responsible for the corruption of the Indian–land relationship, in which the native had merged sympathetically with his environment. By a lockstep process European disease rendered the Indian's control over the supernatural and spiritual realm inoperative, and the disillusioned Micmac apostatized, debilitating taboo and preparing the way for the destruction of wildlife which was soon to occur under the stimulation of the fur trade. For those who believed in it, Christianity furnished a new, dualistic world view, which placed man above nature, as well as spiritual support for the fur trade, and as a result the Micmac became dependent on the European marketplace both spiritually and economically. Within his ecosystem the Indian changed from conservator to exploiter. All of this resulted in the intense exploitation of some game animals and the virtual extermination of others. Unfortunately for the

Indian and the land, this grim tale was to be repeated many times along the moving Indian–white frontier. Life for the Micmac had indeed become more convenient, but convenience cost dearly in much material and abstract culture loss or modification.

The historiography of Indian–white relations is rendered more comprehensible when the Indian and the land are considered together: "So intimately is all of Indian life tied up with the land and its utilization that to think of Indians is to think of land. The two are inseparable."[94] American Indian history can be seen, then, as a type of environmental history, and perhaps it is from this perspective that the early period of Indian–white relations can best be understood.

Notes

1. Reuben Gold Thwaites, ed., *The Jesuit Relations and Allied Documents: Travels and Explorations of the Jesuit Missionaries in New France, 1610–1791* (1896–1901; reprint, New York, 1959), 8: 57.

2. Baron Lahontan, *New Voyages to North America . . . An Account of the Several Nations of that vast Continent . . .* , ed. Reuben Gold Thwaites (Chicago, 1905), 1: 82.

3. Thwaites, ed., *Jesuit Relations,* 5: 25; 6: 297–99; 8: 57; 40: 151; 68: 47, 109–11; 69: 95, 99–113.

4. Ibid., 8: 41.

5. Nicolas Denys, *The Description and Natural History of the Coasts of North America (Acadia),* ed. and trans. William F. Ganong (Toronto, 1908), 1: 187, 199, 209, 219–20.

6. Ibid., 432, 450.

7. Peter Farb, *Man's Rise to Civilization as Shown by the Indians of North America from Primeval Times to the Coming of the Industrial State* (New York, 1968), 82–83.

8. See Wilson D. Wallis and Ruth Sawtell Wallis, *The Micmac Indians of Eastern Canada* (Minneapolis, Minn., 1955), for a thorough ethnographic study of the Micmac, Jacques and Maryvonne Crevel, *Honguedo ou l'Histoire des Premiers Gaspesiens* (Quebec, 1970), give a fairly good general history of the Micmac during the seventeenth century, together with a description of the fishing industry.

9. Julian H. Steward, "The Concept and Method of Cultural Ecology" in his *Theory of Culture Change: The Methodology of Multilinear Evolution* (Urbana, Ill., 1955), 30–42; and Andrew P. Vayda and Roy A. Rappaport, "Ecology, Cultural and Noncultural" in *Introduction to Cultural Anthropology: Essays in the Scope and Methods of the Science of Man,* ed. James A. Clifton (Boston, 1968), 494.

10. W.D. Billings, *Plants, Man, and the Ecosystem,* 2d ed. (Belmont, Calif., 1970), 4.

11. Roy A. Rappaport, *Pigs for the Ancestors: Ritual in the Ecology of a New Guinea People* (New Haven, Conn., 1968).

12. Among the few who have are William Christie MacLeod, "Conservation Among Primitive Hunting Peoples," *Scientific Monthly* 43 (1936): 562–66, and Alfred Goldsworthy Bailey in his little-known book, *The Conflict of European and Eastern Algonkian Cultures, 1504–1700,* 2d ed. (Toronto, 1969).

13. Wilbur R. Jacobs, *Dispossessing the American Indian: Indians and Whites on the Colonial Frontier* (New York, 1972), 25.

14. Billings, *Plants, Man, and the Ecosystem,* 37–38.

15. Sieur de Dièreville, *Relation of the Voyage to Port Royal in Acadia or New France,* trans. Mrs. Clarence Webster and ed. John Clarence Webster (Toronto, 1933), 184. According to the editor, 216, the Malecites later replaced the Micmacs living along the St. John, the latter withdrawing to Nova Scotia. See also Diamond Jenness, *The Indians of Canada,* 3d ed. (Ottawa, 1955), 267.

16. See Rappaport, *Pigs for the Ancestors,* 225–26. If the present article were intended as a more rigorous analysis of the Micmac ecosystem, we would report on the topography of this region, on the soil types, the hydrological characteristics, the climate, the influence of the ocean, and the effects of fires caused by lightning. But since neither the Micmac nor the first Europeans had any appreciable effect on these physical variables—except perhaps that of water relations—we shall pass over the physical environment and go on to the biological. Suffice it to say that the water of numerous rivers and streams was regulated in its flow by beaver dams throughout much of this region, and Indian beaver hunting and trapping certainly upset this control.

17. For a thorough discussion of Micmac plant and animal use see Frank G. Speck and Ralph W. Dexter, "Utilization of Animals and Plants by the Micmac Indians of New Brunswick," Washington Academy of Sciences, *Journal* 41 (1951): 250–59.

18. Father Chrestien Le Clercq, *New Relation of Gaspesia, with the Customs and Religion of the Gaspesian Indians,* ed. and trans. William F. Ganong (Toronto, 1910), 212–13; Thwaites, ed., *Jesuit Relations,* 3: 77; Marc Lescarbot, *The History of New France,* trans. W.L. Grant (Toronto, 1907), 3:93, 194–95. Lescarbot asserts that the Micmac definitely grew tobacco, most likely the so-called wild tobacco, *Nicotiana rustica* (ibid., 252–53).

19. Lescarbot, *History of New France,* 2: 323–25; 3: 158.

20. Thwaites, ed., *Jesuit Relations,* 3: 77–83.

21. Ibid., Denys, *Description of North America,* 2: 403; Lescarbot, *History of New France,* 3: 80; Le Clercq, *New Relation of Gaspesia,* 88–89, 93: Dièreville, *Relation of the Voyage to Port Royal,* 146.

22. Lescarbot, *History of New France,* 3: 219–20, and Thwaites, ed., *Jesuit Relations,* 3: 77–79.

23. Lescarbot, *History of New France,* 3: 222–24. See Horace T. Martin, *Castorologia, or the History and Traditions of the Canadian Beaver* (Montreal, 1892), for a good treatise on the beaver.

24. Le Clercq, *New Relation of Gaspesia,* 276–80; Dièreville, *Relation of the Voyage to Port Royal,* 133–34; Denys, *Description and Natural History,* 2: 429–33; Lescarbot, *History of New France,* 3: 222–24.

25. Lescarbot, *History of New France,* 3: 220–22; Denys, *Description and Natural History,* 2: 426–29; Le Clercq, *New Relation of Gaspesia,* 274–76. Speck and Dexter place caribou before moose in order of importance, but they cite no evidence for such ranking. Speck and Dexter, "Utilization of Animals and Plants by Micmacs," 255.

26. Le Clercq, *New Relation of Gaspesia,* 118–19.

27. Ibid., 93–94; Denys, *Description and Natural History,* 2: 412; Lescarbot, *History of New France,* 3: 133; Speck and Dexter, "Utilization of Animals and Plants by Micmacs," 255.

28. Speck and Dexter, "Utilization of Animals and Plants by Micmacs" 255.

29. Le Clercq, *New Relation of Gaspesia,* 116, 119; Dièreville, *Relation of the Voyage to Port Royal,* 131; Thwaites, ed., *Jesuit Relations,* 3:107–9.

30. Denys, *Description and Natural History,* 2: 433–34.

31. Thwaites, ed., *Jesuit Relations,* 3: 79.

32. Ibid., 81; and Speck and Dexter, "Utilization of Animals and Plants by Micmacs," 251–54.

33. Lescarbot, *History of New France*, 3: 236–37, and Denys, *Description and Natural History*, 2: 436–37.

34. Le Clercq, *New Relation of Gaspesia*, 92, 137; Lescarbot, *History of New France*, 3: 230–31; Denys, *Description and Natural History*, 2: 435–36.

35. Thwaites, ed., *Jesuit Relations*, 3: 83.

36. Ibid.

37. Le Clercq, *New Relation of Gaspesia*, 109–10, 283; and Denys, *Description and Natural History*, 2: 389, 434.

38. Frank G. Speck, "Aboriginal Conservators," *Audubon Magazine* 40 (1938): 260.

39. Denys, *Description and Natural History*, 2: 402–3.

40. Ibid., 426.

41. Speck, "Aboriginal Conservators," 260. Italics in original.

42. Rappaport, *Pigs for the Ancestors*, 237–38; and Vayda and Rappaport, "Ecology, Cultural and Noncultural," 491.

43. See, for example, the writings of Speck, especially "Aboriginal Conservators," 258–61; John Witthoft, "The American Indian as Hunter," *Pennsylvania Game News* 39 (February–April, 1953); George S. Snyderman, "Concepts of Land Ownership among the Iroquois and their Neighbors," *Bureau of American Ethnology Bulletin*, no. 149, ed. William N. Fenton (Washington, D.C., 1951), 15–34; Robert F. Heizer, "Primitive Man as an Ecological Factor," Kroeber Anthropological Society, *Papers* 13 (1955): 1–31. See also William A. Ritchie, "The Indian and His Environment," *Conservationist* (December–January 1955–56): 23–27; Gordon Day, "The Indian as an Ecological Factor in the Northeastern Forest," *Ecology* 24 (1953): 329–46; MacLeod, "Conservation," 562–66.

44. Witthoft, "American Indian" (March 1953), 17.

45. Murray Wax, "Religion and Magic," in *Introduction to Cultural Anthropology*, ed., Clifton, 235.

46. See William Jones, "The Algonkin Manitou," *Journal of American Folk-Lore* 18 (1905): 183–90, and Frederick Johnson, "Notes on Micmac Shamanism," *Primitive Man* 16 (1943): 58–59.

47. See Stansbury Hagar, "Micmac Magic and Medicine," *Journal of American Folk-Lore* 9 (1896): 170–77, and Johnson, "Notes on Micmac Shamanism," 54, 56–57, who report that such beliefs in the supernatural and spiritual survive even in modern times, although in suppressed and attenuated form. Le Clercq, *Relation of New Gaspesia*, 187, 209, 212–14; and Denys, *Description and Natural History*, 2: 117, 442.

48. Witthoft, "American Indian" (February 1953), 16.

49. Dièreville, *Relation of the Voyage to Port Royal*, 139, and Le Clercq, *New Relation of Gaspesia*, 225–29, 276–77.

50. Le Clercq, *New Relation of Gaspesia*, 225–29.

51. Ibid., 226.

52. Ibid., 227–29.

53. Witthoft, "American Indian" (March 1953), 16–22; A. Irving Hallowell, "Bear Ceremonialism in the Northern Hemisphere," *American Anthropologist*, new series 28 (1926): 1–175.

54. Le Clercq, *New Relation of Gaspesia*, 227.

55. Frank G. Speck, "Mistassini Hunting Territories in the Labrador Peninsula," *American Anthropologist*, new series 25 (1923): 464. Johnson, "Notes on Micmac Shamanism," 70–72, distinguishes between the Montagnais, Wabanaki, and Micmac ideas of the "soul."

56. Le Clercq, *New Relation of Gaspesia*, 88–89; Dièreville, *Relation of the Voyage to*

Port Royal, 146; Lescarbot, *History of New France*, 3:80.

57. Denys, *Description and Natural History*, 2: 430, 442; and Le Clercq, *New Relation of Gaspesia*, 192–193.

58. Denys, *Description and Natural History*, 2: 417–18; and Le Clercq, *New Relation of Gaspesia*, 215–18.

59. Thwaites, ed., *Jesuit Relations*, 2: 75; Le Clercq, *New Relation of Gaspesia*, 215–16; George H. Daugherty, Jr., "Reflections of Environment in North American Indian Literature" (Ph. D. diss., University of Chicago, 1925), 31; Johnson, "Notes on Micmac Shamanism," 71–72.

60. Le Clercq, *New Relation of Gaspesia*, 215–18, 296–99; Denys, *Description and Natural History*, 2: 415, 417–18; Hagar, "Micmac Magic," 170–77. Denys, *Description and Natural History*, 2: 418, observed that most of these ailments were (what we would call today) psychosomatic in origin.

61. Billings, *Plants, Man, and the Ecosystem*, 36.

62. Thwaites, ed., *Jesuit Relations*, 2: 75.

63. H.P. Biggar, *The Early Trading Companies of New France: A Contribution to the History of Commerce and Discovery in North America* (1901; reprint New York, 1965), 18–37.

64. John Witthoft, "Archaeology as a Key to the Colonial Fur Trade," *Minnesota History* (1966): 204–5.

65. John Witthoft, *Indian Prehistory of Pennsylvania* (Harrisburg, Pa., 1965), 26–29.

66. Le Clercq, *New Relation of Gaspesia*, 146–52. The Recollet fathers, especially Father Emanuel Jumeau, were able to cause a renaissance of the old traditional religion by encouraging these people to look to the cross once more for their salvation, although, of course, this time it was the Christian cross. We should bear in mind that the cross was an art motif common among non-Christian people, and of independent origin from that of the Christian cross. Whether the cross mentioned in this particular tradition was of Christian or aboriginal origin should make little difference, for the story still serves to illustrate the process of apostatization.

67. Denys, *Description and Natural History*, 2: 415. Estimates of the aboriginal population of North America at the time of European contact are constantly being revised upward. Henry F. Dobyns, "Estimating Aboriginal American Population: An Appraisal of Techniques with a New Hemispheric Estimate," *Current Anthropology* 7 (1966): 395–416, has recently placed the figure at a controversial and fantastically high total of 9 800 000 natives.

68. Dièreville, *Relation of the Voyage to Port Royal*, 116. See Thwaites, ed., *Jesuit Relations*, 1: 177–79.

69. Thwaites, ed., *Jesuit Relations*, 3: 105–7.

70. Ibid., 1: 183.

71. Ibid., 2: 75–77; 3: 123; and Le Clercq, *New Relation of Gaspesia*, 193, 220, 224–25, 227, 239, 253. See also Denys, *Description of North America*, 2: 117, 430, 442.

72. Notice that when a custom in any society becomes a mere formality and loses its practical meaning, it is easily discarded when challenged by detractors, who may or may not replace it with something more meaningful. See Le Clercq, *New Relation of Gaspesia*, 206, 227, and Lescarbot, *History of New France*, 3: 94–95.

73. Jean Baptiste de la Croix Chevrières de Saint–Vallier, *Estat Présent de l'Eglise et de la Colonie Françoise dans la Nouvelle France, par M. l'Evêque de Québec* (Paris, 1688), 36–37; and Thwaites, ed., *Jesuit Relations*, 2: 75–77. See Le Clercq, *New Relation of Gaspesia*, 220–21, where he speaks of converting a noted shaman to Christianity. André Vachon, "L'Eau-de-Vie dans la Société Indienne," *Canadian Historical*

Association, *Report of the Annual Meeting* (1960), 22–32, has observed that the priest replaced the shaman and sorcerer in Indian society by virtue of his superior powers. By discrediting his Indian counterparts (and rivals), the priest became the shaman-sorcerer (i.e., a source of both good and evil power).

74. Lescarbot, *History of New France*, 3: 128, and Le Clercq, *New Relation of Gaspesia*, 133–35.

75. Le Clercq, *New Relation of Gaspesia*, 209, 213–14, and Bailey, *Conflict of European and Eastern Algonkian Cultures*, 47.

76. Denys, *Description and Natural History*, 2: 439.

77. Le Clercq, *New Relation of Gaspesia*, 187, 209, 212–14, 238–39, 303; Lescarbot, *History of New France*, 3: 279, 285; Thwaites, ed., *Jesuit Relations*, 1: 169; Denys, *Description and Natural History*, 2: 437–39; Dièreville, *Relation of the Voyage to Port Royal*, 161.

78. Denys, *Description and Natural History*, 2: 439–41.

79. Le Clercq, *New Relation of Gaspesia*, 125, 193; and Thwaites, ed., *Jesuit Relations*, 1: 165. See Ibid., 2: 89, where baptism was understood by the Micmac (of Port Royal, at least) "as a sort of sacred pledge of friendship and alliance with the French."

80. Lescarbot, *History of New France*, 3: 53–54; Denys, *Description and Natural History*, 2: 117, 430, 442; Le Clercq, *New Relation of Gaspesia*, 116; Dièreville, *Relation of the Voyage to Port Royal*, 161; Thwaites, ed., *Jesuit Relations*, 3: 131–35. See ibid., 2: 75–77, where the shamans complain of having lost much of their power since the coming of the French.

81. Le Clercq observed that since the introduction of Christianity and especially baptism the manitou had not afflicted them to the degree that he did formerly. See Le Clercq, *New Relation of Gaspesia*, 225. See also 229–33, where cases are recorded of native men and women who seemed to feel a divine call and ordination, representing themselves as priests among their fellows.

82. Denys, *Description and Natural History*, 2: 440–41.

83. Samuel de Champlain, *The Voyages of the Sieur de Champlain of Saintoge . . .*, vol. 1 of *The works of Samuel de Champlain*, ed. and trans. H.P. Biggar (Toronto, 1922), passim; and Thwaites, ed., *Jesuit Relations*, 3: 81.

84. Lescarbot, *History of New France*, 2: 281–82, 323–24; 3: 158, 168, 250; Thwaites, ed., *Jesuit Relations*, 3: 75–77; Le Clercq, *New Relation of Gaspesia*, 93–94, 109; Dièreville, *Relation of the Voyage to Port Royal*, 132–33, 139–41.

85. Harold A. Innis, *The Fur Trade in Canada: An Introduction to Canadian Economic History*, rev. ed. (Toronto, 1956), 15–17.

86. Farb, *Man's Rise to Civilization*, 82–83.

87. See Thwaites, ed., *Jesuit Relations*, 1: 175–77, and Denys, *Description and Natural History*, 2:439, for mention of the French lust for furs.

88. Le Clercq, *New Relation of Gaspesia*, 276–77. See also Dièreville, *Relation of the Voyage to Port Royal*, 139.

89. Dièreville, *Relation of the Voyage to Port Royal*, 161.

90. Lescarbot, *History of New France*, 3: 191–92; and Denys, *Description and Natural History*, 2: 399, 442–43.

91. Dièreville, *Relation of the Voyage to Port Royal*, 174, and Denys, *Description and Natural History*, 2: 172, 443–52. If we are to believe Craig MacAndrew and Robert B. Edgerton, *Drunken Comportment: A Social Explanation* (Chicago, 1969), 111, the Micmac encountered by Jacques Cartier along the shores of Chaleur Bay in 1534 were the first historically documented North American tribe to receive European liquor.

92. Saint-Vallier, *Estat Présent*, 36–37, 42; Thwaites, ed., *Jesuit Relations*, 3: 105–9; Denys, *Description and Natural History*, 2: 443–52; Dièreville, *Relation of the Voyage to Port Royal*, 166; Le Clercq, *New Relation of Gaspesia*, 244–45, 254–57. The subject of North American Indian drinking patterns and problems has been the topic of much debate from the seventeenth century to the present. The best current scholarship on the subject, which has by no means been exhausted, is contained in MacAndrew and Edgerton, *Drunken Comportment*; Vachon, "L'Eau-de-Vie," 22–32; Nancy Oestreich Lurie, "The World's Oldest On-Going Protest Demonstration: North American Indian Drinking Patterns," *Pacific Historical Review* 40 (1971): 311–32.

93. Billings, *Plants, Man, and the Ecosystem*, 37–38.

94. See John Collier's report on Indian affairs, 1938, in the *Annual Report of the Secretary of the Interior* (Washington, D.C., 1938), 209–11, as quoted by Wilcomb Washburn, ed., *The Indian and the White Man* (Garden City, N.Y., 1964), 394.

THE ROAD TO AFFLUENCE: A REASSESSMENT OF EARLY HURON RESPONSES TO EUROPEAN CONTACT†

BRUCE G. TRIGGER

Until recently, ethnologists and ethnohistorians believed that the detailed European accounts of Huron life that were produced between 1616 and 1650 were descriptions of a native culture essentially unaltered by European contact. It was acknowledged that Huron culture probably had been enriched and their life transformed in superficial ways by the acquisition of European trade goods, but these changes were not seen as altering their prehistoric culture to any significant degree.[1] This paper reassesses that position and argues for a dramatic effect on Huron life, caused by the growing affluence of the protohistoric period of indirect trade.

The view of changes being superficial reflected the continuing influence of Ralph Linton's distinction between directed and nondirected cultural change.[2] It was widely believed that changes that came about as a result of indirect contact, or in situations where the indigenous people were politically and militarily dominant, were unlikely to disrupt native societies; on the contrary, by means of such changes these societies were able to realize their full cultural potential. Only when Europeans deliberately sought to alter native styles of life and had the power to do so did cultural change become disruptive. This view remains popular and in some cases may be appropriate.[3]

The Archaeological Record

This interpretation, as it pertained to the Hurons, seems to be confirmed in many respects by archaeologists. Prior to European goods reaching southern Ontario, the Hurons, like other Northern Iroquoian-speaking groups, were dependent upon a horticultural economy. Extended families

† Richard F. Salisbury and Elisabeth Tooker, eds., *Affluence and Cultural Survival: 1981 Proceedings of the American Ethnological Society* (1984), 12–25.

lived in longhouses and their villages sometimes had over 1 000 inhabitants. These villages had to be relocated every ten to twenty years, as fields and nearby sources of firewood became exhausted. Many of them were palisaded and located on bluffs, which suggests that warfare was already prevalent. There is also evidence that prisoners were being tortured and that the bones of dead Hurons were being interred periodically in village ossuaries.[4] Nearby villages formed small tribal clusters.[5] Councils had evolved to co-ordinate the activities of at least the larger villages and tribal groupings.[6] All of this was similar to the historic period.

The Hurons claimed in 1640 that two of their tribes, the Attignawantans and Attigneenongnahacs, had formed the nucleus of their confederacy over 200 years before. By contrast, two other tribes, the Arendahronons and the Tahontaenrats, joined only about the beginning of the seventeenth century,[7] following a period that recent archaeological research shows to have been one of unexpectedly great sociocultural change. During that period Huron villages, unlike those of the Five Iroquois Nations, had altered their overall distribution, contracting northward and westward to cluster along the small rivers flowing north into Georgian Bay. Communities and tribal clusters split and merged as part of this process,[8] most likely as localized clan segments—the Hurons' most durable social and political units—realigned themselves. It is likely that the historically known tribes of the Huron confederacy developed only after the Huron had relocated in their seventeenth-century homeland. By contrast, the resilience of clan and moiety affiliations of the Hurons and Tionontatis after their dispersal in 1649 suggests that these groupings, which had social and religious functions, were less responsive to major geographical shifts of location.[9]

All recorded Iroquoian societies in the seventeenth century, including the Hurons, viewed war and trade as alternative forms of intertribal relations. Neighboring tribal groupings either were at peace and traded with each other or engaged in blood feuds of varying intensity. Warfare was essential, since it was the most important way in which Iroquoian men acquired individual prestige.[10] There was also much rivalry between peace, or council, chiefs and war chiefs, even though both types usually came from the same lineages. The former normally had a vested interest in maintaining peaceful relations and trade with neighboring tribes, while the war chiefs sought opportunities to attack them. The latter were supported by the young men, who were anxious to win personal prestige and who viewed the efforts of council chiefs and older men to curtail warfare, not as prudence, but an effort to prevent them from challenging their elders. The relative power of council chiefs and war chiefs tended to vary as the political situation changed.[11] If we assume that similar relations applied in the sixteenth century, the archaeological records of trade and warfare may tell us about the shifting patterns of political power among the Hurons at that time.

Trade before 1609

Archaeologists generally have believed that there was only a limited amount of trade among Iroquoian groups prior to the protohistoric period. A likely exception was the trade between the Hurons, some of whom had lived in northern Simcoe County from earliest times, and the Nipissings, which seems to have been based on the exchange of Huron surplus produce for furs, fish and meat. Elsewhere, the presence of only small amounts of native copper from the Lake Superior region and shells from the Eastern Seaboard of the United States suggests that individual Iroquoian villages remained relatively isolated and that inter-tribal trade was restricted, although it may have been increasing in late prehistoric times.[12] Exotic goods are also rare in prehistoric Huron ossuaries, which generally seem to have been lined with mats rather than with beaver-skin robes as they were in the historic period.

Direct trade between the Hurons and the French began in 1609, bringing with it the period of recorded history. Trigger summarizes the growth of direct trade between Europeans and native peoples during the sixteenth century.[13] Small amounts of European goods seem to have been passing from one native group to another this far inland already in the first half of the sixteenth century. Some may have reached the Iroquoians from the East Coast of the United States, which was visited intermittently by European explorers, traders, and colonists, but their most reliable and important source was the lower St. Lawrence Valley, where there was a gradual increase in the volume of trade throughout the sixteenth century.

European goods were passed from one native group to another. In 1535 native copper was being traded along a route that ran from Lake Superior eastward to Lake Nipissing and the Ottawa Valley and then across the forests of southern Quebec to Tadoussac.[14] A return exchange of European goods could have reached the Hurons by way of the Kichesipirinis, an Algonkin tribe of the upper Ottawa Valley, and the neighboring Nipissings, who must have passed some of them along to their Huron trading partners living at the southeastern corner of Georgian Bay. Ridley shows that close ties had existed between the Nipissings and some Hurons since the earliest development of a horticultural economy in southern Ontario.[15]

The upper St. Lawrence seems to have been less important as a trade route. Though the Stadaconans, or St. Lawrence Iroquoians living in the Quebec City area, obtained limited amounts of European goods before 1534, probably in return for furs,[16] the Hochelagans, who lived on Montreal Island, seem not to have been involved in such trade.[17] No convincing evidence of European goods has so far been found in St. Lawrence Iroquoian sites farther up the St. Lawrence Valley. Suspected European goods have turned out to be made of native copper.[18] It is possible that the St. Lawrence Iroquoians living west of Montreal had been dispersed prior to the 1530s. Documents reveal that later in the sixteenth century Algonkin traders carried European goods up the St. Lawrence Valley to various groups living around the rim of Lake Ontario, including the Hurons of the Trent Valley. This route was closed, around the beginning of the seventeenth century, as a result of Five Nations attacks directed against Algonkins living in the lower part of the Ottawa Valley. It remained closed until after the final dispersal of the Hurons.[19]

The earliest European goods to reach southern Ontario were restricted both in variety and volume. They included rare iron celts, iron awls, and fragments of cut-up brass kettles that were bent by the Indians to make metal beads. It appears that communities that were located close to major trade routes had readier access to these goods than did other groups. Especially during the early stages, some communities probably received no European goods. While the Hurons in Simcoe County continued to exchange their surplus corn, as well as nets and tobacco, first with the Nipissings and later with various Ottawa Valley Algonkin groups, they now also seem to have traded beaver skins, which they continued to trap within their tribal territories until they became depleted about 1630.[20] There is evidence that some Iroquoian groups relocated during the late sixteenth century in order to be closer to good beaver-hunting grounds. One example is the Tionontatis, who moved north into their seventeenth-century homeland in order to be able to hunt beaver in the nearby swamps at the head of the Grand River.[21] Huron communities fragmented when some of their inhabitants decided to move to new locations, while other groups joined together in areas favorable for hunting or trading for European goods.[22]

By 1615, the Hurons were trading corn and European goods for beaver skins with the Algonkins, Nipissings, and Ottawas and European goods for fancy furs and other native luxury goods with the Tionontatis and Neutrals of southwestern Ontario. They were also obtaining wampum directly from the Susquehannocks of Pennsylvania, an Iroquoian group with whom they had concluded an alliance against their common enemies, the Five Nations. This expansion of intertribal trade in native luxury goods late in the sixteenth century appears to have been stimulated by the fur trade.

The Hurons and their neighbors quickly realized that European metal cutting tools, including arrowheads, were technologically and militarily superior to their own stone implements. Yet in the course of the sixteenth century Huron social and political organization underwent changes that seem out of proportion to the utilitarian significance of the small amounts of European goods that they were obtaining. As I observed in *The Children of Aataentsic*, "what appears in the archaeological record as a few scraps of metal seems in fact to have been a sufficient catalyst to realize certain potentials for development that were inherent in prehistoric Huron society, but which otherwise might never have come to fruition."[23] At this period the exotic and perhaps magical properties of these scarce goods and the prestige of possessing them probably remained of greatest importance. Their scarcity may also have enhanced the desire to obtain corresponding categories of native luxuries.

Protohistoric Warfare

Recent interpretations of protohistoric Iroquoian warfare depended heavily upon pottery analysis. Foreign-style pottery found in small amounts in a village site, especially if trace-element analysis shows it to be made of local clays,[24] may indicate that it was manufactured by women captured from a foreign group. Reciprocal presence of foreign-style pottery in two groups more likely indicates mutual bloodfeud and raiding than it does peaceful trade. Imported pottery, especially if it occurs only in particular sections of villages, may attest the forcible or voluntary relocation of extended families as a result of warfare.[25] With caution, such evidence can be used, along with European descriptions of warfare patterns after 1603, to infer the nature of conflict during the preceding century.

On the basis of such pottery distributions, P.G. Ramsden suggests that the disappearance of the St. Lawrence Iroquoians was the final result of wars waged between them and some Huron groups.[26] He proposes that the St. Lawrence Iroquoians at first supplied the Hurons with European goods, but later either cut off this trade or were unable to supply them with enough goods. As a result, the Hurons decided to disperse them and trade directly with the Europeans. Thus the numerically weaker St. Lawrence Iroquoians were destroyed. St. Lawrence Iroquoian artifacts identified in some presumably late sixteenth-century Huron sites are those used by women and not men. Pipes and bone artifacts of St. Lawrence types are said to be absent, which suggests that the men had been killed by the Hurons. Significant amounts of domestic pottery indicate that large numbers of St. Lawrence Iroquoian women had been taken prisoner by the Hurons.[27]

Yet the earliest pottery evidence of contacts, and probably warfare, between St. Lawrence Iroquoians and Hurons clearly precedes the presence of European goods on Huron sites. In addition, European goods are not securely attested on any St. Lawrence Iroquoian sites in the upper St. Lawrence Valley; which could mean that most of the St. Lawrence Iroquoians were dispersed by the early sixteenth century, leaving only those groups that Jacques Cartier encountered at Montreal and around Quebec. The Hurons do not seem to have had a strong motive for attacking and destroying their remaining eastern neighbors in order to gain access to European goods. In part or in whole, they were able to obtain these goods from Algonkian-speaking groups by way of Georgian Bay without them having to pass through St. Lawrence Iroquoian territory. There is also no evidence that the St. Lawrence River west of Quebec City was a major artery of trade while the St. Lawrence Iroquoians lived there. If the Hurons living in the Trent Valley attacked the remaining St. Lawrence Iroquoians in order to remove them as middlemen, why was there no sign of a Huron presence along the St. Lawrence when Champlain explored the river in 1603 or anytime prior to what the French and the Hurons agreed was their first direct encounter in 1609? Why also at this time were Mohawk and Oneida warriors raiding the St. Lawrence Valley below Montreal, preventing the Hurons and Algonkins from using the upper valley, and also raiding the lower Ottawa Valley in order to seize European goods? Champlain's observations seem to accord with early accounts that claim it was the Five Nations (probably specifically the Mohawks and Oneidas) who dispersed the remaining St. Lawrence Iroquoians after 1570 in an effort to capture European axes and other goods from neighboring tribes and probably to gain access to the European trading station at Tadoussac.[28]

If some St. Lawrence Iroquoians sought refuge with the Hurons living in the Trent Valley, oral traditions recorded by the French suggest that others joined a branch of the Petite Nation, an Algonkin tribe living in the lower part of the Ottawa Valley.[29] These refugee groups may have played a vital role in forging the close links that existed in the early historic period between the Petite Nation and the Arendahronon tribe of the Hurons. As long as some, if not all, of the ancestors of the Arendahronons continued to live in the Trent Valley, French goods were probably brought up the St. Lawrence Valley to them by the Petite Nation, who in turn may have obtained them from the Kichesipirinis. After the upper St. Lawrence Valley was closed as an artery of communication by the Five Nations and the Arendahronons moved into Simcoe County, the Petite Nation continued to visit and trade with them by way of Lake Nipissing. Early in the seventeenth century, large numbers of Algonkins were spending each winter living and trading in the Huron country. This trading alliance gradually involved the Hurons in the Algonkins' wars against the Oneidas and the Mohawks, Five Nations groups with whom they had probably formerly had little contact. A few Huron warriors were with the Algonkin and Montagnais war party that, accompanied by Champlain, fought with the Mohawks on the shore of Lake Champlain in 1609. Probably in 1613, and certainly in 1615 and 1638, large war parties made up of Hurons and Algonkins attacked these two eastern Five Nations tribes.[30]

Little is known about warfare among neighboring Iroquoian groups in southern Ontario in prehistoric times, although it may have been common. Ceramic analysis provides little evidence of warfare or of any other kind of mutual contact between the Hurons and the Seneca and Cayuga tribes of the Five Nations prior to about 1550. It is true that by

1609 warfare with these tribes was a significant factor in Huron life. Yet it is questionable that all Hurons had moved north into Simcoe County before 1600 to avoid the attacks of the Five Nations.[31] Even when the Hurons informed Champlain that they had abandoned the Trent Valley in response to Five Nations warfare[32] this does not necessarily mean that they moved into Simcoe County to avoid Five Nations attacks on their villages. Rather it suggests that when the Five Nations cut the trade route running up the St. Lawrence, along which the Algonkins were supplying the Hurons living in the Trent Valley with European goods, these groups may have moved north into Simcoe County to be closer to the Georgian Bay route, which remained open.[33] While this explanation acknowledges Five Nations warfare as one reason for the clustering of all Huron groups in northern Simcoe County by the beginning of the seventeenth century, it interprets the primary aim of this relocation as being to have continuing access to familiar trading partners.

Protohistoric Political Change

The precise movements bringing together the population that constituted the Huron confederacy in the historic period are not yet known. One can, however, speculate about the social and political processes that accompanied these moves. As Huron groups shifted north, they must have settled on land that had belonged to the ancestors of the Attigna-wantan and Attigneenongnahac tribes, whose villages in historic times were confined to the western part of northern Simcoe County. All of the land to the south and east that had been abandoned by Huron settlement remained Huron hunting territory. Yet we do not know to what degree these areas were thrown open to use by all Hurons or were reserved for their former inhabitants. Presumably, the Attignawantans and Attigneenongnahacs received some compensation for relinquishing their own land for settlement by other Huron groups. The newcomers would also have had to learn about the northern trade routes from the original inhabitants of Simcoe County and required the latter's consent in order to use them. As the Huron population became more densely settled, trade for skins and meat with northern hunting groups became an essential part of their economy. We do not know to what degree the newcomers' gaining permission to settle near Georgian Bay and to trade directly with the north was a peaceful process or one that involved intimidation or even conflict between various Huron groups. The Hurons spoke about waging fierce wars in late protohistoric times against the neighboring Tionontatis.[34] They may have had similar conflicts with the Neutrals.[35] These wars ended when the Hurons began to supply European goods to these groups on a regular basis. Neither was ever allowed to join the Huron confederacy, however, or to use the Hurons' northern trade routes.

Archaeologists have not yet traced the origins of the historic Huron tribes, although I have already remarked that none of them seems precisely equivalent to local village clusters observed at an earlier date. The archaeological record suggests that the Huron confederacy was greatly expanded, if (contrary to Huron traditions) it did not come into existence, around the end of the sixteenth century.[36] The councils that managed the affairs of the Huron tribes and confederacy were probably extensions of an older system of village government. Such tribal governments as had existed in the past must have been greatly extended and elaborated as the Huron confederacy expanded to embrace its final membership. The expanded tribal association and the denser Huron settlement pattern required new and more elaborate hierarchies of chiefs and the development of more complex rituals of consultation than had existed previously. Such patterns could not develop without much discussion and bargaining.

While the details remain unclear, the late sixteenth century must have been a period of rapid social and political change for the Hurons. This would have produced considerable tension and an unknown amount of warfare. While the Huron confederacy suppressed such warfare as had previously existed among the Hurons, and expanding trading patterns ultimately eliminated it between them and the Tionontatis and Neutrals, new alliances, possibly new forms of economic competition, and the continuing search for individual prestige created new conflicts with all of the tribes of the Five Nations. Although Huron trading networks had expanded with tribes living to the north and south, during the sixteenth century the volume of intertribal trade remained limited by comparison with trade in the historic period.[37] Only a relatively small number of Hurons would have been engaged in such trade. Hence, during the protohistoric period, expanding trade probably enhanced the power of council or peace chiefs far less than the tensions and dislocations of that period enhanced the power of the war chiefs. Yet we must enquire why this is not reflected in any obvious way in later French descriptions of Huron society.

Historic Trade, 1609–15

The first direct contact between Hurons and French occurred in 1609.[38] That summer, Ochasteguin, an Arendahronon chief, and some of his men accompanied their Petite Nation trading partners to the St. Lawrence ostensibly to join Champlain on an expedition against the Mohawks. The Kichesipirini Algonkins, seeking to remain significant middlemen in the trade between the French and the Huron, sought to discourage the conclusion of a formal trading alliance between them. Nevertheless, in 1611, the chiefs of the recently expanded Huron confederacy council secretly sent presents to Champlain inviting him to visit the Huron country to conclude an alliance with them. In spite of strenuous Kichesipirini opposition, Champlain was able to visit the Huron country in 1615, where a large joint Huron and Algonkin raiding party had assembled to attack the Oneidas or Onondagas. While allegedly going there to join this war party, Champlain was able to visit each Huron village and conclude a formal alliance with its chiefs.[39]

Between 1609 and 1615, the allocation of rights to trade with the French created a major political problem for the Hurons. According to their traditional practice, the right to control the use of a trade route belonged to the man who had first pioneered it, or possibly to the leader of his clan segment. This individual had the right to charge other traders for the privilege of using his route, although there was no effective mechanism for enforcing this.[40] Thus, although Ochasteguin had pioneered the trade with the French, in later years it was Atironta, the highest ranking chief of his tribe, who was the principal trading partner of the French. Even so, direct trade with the French was far too important for one man or even one tribe to control and soon all Huron groups were demanding a share of it. Prior to 1611, the Arendahronons shared the right to trade with the French not only among their own headmen but also with all the headmen in the other tribes of the Huron confederacy. Atironta preserved only his role as the chief Huron ally of the French. Each of the Huron council chiefs now had his own right to trade with the French. It was in that capacity that the many Huron chiefs collectively and individually concluded their alliance with Champlain. Most of the trading with the French was done by the Attignawantans, the largest and most prestigious tribe of the Huron confederacy.

Historic Political Change, 1615–29

Once the Hurons began to trade directly with the French, they were able to obtain a greater amount and variety of European goods than ever before. The Ottawas and Nipissings became satellites of the Hurons, in the sense that these groups collected furs from bands to the west and north, which in turn they traded with the Hurons for cornmeal and European goods, rather than seeking to obtain the latter directly from the French. The unaccustomed wealth that began to reach the Huron country at this time must have greatly enhanced the prestige of the council, or peace chiefs, who either personally traded with the French and with neighboring Indian groups or received substantial presents in return for sanctioning others to do so. This permitted these chiefs to redistribute large amounts of exotic goods, and especially goods of European origin, to their kin, clients, and other Hurons generally.

The increasing economic importance of the Huron peace chiefs and a period of relative tranquillity, both among the Huron tribes and in their relations with their neighbors, including the Five Nations, must have helped these chiefs to regain their prestige at the expense of the war chiefs. It no doubt also helped to stabilize the Huron government after a period of marked instability and rapid change. A possible reminder of the use that the council chiefs had made of the developing trade with the French to recover their authority was the apparently deprecatory nicknames, such as "big stones" and "stay-at-homes," that Jean de Brébeuf recorded in 1636 the Hurons were now applying to their headmen.[41]

The year 1615 marked the beginning of a 15-year period of considerable stability for the Hurons. Their economic life was greatly enriched by trade, but the Huron country was not flooded with European goods. The 800 miles of canoe travel and portages that separated it from the French trading posts along the St. Lawrence River precluded obtaining enough European goods to satisfy fully the growing needs and wants of a large Huron population. By 1630, the Hurons had also exhausted the beaver stock of their own tribal territories and henceforth had to obtain all the furs they traded with the French from other native groups, often in return for new or second-hand European goods. Hence the Hurons never possessed the vast numbers and array of European goods that tribes, such as the Mohawks, who lived closer to European trading posts were able to obtain.[42] Nevertheless, rituals such as the Ononharoia, or winter festival, and the periodically celebrated Feasts of the Dead seem to have been considerably elaborated, as a means both of redistributing goods and of promoting social solidarity. As the latter ritual grew more elaborate, large amounts of goods were exchanged between the community that was burying its dead prior to relocation and the other Huron groups as well as foreign trading partners who were invited to participate as guests. Large numbers of furs, kettles and other trade goods were also buried with the dead or destroyed in the course of this ritual. Obtaining metal cutting tools speeded the work of forest clearance, made it easier to use large posts to construct houses and palisades, and stimulated the elaboration of traditional arts and crafts, such as bone working. Broken metal kettles provided raw material for more extensive metal working, using techniques applied in prehistoric times to native copper. The Hurons and neighboring Iroquoian tribes also modified iron tools for their own purposes.[43] The metal arrowheads that they either purchased from the French or made out of fragments of metal kettles could pierce traditional Iroquoian body armor and hence were essential for keeping militarily abreast of the Five Nations. Yet, while the Hurons clearly recognized the advantages of possessing European cutting tools and metal kettles, the limited supply of these goods kept pottery making and the manufacture of stone and bone tools alive until after the dispersal of the Huron confederacy.

There is no evidence that the right of peace chiefs to control trade routes or to distribute much of the goods brought to the Huron country was being challenged by other Huron traders. Clan solidarity remained an important factor in Huron life. There is also no evidence that these chiefs were attempting to hoard surplus wealth as an end in itself. Their prestige continued to be validated by the redistribution of such wealth. Individuals who refused to participate whole-heartedly in such activities still risked being suspected or even accused of witchcraft.[44] All of this suggests that while Huron social and political structure existed on a vaster scale than in prehistoric times, it continued to be founded upon essentially traditional role concepts. Warfare with the Five Nations continued at a moderate pace but does not appear to have undermined the power of the council chiefs at this period.

Nevertheless, archaeological data make it clear that much of what seems "traditional" in historic Huron society represented a restoration of stability and, in particular, of the roles played by the council chiefs after a long period of change and dislocation. By comparison with 50 years earlier, the Huron settlement pattern had been greatly altered, so that all Huron people were living in close proximity to one another. New tribal structures seem to have emerged, the confederacy was vastly expanded, if, indeed, it had not come into being in the interval, trading networks had proliferated and the volume of trade vastly increased, and crafts and ritual life had been enriched. The new social order was based on an expanded application of principles that must already have been present and applied in embryonic form in Huron society in prehistoric times and, in this sense, was traditional. Yet the new Huron society was larger and more complex than it had been previously and the process of expansion must have been extremely stressful even if the final result was stable. The whole process was nondirected, in the sense that Europeans had not deliberately sought to influence it. The main dislocations had occurred prior to direct contact with them and while the supply of European goods remained extremely limited. The period of relative affluence that followed direct contact was thus a period of renewed stability.

Mission Period and Decline, 1634–49

The moderately well-documented period of prosperity and stability came to an end in 1629 with the temporary expulsion of the French from Quebec by English privateers. This disrupted Huron trading relations and led to a period of renewed crisis in intertribal relations in eastern Canada. The return of the French to the Huron country in 1634 was followed by a series of epidemics that by 1640 had halved the population of the Hurons and of neighboring peoples. There is no evidence of similar epidemics earlier in the seventeenth century in this region.[45] In the course of these epidemics, many of the most experienced chiefs, ritualists, and craftsmen perished. This was followed by increasingly severe attacks by the Five Nations, who were anxious to acquire more furs by raiding and expanding their hunting territories to the north. Finally, the coercive element that the Jesuits forced French traders and government officials to introduce into French–Huron relations in an effort to Christianize the Hurons put additional strain on their political and cultural life prior to their dispersal by the Five Nations in 1649.

Conclusions

No one can doubt the need to interpret ethnographic data in an historical perspective. Yet, especially for the early phases of direct and indirect contact between Europeans and native peoples, only archaeological data can provide adequate historical context. The Hurons, as they were described by European visitors between 1615 and 1650, seemed to be a traditional society, largely unaffected by the presence of European traders in North America. Yet archaeological data reveal that major changes in Huron settlement patterns took place during the century preceding the earliest French descriptions of Huron culture. It seems that these shifts were brought about mainly by a desire to secure and maintain access to sources of European goods. The social and political changes associated with these shifts in settlement must have been accompanied by much uncertainty and tension and probably by overt conflict. Clearly not all change that occurs independently of European control and direction is easy and peaceful. It is also of interest that the main period of crisis preceded the increased flow of European goods into the Huron country that began after the Huron started to trade directly with the French in 1609.

By contrast, the period from 1615 to 1629 was one of social and political stability, accompanied by a higher level of affluence and cultural florescence. The new society remained traditional in the sense that redistribution was highly valued, peace chiefs had reconsolidated their leading role in co-ordinating Huron life, and Huron political behavior remained noncoercive. Yet Huron society was co-ordinated on a larger scale than it had been formerly and the dense nucleation of the Huron population created a social environment not found among the Five Nations, whose tribes continued to live in separate clusters as they had done in prehistoric times. Although the scale of Huron society and Huron cultural life was greatly altered, the new society was able to cope with relative affluence and, indeed, had used this affluence to achieve an impressive level of social and political stability. Yet their achievements were doomed to destruction in 1649 by the Five Nations' need for more abundant supplies of beaver pelts, intertribal and international competition, and French interference in Huron life in support of Jesuit mission policy.

Notes

1. Elisabeth Tooker, *An Ethnography of the Huron Indians, 1615–1649*, Bureau of American Ethnology Bulletin no. 190 (1964), 4; Bruce G. Trigger, *The Huron: Farmers of the North* (New York, 1969).

2. Ralph Linton, ed., *Acculturation in Seven American Indian Tribes* (New York, 1940), 501–2; E.H. Spicer, ed., *Perspectives in American Indian Cultural Change* (Chicago, 1961), 519–20.

3. Trigger, *The Children of Aataentsic: A History of the Huron People to 1660*, 2 vols. (Montreal, 1976); Robin Fisher, *Contact and Conflict: Indian–European Relations in British Columbia, 1774–1890* (Vancouver, 1977); Toby Morantz, "The Fur Trade and the Cree of James Bay," in *Old Trails and New Directions*, ed. C.M. Judd and A.J. Ray (Toronto, 1980), 39–58.

4. J.V. Wright, *The Ontario Iroquois Tradition*, National Museum of Canada Bulletin no. 210 (Ottawa, 1966).

5. P.G. Ramsden, *A Refinement of Some Aspects of Huron Ceramic Analysis*, Mercury Series, no. 68 (Ottawa: Archaeological Survey of Canada, 1977).

6. Trigger, "Inequality and Communication in Early Civilizations," *Anthropologica* 18 (1976): 30–34.

7. Reuben Gold Thwaites, *The Jesuit Relations and Allied Documents*, 73 vols. (Cleveland, 1896–1901), 16: 227–29.

8. Ramsden, *Refinement*.

9. Trigger, *Children of Aataentsic*, 825.

10. Trigger, *The Huron*, 42–53.

11. Thwaites, ed., *Jesuit Relations*, 15:53.

12. W.A. Ritchie, *The Archaeology of New York State* (New York, 1965), 293.

13. Trigger, "Sixteenth Century Ontario: History, Ethnohistory and Archaeology," *Ontario History* 72 (1979): 205–23.

14. H.P. Biggar, *The Voyages of Jacques Cartier*, Publications of the Public Archives of Canada, no. 11 (Ottawa, 1924), 106, 171.

15. Frank Ridley, "The Frank Bay Site, Lake Nipissing, Ontario," *American Antiquity* 20 (1954): 40–50.

16. Trigger, *Children of Aataentsic*, 214.

17. Biggar, *Voyages of Jacques Cartier*, 160–61.

18. J.F. Pendergast and J.V. Wright, personal communications.

19. Trigger, *Children of Aataentsic*, 233–34.

20. Gabriel Sagard, *Histoire du Canada*, 4 vols. (Paris, 1866), 585.

21. Ramsden, *Refinement*, 274.

22. Ibid., 292, 286.

23. Trigger, *Children of Aataentsic*, 245.

24. Trigger, et al., "Trace-Element Analysis of Iroquoian Pottery," *Canadian Journal of Archaeology* 4 (1980): 119–45.

25. Ramsden, "Late Iroquoian Occupations of South-Central Ontario," *Current Anthropology* 20 (1979): 597–98.

26. Ramsden, *Refinement*, 293.

27. Wright, *Ontario Prehistory: An Eleven-Thousand Year Archaeological Outline* (Ottawa: National Museum of Man, 1972), 90; and *Quebec Prehistory* (Toronto, 1979), 71–75; Ramsden, *Refinement*, 293.

28. Trigger, "Hochelaga: History and Ethnohistory," in *Cartier's Hochelaga and the Dawson Site*, ed. J.F. Pendergast and B.G. Trigger (Montreal, 1972), 71–92.

29. Trigger, *Children of Aataentsic*, 225–27.

30. Ibid., 275, 308–15, 559–60.

31. C.E. Heidenreich, "The Indian Occupance of Huronia, 1600–1650," in *Canada's Changing Geography*, ed. R.L. Gentilcore (Scarborough, Ont., 1967), 16.

32. H.P. Biggar, ed., *The Works of Samuel de Champlain*, 6 vols. (Toronto, 1922–36), 3:59.

33. Trigger, "The Historic Location of the Hurons," *Ontario History* 54 (1962): 137–48.

34. Thwaites, ed., *Jesuit Relations*, 20: 43.

35. G.M. Wrong, ed., *The Long Journey to the Country of the Hurons* (Toronto, 1939), 151.

36. Tooker, *Ethnography of the Huron Indians*, 3–4.

37. T.F. McIlwraith, "Archaeological Work in Huronia, 1946: Excavations near Warminster," *Canadian Historical Review* 27 (1946): 400.

38. Trigger, *Children of Aataentsic*, 246–47.

39. Ibid., 246–301.

40. Thwaites, ed., *Jesuit Relations*, 10: 223–25.

41. Ibid., 231–33.

42. J.F. Jameson, ed., *Narratives of New Netherlands, 1609–1664* (New York, 1909), 141.

43. Charles Garrad, "Iron Trade Knives on Historic Petun Sites," *Ontario Archaeology* 13 (1969): 3–15.

44. Trigger, *Children of Aataentsic*, 423–25.

45. Cf. J.A. Dickinson, "The Pre-contact Huron Population: A Reappraisal," *Ontario History* 72 (1980): 173–79.

AMERINDIAN VIEWS OF FRENCH CULTURE IN THE SEVENTEENTH CENTURY†

CORNELIUS J. JAENEN

Our historiography has been more concerned with French and Canadian views of the Amerindians than with aboriginal opinions and evaluations of the French culture with which they came into contact during the seventeenth century.[1] Yet, the most elementary canons of historical interpretation require that the values and belief systems of both parties concerned in the contact experience be considered. In general, it has been assumed by historians that not only did Frenchmen consider their civilization superior to the aboriginal cultures of North America but also that the native tribesmen viewed French culture with awe and admiration, that they often attempted to imitate Europeans, and usually aspired to elevate themselves to the superior level of the white man. This interpretation was firmly established in European and Canadian literature by Charlevoix, Raynal, Chateaubriand, and Bossange.[2]

Not until the mid-nineteenth century was there any notable departure from this accepted approach to French–Amerindian relations. While it is true that a few earlier French writers had been critical of the ideas and ideals of their compatriots in comparison with native behaviour, such critical observations were invariably motivated by desires for political and social reforms, by religious toleration, or by scepticism which related to France more than to North America. Clodoré, Abbeville, de Léry, Boyer, Sagard, and Lescarbot made guarded criticisms of French behaviour and institutions employing Amerindian examples to strengthen their arguments.[3] Maximilien Bibaud was the first French Canadian to depict the Amerindians in a consistently favourable light. He was fully conscious, moreover, that the aborigines had resisted francization and, in

† *Canadian Historical Review* 55, no. 3 (September 1974): 261–91. This is the revised version of a paper read at the seventh annual Northern Great Plains History Conference, University of Manitoba, 20 October 1972.

the majority, had rejected conversion.[4] Napoléon Legendre pleaded eloquently in 1884 for an impartial and just treatment of Amerindian history, but his was still a voice of one crying in the wilderness.[5]

It is therefore only quite recently that the sources for the traditional views of the contact experience have been re-examined more critically and that the accepted interpretations have been challenged. In 1903, Léon Gérin began to study the natives of New France in a new conceptual framework, but his work went largely unnoticed by his contemporaries. In 1925, F.W. Howay attempted to present the aboriginal case and his pioneer work was followed by Diamond Jenness' *The Indians of Canada* (1932) and A.G. Bailey's *The Conflict of European and Eastern Algonkian Cultures, 1504–1700* (1937). More significant still in setting the stage for a thorough-going revision of Amerindian history have been the writings of Jacques Rousseau, Léo-Paul Desrosiers, and André Vachon.[6]

To delineate Amerindian views of French culture and civilization at the time of contact in the seventeenth century is extremely difficult because, first of all, an understanding of both French culture and Amerindian cultures is necessary. More information about French culture in the seventeenth century is available than about Micmac, Montagnais, Algonkin, Huron, and Iroquois cultures which were described by French travellers, missionaries, and traders as seen through their own understanding of such cultures and interpreted according to their values and beliefs. The missionaries, as France's foremost cultural ambassadors at the time, tended to undervalue tribal customs and practices, but they soon found that the Amerindians were secure, well-adjusted and self-reliant peoples. As early as 1616 the report back to France was: "For all your arguments, and you can bring a thousand of them if you wish, are annihilated by this single shaft which they always have at hand, *Aoti Chabaya*, (they say) 'That is the Savage way of doing it. You can have your way and we will have ours; every one values his own wares.' "[7] The historian's task is to attempt to understand both cultures in contact.

Secondly, past events must not only be identified but also be interpreted in the manner seen by each of the participants involved. As the archaeologists have contributed much to an understanding of Amerindian cultures, so the ethno-historians and anthropologists have contributed to an understanding of the moral assumptions and value systems involved. As Wilcomb Washburn has said, "an understanding of conflicting values seems to be a condition of great history, great imaginative writing, and great religious insight."[8] At least one of the missionaries to the Micmacs realized that French and Algonkian value systems and moral assumptions differed greatly. He wrote:

> You must know that they are men like us; that intrinsically they
> reason as all men must think; that they differ only in the manner
> of rendering their thoughts, and that if something appears strange

to us in their way of thinking it is because we have not been educated like them, and we do not find ourselves in a similar situation to theirs, to reach such conclusions.[9]

The inability to understand behaviour and thought as conceived by the various Amerindian cultures was the greatest barrier to French appreciation of native civilization, and it remains a formidable challenge to the modern historian who attempts to explain and evaluate the contact experience.

The Amerindians, as a non-literate society, left few documents to assist in reconstructing their views and concepts. The majority of documentary sources are European and, therefore, although designated as primary sources, are interpretations as well as records of events. On the other hand, it can be argued that the recorders were also participants and that this gave them a distinctive advantage over today's social scientists who are deprived of the experience of being eye-witnesses and participants. It is true that the early observers of native reactions to contact with Frenchmen had commercial, religious and military interests in the Amerindians and that they studied aboriginal society largely in order to discover vulnerable points which could be exploited to the achievement of their objectives. Nevertheless, in their records, which were sometimes quite comprehensive, they unwittingly related incidents and conversations which enable one to reconstruct Amerindian reactions motivated by beliefs and objectives which the chroniclers frequently ignored.

Moreover, there are few model studies to guide one through the labyrinth of traditional views, or of narrowly professional views such as the stress by the anthropologists on material culture. Acculturation is a two-way process, and important as was the French impact on Amerindian cultures, the aboriginal impact on French culture was continuous and significant. These facts cannot be ignored in the study of the Amerindian opinions and evaluations of French culture during the early contact period.

These initial contacts strengthened the Europocentric view of history. In the seventeenth century Europeans invariably assumed that Europe was the centre of the world and of civilization, that its cultures were the oldest, that America was a new continent and that its peoples were necessarily recent immigrants. The literature of the period of exploration was dominated by the theme of a New World populated by peoples of different languages and cultures who conducted European explorers and "discoverers" on tours along well-known and well-travelled water routes and trails to the various centres of aboriginal population. The conceptual frameworks of Europeans — whether Spaniards, French or English, or whether Catholics or Protestants — were remarkably indistinguishable whenever the circumstances of contact were similar. Explorers were fed, sheltered, offered the other amenities of social life, and provided with multilingual guides. In this context Europeans tended to see themselves and their activities as being at the centre of the historical stage.

The French did distinguish, nevertheless, cultural differences among the tribes or "nations" they contacted, although contemporary literature is remarkable for the absence of differentiation on the basis of "race" or pigmentation. On the basis of differences in language and in observable customs and beliefs there was an awareness of the great cultural diversity of the native peoples. It may be postulated, therefore, that the views of Micmacs or Montagnais would differ from the views of the Huron or Iroquois. There are a few indications of differing reactions but these can usually be associated with the context of contact rather than with conceptual variations. The nomadic Algonkian cultures were sufficiently different from the Iroquoian groups to elicit varying responses to the French presence, yet the records available to the historian indicate a similarity of response to European intrusion. As there appears now to have been much more of a common European concept of America — rather than markedly different Spanish, French, and English conceptual frameworks — so there appears to have been more of a common Amerindian reaction to the coming of the Europeans than different Micmac, Huron, or Iroquois responses, with the differences in so-called tribal relations with the French better identified in terms of specific and immediate economic and socio-political problems. In other words, it is as justifiable to conceive of Amerindian views of French culture as of European views of the New World, when examining the conceptual frameworks of a generalized culture contact over a period of a century. Such an approach would be less satisfactory if dealing with more specific contact experiences in restricted time periods.

There were a number of features of French life that the Amerindians found admirable and their curiosity was reinforced by a desire to adapt some of the French ways and equipment to their own culture. First of all, they were interested in observing the Europeans in their day to day activities. Lescarbot recorded that "the savages from all the country round came to look at the ways of the French and willingly came among them."[10] Similarly, the Algonkins were amazed at Champlain's men: "The bulk of the savages who were there had never seen a Christian, and could not get over their wonder as they gazed at our customs, our clothing, our arms, our equipment."[11] The Iroquois who held Father Jogues prisoner questioned him at great length about scientific matters and were so impressed by his wisdom and explanations that they regretted the tortures they had inflicted upon him. The greatest appreciation seems to have been for European technology. All tribes showed an appreciation of the knives, hatchets, kettles, beads, cloth and, eventually, the firearms of the French. Indeed the exchange of the beaver pelt coats worn by the tribesmen of the Atlantic coastal region for European iron goods had been initiated by the Breton, Basque, Norman and other Western European fishermen at least in the fifteenth century, if not earlier. During the sixteenth century Cartier's accounts, among others, recorded the Amerindian desire to pursue barter. His records of the 1534 voyage in the Gaspé region included the following passage about noisy warriors making signs and "holding up skins on the end of sticks" which they obviously wished to exchange for European goods: "two of our men landed to approach them, and bring them knives and other iron-ware, with a red hat to give to their captain. Seeing this, they also landed, carrying these skins of theirs, and began to trade with us, showing great and marvellous joy to possess this ironware and other articles, dancing continually and going through various ceremonies. . . . "[12] In 1536 he recorded that each day natives approached his vessel with eels and fish to exchange for European goods: "in return they were given knives, awls, beads, and other such things, wherewith they were much pleased."[13] In time, the coastal tribes became more exacting in their bartering operations. In 1623, for example, the Montagnais objected to the gift of a few figs which the French sea captain had offered them and seized knives and other trade goods saying they would give a fair price for the articles taken. Sagard, who reported the incident, was amazed that the Montagnais not only left furs in payment but did so in quantities which outstripped the value of the goods they had seized.[14]

It should be remarked that originally the fur trade was a non-economic exchange between fishermen and aborigines, at least in the sense that for the natives non-commercial motives operated. Furs were given to Europeans, because they were desired by the visiting fishermen and it was part of Algonkian culture to view exchange in non-commercial terms.[15] They gave their peltries without apparent demand for return, at least at the time of the initial contacts; nevertheless, whatever the fishermen offered in exchange was gratefully accepted. There is reason to believe that the Amerindians valued European trade goods such as beads, mirrors, bells, and caps, for their aesthetic, magical, or purely decorative and fascinating worth, not their economic value.[16] Furthermore, this exchange, for the Amerindians, had a symbolic or diplomatic meaning and was in reality viewed as an exchange of gifts which established rank and prestige. Cartier's journals seem to indicate this to have been the context of the exchanges in the sixteenth century. This difference between European and Amerindian concepts continued into the seventeenth century and was demonstrated in the special meaning the tribesmen attached to the wampum belt, the calumet, or even the hatchet. The French traders and missionaries, both of whom shared the same economic views, regarded wampum in materialistic terms whereas the Amerindians viewed it in symbolic terms. Amerindian admiration of trade goods brought them inevitably into a position of dependence on the French trade. Denys remarked on the changing values among the Micmacs:

> They have abandoned all their own utensils, whether because of the trouble they had as well to make as to use them, or because of the facility of obtaining from us, in exchange for skins which cost them almost nothing, the things which seemed to them invaluable, not so much for their novelty as for the convenience derived therefrom. Above everything the kettle has always seemed to them, and seems still, the most valuable article they can obtain from us.[17]

He related how a Micmac sent by Governor Razilly to Paris, while passing the street where many coppersmiths were located, asked of his interpreter if they were not "relatives of the King" and if this were not the "trade of the grandest Seigniors of the Kingdom"!

The Amerindians did not always understand French concepts of personal property, their materialistic outlook as evidenced in their desire to accumulate goods, and their fear of losing personal belongings to covetous colleagues. They expected the French to have a better developed sense of kin-group belongings, of sharing of goods, of using the goods or utensils of others if there was urgent need to do so without the formalities of ownership intervening in such cases, and of showing more respect for articles to which ceremonial or magical qualities were attached. Father Sagard reported at Tadoussac in 1617 that the Montagnais were surprisingly honest compared to Frenchmen and saw no risk in leaving their boats unattended over long periods on the beaches and never stole the boats left by the French.[18] Nevertheless, the Micmacs learned, from their experience over a century with European fishermen and traders, that they could exact more and better quality goods for their furs as the competition grew. Lescarbot said:

> so great has been the greed that in their jealousy of one another the merchants have spoiled the trade. Eight years ago, for two biscuits or two knives, one had a beaver, while to-day one must give fifteen or twenty: and in this very year 1610 some have given away to the savages their whole stock in trade, in order to obstruct the holy enterprise of M. de Poutrincourt, so great is human avarice.[19]

The Montagnais who had come to trade at Tadoussac in March 1611 were reported as having brought only poor quality furs "and even these few they are fain to employ to the best advantage while awaiting the arrival of a crowd of vessel[s] . . . to have their goods better cheap; wherein they are all well skilled now that the avarice of our merchants has made itself known in those parts."[20]

Their developing interest in large-scale trade led them to acquire a taste for brandy and other intoxicants which they soon came to demand and to expect as a concomitant of contact. A Dutch version of Denys' history recounted how the aborigines stood along the shores where fishing vessels were known to come and how they made smoke signals to the crews of vessels they sighted inviting them to come to barter for furs: "The skins are bartered for brandy, for which they ever since they have begun to trade with fishermen are very greedy; and they herewith fill themselves up to such an extent that they frequently fall over backwards, for they do not call it drinking unless they overload themselves with this strong drink in a beastly fashion."[21] Whatever the reason for the low tolerance the Amerindians had for alcohol and their eventual social disorganization as a consequence of its nefarious traffic, it is clear from contemporary sources that they developed an inordinate desire for it. It would appear that, although they never liked its taste and they deplored the violence and disorders they committed under its influence, they coveted it in order to obtain release from their cultural and natural inhibitions, to commit unconventional and illegal acts, to attain a new state of spirit possession, and eventually to reduce the tension they experienced as a result of the contact with purveyors of an alien civilization which gradually undermined their ancestral way of life, eroded their belief system, and left them alienated from their traditions. Alcohol was a major contributor to the breakdown of Amerindian cultural patterns; nevertheless, it was employed by some tribesmen to create or symbolize in-group solidarity against the French, a rejection of European standards and values, and a defiance of the teachings of the Catholic church and of the threatening edicts of the French state.

The Amerindians were very impressed with the French regard for ceremonial and for ritual. The French willingness to engage in ceremonial preludes to trading engagements, to military talks, and to parleys brought the two cultures together. There is some indication also that the tribesmen in general were impressed with the ritual and ceremonial of the Catholic religion, although on this score there seems to have been considerable concern among the early Catholic missionaries and Governors that the Amerindians also found the congregational singing of the "songs of Marot" and the participatory worship of the Huguenots very attractive.[22] A missionary wrote with obvious satisfaction:

> I say nothing of the esteem manifested by this new Church for all The outward signs of our Holy Religion. Crosses, medals, and other similar Articles are Their most precious jewels. So fondly do they preserve These that they wear them around their necks, even at preaching in New Holland, where The heretics have never been able to tear from Them a single bead of Their Rosaries.[23]

In addition to the beautiful ritual of the mass, the solemn processions and the adoration of the Blessed Sacrament, the secular celebrations of the French impressed the natives. The celebration in 1639 at Quebec upon receipt of the news of the birth of the future Louis XIV was recorded as follows:

> Bon-fires were built with all possible ceremony, rockets were discharged, Roman candles flared, golden rain descended, the night was illuminated with tapers, and the forest resounded with the thunder of guns. On this occasion the Hurons were present, since they were paying their customary visit to Quebec, which is the market of the whole country. They had never seen the like before and astounded and amazed they put their right hands to their mouths, which is their method of exhibiting joyous emotion.[24]

The French for a long time held to the idea of bringing a few natives from each tribe to France to impress them with their might and civilization. Lahontan told of six *sagamos* at Versailles at one time, all soliciting aid against the English. But Lahontan inferred that the chieftains were less interested in the beauty and grandeur of Versailles than they were in employing French power and wealth for the achievements of their own ends. Eventually the French Crown concluded that the Amerindians were sufficiently aware of the military might of France and that the bringing of representatives to France was unnecessary. The French did sense the native appreciation of presents, however, and they satisfied them in this matter. LeClercq explained this need of recognition, this need for prestige and security:

> They are fond of ceremony and are anxious to be accorded some when they come to trade at French establishments; and it is consequently in order to satisfy them that sometimes the guns and even the canon are fired on their arrival. The leader himself assembles all the canoes near his own and ranges them in good order before landing, in order to await the salute which is given him, and which all the Indians return to the French by the discharge of their guns. Sometimes the leaders and chiefs are invited for a meal in order to show all the Indians that they are esteemed and honoured. Rather more frequently they are given something like a fine coat, in order to distinguish them from the commonalty. For such things as this they have a particular esteem, especially if the article has been in use by the commander of the French.[25]

Here was a fortunate cultural convergence; the French held views of precedence as this related to concepts of rank, estate, dignity, *splendeur.* The Amerindians were very pleased with French commissions, special uniforms, medals, and titles of nobility. The Micmacs regarded medals as "titres de noblesse" and it secured their loyalty, according to the missionaries. Dièreville mentioned the loyalty and devotion to the

French of a chieftain he met at Port Royal whose grandfather had been "ennobled" by Henry IV.[26]

Another aspect of French life which the Amerindian did not comprehend but in the end came rather to admire was the generous and kindly treatment of the sick by the Sisters Hospitallers who arrived in Quebec in 1639. A dreadful smallpox epidemic, alleged to have come from Virginia — as all accursed events seemed to the colonists to have their origins in the English colonies — took a heavy toll of natives and the nuns themselves were "attacked by the malady." Du Creux recorded of these devout women that:

> with scarcely any interruption of their pious labours, they presented such a strange spectacle to the savages, who are quite without the emotion of pity, that they could not restrain their surprise that women could be found eager to encounter so many perils, and to penetrate unknown regions in order to succour those whom the Indians themselves generally abandon or kill.[27]

Actually, the Amerindian could not have been astounded by the willingness of women to serve in evangelical labours in a distant land—that was a marvel to Europeans and a most unusual event in Catholic history —but they were astounded by the care the French lavished on the sick and dying. In the native encampments the terminally ill and the very aged were abandoned to their fate. They expected this treatment and there was no lack of pity attached to such action. The moralizing quality attributed to the treatment of the unfortunates is an example of European value judgments being applied to a different culture.

Indeed, on a wide range of points of contact at the military, social, religious, educational, agricultural, medical, and organizational level the Amerindian evaluation of French culture and civilization was often as unflattering as was the low regard of Frenchmen for Amerindian culture. Each group had its own somatic norm image, or "complex of physical characteristics which are accepted by a group as its norm and ideal," by which it evaluated and analysed other societies.[28] Thus, the French considered themselves aesthetically superior to the Amerindians and held views which would be classified as "racist" today; on the other hand, the Amerindians considered the French inferior to themselves and according to their somatic norm image considered themselves superior aesthetically and otherwise. Pierre d'Avity wrote in 1637 that "although they lack police, power, letters, arts, wealth and other things they despise other nations and esteem themselves highly."[29] He was echoing the sentiments of Father Gabriel Sagard, who had spent the winter of 1623– 24 among the Hurons, and who reported that the Hurons esteemed the French "to possess little intelligence in comparison to themselves." Although they respected the knowledge of the Recollet missionaries they "did not have this opinion or belief concerning other Frenchmen in comparison with whom they estimated their own children wiser and more intelligent."[30] The Jesuits were no more highly regarded than the Recollets, the native children sometimes scorning them and ridiculing them "because they do not see in a Frenchman any of the perfections of a Savage and cannot recognize the virtues of a generous Christian."[31] Frenchmen, it would seem, seldom attained the intellectual and moral qualities demanded by the Amerindian somatic norm image.

Furthermore, Frenchmen generally were regarded as physically inferior, as weak and unfitted to stand up to the rigours of arduous canoe journeys, hunting expeditions, and forest warfare. When Champlain proposed to Chief Iroquet of the Algonkins to send young men to live among them there was immediate opposition: "the other savages raised objections, fearing that harm might come to the youth, who was not accustomed to their manner of life, which is in all respects hard, and that if any accident befell him the French would be their enemies."[32] Only after Champlain remonstrated angrily, and agreed to accept in exchange an Algonkian youth to be sent to France to be educated, could Iroquet accept the proposal.

If Frenchmen were regarded as "soft" it was because they were raised in a country which reportedly encouraged the development of effeminacy. Two young Algonkins who had spent a year in France, upon their return to Canada, were loud in their praises of the treatment they had been accorded, but one of them did admit that he would find it extremely difficult to readjust to his "former hard life" among his compatriots.[33] Savignon, one of the youths Champlain had sent to France, "when he saw two men quarrelling without coming to blows or killing one another, would mock at them, saying they were nought but women, and had no courage."[34] Indeed, for an Amerindian to marry a European was not a socially desirable union. When an "honest French surgeon" asked to marry an Amerindian maiden in 1618 the native council refused his request.[35] Le Jeune's *Relation* of 1633 recorded another incident which the natives interpreted as proof of French effeminacy: "Our Savage, seeing Father de Noue carrying wood began to laugh, saying: 'He's really a woman,' meaning that he was doing a woman's work."

The first Frenchmen to inhabit the New World must have appeared singularly ill-equipped to cope with their new environment. It was not long before they stripped off their cumbersome European dress for the hunting shirt and moccasins. The Frenchman learned to travel by canoe and snowshoes, to portage and shoot rapids, to fish through the ice and eat *sagamite* in order to survive. But in the official French view they did this in order to establish good relations with the natives, to advance the economic and cultural objectives of the leaders. This temporary "Indianization" involved a cultural step backward in order to make possible a cultural leap forward later. The Amerindians could only interpret this "going native" by Frenchmen in increasing numbers as a reasonable adjustment to conditions in the New World, as a wise acceptance of folk wisdom, and as an accommodation learned by the *naturels* over centuries of American habitation. Nicolas Perrot maintained that the Hurons, Ottawas, Fox, and Sioux became much aware of this accommodation on the part of the French; therefore they became insolent and desired "to dominate us and be our superiors; they even regard us as people who are in some manner dependent on them."[36]

In addition to reproaching Frenchmen for their physical weakness, the Amerindians found them ugly, especially because of their excessive hairiness, and their frequent deformities and infirmities. Sagard related how "one of the ugliest savages in the district" laughed at the bearded Europeans and wondered how any woman could look with favour on such ugly creatures. He added: "They have such a horror of a beard that sometimes when they try to insult us they call us Sascoinronte, that is to say, Bearded, you have a beard; moreover, they think it makes people more ugly and weakens their intelligence."[37] Father Biard sent a similar report from Acadia: "They have often told me that at first we seemed to them very ugly with hair both upon our mouths and heads; but gradually they have become accustomed to it, and now we are beginning to look less deformed."[38] In addition to this common Mongoloid abhorrence of the hairiness of Europeans, the Micmacs showed no compassion for "the one-eyed, and flat-nosed" Frenchmen whom they derided. Biard continued:

> For they are droll fellows, and have a word and a nickname very readily at command, if they think they have any occasion to look down upon us. And certainly (judging from what I see) this habit of self-aggrandizement is a contagion from which no one is exempt, except through the grace of God. You will see these poor barbarians, notwithstanding their great lack of government, power, letters, art and riches, yet holding their heads so high that they greatly underrate us, regarding themselves as our superiors.[39]

Lahontan, who was generally very sympathetic in his appraisal of aboriginal views, remarked on "their fanatical Opinions of things, which proceeded from their Prepossession and Bigotry with reference to their own customs and ways of living."[40]

There was much about Catholicism that seemed incongruous and dangerous to the Amerindians. From the first contacts with missionaries, whether seculars or regulars, the zeal for the baptism of dying infants led to a confirmed belief that baptism was the cause of death. The French were responsible for the epidemics of measles, smallpox, influenza and related bronchial disorders which decimated the encampments and villages, and the natives without being able to understand the precise relationship between contact and infection did realize that there was such a cause–effect relationship. As early as 1616, Biard sent the following observations from Acadia:

> They are astonished and often complain that since the French mingle with and carry on trade with them, they are dying fast, and the population is thinning out. For they assert that, before this association and intercourse, all their countries were very populous, and they tell how one by one the different coasts, according as they have begun traffic with us have been more reduced by disease; adding, that the reason the Armouchiquois do not diminish in population is because they are not at all careless. Thereupon they often puzzle their brains, and sometimes think that the French poison them . . . .[41]

All the tribes contacted by the French in the early seventeenth century —the Micmacs, Montagnais, Algonkins, Hurons and Iroquois—charged the French with bringing pestilence and death. The Algonkins went so far as to tell the Hurons infection was a deliberate policy of the French to destroy all the Amerindian nations. By 1647 the Jesuits made the following admission:

> The Algonquins and Hurons — and next the Hiroquois, at the solicitation of their captives — have had, and some have still, a hatred and an extreme horror of our doctrine. They say that it causes them to die, and that it contains spells and charms which effect the destruction of their corn and engender the contagious and general diseases wherewith the Hiroquois now begin to be afflicted.[42]

The missionaries taught those who would give them a hearing, among other things, the wonder-working power of the sacraments, novenas, and relics. They taught a reverence for the cross, religious images and pious practices. In the adversities which often accompanied the coming of the missionaries to their villages, the tribesmen concluded that the supernatural invoked for good could also be invoked to produce harmful effects. The missionary report of 1653 from the Huron country included the following observation: "They said the same thing about some images, etc. the prayers that we made, and the masses which we said at an early hour, with closed doors; the litanies; even walking abroad—a new thing in these countries — were superstitions which we practiced in order to destroy them."[43] Every unaccustomed, unusual or secretive act became the object of intense suspicion.

Religious symbols were greatly distrusted. In 1635 the Hurons insisted that a cross atop the mission-house be removed as the cause of that summer's drought: "When the Indians gathered from the surrounding villages and insisted that the Fathers should remove the cross, they told them that should the drought wither the crops there was danger that the infuriated Hurons would attack them as sorcerers and poisoners and beat them to death."[44] The following year, the villagers had cause for further alarm, as an epidemic spread rapidly through the lodges taking a heavy toll. The Jesuits had displayed in their chapel two life-size images, one of Jesus and the other of the Virgin Mary, for the edification of their hearers. The rumour spread quickly that the images were the cause of the pestilence:

> This unfounded suspicion, which should have been dismissed with a laugh, spread so rapidly in a few days that throughout the length and breadth of the land it was soon reported that the French priests were the cause of the trouble; and although we may conjecture that those from whom this ridiculous falsehood emanated were not so foolish as to persuade themselves to accept what they wished others to believe, still they told their lie so cunningly that the majority who heard the report had no doubt that the thing was true. For the most part they gradually refused to associate with the Fathers, and the women and children, otherwise of no account but ready to believe anything, execrated them as public male-factors. In all the gatherings and meetings the talk was against the Fathers, who, it was said, had come to the Huron country on an evil day and who were destined to be the ruin of the whole race. The inhabitants of Ihonatiria alone at first zealously defended their cause, but they too, when the conflagration of unpopularity burned more fiercely, whether they were afraid or whether they were tired of the task, ceased to protect them and began to excuse their former conduct with their neighbours as if it had been a serious crime.[45]

The prophets of doom were correct in their predictions, of course, for the French presence in Huronia precipitated their subjugation by the Iroquois.

The Amerindian charge against the missionaries was of engaging in sorcery and witchcraft. Obsessive fear appears to have outweighed hatred as the motive for the "persecution" reported by Mother Marie de l'Incarnation:

> They were on the dock as criminals in a council of the savages. The fires were lit closer to each other than usual and they seemed to be so only for them, for they were esteemed convicted of witchcraft, and of having poisoned the air which caused the pestilence throughout the country. What put the Fathers in extreme peril was that the Savages were as it were convinced that these misfortunes would cease with their death.[46]

"Great assemblies" were called throughout Huronia to deliberate on appropriate protective measures. The oldest and most prominent woman of the nation was reported to have harangued the consultative assembly of the four tribes in the following manner:

> It is the Black Robes who make us die by their spells; listen to me, I prove it by the reasons you are going to recognize as true. They lodged in a certain village where everyone was well, as soon as they established themselves there, everyone died except for three or four persons. They changed location and the same thing happened. They went to visit the cabins of the other villages, and only those where they did not enter were exempted from mortality and sickness. Do you not see that when they move their lips, what they call prayers, those are so many spells that come forth from their mouths? It is the same when they read in their books. Besides, in their cabins they have large pieces of wood (they are guns) with which they make noise and spread their magic everywhere. If they are not promptly put to death, they will complete their ruin of the country, so that there will remain neither small nor great.[47]

The Ursuline correspondent opined that wherever the missionaries travelled in their apostolic labours they carried the epidemic "to purify the faith of those they have converted." News of the alleged French practice of witchcraft and sorcery travelled rapidly to neighbouring tribes and forestalled plans Chaumonot and his companion had of carrying the gospel farther afield:

> As for the adults, not only have they not been willing to listen to the good news, but they even prevented us from entering their villages, threatening to kill and eat us, as they do with their most cruel enemies. The reason of this great aversion arose from the calumnies disseminated by some evil inhabitants of the country from which we came. In consequence of these calumnies, they were convinced that we were sorcerers, imposters come to take possession of their country, after having made them perish by our spells, which were shut up in our inkstands, in our books, etc. — inasmuch that we dared not, without hiding ourselves, open a book or write anything.[48]

Association with the new religion meant certain sterility of hunting and fishing. Iroquois captives brought to the Huron villages were forced to kneel before wooden crosses, symbols which filled them with terror. A report of 1647 indicates the extent of the fear Catholicism inspired among the Iroquois: "It is further said that they have seen issuing from the lips of a Christian, whom they were burning, a strange brightness which has terrified them; so indeed, they have knowledge of our doctrine, but they regard it with horror, as of old the Pagans in the early age of Christianity."[49] This obsessive fear attached itself not only to the external symbols of the new religion and its practices but also to the Eucharist itself. Some of the pagans asked to see the corpse of Christ which the priests were said to bring to life at mass. Eventually, even purely secular objects such as weather-vanes and clocks were shunned as evil spirits associated with the religion of the French.

Although the missionaries, almost without exception, complained of the inadequacies of the Amerindian languages for expressing their religious message and noted the great difficulty in compiling vocabularies of equivalents to common French terms, modern linguistic experts do not find the Amerindian languages deficient for expressing the abstract and symbolic. Nevertheless, the aboriginal tongues did not always have precise equivalents, as Lescarbot emphasized:

> For they have no words which can represent the mysteries of our religion, and it would be impossible to translate even the Lord's prayer into their language save by paraphrase. For of themselves they do not know what is sanctification, or the kingdom of Heaven, or super-substantial bread (which we call daily), or to lead into temptation. The words glory, virtue, reason, beatitudes, Trinity, Holy Spirit, baptism, faith, hope, charity, and an infinity of others are not in use among them. So that at the beginning there will be no need of great Doctors.[50]

The world expressed by the French language was one world and the world expressed by the Huron language, for example, was a distinct world; each were distinct worlds and not merely the same world with different labels attached. LeClercq commended the Micmac language as being "very beautiful and very rich in its expressions," adding that it had a greater range of expression than European languages and that there were distinct styles for solemn and less formal occasions.[51] The Jesuits later asserted on the basis of their experience among both Algonkian and Iroquoian linguistic groups that the languages were definite in meaning, beautiful and regular in expression, "not at all barbarous," and full of force.[52]

The deficiency arose more out of the cultural approach and the implications of evangelization for Amerindian society than from linguistic difficulties. The natives saw some danger in divulging their religious vocabulary to the evangelists of the new religion, therefore they refused to co-operate extensively in the linguistic task of compiling dictionaries and grammars, and of translating religious books.[53] Gravier reported at the close of the century of the Illinois tribes that they were "so secret regarding all the mysteries of their Religion that the Missionary can discover nothing about them."[54] What the pagans refused the neophytes later supplied, although the continued refusal of some coureurs-de-bois to assist in missionary translation suggests that there was pressure in the native encampments to offer no assistance to the missionaries in this aspect of their evangelical labours.

Most natives, seeing the Europeans determined to learn their languages, felt no necessity to learn French; this fact elicited the accusation from one royal official that the Amerindians were too proud to learn French. The Amerindians did not find the Jesuits particularly good linguists, although by any measure that can be applied today to their efforts they appear to have been brilliant. Du Creux recounted that the Hurons "thought it was a joke to ask Le Jeune to speak, and when he made a stammering attempt at their language, laughter and derision greeted his childish efforts."[55]

The religious differences in the French community did not escape Amerindian notice, although the religious chroniclers may have exaggerated this so-called scandal in order to advance their own demands for enforced religious uniformity. Sagard wrote about the intestine quarrels between Huguenot and Catholic seamen, fishermen, traders, and ministers of religion which tended to confirm the natives in their skepticism.[56] The natives were never slow to point out the weaknesses in the French character, the divergence between the missionaries' ideals and the colonists' practices, and the greater severity with which the clergy sought to repress drunkenness among them than among the French. Governor Montmagny sought to answer one such remonstrance with an unconvincing "don't plead the French as an excuse when they sometimes fall into intemperance themselves; those who do so are stupid fools, and are regarded as trash and a disgrace to the light of day."[57]

Be that as it may, the greatest obstacles to evangelization of the Amerindians remained native religion, the world view of the tribesmen, and (under pressure to convert to Catholicism) the emergence of counter-innovative techniques. Native religion was completely integrated into Amerindian cultures and permeated all aspects of daily living as well as the ideology. Conversion to Catholicism required a rejection of the whole traditional way of life, belief system and tribal ideals of behaviour and relationships. When the Jesuits sought to establish a model Catholic "republic" among the Hurons, the medicine-men and elders developed counter-innovative techniques: a version of baptism, for example, was initiated as a part of a healing cult said to be inspired by a deity who revealed himself as "the real Jesus," and anti-Catholic cults spread rapidly throughout Huronia to provide an ideological resistance to the new European religion.[58]

Dreams, both of a symptomatic and visitation variety, played an important role in Amerindian religion and not infrequently turned against the threatening tide of the "French religion." During an epidemic of smallpox among the Hurons in 1640, a young fisherman had a dream in which the spirit appeared to him to advise the tribe in its distress. Jerome Lalemant reported the "demon" as having issued the following warning:

> I am the master of the earth, whom you Hurons honor under the
> name of Iouskeha. I am the one whom the French wrongly call

Jesus, but they do not know me. I have pity on your country, which I have taken under my protection; I come to teach you both the reasons and the remedies for your fortune. It is the strangers who alone are the cause of it; they now travel two by two through the country, with the design of spreading the disease everywhere. They will not stop with that, after this smallpox which now depopulates your cabins, there will follow certain colics which in less than three days will carry off all those whom this disease may not have removed. You can prevent this misfortune; drive from your village the two black gowns who are there.[59]

Just as the French tended to fashion God in their own image, so one is assured that Iouskeha spoke as a "true" Huron.

Each culture had its own conception of supernatural intervention in human affairs. On occasion there was a cultural convergence: in such situations the Amerindians held French religious powers, or "good medicine," in high esteem. When in 1673 at Folle Avoine on the Menominee river Louis André replaced sacrifices offered to the sun in order to assure good fishing by a crucifix he invited a contest between the deities. The fact that the following morning a large number of sturgeon entered the river suddenly gave him attentive hearers.[60] The following year, Pierre Millet reported that an Iroquois chieftain exhorted his compatriots to hold prayer in esteem "as Monsieur the governor had recommended them to do at Catarakoui," but far more effective was the fact that the missionary correctly predicted an eclipse of the moon a few days earlier.[61] Paul Le Jeune attempted to convince the Huron that neither the French nor any other people could bring rain or fine weather, but that the Creator alone was master of these elements and therefore "recourse must be had only to him." His hearers remained unconvinced and persisted in their belief that the Europeans had influenced the supernatural to bring unfavourable weather. An incident that had occurred when the Recollets had first gone into Huron country probably lived on in their oral history. Sagard recorded that the Recollets had been asked to pray God to stop a long and devasting rain. "And God looked with favour on our prayers, after we had spent the following night in petitioning Him for His promises, and heard us and caused the rain to cease so completely that we had perfectly fine weather; whereat they were so amazed and delighted that they proclaimed it a miracle, and we rendered thanks to God for it."[62]

It was only a short step from belief in beneficial supernatural intervention to belief in malignant and malicious intervention from the spirit world.

The Amerindians soon came to hold a low opinion of French standards of morality. As early as Verrazano's expedition of 1524 it was remarked that contact with European fishing fleets had taught the coastal Algonkian tribes to take appropriate protective measures. Verrazano reported

"Every day the people came to see us at the ship; bringing their women of whom they are very careful; because, entering the ship themselves, remaining a long time, they made their women stay in barges and however many entreaties we made them, offering to give them various things, it was not possible that they would allow them to enter the ship."[63] Similarly Biard observed that the Micmac girls and women were "very modest and bashful" and that the men were well behaved and "very much insulted when some foolish Frenchman dares meddle with their women." This Jesuit missionary related an incident to illustrate his judgment: "Once when a certain madcap took some liberties, they came and told our Captain that he should look out for his men, informing him that any one who attempted to do that again could not stand much of a chance, that they would kill him on the spot."[64]

The Jesuit missionaries seem to have expected the tribesmen to respect them for their sacrifices and sufferings in bringing them the gospel under unattractive conditions, especially when compared to life in the elitist colleges of France where they had taught previously. They also expected to be honoured for their vows of poverty and chastity. The natives felt quite otherwise about the missionary mode of life. Sagard observed: "One of the great and most bothersome importunities which they caused us at the beginning of our stay in the country was their continual pursuit of pleas to marry us, or at least that we should join ourselves to them, and they could not understand our manner of Religious life . . . ."[65] The Hurons told the Recollets it was unnatural to remain celibate, that they were abnormal, that conditions could not be as favourable in France as they pretended or they would have remained there, and that they were out of touch with the rhythm of natural provisions the supernatural powers bestowed on mankind. What other conclusion could aborigines, especially the nomadic Algonkian bands, come to in seeking a rational explanation of apostolic poverty, celibacy and calendar-oriented fasting?

There is sparse documentation dealing with Amerindian reactions to French agriculture, or to life in the towns of Quebec and Montreal. The French diet, as reflected in the kitchen gardens and field crops of the riparian clearings, was a varied one but native palates did not respond well to salted meat and vegetables. Upon being offered a barrel of bread and biscuits, the Hurons examined it, found it tasteless, and threw it into the St. Lawrence: "Our Savages said the Frenchmen drank blood and ate wood, thus naming the wine and biscuits."[66] A chieftain at Isle Percée told Chrestien LeClercq that French contributions in the dietary and culinary realm were not appreciated.

> It is true . . . that we have not always had the use of bread and of wine which your France produces; but, in fact, before the arrival of the French in these parts, did not the Gaspesians live much longer than now? And if we have not any longer among us any of those old men of a hundred and thirty to forty years, it is only

because we are gradually adopting your manner of living, for experience is making it very plain that those of us live longest who,
despising your bread, your wine, and your brandy, are content
with their natural food of beaver, of moose, of waterfowl, and fish,
in accord with the custom of our ancestors and of all the Gaspesian
nation. Learn now, my brother, once for all, because I must open
to thee my heart: there is no Indian who does not consider himself
infinitely more happy and more powerful than the French.[67]

The same attitudes prevailed with respect to French clothing which the
natives found inadequate to keep out the winter's cold. Only the decorative aspects held appeal for them.

Although they were impressed by the tall stone buildings erected by
the French, and marvelled at the layout of their towns, there remained
an attachment to the traditional style of building and of life. The Micmac
chieftain just cited made the following observations:

But why now, do men of five or six feet in height need houses
which are sixty to eighty? For, in fact, as thou knowest very well
thyself, Patriarch—do we not find in our own all the conveniences
and advantages that you have with yours, such as reposing, drinking, sleeping, eating, and amusing ourselves with our friends when
we wish? This is not all. My brother, hast thou as much ingenuity
and cleverness as the Indians, who carry their houses and their
wigwams with them so they may lodge wheresoever they please,
independently of any seignior whatsoever? Thou art not as bold or
as stout as we, because when thou goest on a voyage thou canst
not carry upon thy shoulders thy buildings and thy edifices. Therefore it is necessary that thou preparest as many lodgings as thou
makest changes of residence, or else thou lodgest in a hired house
which does not belong to thee. As for us, we find ourselves secure
from all inconveniences, and we are at home everywhere, because
we set up our wigwams with ease wheresoever we go, and without
asking permission of anybody.[68]

If they were impressed by French tools and implements there is little
record of their adopting any of these in their own house-building or
agriculture. One enterprising convert, Manitougache, used a hatchet and
some nails salvaged from an old boat to build a board cabin for himself,
but he seems to have been exceptional.[69] In point of fact, the fur-covered
wigwams of the natives were superior to the later linen tents. The only
goods the domiciled reservation natives asked of the Hôtel-Dieu in 1643,
for example, were blankets and copper kettles—other furnishings apparently had little appeal for them.[70]

In general, the Amerindians do not seem to have retained a favourable
impression of the social organization of French life. They were quite
unable to understand that in France, where, according to the tales of the

Europeans and the few Amerindians who had visited the country and returned to North America, there was apparently an abundance of food, many large towns and many people yet there were also poor people and beggars. Montaigne said that the astonished visitors "thought it strange that these needy halves should endure such an injustice, and did not take the others by the throat, or set fire to their houses."[71] The Recollet missionaries found no beggars in the Huron and Montagnais encampments and whatever food was available was always shared, open hospitality being offered to all travellers, Sagard said:

> those of their Nation, . . . offer reciprocal Hospitality, and help each other so much that they provide for the needs of all so that there is no poor beggar at all in their towns, bourgs and villages, as I said elsewhere, so that they found it very bad hearing that there were in France a great number of needy and beggars, and thought that it was due to a lack of charity, and blamed us greatly saying that if we had some intelligence we would set some order in the matter, the remedies being simple.[72]

To Frenchmen, who thought they had a well-disciplined society, a rational order and civilized community, it came as quite a shock to be reproved by the aborigines, whom they often regarded as being devoid of "right reason" and "right religion," for their injustice, improvidence and inequality. LeClercq was told bluntly how the Micmacs regarded French notions of superiority:

> Thou reproachest us, very inappropriately, that our country is a little hell in contrast with France, which thou comparest to a terrestrial paradise, inasmuch as it yields thee, so thou sayest, every kind of provision in abundance. Thou sayest of us also that we are most miserable and most unhappy of all men, living without religion, without manners, without honour, without social order, in a word, without any rules, like the beasts in our woods and our forests, lacking bread, wine, and a thousand other comforts which thou hast in superfluity in Europe. Well, my brother, if thou dost not yet know the real feelings which our Indians have toward thy country and toward all thy nation, it is proper that I inform thee at once. I beg thee now to believe that all miserable as we seem in thine eyes, we consider ourselves nevertheless much happier than thou in this, that we are content with the little that we have; and believe also, once for all, I pray, that thou deceivest thyself greatly if thou thinkest to persuade us that thy country is better than ours. For if France, as thou sayest, is a little terrestrial paradise, art thou sensible to leave it?[73]

To this rebuke was added the observation that Frenchmen were often inhospitable and parsimonious.

Amerindian hospitality and sharing of goods, on the other hand, were regarded as the most praiseworthy qualities of the aborigines by the fur traders, soldiers and coureurs-de-bois who were so often the beneficiaries of these traits and whose survival and success depended frequently on the goodwill of the natives. Nicolas Perrot reported that unfortunately the Amerindians soon came to understand and imitate French ways:

> This sort of reception is ordinary among the savages; in point of hospitality, it is only the Abenakis, and those who live with the French people, who have become somewhat less liberal, on account of the advice that our people have given them by placing before them the obligations resting on them to preserve what they have. At the present time, it is evident that these savages are fully as selfish and avaricious as formerly they were hospitable. . . . Those of the savages who have not been too much humoured (by the French) are attached to the ancient custom of their ancestors, and among themselves are very compassionate.[74]

Contact with Europeans had resulted in an erosion of both native hospitality and liberality.

There is some indication that the converted Amerindians resented the segregationist practices of the French. Why did the French insist on separate villages, separate churches, separate schools or classes, separate hospital wards, and even separate burial grounds? Sagard reported that the Hurons were not happy when he and his companion came to them and proposed to build their cabin apart from their lodges. The chief and council tried to dissuade them, insisting that it would be preferable if they lodged with Huron families in order to be better cared for than if they remained apart.[75] Had they followed the council's advice, all their food would have been provided by the hunters. However, they preferred privacy to provisions.

Although segregationist practices were not well received, overt attempts to assimilate and dominate the tribesmen were also resented. The decision of the French authorities to provide some tangible encouragement to miscegenation as a means of assimilating the Amerindians met with some resistance in native quarters. When one fur trader had pledged the Ursulines a sizeable donation in order to marry one of their native pupils "it was found that the girl did not want him at all, and preferred a savage and to follow the wishes of her parents."[76] The natives were interested in the provision by the French state of dowries for native women who married Frenchmen and made astute inquiries concerning specific terms of the plan:

> They would be very glad to know what a husband would give his wife; that among the Hurons the custom was to give a great deal besides — that is to say — a beaver robe, and perhaps a porcelain collar. Second, whether a wife would have everything at her dis-

posal. Third, if the husband should decide to return to France whether he would take his wife with him; and in case she remained, what would he leave her on his departure. Fourth, if the wife failed in her duty and the husband drove her away, what she could take with her. . . . [77]

The commissioner general of the Company of New France reproached the natives in the vicinity of Trois Rivières for marrying only within their own tribe and for avoiding marriage alliances with Frenchmen.[78] The following year, a chief from Tadoussac replied to French charges that his people "were not yet allied with the French by any marriage" and that their dislike of the French was evident because "they did not care to be one people with us, giving their children here and there to their allied Nations, and not to the French." He told an assembly at Quebec that when young Frenchmen joined with the Montagnais warriors in war and returned "after the massacre of our enemies" they would find native girls to marry. As for the placement of children in French homes to be raised in the European fashion, he retorted boldly that "one does not see anything but little Savages in the houses of the French." He concluded with a strong argument: "what more do you want? I believe that some of these days you will be asking for our wives. You are continually asking us for our children, and you do not give yours; I do not know any family among us which keeps a Frenchman with it."[79] The Amerindians continued to think of the mutual exchange of children as tokens of unity and alliance, and had no doubt so accepted Champlain's sending of youths to learn native customs and languages in the early decades of the seventeenth century. The one-way placement of children was interpreted as either a demand for hostages or an attempt to assert dominance over them.

They held French medical practices—bleeding and purges, in particular—in low esteem and preferred their own treatments. Lescarbot told of one Micmac warrior who upon being treated by Poutrincourt's surgeon for a badly cut heel returned two hours later "as jaunty as you please, having tied round his head the bandage in which his heel had been wrapped."[80] In 1640, the annalist of the hospital at Quebec reported that the natives avoided the institution, holding it in horror and calling it "the house of death," and refused to submit to medical treatments there.[81] There is no reason to doubt that the anxious relatives who urged a converted widow to abandon French medical treatments for her ailing son, "and told her that she was more like a cruel beast than a loving mother in deserting her boy at such a time; that his recovery depended upon her allowing the remedies to be employed which all their tribe had always used before the coming of those cursed Europeans," did so in all good faith and out of genuine concern for their fellows.[82]

In the domain of personal hygiene the Amerindians appear to have been more advanced than the French, especially in matters concerning bathing which the French avoided as both unhealthy and immodest. Some French practices earned open ridicule, such as the use of handkerchiefs:

> Politeness and propriety have taught us to carry handkerchiefs. In this matter the Savages charge us with filthiness because, they say, we place what is unclean in a fine white piece of linen, and put it away in our pockets as something very precious, while they throw it upon the ground. Hence it happened that, when a Savage one day saw a Frenchman fold up his handkerchief after wiping his nose, he said to himself laughingly, "if thou likest that filth, give me thy handkerchief and I will soon fill it."[83]

There is every indication that the natives were willing to pass on their considerable knowledge and skill in the use of medicinal herbs, ointments, potions, emetics, the practice of quarantining, and the taking of steam baths. Jogues had an abscess lanced by the Iroquois, Crépieul was skilfully bled by an Eskimo, and a French captive had shot removed from a deep wound.[84]

One of the difficulties inherent in relying largely on European documentation for an interpretation of Amerindian views is demonstrated in the discussions on child-rearing. The reported reactions of the aborigines were sometimes literary devices of French authors to criticize French customs and conventions. Lescarbot, for example, deplored the French custom of employing "vicious nursemaids" from whom the infants "sucked in with their milk corruption and bad nature."[85] While there are numerous reports of Amerindian surprise and disdain for French methods of child-rearing, these accounts must be placed in the literary and historical contexts of a period when criticism of government, religion and social conventions in France was severely circumscribed. Both Lescarbot and Denys extended the idealization of the "noble savage," established in France by such writers as Clodoré, d'Abbeville, Montaigne, Du Tertre, Boyer, and de Léry, to an idealization of the New World as a land of opportunity and freedom. The report, therefore, that native women demonstrated more affection to their offspring than French mothers and that they regarded the latter as callous and unfeeling may have been an extension of utopianism in order to criticize metropolitan society. D'Abbeville reported: "They take care not to do like many mothers here, who scarcely can await the birth of their children to put them out to nursemaids. . . . The Savage women would not want to imitate them in that for anything in the world, desiring their children to be nourished with their own milk."[86] The association between nature and nurture may have been more significant to the authors who reported it than to the Amerindians who purportedly emphasized it.

Certainly all the tribes had a very great love for their children and raised them in what might be termed a permissive manner. As Nicolas Denys noted: "Their children are not obstinate, since they give them everything they ask for, without ever letting them cry for that which they want. The greatest persons give way to the little ones. The father and mother draw the morsel from the mouth if the child asks for it. They love their children greatly."[87] They were quite unable to understand the harsher disciplinary methods of the French, the "porcupine-like" affection of French mothers who so readily accepted the separation of their children, and the practice of confining children for months in boarding schools. Marie de l'Incarnation said of the Amerindian children she tried to instruct that "they cannot be restrained and if they are, they become melancholy and their melancholy makes them sick."[88] Education in Amerindian society was part of the everyday life of work and play; unlike French education, it was completely integrated to the rhythm of the adult community. This is the reason for the failure of the early schools to retain their pupils, who, sooner or later, returned home or escaped to the forests.

Marie Arinadsit, a Huron pupil at the Ursuline convent in Quebec, encouraged some Iroquois visitors in 1655 to send their daughters to be educated by the nuns:

> Live, she said to them, with us henceforth as with your brothers, let us be only one people, and as a mark of your affection send some of your daughters to the Seminary; I will be their elder daughter, I will teach them to pray to God, and all the other things our Mothers taught me. And thereupon she started to read before them in Latin, in French and in Huron; then she sang spiritual hymns in those three languages. Thereat those good people were quite taken aback, asked how long it took to learn so many things and to francize well a Savage girl, promising they would not miss sending their children to such a good school.[89]

Within two decades the Superior of the "seminary" for Amerindian girls had to admit that the response from all the tribes had been most discouraging. She confided to a correspondent in France:

> Others are here only as birds of passage and stay with us only until they are sad, something which savage humour cannot suffer; the moment they become sad, the parents take them away for fear they will die. We leave them free on this point, for we are more likely to win them over in this way than by keeping them by force or entreaties. There are others who go off by whim or caprice; they climb our palisades like squirrels, which is as high as a stone wall, and go to run in the woods.[90]

French education was designed to assimilate Amerindian youth and therefore was unsuitable to fit them for life and leadership in their tribal community. The French educators came to understand that their classroom techniques, discipline, curriculum and aims were at complete variance with Amerindian methods and objectives. "The savage life is so charming to them because of its liberty, that it is a miracle to be able to captivate them to the French way of doing things which they esteem unworthy of them, for they glory in not working except at hunting or navigation, or making war."[91] Talon reported in 1670 that on his return to the colony he found the number of native children in the schools established by Bishop Laval and the Jesuits "greatly diminished" but added "they are going to seek new subjects to raise in our ways, our customs, our language and our teaching."[92] These were the very objectives of schooling which so repelled the native children.

Donnacona had offered Cartier three young girls to take to France in 1536 but his people were incensed by this act and managed to free one of the girls from the French vessel. The chieftain intervened and had her returned with the explanation "that they had not advised her to run off, but that she had done so because the ships' boys had beaten her . . . ,"whereupon the unfortunate child was returned with her two companions to the tender care of the French crew.[93] Champlain's astonishment at being offered three little native girls to raise in January 1628 arose out of his experience that the Amerindians did not readily part with their children, that they did not respect French methods of childrearing or education; he could only conclude that the offer was motivated by a desire to cement an alliance or to compensate for the murder of two Frenchmen.[94] The case of the three little girls being offered to Marguerite Bourgeoys at Montreal to be educated was virtually an abduction.[95]

The Amerindian distaste for French educational procedures carried over into a general lack of appreciation for French judicial procedures, law and government. The rigidity, lack of flexibility, authoritarianism and excessive concentration of power at the top of administrative pyramids contrasted unfavourably with the democratic procedures in Huron and Iroquois cantons. In their leaders the Algonkins looked for such traits as emotional restraint, stoicism, practicality, personal resourcefulness, and bravery. The French seem to have misunderstood the value they placed on deference in interpersonal relationships. Father Le Jeune observed that the Montagnais could not "endure in the least those who seem desirous of assuming superiority over others."[96] It is interesting to recall that the Europeans who came into contact with these democratic native societies were members of a paternalistic monarchy and a hierarchical church, both being authoritarian, highly centralized pyramids of secular and religious power respectively. Paul Boyer wrote enthusiastically of the equality of the people encountered in the New World: "They do not know what are extortions, or subsidies, nor brigandry; no avarice, no cupidity, no lawsuits, no quarrels, no savants, no masters, no unfortunates, no beggars, not so much as an inkling of covetousness, which things should make us blush with shame. No distinctions of estates among them, and they consider men only by the actions they accomplish."[97] The greater measure of liberty and of equality in Amerindian life was a comparison that Frenchmen were more apt to make than were Amerindians because the latter had less experience of both cultural milieux on which to base such conclusions.

French justice did not appeal to the Iroquois because it restricted itself to punishing the wrongdoer, while neglecting to give satisfaction to the wronged. Galinée described the fear which his party had in 1669–70 about passing near a Seneca village because shortly before his party had murdered a Seneca hunter and stolen his furs. The culprits were brought to trial and were executed in public in the presence of several Senecas. Nevertheless, as Galinée said, "although the bulk of the nation was appeased by this execution, the relatives of the deceased did not consider themselves satisfied and wished at all hazards to sacrifice some Frenchmen to their vengeance, and loudly boasted of it. . . ."[98]

During the years of initial contact the Amerindians had every reason to fear kidnapping under the guise of taking "volunteers" to France to be educated as interpreters or trained as a native clergy. From the earliest fishing voyages which made contact through to Cartier and Dupont-Gravé, tribesmen had been taken off to France.[99] In 1622 an Indian who had been taken to Dieppe where he fell ill but showed no desire for baptism, although often encouraged by Huguenots to submit to this rite, returned to Canada in the company of the Recollet, Father Irenée Piat. He died shortly after receiving baptism and was buried at sea with full Catholic rites. However, the missionary later regretted not having kept locks of his hair and pieces of his nails to offer relatives proof of his decease because he knew they would suspect foul play and demand compensation: "We did not omit nevertheless to make presents to the closest relatives of the deceased, to remove from them all subject of complaint, and to assure our position in the matter."[100]

Although the French and Amerindians shared a high esteem for qualities considered exclusively masculine — skill in hunting and prowess in war — their cultures were far apart in their concepts of warfare, its objectives, its proper conduct, the treatment of prisoners, and the significance of alliances. The Amerindians never did understand the long-range objectives of European warfare, the sustained campaigns and the highly centralized and authoritarian military organization. They fought their wars for vengeance, for the adoption of prisoners so as to increase their population, and for reasons of prestige. The idea that North Americans were at war with each other because motherlands across the ocean were at war was incomprehensible unless immediate local issues were clearly involved. The humane treatment of prisoners of war by the French was also a mystery to the Amerindian mind: prisoners either should become objects of vengeance or they should be adopted to strengthen or maintain one's manpower. French outrage at scalping, platform torture, and ritual cannibalism was not understood by natives, especially when French warfare was obviously more destructive than Amerindian action. On the other hand, Iroquois prisoners brought back to the Christian reservation in 1645 were greeted by Jean-Baptiste Etinechikawat who received his warriors with praise, saying to the war captain: "Thou knowest well that we now proceed in a different fashion than we formerly did. We have overturned all our old customs. That is why we receive you quietly, without harming the prisoners, without striking or injuring them in any way."[101] The startled prisoners, expecting the traditional torture stake and platform and prepared to sing their death-songs, were well treated in spite of the urgent pleadings of two women, sole survivors of families killed by the Iroquois, to be permitted to avenge themselves on the pagans. This incident proved to be the exception for French attitudes were unable to supplant [the] Amerindian motivations, value system, or ritualistic satisfaction in this domain. Even treaties of peace and non-aggression signed with the French or English were interpreted in Amerindian terms of adoption. They spoke of the French monarch as their "father" and themselves as his "adopted children" upon entering what the French considered a military alliance and a political protectorate.[102]

In almost every sphere of activity the Amerindians differed greatly from the French not only in their practices and traditions, but more especially in their conceptualization. Apart from concessions to French material civilization, technology and military force, they felt equal to, or superior to, the Europeans at the time of contact in the seventeenth century, The fact that the French tended on contact to learn their languages, to adopt to some degree their ways of living, travelling, hunting, and fighting, and to rely heavily on them for their economic and military success confirmed them in their belief that their way of life had advantages over the French life-style. In 1685 Governor Denonville wrote to Seignelay, Minister of the Marine responsible for the colonies, that French attempts to assimilate the proud, self-reliant, and dignified Amerindians had had unfortunate consequences:

> It was believed for a very long time that domiciling the savages near our habitations was a very great means of teaching these peoples to live like us and to become instructed in our religion. I notice, Monseigneur, that the very opposite has taken place because instead of familiarising them with our laws, I assure you that they communicate very much to us all they have that is the very worst, and take on likewise all that is bad and vicious in us. . . . [103]

But already the eroding effects of the new religion, the new economic pressures, the new diseases and alcohol addiction, the new military alignments and the new immigration were beginning to undermine the dignity, self-reliance, and self-assurance of the Amerindians. It was not contact per se, nor the comparisons which Frenchmen and aborigines inevitably made between the two types of civilizations, which proved so destructive to aboriginal belief systems, an integrated social pattern, and self-image, but rather it was the more pervasive long-term concomitants of a permanent and expansionist European presence which undermined the cohesiveness and viability of Amerindian cultures during the ensuing generations and centuries.

While there can be no doubt that the French regarded their own culture as infinitely superior both in material and intellectual aspects to the aboriginal cultures they encountered in North America, it would be a fundamental error to assume that the Amerindians entertained or accepted such a comparative evaluation. Despite the paucity of "Indian sources" there is sufficient primary evidence to indicate that the various tribes were selective in their adaptation of European technology and cultural patterns, that they rejected outright many behavioural and conceptual innovations, that they developed counter-innovative devices and behaviour as a consequence of their contact experience, and that they maintained their own somatic norm image. While there was much in French life and culture that impressed or intrigued the aboriginal tribesmen, it would be inaccurate to assume that they invariably acknowledged the superiority of European culture, much less that they adopted or imitated uncritically French beliefs and behaviour. The Amerindian and French folkways and belief systems tended rather to remain parallel and concurrent with a much greater degree of accommodation of French culture to native life and environmental considerations than of Amerindian cultures to French life-style. While there is evidence to indicate that French accommodation and adaptation to New World circumstances incorporated a degree of barbarization or "Indianization" on the contrary, assimilationist and adaptive responses on the part of aboriginals usually led to alienation from traditional life-style and beliefs, to a rejection of their past and to a close identification of religious conversion with "Frenchification." Few Amerindians crossed the cultural chasm to become identified as domiciled francized converts; on the other hand, new social types, identified as coureurs-de-bois and voyageurs evolved in New France and the more comprehensive social groups identified as habitants, militiamen, and missionaries all experienced significant adaptation to the aborigines and environment of North America which distinguished them from their metropolitan French counterparts.

In the past Canadian historiography has taken little account of these primordial facts concerning initial European-Amerindian relations. Our knowledge of both the facts and fantasies of this cultural contact is now sufficiently advanced to make a revision of interpretations both imperative and credible. There is no longer place for the uncritical assumption that the Europocentric evaluations and comparisons of the French seventeenth-century contemporary sources represented accurately the social realities of the time, much less Amerindian views of events and values. The corrective considerations and the long overdue reappraisal suggested herein can only have the beneficial and stimulating consequence for Canadian historical writing of challenging description, exposition, and evaluation which depict the Amerindians as part of an American environment to be overcome and subdued to European purposes and policies, which relegate the aborigines to the background and stage-setting of national history, or which represent them as awe-stricken inferiors overwhelmed by the impact of a superior civilization which they aspired to acquire but which their own inadequacies denied them as an elusive and unattainable objective.

Notes

1. This orientation is illustrated in the following important writings: Henri Baudet, *Paradise on Earth. Some Thoughts on European Images of Non-European Man* (New Haven, 1965); Gilbert Chinard, *L'Amérique et le rêve exotique dans la littérature française au XVIIe et au XVIIIe siècle* (Paris, 1913); René Gonnard, *La légende du bon sauvage* (Paris, 1946); George R. Healy, "The French Jesuits and the Idea of the Noble Savage," *William and Mary Quarterly* 15, no. 2 (April 1958): 143–67; Douglas Leechman, "The Indian in Literature," *Queen's Quarterly* 50, no. 2 (Summer 1943): 155–63; Roy Harvey Pearce, *The Savages of America. A Study of the Indian and the Idea of Civilization* (Baltimore, 1953); Donald Boyd Smith, *French Canadian Historians' Images of the Indian in the "Heroic Period" of New France, 1534–1663* (M.A. thesis, Université Laval, 1969).

2. Adolphe Bossange [D. Dainville, pseud.], *Beautés de l'histoire du Canada ou époques remarquables, traits intéressans, moeurs, usages, coutumes des habitans du Canada, tant indigènes que colons, depuis sa découverte jusqu'à ce jour* (Paris, 1821); F.-X. Charlevoix, *Histoire et description générale de la Nouvelle-France avec le journal historique d'un Voyage fait par ordre du Roi dans l'Amérique septentrionale,* 3 vols. (Paris, 1744); F.R. Chateaubriand, *Le Génie du Christianisme* (Paris, 1802); J.F.X. Lafitau, *Moeurs des Sauvages amériquains comparés aux moeurs des premiers temps* (Paris, 1724); G.-T. Raynal, *Histoire philosophique et politique des établissements et du commerce dans les deux Indes* (Genève, 1780).

3. Claude d'Abbeville, *Histoire de la Mission des Pères Capucins en l'Isle de Maragnan et terres circonvoisines* (Paris, 1614); Paul Boyer, *Véritable Relation de tout ce qui s' est fait et passé au voyage que Monsieur Bretigny fit à l'Amérique Occidentale* (Paris, 1654); J. de Clodoré, *Relation de ce qui s'est passé dans les Isles et Terre ferme de l'Amérique* (Paris, 1671); Jean de Léry, *Histoire d'un Voyage fait en le Terre du Brésil, autremont dite Amérique* (La Rochelle, 1578); Marc Lescarbot, *Histoire de la Nouvelle France* (Paris, 1609); Gabriel Sagard-Théodat, *Le Grand Voyage du Pays des Hurons* (Paris, 1632).

4. Maximilien Bibaud, *Biographie des Sagamos Illustres de l'Amérique septentrionale* (Montréal, 1848).

5. Napoléon Legendre, "Les races indigènes de l'Amérique devant l'histoire," *Mémoires de la Société Royale du Canada,* vol. 2 (1884), sec. i, 25–30.

6. Léo-Paul Desrosiers, *Iroquoisie*, 1534–1646 (Montréal, 1947); Jacques Rousseau, L'Indien et notre milieu (mimeographed Laval University televised course, 1966); André Vachon, "L'Eau-de-vie dans la société indienne," Canadian Historical Association, *Annual Report* (1960), 22–32. The author has been much encouraged in this line of research by Wilcomb E. Washburn. The debt to the writings of Clark Wissler, Harold Driver, Edward Spicer, Anthony F.C. Wallace, Bruce Trigger, and William Fenton is also acknowledged.

7. R.G. Thwaites, ed., *The Jesuit Relations and Allied Documents*, 73 vols. (Cleveland, 1896–1901), 3: 123.

8. Wilcomb E. Washburn, "A Moral History of Indian–White Relations: Needs and Opportunities for Study," *Ethnohistory* 4, no. 1 (Winter 1957): 48.

9. P.A.S. Maillard, "Lettre sur les missions de l'Acadie et particulièrement sur les missions Micmaques," *Les Soirées Canadiennes* 3 (1863): 299.

10. W.L. Grant, ed., *The History of New France by Marc Lescarbot* (Toronto, 1911), 2: 247.

11. Ibid., 3: 21.

12. Ibid., 2: 45–46.

13. Ibid., 2: 146.

14. Gabriel Sagard-Théodat, *Histoire du Canada et Voyages que les Frères Mineurs Recollects y ont faicts pour la Conuersion des infidelles* (Paris, 1636), 154.

15. E.E. Rich, "Trade Habits and Economic Motivation among the Indians of North America," *Canadian Journal of Economics and Political Science* 26 (February 1960): 35–53.

16. Wilcomb E. Washburn, "Symbol, Utility, and Aesthetics in the Indian Fur Trade," *Aspects of the Fur Trade, Selected Papers of the 1965 North American Fur Trade Conference* (St. Paul, 1967), 50–54.

17. William F. Ganong, ed., *The Description and Natural History of the Coasts of North America (Acadia) by Nicholas Denys* (Toronto, 1908), 442–43.

18. Sagard, *Histoire du Canada*, 36.

19. Grant ed., *History of New France*, 3: 3.

20. Ibid., 25.

21. Nicholas Denys, *Geographische en Historische Beschrijving den Kusten van NoordAmerica. Met de Naturirlijke Historie des Lendts* (Amsterdam, 1688), 67.

22. William F. Ganong, ed., *New Relation of Gaspesia with the Customs and Religion of the Gaspesian Indians by Father Chrestien LeClercq* (Toronto, 1910), 101–2; also Thwaites, *Jesuit Relations*, 3: 81.

23. Thwaites ed., *Jesuit Relations*, 57: 95–97.

24. James B. Conacher, ed., *The History of Canada or New France by Father François du Creux, S.J.* (Toronto, 1951). 267–68.

25. Ganong, ed., *New Relation of Gaspesia*, 246.

26. J.C. Webster, ed., *Sieur de Dièreville, Relation of the Voyage to Port Royal in Acadia or New France* (Toronto, 1933), 150.

27. Conacher ed., *History of Canada*, 274.

28. Harry Hoetink, *Thw Two Variants in Caribbean Race Relations* (New York, 1967), 120–59.

29. Pierre d'Avity, *Description générale de l'Amérique, troisième partie du Monde* (Paris, 1637), 30.

30. Sagard, *Le Grand Voyage du Pays des Hurons*, 176–77.

31. Thwaites, ed., *Jesuit Relations*, 27: 215.

32. Grant, ed., *History of New France*, 3: 22.

33. Ibid., 27.

34. Ibid., 22.

35. Conacher, *History of Canada,* 1: 36.

36. Nicolas Perrot, "Memoir on the Manners, Customs, and Religion of the Savages of North America," in *The Indian Tribes of the Upper Mississippi Valley and Region of the Great Lakes,* ed. E.H. Blair (Cleveland, 1911), 1:145.

37. George M. Wrong, ed., *The Long Journey to the Country of the Hurons by Father Gabriel Sagard* (Toronto, 1939), 137.

38. Thwaites, ed., *Jesuit Relations,* 3: 22.

39. Ibid., 3: 75.

40. R.G. Thwaites, ed., *New Voyages to North America by Baron de Lahontan* (Chicago, 1905), 2: 471.

41. Thwaites, ed., *Jesuit Relations,* 3: 105.

42. Ibid., 31: 121.

43. Ibid., 39: 129–31.

44. Conacher, ed., *History of Canada,* 1: 194.

45. Ibid., 1: 227.

46. Dom Guy Oury, *Marie de l'Incarnation, Ursuline (1599–1672). Correspondence* (Solesmes, 1971), 67–68.

47. Thwaites, ed., *Jesuit Relations,* 1: 117–18.

48. Ibid., 18: 41.

49. Ibid., 31: 123.

50. Grant, ed., *History of New France,* 179–80.

51. Ganong, ed., *New Relation of Gaspesia,* 140–41.

52. Thwaites, ed., *Jesuit Relations,* 6: 289; 10: 119; 15: 155; 39: 119; 67: 145.

53. Ibid., 63: 299.

54. Ibid., 65: 131.

55. Conacher, ed., *History of Canada,* 1: 160.

56. Sagard, *Histoire du Canada,* 9.

57. Conacher, ed., *History of Canada,* 1: 313–14.

58. Thwaites, ed., *Jesuit Relations,* 20: 27–31; 30: 27, 29–31.

59. Ibid., 20: 27–29.

60. Ibid., 58: 275.

61. Ibid., 58: 201.

62. Wrong, ed., *Long Journey,* 78.

63. Alessandro Bacchiani, "Giovanni da Verrazzano and His Discoveries in North America, 1524, according to the Unpublished Contemporaneous Cellère Codex of Rome, Italy," *Fifteenth Annual Report, 1910, of the American Scenic and Historic Preservation Society* (Albany, 1910), Appendix A, 192.

64. Thwaites, ed., *Jesuit Relations,* 3: 103–5.

65. Sagard, *Histoire du Canada,* 165.

66. Thwaites, ed., *Jesuit Relations,* 5: 119–21.

67. Ganong, ed., *New Relation of Gaspesia,* 106.

68. Ibid., 103–4.

69. Thwaites, ed., *Jesuit Relations,* 5: 121.

70. Dom Albert Jamet, ed., *Les Annales de l' Hôtel-Dieu de Québec, 1636–1716* (Quebec, 1939), 47.

71. Donald H. Frame, ed., *Montaigne's Essays and Selected Writings* (New York, 1963), 117. The account is given in much more detail in an unlikely source: Michel Baudier, *Histoire de la Religion des Turcs* (Paris, 1625), 122.

72. Sagard, *Histoire du Canada,* 241–42.

73. Ganong, ed., *New Relation of Gaspesia,* 104.

74. Perrot, "Memoir," 134–35.

75. Sagard, *Histoire du Canada*, 219.

76. C.H. Laverdière and H.-R. Casgrain, eds., *Le Journal des Jésuites* (Quebec, 1871), 77–78.

77. Thwaites, ed., *Jesuit Relations*, 14: 19–21.

78. Ibid., 9: 216–18.

79. Ibid., 9: 233.

80. Grant, ed., *History of New France*, 2: 326.

81. Jamet, ed., *Annales*, 25.

82. Conacher, ed., *History of Canada*, 2: 651.

83. Thwaites, ed., *Jesuit Relations*, 44: 297.

84. Ibid., 5: 143; 17: 213; 39: 73; 49: 121; 61: 85; 68: 61; F. Speiser, K.R. Andrae, and W. Krickberg, "Les Peaux-Rouges et leur médecine," *Revue Ciba*, no. 10 (April 1940): 291–318.

85. Marc Lescarbot, *Histoire de la Nouvelle-France* (Paris, 1609), 667.

86. d'Abbeville, *Histoire de la Mission*, 281.

87. Ganong, ed., *Description and Natural History*, 404.

88. Joyce Marshall, ed., *Word from New France. The Selected Letters of Marie de l'Incarnation* (Toronto, 1967), 341.

89. Oury, *Marie de l'Incarnation*, 995.

90. Ibid., 801–2.

91. Ibid., 828.

92. Pierre Margry, ed., *Découvertes et Etablissements des Français dans l'Ouest et dans le Sud de l'Amérique septentrionale* (Paris, 1879), 1:92, Talon to Colbert, 10 November 1670.

93. Conacher, ed., *History of Canada*, 35–36.

94. Grant, ed., *History of New France*, 2: 146–48.

95. Public Archives of Canada (hereafter PAC), MG 17/A, 7–1, St. Sulpice, Mélanges, carton B, no. 28 (h), 199–200.

96. Thwaites, ed., *Jesuit Relations*, 6: 165.

97. Paul Boyer, *Véritable Relation de tout ce qui s'est fait et passé au voyage que Monsieur de Bretigny fit à l'Amérique Occidentale* (Paris, 1654), 227.

98. James H. Coyne, "Dollier de Casson & De Bréhaut de Gallinée: Exploration of the Great Lakes, 1669–1670," *Ontario Historical Society Papers and Records* 4 (1903): 19.

99. PAC, MG 2, Archives de la Marine, Series B³, IX, Sieur de Narp to Minister of the Marine, 3 September 1671, fol. 374.

100. Sagard, *Histoire du Canada*, 95.

101. Thwaites, ed., *Jesuit Relations*, 27: 235.

102. Ibid., 42: 121–23; G. Snyderman, "Behind the Tree of Peace: A Sociological Analysis of Iroquois Warfare," *Pennsylvania Archaeologist* 18, nos. 3 and 4 (1948): 30–37.

103. PAC, MG I, Archives des Colonies, Series C¹¹A, VII, Denonville to Seignelay, 13 September 1685, 45–46.

INDIANS AS CONSUMERS IN THE EIGHTEENTH CENTURY†

ARTHUR J. RAY

You told me Last year to bring many Indians, you See I have not Lyd. here is a great many young men come with me, use them Kindly! use them Kindly I say! give them good goods, give them good Goods I say! — we Livd. hard Last winter and in want. the powder being short measure and bad, I say! — tell your Servants to fill the measure and not to put their finger's within the Brim, take pity of us, take pity of us, I say! — we came a Long way to See you, the french sends for us but we will not here, we Love the English, give us good black tobacco (brazl. tobacco) moist & hard twisted, Let us see itt before op'n'd, — take pity of us, take pity of us I say! — the Guns are bad, Let us trade Light guns small in the hand, and well shap'd, with Locks that will not freeze in the winter, and Red gun cases. . . . Let the young men have Roll tobacco cheap, Ketles thick high for the shape and size, strong Ears, and the Baile to Lap Just upon the side, — Give us Good measure, in cloth, — Let us see the old measures, Do you mind me!, the young men Loves you by comming to see you, take pity, take pity I say! . . . they Love to Dress and be fine, do you understand me! — .

According to James Isham, a Hudson's Bay Company trader, the foregoing address was typical of those given by Indian trading leaders during the smoking of the calumet that preceded trade at the bayside posts in the early eighteenth century.[1] Isham's account of the Indian trading speech gives us a rare, fleeting picture of what the Indian was like as a consumer. While politely couching their demands in the form of a plea "take pity of us" and professing that they "love the English" the Indian leaders let the English traders know they expected favourable rates of exchange, good quality merchandise, items stylistically pleasing and well suited to their nomadic life-style in the harsh subarctic environment.

† From Carol M. Judd and Arthur J. Ray, eds., *Old Trails and New Directions: Papers of the Third North American Fur Trade Conference* (Toronto: University of Toronto Press, 1980), 255–71.

To what extent were the Indians able to press these demands? Did the Hudson's Bay Company make a concerted effort to meet them? By seeking answers to these basic questions we should be able to fill out our sketchy image of the Indian as a consumer, and obtain a clearer picture of his English counterpart and of the nature of Indian–European exchange. This paper will consider the Indians' concern with the quality of merchandise offered by Europeans and its suitability for their needs[2] and the efforts of the Hudson's Bay Company during its first century of operations to develop an inventory of goods acceptable to the Indians.

When the Hudson's Bay Company was chartered in 1670, the founders addressed a number of difficult problems in their efforts to establish trade. In Europe, contacts had to be developed with reliable suppliers of suitable merchandise. In North America, the company faced the difficult task of luring the Indians away from the French. The Indians of the James Bay area and the shield uplands to the south toward the Great Lakes had been receiving French trade goods for a considerable period of time prior to 1668 when the first English trading expedition was sent into the bay.[3] Therefore, in the beginning the company was at a considerable disadvantage; the French had considerably more experience dealing with the Indians of central Canada, and the Indians had grown accustomed to their merchandise.

The English handicap was offset somewhat by the fact that the two famous French traders and explorers, Médard Chouart, Sieur des Groseilliers, and Pierre Esprit Radisson, played active roles in the early history of the Hudson's Bay Company. Both helped the company establish its policies for dealing with the Indians and helped set the first standards of trade for the exchange of goods and furs. Besides assisting the company in its early contact with the Indians, they helped the governor and committee in London select trade goods. Radisson appears to have played the more important role.[4]

At its meeting of 4 March 1671, the governor and committee ordered:

> Mr. Bailey with the Advise of Mr. Radisson & Mr. Groseleyer treate with such persons as they think fitt for Such goods as may bee needfull for Supplyeing a Cargo for the next years expedition for Hudson's Bay, that is to Say, two hundred fowleing pieces & foure hundred powder hornes, with a proportionable quantity of Shott fitt thereunto, first bringing patterns of the gunns to bee bought unto the next Committee & . . . two Hundred Brass Kettles Sizeable of from two to Sixteene gallons a piece, twelve grosse of French knives & two Grosse of Arrow head & about five or Six hundred hatchets.

The order consisted of arms, ammunition, and metal goods, and at least the knives were said to be French. The hatchets were perhaps of French origin judging from instructions that Radisson received from the London committee the following year. On 21 May 1672 they ordered: "that Mr. Raddison attende Mr. Millington forthwith with a pattern of biscay hatchetts to be provided for this Company, such as are usually sent from thence to France to Serve the Indians in & about Canada, & that Mr. Millington bee desired to give order for two thousand hatchetts to be brought from Biscay by the first opportunity." Since the Biscay hatchet was an important trade item, the company's directors hoped to get them manufactured in England. On 4 December 1673 they instructed a Mr. Rastell to: "make enquiry among the mchants [sic] if hee can finde any Biscay hatchets to bee bought to the ende that by the Samples of them Such hatchets may be provided here as may be most agreeable to the minde of the Indians and that Mr. Millington gett patternes forthwith from Biscay of three . . . Seizes, Vizt of 1¼, 1½ & 2 lb a piece."[5]

This sequence of events with the Biscay hatchets highlights a pattern that developed very early. The company attempted to obtain goods the Indians were already accustomed to in type, style or pattern. They drew on the considerable experience of Radisson, who advised the company what to buy and assessed the quality of the merchandise obtained for shipment to the bay. Although several key items in the early inventories were of French origin, the company quickly turned to British manufacturers to produce copies. By 1679 an English ironmonger, Robert Carnor, was supplying most of the hatchets. In 1683, the company placed an order for knives with Samuel Bannor. Between that date and 1715, Bannor supplied the company with the bulk of its knives, hatchets, awls, and fire steels. As late as 1697, Bannor was still using French patterns to make some of the company's knives.[6]

English manufacturers also copied other French trade goods. For example, on 25 January 1682, the governor and committee ordered two of their suppliers to contact agents in France to buy samples of blankets so that the company could have similar ones made in England. Six French blankets were eventually bought at a cost of £4 13s. A wide variety of French goods were copied at various times, including awls, vermilion, ice chisels, firearms, and gunpowder.[7]

While the company was thus obtaining patterns for goods, and developing contacts with suppliers in England, its men in the bay were gaining experience in the conduct of trade with Indians. Increasingly these men were able to offer advice to augment that of Radisson and they were able to assess the degree to which the company was meeting Indian consumer demand. Indeed, at an early date the men in the bay were required to provide the governor and committee with this information. For example, in their letter to Governor John Nixon dated 29 May 1680 they informed him that he was supposed to:

> send us home by every return of our Ships all such goods as are either defective or not acceptable to the Natives and to inform us

wherein they are deficient And also to direct us exactly as you can of what form, quality and conditions [of] every sort of goods wch is demanded there for the best satisfaction of the Indians, And wee will do our utmost that you shall be supplied with every species of Commodity in perfection.[8]

This order became standing policy and it was often repeated in later letters with only slight revisions. The revisions were designed to give the governor and committee more precise information. For instance, the traders were ordered to give an exact accounting of the quantity of each good sold (including sizes, shapes, colours, etc., wherever appropriate); samples of goods the Indians disliked were to be sent back to London; and examples of items highly prized were also to be returned.[9]

In spite of its concerted effort, the company still fell short of achieving its objective of supplying the Indians with the variety and quality of goods demanded. In 1682, Governor Nixon filed a report to the governor and committee recommending a series of policies be implemented to improve trade. Many of the goods manufactured in England were of such poor quality that he believed the company should consider sending raw materials and tradesmen to the posts and manufacturing many trade goods in Hudson Bay. "It is a great vexation to me," Nixon wrote,

> to see a poore Indiane with his coat all seem-rent, in less than 6 weeks tyme, and when they are torne, the poore rogues can not mend them, but must suffer could in winter, and just occasione have they to say we have stole their beaver, to my great shame and your loss, I humbly conceave that if yow had taylers in the country they would benefit yow. . . . The lyk of your smiths. It is a wonder to me that for all our wryting since the country hath been settled, that England can not furnish us with good edge toules, you have verry bad fortoun that you can find non, I have seen good edge tweles made in England, but I feare it is your fate to be cheated.
>
> Wherefore it be a great deall better that they were to be made by the smithes in the country. I am sure that 5d worth of stuff will mak a hatchet . . . as for the smith we must have hime (whither he make your iron worke or not) for the use of the factories . . . so that I conclud the smiths will pay their wages by their worke, and the ware too the Indian's minds, the ice chissels nor indeed no other iron worke that yow send over is to their mindes, and that is the great cause that a great deall of beaver goeth to the frens which otherways would come to us. . . .

Nixon considered the company's goods to be of such poor quality that he lowered the standard of trade without obtaining the prior approval of the governor and committee.[10]

The London directors were so upset by Nixon's actions that they met three times in June 1684 to discuss the matter. Soon after they wrote to Governor Henry Sergeant, Nixon's successor, and informed him:

> We are heartily troubled that Governor Nixon has altered the Standard of Trade . . . we have strickly examined him and finde that he gives us a very slender account of that alteration, take all those arguments he musters up in his Councell booke as he calls it & you will finde them but weake. Likewise we have examined Geo. Geyer (upon the premisses who was Chiefe at Rupert River, who assures us that the Indians he Traded with . . . (who Lye nerer the French then any factorey) were all pleased with the Goods they bought & the Quantety and no murmuring amongst them or craveing more goods then at other times . . . we have at this time sent you very good goods, choise goods as can be bought for money especially the Guns, Kettles, hatchets & knives in which we thinke we doe very much outvey the French. . . .
>
> The Goods we have now sent you are very good cost us much more then formerly as we have mentioned in the former parte of our letter. Therefore, we wold have you indeavor what leyes in your power to bring our goods to the old Standard.[11]

For the time being, then, the governor and committee decided not to try to improve the quality of their merchandise by having some articles manufactured in the bay. Rather, they decided the best way to upgrade their trade goods was to offer higher prices to English suppliers. It was for this reason that the committee members took exception to Nixon's action of lowering the standard of trade. In fact, one committee member believed that Nixon's action was so prejudicial to the company's interest that he opposed the committee's decision to pay Nixon the £305 salary they owed him[12]

Despite selling imitations of many French goods and paying higher prices for its commodities in England, the committee received an unabated stream of complaints from the bayside. Even George Geyer, who in 1682 had said the Indians were pleased with company goods, reported widespread dissatisfaction eight years later. This prompted the governor and committee to order that: "all persons against whome Complaints has been Made by Governr Geyer in his Generall Letter [of 1690], shall not furnish the Compa[ny] with any goods, untill the Comittee are satisfied in that Matter & have otherwise determined it."[13]

Judging from Indian complaints, of all of the goods sold in the early years of the company's operations, those manufactured from metal were the least satisfactory. Most of the Indians' basic tools had traditionally been fashioned from stone, bone, or wood, and if they broke, the hunter could easily repair or replace them. However, the situation was quite different when the Indian was using firearms, metal hatchets, knives, awls, firesteels, and kettles. If a blacksmith or gunsmith were not available, metal tools could not be repaired. Since few Indians lived near the posts in the seventeenth and early eighteenth centuries, tools could only be repaired or replaced once a year. The record clearly shows that the Indians for these reasons became very critical of the firearms, metal tools, and utensils the English and French offered them in trade. There is also reason to believe that European manufacturers did not have the technological capability to make metal goods that met exacting Indian requirements and local environmental conditions.

In the case of firearms, Indian complaints were most frequent in the 1670s and 1680s, but declined thereafter. Between 1700 and 1745 comparatively few criticisms were made. Thereafter, until the close of the period, they were more common. Complaints generally centered around apparent defects in the metal which the Indians believed caused gun barrels to burst. For example, on 22 August 1748 George Spence wrote from Fort Albany: "Our armourer hath over hauld the Guns & can find no fault with them, but our Indians complain last Year that the Barrels are not so good as usual, they are full of flaws and apt to burst." The governor and committee considered the matter and concluded that the fault did not lie with the guns, but with the Indians. Accordingly, on 16 May 1749 they responded: "Upon examining Strictly into the Complaints made of the Guns We find it is chiefly the Indians Own faults by not putting Dry and Proper Wads in when they charge them or by firing them when the Muzzel is Slopt with Snow which will burst the best Gun that can be made, but as to the flaws, We have given such Strict Orders that we hope you will hear no farther complaints in that Head."[14] The attitude of the London committee is understandable given that all of the guns were viewed by a gunsmith in London before they were packed. In addition, the gunsmiths at the posts were supposed to open the gun cases as soon as they arrived in the bay, examine the guns, immediately return those that were defective, and oil and repack the others.[15] Therefore, any guns the Indians received should have been inspected at least twice.

Most probably some of the problems the Indians experienced with firearms stemmed from harsh usage, given their life-style and their early stage in acquiring an iron-age technology. The Indians may not have fully appreciated that care and prescribed procedures had to be followed when they used their guns. However, the problems the Indians experienced with their firearms were more complicated than the governor and committee suspected. On 10 August 1749 Spence responded to the committee: "We agree with Your Hons in Opinion that the Guns proving bad is in a Great measure owing to the Carelessness of the Indians, we had Several Gun Barrels brought to us to mend this Summer that were Traded last Year and our Armourer thinks that it is owing to the Stuff [metals used in manufacture] and Likewise being filed too thin."

In their final comment to Spence on this subject the governor and committee replied on 21 May 1750:

> We are still not withstanding your Armourers Sentiments of Opin-ion that the Bursting of some of the Guns is entirely owing to the Indians Mismanagement either by Over charging, Improperly Wad-ing, or Suffering Snow to get into them, and not to the Badness of the Shaft which is the same it allways was. And as to the Barrels being filed too thin it has been done by express desire of the Natives themselves to make them more portable if you are of the same opinion as your Armourer, you shall in future have the Barrels thick if you think it needfull, but then we are Convinced you will not be able to Trade them on account of their being To heavy, besides We have no Such Complaints from the Northward and your Guns are equall in strength and goodness to theirs.[16]

This episode underscores the problems the company faced when trying to cater to Indian demands regarding metal goods. The Indians wanted goods as lightweight as possible, that could withstand hard usage and the severe climate. English manufacturers had had little prior experience designing for such conditions. Indeed, the patterns for some goods, such as firearms, were simply copied from those used by other exporting companies which often traded into temperate or tropical areas. For instance, the early firearms were patterned after those of the East India Company. However, goods well suited to those areas were often inad-equate for the Canadian environment.

Experience had taught the Indians that even the most minute flaws in metal were potential sources of trouble during the winter when temper-atures plummeted and made the iron very brittle. Accordingly, they would not accept any goods with cracks or other apparent defects no matter how minor they appeared to the traders. For instance, in 1750 James Isham returned a considerable number of guns from York Factory saying that they were untradeable. The governor and committee exam-ined them and wrote back to Isham the following year:

> We were much concerned on reading your General Letter to find you had returned so many guns so defective as not fit for Trade . . . but how great was our Surprize when on Strict Examination and the most close Inspection we could not find above four of the guns that had any thing like a fault to make them Untradeable the rest being altogether marked wherever there was a fire flaw/a Scratch as tho made with the Point of a Pin/which no Gun Barrel ever was or can be made without.

The following year Isham returned four more firearms saying that they were substandard because of "fire flaws" in the barrels. Isham's action provoked the ire of the committee. In their 1752 letter to Isham, the governor and committee said they thought it extraordinary that he should have sent the guns back in view of their letter of the previous year and added:

> the Defects that you Condem them for are only Fire flaws as we said before which/were we to give ever so much for our Guns/it is impossible to get them without, therefore we cannot still help imputing it to the Ignorance of your Armourer, more especially as the Guns sent to your Factory are equal in goodness to any we now send or ever did and it is Surprizing to us that the Trading Indians that came to York Fort should be more Curious than any of the other Natives, and more so within these two years then ever they were before.[17]

The problem of "fire flaws" was not limited to guns. Other metal goods were said to have the same defect. As with firearms, the governor and committee insisted these blemishes were not serious. In 1753 the traders at Fort Churchill returned some knives and firesteels as unacceptable to the Indians. The London committee considered the matter and the following year wrote Ferdinand Jacobs and the council at Fort Churchill telling them: "the flaws you mention in the Knives and Steels we apprehend to be Fire Flaws which are not any real defect but a Mark of their Hardness."[18] It is unclear what the "fire flaws" were. Presumably they were small holes resulting from the casting processes used. It is uncertain whether they seriously affected the durability of arms and metal goods. Perhaps such minor defects were not a problem in England but were sources of difficulty in the subarctic. In any event, the company clearly had problems obtaining metal goods without them and the Indians tended to reject items with these flaws.

As early as 1682, Governor Nixon had suggested one solution would be to have some articles manufactured at company posts. Although the governor and committee did not accept Nixon's suggestion, they eventually decided to pursue this course after other traders made similar suggestions. For example, in his letter of 16 August 1724 from York Factory, Thomas McCliesh informed the governor and committee: "We desire that no more ice chisels nor scrapers be sent out of England, our smiths' making here being preferable . . . and more taken with [sic] the Indians." The Governor and committee complied with McCliesh's request and sent bar iron in place of the chisels and scrapers.[19]

The company also confronted similar problems in its efforts to obtain other staple goods acceptable to the Indians. Only one other item, Brazil tobacco, will be considered here. Brazil tobacco ranked high on the Indians' list of priorities; therefore, it indicates the demanding consumer taste the Indian had, even for items not affecting his livelihood. The governor and committee devoted more attention to securing a suitable supply of this commodity than they did for any other item.

Initially the company shipped English tobacco (probably Virginia) to its posts. Its first order for Brazil tobacco, a twisted tobacco treated with molasses, was placed on 7 January 1684.[20] The shipment was received in February and placed on board the company's ships in May 1685. In their 22 May 1685 letter to Governor Sergeant, the governor and committee wrote:

> We are sorry the Tobacco last sent to you proves so bad, we have made many yeares tryall of Engleish Tobacco, by several persons & whiles we have Traded, we have had yearly complaints thereof. We have made search, [of] what Tobacco the French vends to the Indians, which you doe so much extoll, and have this yeare bought the like (vizt) Brazeele Tobacco, of which we have sent for each Factorey a good Quantity, that if approved of we are resolved in the future to supply [you] with the like, as you have occasion.[21]

The Indians heartily approved of this innovation and the company was soon engaged in a continuing search for the best Brazil tobacco that could be purchased in European markets. Initially the company ordered its tobacco from London merchants. Typical of these early orders was one that was placed with the firm of Brooke and Gulston on 27 February 1712. On that date the company's secretary, John Perry, indicated: "The Hudsons Bay Compn will have ocasion for about one thousand weight of the Choicest Brazill Tobacco of the Sweetest Smell, but of a Small Role, about the Size of a Mans Little finger."[22]

After receiving an unsatisfactory shipment of Brazil tobacco from their London supplier in 1722, the governor and committee decided to deal directly with Lisbon tobacco merchants. Since Lisbon was one of the leading Brazil tobacco importing cities, they believed they would have a better chance of getting the best tobacco available. The record suggests this was a wise decision. In 1735 the Lisbon firm of John and James Wats informed the company that 8 335 rolls of Brazil tobacco had been landed in November and they intended to select twenty of the best for the company. Thereafter, the company had with its Lisbon suppliers a standing order for the twenty best rolls of tobacco as soon as the Bahia fleet arrived in port.[23]

Dealing directly with Lisbon merchants helped the company obtain better tobacco, but the governor and committee still had to check its tobacco cargoes closely to prevent abuses and maintain quality. For instance, Mawman and Company of Lisbon was a major supplier between 1735 and 1743. On 29 March 1743 the governor and committee wrote: "the Tobacco is received, but find on looking into some of the Rolls, they are the worst they have had for some Years past, as being of a very bad Staple much of it wilted and to a great fault Loaded with Melosses which they are informed is done since it came from the Brazils together with a bad scent and too Large a twist for their Trade."[24]

The next year the company turned to a different merchant and apparently had no further dealings with Mawman and Company. Suppliers who failed to meet the company's rigid specifications lost its business.

The company closely watched Indian reactions to its goods, kept a watchful eye on the quality and variety of articles their French competitors were selling, and secured the best merchandise available in Europe; but the Indians were still not satisfied. In fact, judging from the record, Indian discontent was increasing toward the middle of the eighteenth century. For instance, on 8 August 1728, Thomas McCliesh wrote the governor and committee from York Factory informing them:

> I have sent home two bath rings as samples, for of late most of the rings sent are too small, having now upon 216 that none of the Indians will Trade. I have likewise sent home 59 ivory combs that will not be traded, they having no great teeth, and 3900 large musket flints and small pistol flints, likewise one hatchet, finding at least 150 such in three casks that we opened this summer which causes great grumbling amongst the natives. We have likewise sent home 18 barrels of powder that came over in 1727, for badness I never saw the like, for it will not kill fowl nor beast at thirty yards distance: and as for kettles in general they are not fit to put into a Indian's hand being all of them thin, and eared with tender old brass that will not bear their weight full of liquid, and soldered in several places. Never was any man so upbraided with our powder, kettles and hatchets, than we have been this summer by all the natives, especially by those that borders near the French. Our cloth likewise is so stretched with the tenter-hooks, so as the selvedge is almost tore from one end of the pieces to the other. I hope that such care will be taken so as will prevent the like for the future, for the natives are grown so politic in their way of trade, so as they are not to be dealt by as formerly . . . and I afirm that a man is not fit to be entrusted with the Company's interest here or in any of their factories that does not make more profit to the Company in dealing in a good commodity than in a bad. For now is the time to oblige the natives before the French draws them to their settlement.[25]

In their response, the governor and committee indicated that steps had been taken to rectify the problems detailed.[26]

Writing from the same post eleven years later, James Isham sent a long list of Indian complaints. In a letter of 1739, Isham indicated that the Indians disliked the colour and size of the large pearl beads; complained that the kettles were too heavy for their size and the wrong shape; and claimed the gunpowder was very weak, foul smelling, and an objectionable ashy colour. Although they liked the shape, quality, and colour of the blankets, the Indians said they were too short. Cloth, on the other hand, was said to be of little service because it was too narrow, weak, and thin. Despite liking their design, the Indians also considered the buttons and combs to be too weak. The fire steels were faulty, giving little fire, the gun worms too big for the ramrods, the French flints the wrong shape, the yarn gloves useless, and the knives very displeasing, with bad blades and worse handles. The twine was weak and uneven, as thick as packthread in some places and as thin as sewing thread in others. Powder horns were the wrong shape and rings were too wide for women's fingers. Isham concluded his list of Indian criticisms by remarking: "Those are the only things of dislike of trading goods to the best of my knowledge, and according to your honours' desire, [I] have sent home samples of most part which is pleasing to the Indians, and most conducive to your honours' interest." Isham must have sent home few examples of articles that pleased the Indians! Only the hatchets were said to be extraordinarily good.[27]

Indian dissatisfaction with many goods continued. Owing to the quantity and variety of goods imported, the governor and committee could not maintain complete control over all of their suppliers in any given year. Some defective merchandise probably slipped their notice every year. English manufacturers had probably still not come to grips with the problem of making light-weight durable goods. McCliesh said the Indians found the kettles thin and weak. Eleven years later Isham reported they thought them too heavy for their size. There was apparently some difficulty making articles stylistically pleasing and sturdy. Isham said the Indians found the combs and buttons pleasing in design but too weak; the governor and committee wrote: "Buttons and Combs are made Neat but if made to Strong will look Clumsy and heavy."[28]

Another aspect of Indian complaints cannot be overlooked. These criticisms were part of the bargaining ploys the Indians used to pressure the traders to lower the prices of goods. Since this strategy was most effective when European trading rivalries were strong, there should perhaps be some correlation between the frequency of Indian complaints and the intensity of English–French competition. This was probably the case.

French opposition was strongest between 1730 and 1755 when the company was forced to relax the standards of trade at all posts except Fort Churchill.[29] During this period Indian criticisms of company trade goods were most prevalent. McCliesh noted in his 1728 letter that it was particularly the Indians living near the French who "upbraided" him for the poor quality of company merchandise; also, the Indians were becoming increasingly "politic" in their way of trade as the French drew near.[30]

Besides holding McCliesh and other company traders up to ridicule for the "substandard" trade goods offered for exchange, these "Frenchified" Indians, as they were called, claimed that the French traded superior merchandise.[31] The governor and committee were puzzled as to why the Indians seemed to prefer French articles to those of the company — many company goods had been copied from French patterns and subsequently improved. Accordingly, on 18 May 1738 they wrote to Thomas Bird at Fort Albany: "Wee Shall Expect by the return of the Ship this Year Samples of Such Sorts of Commodities which the French furnish the Indians . . . that you not only say are better than ours but also more acceptable to the Natives, And also your remarks thereon." Bird sent to London a variety of French goods obtained from the Indians. After inspecting these articles, the governor and committee wrote back in 1739:

> We have received the two pieces of Cloth and the Samples of other knives you sent us which you say are French, the worst piece is very coarse and loose and Narrow and not near so good or broad as what we have formerly & do now send, and therefore we do Expect you will write us the reasons why the Indians like the French better then ours which you have omitted to do, the Finest piece is also narrow. As to the knives the Difference is only in the handles. Wherefore we have sent you Six hundred large Long Knives with box handles over and above ye Quantity you Indented for.[32]

The governor and committee clearly believed the cloth they were shipping to the bay superior to that of the French; nonetheless they took steps to improve the quality. On 1 May 1740 they wrote to Rowland Waggoner at Moose Factory: "we have taken very great care about the cloth for it is thick and Strong of good wool and Spinning full Breadth & well dyed, much better then the french cloth, so do not Doubt but it will be very pleasing to the Indians. . . . The flannell now sent is thicker and better then what was sent heretofore, therefore let us know how it is approved of.[33] Similar letters were sent to the factors at Fort Albany and York Factory. Thus the Indians not only successfully pressured the company to relax the standards of trade, but also brought about an improvement in the quality of goods offered to them. They effected change in this and many other instances even though company officials were convinced the merchandise they offered was the best available locally.

The Indians apparently used the same tactics in their dealings with the French. For example, the French were convinced that English woollens were better and cheaper than French and were preferred by the Indians. In the early eighteenth century over 21 000 yards of English strouds were imported into New France annually from New York for the Indian trade.[34] At mid-century, the governor and intendant of New France wrote to the French government: "The English have the better of us in the quality of merchandise in two important articles. The first is kettles — the second is cloth. They [the traders] believe that up to the present the Indians wish only English cloth and they become so well accustomed to it that it would be difficult to introduce others.''[35] The governor's remarks are interesting given that French manufacturers had been producing imitations of English cloth for the Indian trade since the 1720s.[36] His comments were made during the very period when the Indians were telling company traders English woollens were not equal to French. Ironically, the cloth the Indians brought to the bay from the French posts may well have been made in England or copies of yard goods formerly sold by the company. The Indians were clearly successful in pitting the two European groups against each other, forcing them to lower prices, and getting them to make copies and improvements of each other's merchandise.

In conclusion, an examination of the early Hudson's Bay Company fur trade reveals the Indians as shrewd consumers who knew how to take full advantage of the economic opportunities offered to them. In this respect the Indians were clearly equal to their European counterparts. The old stereotype of the Indians being a people easily tricked by crafty Europeans and made to part with valuable furs for worthless trinkets obviously does not apply to the central subarctic before 1763.

In casting away the old stereotype and searching the rich historical record we find a consistent and logical pattern to Indian consumer demand. They wanted to barter their furs at the most favourable rates of exchange that competitive conditions permitted. They wanted lightweight durable goods well suited to the harsh subarctic environment. Given the widely scattered posts, Indians were usually unable to have their European-manufactured tools repaired or replaced more than once a year. Therefore, they expected more from these tools than from those they traditionally made from local materials. Indeed, the Indians needed more reliable metal tools than did the European traders, who had access to blacksmiths and gunsmiths or to warehouses for replacements when the smiths could not effect needed repairs.

Perhaps we have dwelt too long on the sorry tale of the European abuse of Indians in the fur trade after 1763 — a well-known tale which usually casts the Indians as passive figures pushed around by different trading companies. By looking at an earlier period, when a more equal partnership existed between the Indian and the trader, the active role of the Indian is more readily apparent. In this instance, by recognizing that the Indians had well-defined demands and a critical eye to assess trade goods, we find that the Indian was probably an agent of technological change even though his culture was not as advanced technologically as that of his European partners. The latter were forced to make a number of changes in the manufacture of firearms and metal goods. The tempering and casting of metal had to be improved to produce knives, hatchets, kettles, ice chisels, and guns that were less prone to breaking in the severe cold. The record indicates that some of the craftsmen working at the trading posts were able to make certain tools that were more to the Indians' liking than those manufactured in Europe. The nature and importance of technological innovations resulting from attempts to meet the consumer demands of the Indian is a story that has yet to be told.

Notes

1. E.E. Rich, ed., *James Isham's Observations on Hudson's Bay, 1743* (Toronto, 1949), 83–87.

2. See also, Arthur J. Ray and D.B. Freeman, *"Give Us Good Measure": An Economic Analysis of Relations Between the Indians and the Hudson's Bay Company Before 1763* (Toronto, 1978), 163–97.

3. For discussions of early trade into this region see: Charles A. Bishop, *The Northern Ojibwa and the Fur Trade. An Historical and Ecological Study* (Toronto, 1974); Conrad Heidenreich and Arthur J. Ray, *The Early Fur Trades: A Study in Cultural Interaction* (Toronto, 1976); Arthur J. Ray, *Indians in the Fur Trade: Their Role as Trappers, Hunters, and Middlemen in the Lands Southwest of Hudson Bay 1660–1880* (Toronto, 1974), 3–26.

4. E.E. Rich, ed., *Hudson's Bay Copy-Book of Letters Outward etc., Begins 29th May, Ends 5 July 1687* (Toronto, 1948), 147.

5. E.E. Rich, ed., *Minutes of the Hudson's Bay Company 1671–1674* (Toronto, 1942), 26–27, 58–59, 61.

6. On 3 February 1679 the company ordered 300 hatchets from Robert Carnor at a price of ten pennies per hatchet (ibid., 32). The first order with Bannor appears to have been placed on 7 December 1683 (Rich, ed., *Minutes of the Hudson's Bay Company, 1679–84, Second Part, 1682–1684* (Toronto, 1945), 171–72. In a letter of 24 February 1697 the company secretary informed Bannor that the company wanted him to make 1 200 Jack Knives "imitating the French" (Hudson's Bay Company Archives (hereafter HBCA), A6/3, 37, Letters Outward).

7. Rich, ed., *Minutes 1679–84*, 1st part, 177; 2nd part, 9. The common practice was to have the men buy French goods from the Indians. These goods would then be sent to London and used as samples. For evidence that French patterns were being followed, see the various minutes of the company edited by E.E. Rich. Other examples can be found in the unpublished minutes and outward correspondence books of the company.

8. Rich, ed., *Letters Outward*, 8.

9. The first order was sent to John Bridgar on 27 April 1683 and became standing policy (ibid., 86–89). The second policy was implemented in 1680 (ibid., 8). The governor and committee initiated the third policy to prevent confusion in the indents (HBCA, A6/3, 31, Letters Outward, 31 May 1697 to York Factory).

10. Rich, ed., *Minutes 1679–84*, 1st part, 251–52. The governor and committee questioned Nixon's right to take such action (Rich, ed., *Minutes 1679–84*, 2nd part, 251).

11. Rich, ed., *Letters Outward*, 120–21. For the three meetings, see Rich, ed., *Minutes 1679–84*, 2nd part, 251–52 and 256.

12. Rich, ed., *Minutes 1679–84*, 2nd part, 256. Sir Edward Dering was in opposition.

13. HBCA, A 1/13, 4, Minutes, Meeting of 3 December 1690.

14. HBCA, A 11/2, 136, Letters Inward; HBCA, A 6/8, 9, Letters Outward.

15. The company had been doing these inspections since the early 1670s. On 24 March 1674 an attempt was made to enlist the services of the East India Company's gun surveyor (Rich, ed., *Minutes 1671-74*, 91). In their general letter of 3 May 1745, the governor and committee wrote: "We do direct that you take all the Guns out of the Chests immediately [upon receipt] and that they be overlooked by the Armourer and then Oiled and repacked and in case of any Defect to give the Committee the number on the Case and the Name of the maker of the Gun and . . . what the defects are that we may get them rectifyed" (HBCA, A 6/7, 71, Letters Outward). This became a standing policy thereafter.

16. HBCA, A 11/2, 140, Correspondence Inward, Fort Albany, 10 August 1749; HBCA, A 6/8, 36, Correspondence Outward, 21 May 1750.

17. HBCA, A 6/8, 67, Correspondence Outward, 16 May 1751; HBCA, A 6/8, 95, Correspondence Outward, 12 May 1752. When he sent the guns in question, Isham sent a covering letter in which he informed the committee, "the reason of our sending no others home have My self/as I did those/examined them very carefully & find several [4] that has flaws in the Barrells, which no Indian will trade" (HBCA, A 11/114, 146-50, Correspondence Inward, York Factory, 8 August 1751).

18. HBCA, A 6/8, 120, Correspondence Outward, 24 May 1753.

19. K.G. Davies, ed., *Letters from Hudson Bay, 1703-40* (London, 1965), 99-100; HBCA, A 6/4, 95-96, Correspondence Outward, 19 May 1725.

20. HBCA, A 1/8, 9, Meeting of 7 January 1684.

21. Rich, ed., *Letters Outward*, 140-42.

22. HBCA, A 6/3, 120, Correspondence Outward, 27 February 1712.

23. The company had ordered the tobacco from a London merchant named Edward Bridgon. On 22 November 1723 the company's secretary wrote Bridgon informing him: "Complaint having been made to the Comitte that the Brazil Tobacco Imported last yeare by Mess Gutson Simens & Co of Lisbone for ye Comp account was not soe good as formerly I am ordered by them to acquaint you therewith, desiring you would informe those Gent. of it" (HBCA, A 6/4, 82, Correspondence Outward). On 14 July 1724 the company began dealing with the firm of Lewsen, Gibbs and Potter of Lisbon (HBCA, A 6/4, 82, Correspondence Outward, 14 July 1724).

The merchants, Lewsen, Gibbs and Potter, had suggested to the governor and committee that tobacco be specially ordered in Brazil to meet their requirements. However, the committee believed that this arrangement would not be as satisfactory as selecting from the best that was available in Lisbon (HBCA, A 6/4, 94, Correspondence Outward, 27 October 1724).

For John and James Wats see HBCA, A 6/5, 103, Correspondence Outward, 25 November 1735.

In their yearly letters to their tobacco suppliers, the governor and committee repeatedly stressed that the Brazil tobacco had to be the newest and freshest available or their Indian customers would refuse to buy it.

24. HBCA, A 6/7, 13, Correspondence Outward, 29 March 1743. The London correspondence indicates that the company began dealing with Chase and Company of Lisbon (HBCA, A 6/7, 32, Correspondence Outward, 22 December 1743).

25. Davies, ed., *Letters*, 136.

26. The governor and committee responded to McCliesh saying: "We take notice of the complaints mady [sic] by the Indians of ye unsizeableness and badness of some of our trading goods and have given such orders and directions to the persons that serve us with those goods that we hope will prevent the like complaints for the future" (HBCA, A 6/5, Correspondence Outward, 21 May 1729, 26-28).

27. Davies, ed., *Letters*, 278–80.

28. HBCA, A 6/6, 74–75, Correspondence Outward, 1 May 1740. The governor and committee added in their letter that they would again contact their suppliers to correct the defects in the other merchandise.

29. Ray and Freeman, *"Give us Good Measure,"* 163–97.

30. Pierre Gaultier de Varennes de La Vérendrye had been placed in command of the northern posts of the French in 1728. Under his direction the French began pushing into the hinterland of York Factory in the late 1720s and 1730s. Heidenreich and Ray, *Early Fur Trades*, 41–43. As noted earlier in the paper, guns were an exception to the escalation of complaints.

31. This term was used as early as 1703 to describe Indians who also traded with the French. In a letter from Fort Albany dated 2 August 1703, John Fullartine wrote "there came an abundance of Indians down who used the French and were so much Frenchified that they asked for the goods which they traded in French" (Davies, ed., *Letters*, 8).

32. HBCA, A 6/6, 9–15, Correspondence Outward, 18 May 1738; HBCA, A 6/6, 31–35, Correspondence Outward, 17 May 1739.

33. HBCA, A 6/6, 66, Correspondence Outward, 1 May 1740. A letter to Richard Staunton at Moose Factory indicated that he had sent a French coat along with the French cloth the previous year. Many of the company goods were made in the bay and there is no indication that the Governor and Committee attempted to copy the coat Staunton sent (HBCA, A 6/6, 71, Correspondence Outward, 1 May 1740).

34. Peter Wraxall, *An Abridgement of the Indian Affairs Contained in Four Folio Volumes, Transacted in the Colony of New York from the Year 1678 to the Year 1751*, ed. C.H. McIlwain (Cambridge, 1915), lxvii. According to Thomas E. Norton, Montreal-based traders had a preference for many English goods and French smugglers made their largest profits bringing strouds into Canada from New York (T.E. Norton, *The Fur Trade in Colonial New York 1686–1776* (Madison, 1974), 126).

35. Quoted in Harold Innis, *The Fur Trade in Canada, An Introduction to Canadian Economic History* (Toronto, 1956), 85. According to Innis, English-manufactured trade goods were generally cheaper and superior to those made in France in the early eighteenth century. For this reason a considerable trade developed between merchants in Montreal and the colony of New York (ibid., 84–85).

36. Wraxall, *Indian Affairs*, lxxii.

"WOMEN IN BETWEEN": INDIAN WOMEN IN FUR TRADE SOCIETY IN WESTERN CANADA†

SYLVIA VAN KIRK

In attempting to analyse the life of the Indian woman in fur trade society in Western Canada, especially from her own point of view, one is immediately confronted by a challenging historiographical problem. Can the Indian woman's perspective be constructed from historical sources that were almost exclusively written by European men? Coming from a non-literate society, no Indian women have left us, for example, their views on the fur trade or their reasons for becoming traders' wives.[1] Yet if one amasses the sources available for fur trade social history, such as contemporary narratives, journals, correspondence and wills, a surprisingly rich store of information on Indian women emerges. One must, of course, be wary of the traders' cultural and sexual bias, but then even modern anthropologists have difficulty maintaining complete objectivity. Furthermore, the fur traders had the advantage of knowing Indian women intimately — these women became their wives, the mothers of their children. Narratives such as that of Andrew Graham in the late eighteenth century and David Thompson in the nineteenth, both of whom had native wives, comment perceptively on the implications of Indian–white social contact.[2] The key to constructing the Indian woman's perspective must lie in the kinds of questions applied to the data;[3] regrettably the picture will not be complete, but it is hoped that a careful reading of the traders' observations can result in a useful and illuminating account of the Indian woman's life in fur trade society.

The fur trade was based on the complex interaction between two different racial groups. On the one hand are the various Indian tribes, most importantly the Ojibway, the Cree and the Chipewyan. These Indians may be designated the "host" group in that they remain within their traditional environment. On the other hand are the European traders, the "visiting" group, who enter the Northwest by both the

† Canadian Historical Association, *Historical Papers* (1977): 31–46.

Hudson Bay and St. Lawrence–Great Lakes routes. They are significantly different from the Indians in that they constitute only a small, all-male fragment of their own society. For a variety of factors to be discussed, this created a unique situation for the Indian women. They became the "women in between" two groups of males. Because of their sex, Indian women were able to become an integral part of fur trade society in a sense that Indian men never could. As country wives[4] of the traders, Indian women lived substantially different lives when they moved within the forts. Even within the tribes, women who acted as allies of the whites can also be observed; certain circumstances permitted individual women to gain positions of influence and act as "social brokers" between the two groups.

It is a major contention of this study that Indian women themselves were active agents in the development of Indian–white relations.[5] A major concern then must be to determine what motivated their actions. Some themes to be discussed are the extent to which the Indian woman was able to utilize her position as "woman in between" to increase her influence and status, and the extent to which the Indian woman valued the economic advantage brought by the traders. It must be emphasized, however, that Indian–white relations were by no means static during the fur trade period.[6] After assessing the positive and negative aspects of the Indian woman's life in fur trade society, the paper will conclude by discussing the reasons for the demise of her position.

Miscegenation was the basic social fact of the western Canadian fur trade. That this was so indicates active co-operation on both sides. From the male perspective, both white and Indian, the formation of marital alliances between Indian women and the traders had its advantages. The European traders had both social and economic reasons for taking Indian mates. Not only did they fill the sexual void created by the absence of white women,[7] but they performed such valuable economic tasks as making moccasins and netting snowshoes that they became an integral if unofficial part of the fur trade work force.[8] The traders also realized that these alliances were useful in cementing trade ties; officers in both the Hudson's Bay and North West companies often married daughters of trading captains or chiefs.[9] From the Indian point of view, the marital alliance created a reciprocal social bond which served to consolidate his economic relationship with the trader. The exchange of women was common in Indian society where it was viewed as "a reciprocal alliance and series of good offices . . . between the friends of both parties; each is ready to assist and protect the other."[10] It was not loose morality or even hospitality which prompted the Indians to be so generous with their offers of women. This was their way of drawing the traders into their kinship circle, and in return for giving the traders sexual and domestic rights to their women, the Indians expected equitable privileges such as free access to the posts and provisions.[11] It is evident that the traders often did not understand the Indian concept of these alliances and a flagrant violation of Indian sensibilities could lead to retaliation such as the Henley House massacre in 1755.[12]

But what of the women themselves? Were they just pawns in this exchange, passive, exploited victims? Fur trade sources do not support this view; there are numerous examples of Indian women actively seeking to become connected with the traders. According to an early Nor'Wester, Cree women considered it an honour to be selected as wives by the voyageurs, and any husband who refused to lend his wife would be subject to the general condemnation of the women.[13] Alexander Ross observed that Chinook women on the Pacific coast showed a preference for living with a white man. If deserted by one husband, they would return to their tribe in a state of widowhood to await the opportunity of marrying another fur trader.[14] Nor'Wester Daniel Harmon voiced the widely held opinion that most of the Indian women were "better pleased to remain with the White People than with their own Relations," while his contemporary George Nelson affirmed "some too would even desert to live with the white."[15] Although Alexander Henry the Younger may have exaggerated his difficulties in fending off young Indian women, his personal experiences underline the fact that the women often took the initiative. On one occasion when travelling with his brigade in the summer of 1800, Henry was confronted in his tent by a handsome woman, dressed in her best finery, who told him boldly that she had come to live with him as she did not care for her husband or any other Indian. But Henry, anxious to avoid this entanglement partly because it was not sanctioned by the husband whom he knew to be insatiably jealous, forced the woman to return to her Indian partner.[16] A year or so later in the lower Red River district, the daughter of an Ojibway chief had more luck. Henry returned from New Year's festivities to find that "Liard's daughter" had taken possession of his room and "the devil could not have got her out."[17] This time, having become more acculturated to fur trade life, Henry acquiesced and "Liard's daughter" became his country wife. The trader, however, resisted his father-in-law's argument that he should also take his second daughter because all great men should have a plurality of wives.[18]

The fur traders also comment extensively on the assistance and loyalty of Indian women who remained within the tribes. An outstanding example is the young Chipewyan Thanadelthur, known to the traders as the "Slave Woman."[19] In the early eighteenth century after being captured by the Cree, Thanadelthur managed to escape to York Factory. Her knowledge of Chipewyan made her valuable to the traders, and in 1715–16, she led an H.B.C. expedition to establish peace between the Cree and the Chipewyan, a necessary prelude to the founding of Fort Church-ill. Governor James Knight's journals gives us a vivid picture of this woman, of whom he declared: "She was one of a Very high Spirit and of the Firmest Resolution that ever I see any Body in my Days."[20]

Post journals contain numerous references to Indian women warning the traders of impending treachery. In 1797, Charles Chaboillez, having been warned by an old woman that the Indians intended to pillage his post, was able to nip this intrigue in the bud.[21] George Nelson and one of his men only escaped an attack by some Indians in 1805 by being "clandestinely assisted by the women."[22] It appears that women were particularly instrumental in saving the lives of the whites among the turbulent tribes of the Lower Columbia.[23] One of the traders' most notable allies was the well-connected Chinook princess known as Lady Calpo, the wife of a Clatsop chief. In 1814, she helped restore peaceful relations after the Nor'Westers had suffered a raid on their canoes by giving them important information about Indian custom in settling disputes. Handsome rewards cemented her attachment to the traders with the result that Lady Calpo reputedly saved Fort George from several attacks by warning of the hostile plans of the Indians.[24]

The reasons for the Indian women's action are hinted at in the traders' observations. It was the generally held opinion of the traders that the status of women in Indian society was deplorably low. As Nor'Wester Gabriel Franchère summed it up: "Some Indian tribes think that women have no souls, but die altogether like the brutes; others assign them a different paradise from that of men, which indeed they might have reason to prefer . . . unless their relative condition were to be ameliorated in the next world."[25] Whether as "social brokers" or as wives, Indian women attempted to manipulate their position as "women in between" to increase their influence and status. Certainly women such as Thanadelthur and Lady Calpo were able to work themselves into positions of real power. It is rather paradoxical that in Thanadelthur's case it was her escape from captivity that brought her into contact with the traders in the first place; if she had not been a woman, she would never have been carried off by the Cree as a prize of war. Once inside the H.B.C. fort, she was able to use her position as the only Chipewyan to advantage by acting as guide and consultant to the Governor. The protection and regard she was given by the whites enabled Thanadelthur to dictate to Indian men, both Cree and Chipewyan, in a manner they would not previously have tolerated. Anxious to promote the traders' interests, she assaulted an old Chipewyan on one occasion when he attempted to trade less than prime furs; she "ketcht him by the nose Push'd him backwards & call'd him fool and told him if they brought any but Such as they ware directed they would not be traded."[26] Thanadelthur did take a Chipewyan husband but was quite prepared to leave him if he would not accompany her on the arduous second journey she was planning to undertake for the Governor.[27] It is possible that the role played by Thanadelthur and subsequent "slave women" in establishing trade relations with the whites may have enhanced the status of Chipewyan women. Nearly a century later, Alexander Mackenzie noted that, in spite of their burdensome existence, Chipewyan women possessed "a very considerable influence in the traffic with Europeans."[28]

Lady Calpo retained a position of influence for a long time. When Governor Simpson visited Fort George in 1824, he found she had to be treated with respect because she was "the best News Monger in the Parish"; from her he learned "More of the Scandal, Secrets and politics both of the out & inside of the Fort than from Any other source."[29] Significantly, Lady Calpo endeavoured to further improve her rank by arranging a marriage alliance between the Governor and her carefully raised daughter. Although Simpson declared he wished "to keep clear of the Daughter," he succumbed in order "to continue on good terms with the Mother."[30] Many years later, a friend visiting the Columbia wrote to Simpson that Lady Calpo that "'fast friend' of the Whites" was still thriving.[31]

As wives of the traders, Indian women could also manoeuvre themselves into positions of influence. In fact, a somewhat perturbed discussion emerges in fur trade literature over the excessive influence some Indian women exerted over their fur trader husbands. The young N.W.C. clerk George Nelson appears to have spent long hours contemplating the insolvable perplexities of womankind. Nelson claimed that initially Cree women when married to whites were incredibly attentive and submissive, but this did not last long. Once they had gained a little footing, they knew well "how to take advantage & what use they ought to make of it."[32] On one of his first trips into the interior, Nelson was considerably annoyed by the shenanigans of the Indian wife of Brunet, one of his voyageurs. A jealous, headstrong woman, she completely dominated her husband by a mixture of "caresses, promises & menaces." Not only did this woman render her husband a most unreliable servant, but Nelson also caught her helping herself to the Company's rum. Brunet's wife, Nelson fumed, was as great "a vixen & hussy" as the tinsmith's wife at the market place in Montreal: "I now began to think that women were women not only in civilized countries but elsewhere also."[33]

Another fur trader observed a paradoxical situation among the Chipewyan women. In their own society, they seemed condemned to a most servile existence, but upon becoming wives of the French-Canadian voyageurs, they assumed "an importance to themselves and instead of serving as formerly they exact submission from the descendants of the Gauls."[34] One of the most remarkable examples of a Chipewyan wife rising to prominence was the case of Madam Lamallice, the wife of the brigade guide at the H.B.C. post on Lake Athabasca. During the difficult winter of 1820-21, Madam Lamallice was accorded a favoured position because she was the post's only interpreter and possessed considerable influence with the Indians.[35] George Simpson, then experiencing his first winter in the Indian Country, felt obliged to give in to her demands for extra rations and preferred treatment in order to prevent her defection. He had observed that the Nor'Westers' strong position was partly due to the fact that "their Women are faithful to their cause and good Interpreters whereas we have but one in the Fort that can talk Chipewyan."[36] Madam Lamallice exploited her position to such an extent that she even defied fort regulations by carrying on a private trade in provisions.[37] A few years later on a trip to the Columbia, Governor Simpson was annoyed to discover that Chinook women when married to the whites often gained such an ascendancy "that they give law to their Lords."[38] In fact, he expressed general concern about the influence of these "petticoat politicians" whose demands were "more injurious to the Companys interests than I am well able to describe."[39] The Governor deplored Chief Factor James Bird's management of Red River in the early 1820s because of his habit of discussing every matter "however trifling or important" with "his Copper Cold. [coloured] Mate," who then spread the news freely around the colony.[40] Too many of his officers, Simpson declared, tended to sacrifice business for private interests. Particular expense and delay were occasioned in providing transport for families. Simpson never forgave Chief Factor John Clarke for abandoning some of the goods destined for Athabasca in 1820 to make a light canoe for his native wife and her servant.[41]

It is likely that Simpson's single-minded concern for business efficiency caused him to exaggerate the extent of the Indian women's influence. Nevertheless, they do seem to have attempted to take advantage of their unique position as women "in between" two groups of men. This fact is supported by the traders' observation that the choice of a husband, Indian or white, gave the Indian woman leverage to improve her lot. Now she could threaten to desert to the whites or vice-versa if she felt she were not being well-treated: "She has always enough of policy to insinuate how well off she was while living with the white people and in like manner when with the latter she drops some hints to the same purpose."[42] Although Chipewyan women who had lived with the voyageurs had to resume their former domestic tasks when they returned to their own people, they reputedly evinced a greater spirit of independence.[43] Considerable prestige accrued to Chinook women who had lived with the traders; upon rejoining the tribes, they remained "very friendly" to the whites and "never fail to influence their connections to the same effect."[44]

From the Indian woman's point of view, material advantage was closely tied to the question of improved influence or status. The women within the tribes had a vested interest in promoting cordial relations with the whites. While George Nelson mused that it was a universal maternal instinct which prompted the women to try to prevent clashes between Indian and white,[45] they were more likely motivated by practical, economic considerations. If the traders were driven from the country, the Indian woman would lose the source of European goods, which had revolutionized her life just as much if not more than that of the Indian man. It was much easier to boil water in a metal kettle than to have to laboriously heat it by means of dropping hot stones in a bark container. Cotton and woolen goods saved long hours of tanning hides. "Show them an awl or a strong needle," declared David Thompson, "and they will gladly give the finest Beaver or Wolf skin they have to purchase it."[46]

Futhermore, it can be argued that the tendency of the Indians to regard the fur trade post as a kind of welfare centre was of more relevance to the women than to the men. In times of scarcity, which were not infrequent in Indian society, the women were usually the first to suffer.[47] Whereas before they would often have perished, many now sought relief at the companies' posts. To cite but one of many examples: at Albany during the winter of 1706, Governor Beale gave shelter to three starving Cree women whose husband had sent them away as he could only provide for his two children.[48] The post was also a source of medical aid and succour. The story is told of a young Carrier woman in New Caledonia who, having been severely beaten by her husband, managed to struggle to the nearest N.W.C. post. Being nearly starved, she was slowly nursed back to health and allowed to remain at the post when it became apparent that her relatives had abandoned her.[49] The desire for European goods, coupled with the assistance to be found at the fur trade posts, helps to explain why Indian women often became devoted allies of the traders.

In becoming the actual wife of a fur trader, the Indian woman was offered even greater relief from the burdens of her traditional existence. In fact, marriage to a trader offered an alternative lifestyle. The fur traders themselves had no doubt that an Indian woman was much better off with a white man. The literature presents a dreary recital of their abhorrence of the degraded, slave-like position of the Indian woman. The life of a Cree woman, declared Alexander Mackenzie, was "an uninterrupted success[ion] of toil and pain."[50] Nor'Wester Duncan McGillivray decided that the rather singular lack of affection evinced by Plains Indian women for their mates arose from the barbarous treatment the women received.[51] Although David Thompson found the Chipewyan a good people in many ways, he considered their attitudes toward women a disgrace; he had known Chipewyan women to kill female infants as "an act of kindness" to spare them the hardships they would have to face.[52]

The extent to which the fur traders' observations represent an accurate reflection of the actual status of Indian women in their own societies presents a complex dilemma which requires deeper investigation. The cultural and class biases of the traders are obvious. Their horror at the toilsome burdens imposed upon Indian women stems from their narrow, chivalrous view of women as the "frail, weaker sex." This is scarcely an appropriate description of Indian women, particularly the Chipewyan who were acknowledged to be twice as strong as their male counterparts.[53] Furthermore, while the sharp sexual division of labour inflicted a burdensome role upon the women, their duties were essential and the women possessed considerable autonomy within their own sphere.[54] Some traders did think it curious that the women seemed to possess a degree of influence in spite of their degraded situation; indeed, some of the bolder ones occasionally succeeded in making themselves quite independent and "wore the breeches."[55]

A possible way of explaining the discrepancy between the women's perceived and actual status is suggested in a recent anthropological study of the Mundurucú of Amazonian Brazil. In this society, the authors discovered that while the official (male) ideology relegates women to an inferior, subservient position, in the reality of daily life, the women are able to assume considerable autonomy and influence.[56] Most significantly, however, Mundurucú women, in order to alleviate their onerous domestic duties, have actively championed the erosion of traditional village life and the concomitant blurring of economic sex roles which have come with the introduction of the rubber trade. According to the authors, the Mundurucú woman "has seen another way of life, and she has opted for it."[57]

This statement could well be applied to the Indian woman who was attracted to the easier life of the fur trade post. In the first place, she now became involved in a much more sedentary routine. With a stationary home, the Indian woman was no longer required to act as a beast of burden, hauling or carrying the accoutrements of camp from place to place. The traders often expressed astonishment and pity at the heavy loads which Indian women were obliged to transport.[58] In fur trade society, the unenviable role of carrier was assumed by the voyageur. The male servants at the fort were now responsible for providing firewood and water, although the women might help. In contrast to Indian practice, the women of the fort were not sent to fetch home the produce of the hunt.[59] The wife of an officer, benefiting from her husband's rank, enjoyed a privileged status. She herself was carried in and out of the canoe[60] and could expect to have all her baggage portaged by a voyageur. At Fond du Lac in 1804 when the wife of N.W.C. *bourgeois* John Sayer decided to go on a sugar-making expedition, four men went with her to carry her baggage and provisions and later returned to fetch home her things.[61]

While the Indian woman performed a variety of valuable economic tasks around the post, her domestic duties were relatively lighter than they had traditionally been. Now her energies were concentrated on making moccasins and snowshoes. As one Nor'Wester declared, with the whites, Indian women could lead "a comparatively easy and free life" in contrast to the "servile slavish mode" of their own.[62] The prospect of superior comforts reputedly motivated some Spokan women to marry voyageurs.[63] The ready supply of both finery and trinkets which *bourgeois* and voyageurs were seen to lavish on their women may also have had an appeal.[64] Rival traders noted that luxury items such as lace, ribbons, rings, and vermilion, which "greatly gain the Love of the Women," were important in attracting the Indians to trade.[65] The private orders placed by H.B.C. officers and servants in the 1790s and later include a wide range of cloth goods, shawls, gartering, earrings and brooches for the women.[66] When taken by a trader *à la façon du pays*, it became common for an Indian woman to go through a ritual performed by other women of the fort; she was scoured of grease and paint and exchanged her native garments for those of more civilized fashion. At the N.W.C. posts, wives were clothed in "Canadian fashion" which consisted of a shirt, short gown, petticoat and leggings.[67]

The traders further thought that Indian women benefited by being freed from certain taboos and customs which they had to bear in Indian society. Among the Ojibway and other tribes, for example, the choicest part of an animal was always reserved for the men; death it was believed would come to any woman who dared to eat such sacred portions. The Nor'Westers paid little heed to such observances. As Duncan Cameron sarcastically wrote: "I have often seen several women living with the white men eat of those forbidden morsels without the least inconvenience."[68] The traders were also convinced that Indian women welcomed a monogamous as opposed to a polygamous state. Polygamy, several H.B.C. officers observed, often gave rise to jealous and sometimes murderous quarrels.[69] It is possible, however, that the traders' own cultural abhorrence of polygamy[70] made them exaggerate the women's antipathy toward it. As a practical scheme for the sharing of heavy domestic tasks, polygamy may in fact have been welcomed by the women.

Thus far the advantages which the fur trade brought to Indian women have been emphasized in order to help explain Indian women's reactions to it. It would be erroneous, however, to paint the life of an Indian wife as idyllic. In spite of the traders' belief in the superior benefits they offered, there is evidence that fur trade life had an adverse effect on Indian women. Certainly, a deterioration in her position over time can be detected.

First there is the paradox that the supposedly superior material culture of the fur trade had a deleterious effect on Indian women. It was as if, mused Reverend John West, the first Anglican missionary, "the habits of civilized life" exerted an injurious influence over their general constitutions.[71] Apart from being more exposed to European diseases, the

Indian wives of traders suffered more in childbirth than they had in the primitive state.[72] Dr. John Richardson, who accompanied the Franklin Expedition of the 1820s noted, that not only did Indian women now have children more frequently and over longer periods of time, but that they were more susceptible to the disorders and diseases connected with pregnancy and childbirth.[73] It was not uncommon for fur traders' wives to give birth to from eight to twelve children, whereas four children were the average in Cree society.[74]

The reasons for this dramatic rise in the birth rate deserve further investigation, but several reasons can be advanced. As recent medical research has suggested, the less fatiguing lifestyle and more regular diet offered the Indian wife could have resulted in greater fecundity.[75] The daily ration for the women of the forts was four pounds of meat or fish (one half that for the men);[76] when Governor Simpson jokingly remarked that the whitefish diet at Fort Chipewyan seemed conducive to procreation he may have hit upon a medical truth.[77] Furthermore, sexual activity in Indian society was circumscribed by a variety of taboos, and evidence suggests that Indian men regarded their European counterparts as very licentious.[78] Not only did Indian women now have sex more often, but the attitudes of European husbands also may have interfered with traditional modes of restricting family size. The practice of infanticide was, of course, condemned by the whites, but the Europeans may also have discouraged the traditional long nursing periods of from two to four years for each child.[79] In their view this custom resulted in the premature aging of the mothers,[80] but the fact that Indian children were born at intervals of approximately three years tends to support the recent theory that lactation depresses fertility.[81]

The cultural conflict resulting over the upbringing of the children must have caused the Indian women considerable anguish. An extreme example of the tragedy which could result related to the Chinook practice of head-flattening. In Chinook society, a flat forehead, achieved by strapping a board against the baby's head when in its cradle, was a mark of class; only slaves were not so distinguished. Thus it was only natural that a Chinook woman, though married to a fur trader, would desire to bind her baby's head, but white fathers found this custom abhorrent. The insistence of some fathers that their infants' heads not be flattened resulted in the mothers murdering their babies rather than have them suffer the ignominy of looking like slaves. Gradually European preference prevailed. When Governor Simpson visited the Columbia in the early 1820s, he reported that Chinook wives were abiding by their husbands' wishes and no cases of infanticide had been reported for some years.[82]

In Indian society, children were the virtual "property" of the women who were responsible for their upbringing;[83] in fur trade society, Indian women could find themselves divested of these rights. While the traders acknowledged that Indian women were devoted and affectionate mothers, this did not prevent them from exercising patriarchal authority, particularly in sending young children to Britain or Canada so that they might receive a "civilized" education.[84] It must have been nearly impossible to explain the rationale for such a decision to the Indian mothers; their grief at being separated from their children was compounded by the fact that the children, who were especially vulnerable to respiratory diseases, often died.[85]

It is difficult to know if the general treatment accorded Indian women by European traders met with the women's acceptance. How much significance should be attached to the views of outside observers in the early 1800s who did not think the Indian woman's status had been much improved? Some of the officers of the Franklin Expedition felt the fur traders had been corrupted by Indian attitudes toward women; Indian wives were not treated with "the tenderness and attention due to every female" because the Indians would despise the traders for such unmanly action.[86] The first missionaries were even stronger in denouncing fur trade marital relations. John West considered the traders' treatment of their women disgraceful: "They do not admit them as their companions, nor do they allow them to eat at their tables, but degrade them *merely* as slaves to their arbitrary inclinations."[87] Such statements invite skepticism because of the writers' limited contact with fur trade society, and in the case of the missionaries because of their avowedly hostile view of fur trade customs. Furthermore, the above statements project a European ideal about the way women should be treated, which apart from being widely violated in their own society, would have had little relevance for Indian women. It is doubtful, for example, that the Indian women themselves would have viewed the fact that they did not come to table, a custom partly dictated by the quasi-military organization of the posts, as proof of their debased positon.[88] The segregation of the sexes at meals was common in Indian society, but now, at least, the women did not have to suffice with the leftovers of the men.[89]

Nevertheless, there is evidence to suggest that Indian women were misused by the traders. In Indian society, women were accustomed to greater freedom of action with regard to marital relationships than the traders were prepared to accord them. It was quite within a woman's rights, for example, to institute a divorce if her marriage proved unsatisfactory.[90] In fur trade society, Indian women were more subject to arbitrary arrangements devised by the men. Upon retiring from the Indian Country, it became customary for a trader to place his country wife and family with another, a practice known as "turning off." Although there was often little they could do about it, a few cases were cited of women who tried to resist. At a post in the Peace River district in 1798, the Indian wife of an *engagé*, who was growing tired of wintering *en derouine*, absolutely rejected her husband's attempt to pass her to the man who agreed to take his place.[91] At Fort Chipewyan in 1800, the estranged wife of the voyageur Morin foiled the attempt of his *bourgeois* to find her a temporary "protector"; she stoutly refused three different prospects.[92] Indian women also did not take kindly to the long separations which fur trade life imposed on them and their European mates. Although the Indian wife of Chief Factor Joseph Colen was to receive every attention during his absence in England in the late 1790s, Colen's successor could not dissuade her from taking an Indian lover and leaving York Factory.[93]

Indian wives seem to have been particularly victimized during the violent days of the trade war when rivals went so far as to debauch and intimidate each other's women. In 1819 at Pelican Lake, for example, H.B.C. servant Deshau took furs from an N.W.C. servant and raped his wife in retaliation for having had his own wife debauched by a Nor'Wester earlier in the season.[94] A notorious instance involved the Indian wife of H.B.C. servant Andrew Kirkness at Isle à la Cross in 1810–11. In the late summer, this woman in a fit of pique had deserted her husband and sought refuge at the Nor'Westers' post. She soon regretted her action, however, for she was kept a virtual prisoner by the Canadians, and all efforts of the H.B.C. men to get her back failed. The upshot was that Kirkness himself deserted to the rival post, leaving the English in dire straits since he was their only fisherman. Kirkness was intimidated into remaining with the Nor'Westers until the spring with the threat that should he try to leave "every Canadian in the House would ravish his woman before his eyes." Eventually Kirkness was released, but only after his wife had been coerced into saying that she did not want to accompany him. As the H.B.C. party were evacuating their post, the woman tried to escape but was forcibly dragged back by the Nor'Westers and ultimately became the "property" of an *engagé*.[95]

Such abusive tactics were also applied to the Indians. By the turn of the century, relations between the Indians and the Nor'Westers in particular showed a marked deterioration. In what seems to have been a classic case of "familiarity breeding contempt," the Nor'Westers now retained their mastery through coercion and brute force and frequently transgressed the bounds of Indian morality. An especially flagrant case was the Nor'Westers' exploitation of Chipewyan women at its posts in the Athabasca district. By the end of the eighteenth century, they had apparently built up a nefarious traffic in these women; the *bourgeois* did not scruple at seizing Chipewyan women by force, ostensibly in lieu of trade debts, and then selling them to the men for large sums.[96] The situation became so bad that the Chipewyan began leaving their women behind when they came to trade, and when Hudson's Bay traders appeared on Lake Athabasca in 1792, the Indians hoped to secure their support and drive out their rivals. The English, however, were too weak to offer any effective check to the Nor'Westers, who continued to assault both fathers and husbands if they tried to resist the seizure of their women. Since they were not powerful enough to mount an attack, the Chipewyan connived at the escape of their women during the summer months when most of the traders were away. Resentful of their treatment, many of the women welcomed the chance to slip back to their own people so that the summer master at Fort Chipewyan was almost solely preoccupied with keeping watch over the *engagés'* women.[97] By 1800 at least one voyageur had been killed by irate Chipewyans, and the *bourgeois* contemplated offering a reward for the hunting down of "any d—nd rascal" who caused a Frenchman's woman to desert.[98]

The Indians appear to have become openly contemptuous of the white man and his so-called morality. A northern tribe called the Beaver Indians took a particularly strong stand. At first they had welcomed the Canadians but, having rapidly lost respect for them, now forbade any intercourse between their women and the traders.[99] Elsewhere individual hunters boycotted the traders owing to the maltreatment of their women.[100] Sporadic reprisals became more frequent. Whereas Indian women had previously played a positive role as a liaison between Indian and white, they were now becoming an increasing source of friction between the two groups. Governor Simpson summed up the deteriorating situation: "It is a lamentable fact that almost every difficulty we have had with Indians throughout the country may be traced to our interference with their Women or their intrigues with the Women of the Forts in short 9 murders out of 10 Committed on Whites by Indians have arisen through Women."[101]

Although there is little direct evidence available, it is possible that the Indian women themselves were becoming increasingly dissatisfied with their treatment from the whites. In spite of the initiative which the women have been seen to exercise in forming and terminating relationships with the traders, there were undoubtedly times when they were the unwilling objects of a transaction between Indians and white men. Certainly not all Indian women looked upon the whites as desirable husbands, a view that was probably reinforced with experience. George Nelson did observe in 1811 that there were some Indian women who showed "an extraordinary predilection" for their own people and could not be prevailed upon to live with the traders.[102]

The increasing hostility of the Indians, coupled with the fact that in well established areas marriage alliances were no longer a significant factor in trade relations, led to a decline in the practice of taking an Indian wife. In fact in 1806, the North West Company passed a ruling prohibiting any of its employees from taking a country wife from among the tribes.[103] One of the significant factors which changed the traders' attitudes toward Indian women, however, was that they were now no longer "women in between." By the turn of the century a sizeable group of mixed-blood women had emerged and for social and economic reasons, fur traders preferred mixed-blood women as wives.[104] In this way the Indian women lost their important place in fur trade society.

The introduction of the Indian woman's perspective on Indian–white relations serves to underscore the tremendous complexity of inter-cultural contact. It is argued that Indian women saw definite advantages to be gained from the fur trade, and in their unique position as "women in between," they endeavoured to manipulate the situation to improve their existence. That the limits of their influence were certainly circum-scribed, and that the ultimate benefits brought by the traders were questionable, does not negate the fact that the Indian women played a much more active and important role in the fur trade than has previously been acknowledged.

Notes

1. The lack of written Indian history is, or course, a general problem for the ethnohistorian. Indeed, all social scientists must rely heavily on the historical observations of the agents of white contact such as fur traders, explorers and missionaries. Little seems to have been done to determine if the oral tradition of the Indians is a viable source of information on Indian–white relations in the fur trade period.

2. Glyndwr Williams, ed., *Andrew Graham's Observations on Hudson's Bay 1769–91*, vol. 27 (London: Hudson's Bay Record Society, 1969); Richard Glover, ed., *David Thompson's Narrative 1784–1812*, vol. 40 (Toronto: Champlain Society, 1962).

3. A fascinating study which indicates how the application of a different perspective to the same data can produce new insights is *Women of the Forest* by Yolanda and Robert Murphy (New York, 1974). Based on field work conducted twenty years earlier in Amazonian Brazil, the authors found that by looking at the life of the Mundurucú tribe from the woman's point of view, their understanding of the actual as opposed to the official functioning of that society was enlarged.

4. Marriages between European traders and Indian women were contracted according to indigenous rites derived from Indian custom. For a detailed explanation, see Sylvia Van Kirk, " 'The Custom of the Country': An Examination of Fur Trade Marriage Practices" in *Essays in Western History*, ed. L.H. Thomas (Edmonton, 1976), 49–70.

5. See Murphy, *Women of the Forest*, ch. 6 for a useful comparison. Mundurucú women actively welcomed the social change brought about by the introduction of the rubber trade into their traditional economy.

6. An instructive study of the Indians' economic role in the fur trade is provided by Arthur Ray in *Indians in the Fur Trade* (Toronto, 1974). He shows that the Indian played a much more active, although changing role in the dynamics of the fur trade than had previously been acknowledged.

7. H.B.C. men were prohibited from bringing women to Hudson Bay. It was not until the early nineteenth century that the first white women came to the Northwest.

8. In 1802, H.B.C. men defended their practice of keeping Indian women in the posts by informing the London Committee that they were "Virtually your Honors Servants" (Hudson's Bay Company Archives (hereafter HBCA), B.239/b/79, fos.

40d–41). For a discussion of the important economic role played by native women in the fur trade, see Sylvia Van Kirk, "The Role of Women in the Fur Trade Society of the Canadian West, 1700–1850" (Ph.D. dissertation, University of London, 1975).

9. HBCA, Albany Journal, 24 January 1771, B.3/a/63, f. 18d; Connolly vs. Woolrich, Superior Court, 9 July 1867, *Lower Canada Jurist* 11 (1867): 234.

10. Charles Bishop, "The Henley House Massacres," *The Beaver* (Autumn 1976): 40.

11. Ibid., 39. For a more technical look at the socio-economic relationship between the Indians and the traders, see the discussion of "balanced reciprocity" in Marshall Sahlins, *Stone Age Economics* (Chicago, 1972), ch. 5.

12. In this instance the Indian captain Woudby attacked Henley House because the master was keeping two of his female relatives but denying him access to the post and its provisions.

13. Alexander Henry, *Travels and Adventures in Canada and the Indian Territories 1760-1766*, ed. Jas Bain (Boston, 1901), 248.

14. Alexander Ross, *The Fur Hunters of the Far West* (London, 1855), 1: 296–97.

15. W. Kaye Lamb, ed., *Sixteen Years in the Indian Country: The Journal of Daniel Williams Harmon 1800-1816* (Toronto, 1957), 29; Toronto Public Library (hereafter TPL), George Nelson Papers, Journal 1810-11, 24 April 1811, 42.

16. Elliot Coues, ed., *New Light on the Early History of the Greater North West: The Manuscript Journals of Alexander Henry and David Thompson 1799-1814* (Minneapolis, 1965), 71–73.

17. Ibid., 163.

18. Ibid., 211.

19. For a detailed account of the story of this woman, see Sylvia Van Kirk, "Thanadelthur," *The Beaver* (Spring 1974): 40–45.

20. Ibid., 45.

21. Public Archives of Canada (hereafter PAC), Masson Collection, Journal of Charles Chaboillez, 13 December 1797, 24.

22. TPL, Nelson Papers, Journal and Reminiscences 1825–26, 66.

23. Ross, *Fur Hunters*, 1: 296.

24. Coues, ed., *New Light*, 793; Frederick Merk, ed., *Fur Trade and Empire: George Simpson's Journal, 1824-25* (Cambridge, Mass., 1931), 104.

25. Gabriel Franchère, *Narrative of a Voyage to the Northwest Coast of America 1811-14*, ed. R.G. Thwaites (Cleveland, Ohio, 1904), 327.

26. Van Kirk, "Thanadelthur," 44.

27. Ibid., 45.

28. W. Kaye Lamb, ed., *The Journals and Letters of Sir Alexander Mackenzie* (Cambridge, Eng., 1970), 152.

29. Merk, *Fur Trade and Empire*, 104.

30. Ibid., 104–5.

31. HBCA, R. Crooks to G. Simpson, 15 March 1843, D. 5/8, f. 147.

32. TPL, Nelson Papers, Journal 1810-11, 41–42.

33. TPL, Nelson Papers, Journal 1803–04, 10–28 passim.

34. PAC, Masson Collection, "An Account of the Chipwean Indians," 23.

35. E.E. Rich, ed., *Simpson's Athabasca Journal and Report 1820-21* (London: Hudson's Bay Record Society, 1938), 1:74.

36. Ibid., 231.

37. HBCA, Fort Chipewyan Journal 1820-21, B.39/a/16, fos. 6–21d, passim.

38. Merk, *Fur Trade and Empire*, 99.

39. Ibid., 11–12, 58.

40. HBCA, George Simpson's Journal 1821–22, D. 3/3, f. 52.

41. Rich, ed., *Simpson's Athabasca Journal*, 23–24; see also Merk, *Fur Trade and Empire*, 131.

42. PAC, Masson Collection, "Account of Chipwean Indians," 23–24.

43. Ibid., 23.

44. Ross, *Fur Hunters*, 1: 297.

45. TPL, Nelson Papers, Journal and Reminiscences 1825-26, 66. Nelson claimed that around 1780 some Indian women had warned the Canadian pedlars of impending attack because in their "tender & affectionate breast (for women are lovely all the world over) still lurked compassion for the mothers of those destined to be sacrificed."

46. Glover, ed., *David Thompson's Narrative*, 45. Cf. with the Mundurucú women's desire for European goods, Murphy, *Women of the Forest*, 182.

47. Samuel Hearne, *A Journey to the Northern Ocean*, ed. Richard Glover (Toronto, 1958), 190.

48. HBCA, Albany Journal, 23 February 1706, B.3/a/1, f. 28.

49. Ross Cox, *The Columbia River*, ed. Jane and Edgar Stewart (Norman, Okla., 1957), 377.

50. Lamb, ed., *Journals and Letters*, 135.

51. A.S. Morton, *The Journal of Duncan McGillivray . . . at Fort George on the Saskatchewan 1794–95* (Toronto, 1929), 60.

52. Glover, ed., *David Thompson's Narrative*, 106.

53. Hearne, *Journey to the Northern Ocean*, 35: "Women," declared the Chipewyan chief Matonabee, "were made for labour; one of them can carry, or haul, as much as two men can do."

54. There has been a trend in recent literature to exalt the Indian woman's status by pointing out that in spite of her labour she had more independence than the pioneer farm wife. See Nancy O. Lurie, "Indian Women: A Legacy of Freedom," *The American Way* 5 (April 1972): 28–35.

55. Morton, *Journal of Duncan McGillivray*, 34; L.R.F. Masson, *Les Bourgeois de la Compagnie du Nord-Ouest*, (n.p., 1889), 1: 256.

56. Murphy, *Women of the Forest*, 87, 112.

57. Ibid., 202.

58. Lamb, ed., *Journals and Letters*, 254; Glover, ed., *David Thompson's Narrative*, 125.

59. PAC, Masson Collection, Journal of John Thomson, 15 October 1798, 10.

60. J.B. Tyrrell, *Journals of Samuel Hearne and Philip Turnor 1774–92* (Toronto: Champlain Society, 1934), 21: 252.

61. Michel Curot, "A Wisconsin Fur Trader's Journal 1803–04," *Wisconsin Historical Collections* 20 (1911): 449, 453.

62. TPL, Nelson Papers, Journal 1810–11, 41, and Reminiscences, Part 5, 225.

63. Cox, *Columbia River*, 148.

64. Coues, ed., *New Light*, 914; Ross, *Fur Hunters*, 11: 236.

65. Tyrrell, *Journals of Samuel Hearne*, 273.

66. HBCA, Book of Servants Commissions, A. 16/111 and 112 passim.

67. Lamb, ed., *Sixteen Years*, 28–29.

68. Masson, *Les Bourgeois*, 2: 263.

69. Hearne, *Journey to the Northern Ocean*, 80; Williams, ed., *Andrew Graham's Observations*, 158.

70. Alexander Ross, *Adventures of the First Settlers on the Oregon or Columbia River* (London, 1849), 280–81: Glover, ed., *David Thompson's Narrative*, 251.

71. John West, *The Substance of a Journal during a residence at the Red River Colony 1820-23* (London, 1827), 54.

72. The traders were astonished at the little concern shown for pregnancy and childbirth in Indian society, see for example Lamb, ed., *Journals and Letters*, 250 and Williams, ed., *Andrew Graham's Observations*, 177.

73. John Franklin, *Narrative of a Journey to the Shores of the Polar Sea 1819–22* (London, 1824), 86.

74. Ibid., 60. The Indian wives of Alexander Ross and Peter Fidler, for example, had thirteen and fourteen children respectively.

75. Jennifer Brown, "A Demographic Transition in the Fur Trade Country," *Western Canadian Journal of Anthropology* 6, no. 1 (1976): 68.

76. Cox, *Columbia River*, 354.

77. J.S. Galbraith, *The Little Emperor* (Toronto, 1976), 68.

78. TPL, Nelson Papers, Reminiscences, Part 5, 225.

79. Brown, "A Demographic Transition," 67.

80. Margaret MacLeod, ed., *The Letters of Letitia Hargrave* (Toronto: Champlain Society, 1947), 94–95; Alexander Ross, *The Red River Settlement* (Minneapolis, 1957), 95, 192.

81. Brown, "A Demographic Transition," 65.

82. Merk, *Fur Trade and Empire*, 101.

83. Williams, ed., *Andrew Graham's Observations*, 176, 178.

84. Ross, *Adventures of the First Settlers*, 280; W.J. Healy, *Women of Red River* (Winnipeg, 1923), 163–66.

85. Lamb, ed., *Sixteen Years*, 138, 186.

86. Franklin, *Narrative of a Journey*, 101, 106.

87. West, *Substance of a Journal*, 16.

88. Cox, *Columbia River*, 360.

89. Hearne, *Journey to the Northern Ocean*, 57.

90. Williams, ed., *Andrew Graham's Observations*, 176.

91. PAC, Masson Collection, Journal of John Thomson, 19 November 1798, 20.

92. Masson, *Les Bourgeois*, 2: 384–85. We are not told whether she also escaped being sold when the brigades arrived in the spring as the *bourgeois* intended.

93. HBCA, York Journal, 2 December 1798, B.239/a/103, f. 14d.

94. HBCA, Pelican Lake Journal, 18 January 1819, D. 158/a/1, f. 7d.

95. This account is derived from HBCA, Isle à la Crosse Journal, B.89/a/2, fos. 5–36d passim.

96. Tyrrell, *Journals of Samuel Hearne*, 446n, 449.

97. Ibid., 449–50.

98. Masson, *Les Bourgeois*, 2: 387–88.

99. Lamb, ed., *Journals and Letters*, 255; Rich, ed., *Simpson's Athabasca Journal*, 388.

100. PAC, Masson Collection, Journal of Ferdinand Wentzel, 13 January 1805, 41.

101. Merk, *Fur Trade and Empire*, 127.

102. TPL, Nelson Papers, Journal 1810-11, 41-42.

103. W.S. Wallace, *Documents relating to the North West Company* (Toronto: Champlain Society, 1934), 22: 211. This ruling was not enforced in outlying districts such as the Columbia. Even after the union in 1821, Governor Simpson continued to favour the formation of marital alliances in remote regions as the best way to secure friendly relations with the Indians, see Rich, ed., *Simpson's Athabasca Journal*, 392.

104. For a discussion of the role played by mixed-blood women in fur trade society, see Van Kirk, "Role of Women in Fur Trade Society."

THE IMAGE OF THE INDIAN†

ROBIN FISHER

> The prevailing idea which exists amongst the later arrivals and present population as to the character of the Indian tribes in those early days, is not, in my experience, borne out by facts. I have heard such terms as treacherous, vindictive, revengeful, and murderous applied to them; possibly some may have deserved the epithets; but taken as a whole, I submit that, with the opportunities they had, we may consider them fairly entitled to a more lenient verdict.[1]

Students of race relations now recognize that images are frequently more potent determinants of behaviour than "reality" and that Europeans in contact with indigenous people act according to perceptions which are often quite different from what "actually exists." Indigenous society and behaviour is viewed through a cultural filter that distorts "reality" into an image that is more consistent with European preconceptions and purposes. The process is complete when the image becomes more real than "reality" as the basis for policy and action.

Before looking at the wider impact of the change from fur trade to settlement on the Indians of British Columbia, it is important, therefore, to examine the image of the Indian that had already built up in the mind of the European and the extent to which it changed with the coming of the settlers. There were, of course, as many images of the Indian as there were Europeans in British Columbia. Furthermore, it is a "well-known but elusive fact that a person can hold contradictory ideas towards the same thing at different times,"[2] and even more elusive is the ambivalence of many racial attitudes. Neither individuals nor groups were necessarily consistent in the opinions that they expressed about the Indians. Yet common attitudes do emerge from the collection of individual views, and it is the consensus that this chapter will try to isolate and describe.

† *Contact and Conflict: Indian–European Relations in British Columbia, 1774–1890* (Vancouver: University of British Columbia Press, 1977), 73–94.

In their evaluations of various Indian groups fur traders and settlers sometimes shared opinions, but the differences in their attitudes towards the Indians were more significant than the similarities. The maritime fur traders were transient visitors to the coast with only limited opportunity or inclination to understand the Indians, but the land-based fur traders lived amongst the Indians for extended periods and so could be much more objective in their assessment of Indian behaviour. When the settlers arrived there was a definite change in the tone of writing about the Indians. In the sense that they had preconceptions about the Indians and their cultures and refused to change their opinion on the basis of new experience, the settlers as a group were more prejudiced than the fur traders. Frequently settler images were in large part the consequence of events and currents of thought in the metropolis, whereas traders' attitudes were more a product of life on the frontier. That is, generally traders reacted to what they saw, while settlers tended to react to what they expected to see.

From the first European contacts with the Indians of British Columbia layers of misunderstanding were laid down by the reports of uninterested and unskilled observers. We have no firsthand information about Indian culture before the Europeans arrived, and even the earliest visitors saw a culture that was undergoing change as a result of their presence.

Some early traders and explorers remained ignorant about Indian culture because they assumed that there was nothing worth studying. One of the first traders to come to the coast, James Strange, who led an expedition in 1786, considered that "such is the savage state of the Inhabitants" that knowledge of their social usages was unlikely to afford any edification to even the most curious reader. He was, however, prepared to broach the subject in so far as it would "admit of Entertainment."[3] Other traders had more pressing reasons for not recording their impressions of the coastal Indians. Because their activities were of dubious legality, many fur-trading captains were anxious not to leave any reports at all.

Among the early visitors, however, there were some Europeans who took a lively interest in the Indians. In an age of scientific exploration, the nations of Europe sent expeditions to the Pacific expecting them to return with a fund of information on the places that they had visited, including accounts of the "manners and customs" of the inhabitants. Spanish navigators, for example, received instructions to record the customs, political systems, religion, and barter of the northwest coast Indians. Some explorers had both a natural curiosity and many years of experience in examining the behaviour of indigenous people. Their experience made men like James Cook acute and relatively dispassionate commentators on other cultures. But even those who took an interest encountered almost insurmountable obstacles. The lack of a common language as well as conceptual barriers meant that many aspects of Indian culture could not be enquired into. Europeans often had to rely on outward behaviour to assess inner motivation, a procedure that was bound to produce misconceptions.

Even at the time of the early voyages it was apparent to some that the evidence being used to make judgments about the nature of the Indians could easily be manipulated to conform to preconceived notions. Meares, for instance, claimed that Maquinna was a cannibal. He gave as evidence of anthropophagy the fact that he had seen the chief sucking blood from a wound in his leg and declaring it to taste good. But Peter Puget rightly pointed out that if "all Mens characters were drawn from such vague & Shallow Conclusions . . . few would be found free from injurious slander."[4] James King, who came to the coast with Cook in 1778, noted that the superficiality of their observations meant that Europeans could come to quite contrary conclusions about the character and disposition of the Indians. Judgments were based on personal experience, and clearly the experience and reactions of individuals varied greatly. Consequently, while some concluded that the Indians were sullen, obstinate, and mistrustful, others said that they were docile, good-natured, and unsuspicious.[5] Other distortions of reality were created when assessments were based on fantasy rather than empiricism. The chronicler of Dixon's voyage was taken to task by another explorer because of his imagination which was "much disposed to be startled and take the alarm."[6] For the objective individual it was difficult enough to represent Indian culture accurately, but for the fanciful person it was virtually impossible. And for all Europeans, whatever their frame of mind, the recording of impressions of the Indian way of life was incidental to the primary concerns of exploration or trade.

Early European visitors to the coast tended to be superficial observers. Their journals make much of physical differences between Indians and Europeans. On the northern coast perhaps the most frequently emphasized feature in the trading journals was the labret worn by Indian women, while in the south the practice of flattening the forehead received great attention. Descriptions of physical appearance were often accompanied by expressions of revulsion, and aversion to the Indians' physical appearance began to assume the tone of a moral judgment. Vancouver, who was less tolerant than Cook, his former captain, had been, considered the labret to be "an instance of human absurdity" that had to be seen to be believed.[7] Not only did many visitors consider the Indians to be "the nastyest race of people under the sun,"[8] but there were also strong suggestions that they barely qualified as humans at all. Comments about "that savage inhumanity which distinguishes these People from the race of Human Kind" and about individual Indians behaving "more like a brute animal than a rational Creature"[9] reveal this tendency to dehumanize the Indians.

By their lengthy physical descriptions, which emphasized the ways in which the Indians differed from themselves, Europeans were exaggerating the separation of the two races. They were making the point, for their own benefit, that the Indians were something distinct and other than themselves. The Indians were not only different but inferior. Europeans always feared being reduced to the level of "savages," and so from the first contacts on the northwest coast they tended to emphasize traits that established their separateness from the Indians, rather than those that demonstrated their common humanity.

Aspects of the Indian way of life that were less clearly manifest than physical appearance were not so well documented in the journals. Apart from the fact that early visitors could not converse with the Indians in their own language, many Indians were reluctant to reveal much of their private knowledge anyway. Moreover, when Indians did divulge private information, they tended to tell the European inquirer what they thought he wanted to hear rather than what was actually true. Voyagers often found this attitude exasperating, and sometimes concluded that the Indians were a people who had little respect for the truth.[10] Several commentators noted the difficulty of investigating the political organization of the Indians.[11] When their social structure was described, it was often in terms of crude analogies to European patterns, such as comparing Indian government to the feudal system. Because religious beliefs and customs also proved very difficult to investigate,[12] it was often simply assumed that the Indians lacked any concept of religion. In the area of Indian ceremonial life, Europeans stressed the distinctive and bizarre, again demonstrating that the Indians were unlike themselves. Some Indian customs both shocked and fascinated observers and thus received much attention. Others, such as the dances of the Nootka women, so scandalized Europeans that "decency" compelled them to omit detailed descriptions.[13]

Comments about the role of Indian women in trading and in society in general are an interesting and puzzling aspect of the journals. There are frequent references to the control that Indian women had over bartering, and sometimes this fact was extended into assertions that Indian society was ruled by a "petticoat government."[14] These conclusions are too frequent for traders to be merely generalizing from a few isolated examples or reading each others' journals and repeating mistakes. Yet the statements are difficult to explain through the ethnographies. Many, although not all, of the accounts of the importance of the role of Indian women come from the northern coast where the Indians had a matrilineal social organization. But a matrilineal society is not necessarily matriarchal, and, in any case, there need be nothing in the transactions of traders to reveal the society as matrilineal. Moreover, some accounts of the crucial role of women in trading came from the south where society was organized patrilineally. The most likely explanation seems to be that the voyagers were seeing women in an unaccustomed role.

Europeans were perhaps surprised by the assertiveness of Indian women, and here again they exaggerated the difference between the Indians and themselves.

It is certain that the cultural baggage that the Europeans brought with them to the northwest coast included preconceptions about Indian behaviour. Pre-eminently they expected the Indians to be both hostile and treacherous. Juan Pérez, perhaps the first European to record his impressions of the Indians of British Columbia, rejected Indian invitations to come ashore because he feared treachery. Fourteen years later Dixon was similarly suspicious when some Haida indicated that his crew would be welcome in their village, and he assumed that once ashore his men would be "instantly butchered." Even present day historians have judged this caution to be well advised given the Haida's "subsequent record of attempting to overpower trading vessels without provocation."[15] Europeans expecting such total hostility naturally found evidence to support their prejudice. Any Indian attack, or suspected attack, was reported in the journals for others to read. Accounts of individual acts of aggression produced racial generalizations that all Indians were warlike. Even when Indians approached them in an outwardly friendly way, Europeans often believed that they were just more devious than most and were therefore especially untrustworthy. Although it was conceded that sometimes Indians were friendly and co-operative — it was said, for example, that Cook "met with remarkable sivel treatment from the natives"[16] — Europeans tended to believe the worst about the Indians. Cleveland knew when he met the Haida chief named Altatsee off Langara Island that two years earlier the Indian had been present when an American captain named Newberry had been accidentally killed. But the demeanour of Altatsee caused Cleveland to very much doubt that the death was an accident.[17] It was the pejorative rather than the complimentary that was remembered from the descriptions of the Indians, and the coastal Indians generally emerged from the initial contact period with an unenviable reputation. The familiar stereotype of the Indians as filthy, treacherous, lazy, lascivious, and dishonest was already established by the maritime fur traders. Such judgments were not always absolute: frequently the northwest coast Indians were being evaluated relatively, often in comparison with the apparently more appealing people of the Pacific Islands.

A pattern of misunderstanding had already been laid down, but it might be expected that with the shift to a land-based fur trade, a more sympathetic, or at least a more impartial, picture of the Indian might emerge. The employees of the fur-trading companies had closer contact with the Indians over extended periods of time. They could, therefore, observe aspects of the Indians' way of life that ships' crews, because of their limited contact, were unable to see. The annual pattern of activities, for example, could only be documented by someone who lived among the Indians for a year. There were, of course, still obstacles in the way of factual objectivity. The Indians remained reluctant to divulge information on certain subjects, sometimes believing that the fur traders' inquiries were "directed by improper motives."[18] At times the Indians still gave answers to please the questioner and so retained their reputation for being unreliable. Nor were the traders entirely free of prejudice. In fact, their very closeness to the Indians often forced them to accentuate ideas of Indian inferiority and to make every effort to ensure that the Indians recognized white superiority. The first of the fur traders to cross the Rockies later recorded his opinion that it was easier "for a civilised people to deviate into the manners and customs of savage life, than for savages to rise into a state of civilisation."[19] Obliged to forego the "pleasures of polished . . . society," the traders expressed a concern that they would tend to assimilate with those whom they lived closest to, "viz — the wretched aborigines."[20] The traders were very much concerned about their own image and needed to define clearly the boundary between "civilization" and "savagery." Nevertheless, in spite of all these impediments, the land-based fur traders did record a great deal of information about the Indian that was relatively unbiased.[21]

Company traders had little truck with notions of the noble savage. That concept was a metropolitan literary convention not typically held by those in close contact with the Indians on the frontier. Yet sometimes the vision of the man on the spot was so limited that his opinions of the Indians are no more reliable than those of the European novelist. Alexander Caulfield Anderson, in an article published in 1863, cautioned that generalizations about the Indians should not be based on extreme examples. He wrote:

> Such of my readers as in the absence of other opportunity, may have formed their impressions of Indian life and character from the alluring fictions of Mr. Cooper; or those who, on the opposite hand, have imbibed well founded prejudices from communication with the wretched fish eaters of the Columbia and its neighbouring coast, will do well to pause as regards the majority, between both extremes.[22]

In a book entitled *Traits of American-Indian Life and Character* written by "A Fur Trader," the author tried to correct certain false impressions conveyed by recent publications. He pointed out from the start the vast difference "between those who travel in pursuit of amusement or science, and men like us who only encounter these hardships for vile lucre." The implication throughout this book is that the traders were closer to frontier realities and therefore more objective. According to this particular "Fur Trader" the Indians did not possess all the fine qualities often attributed to them in popular literature and not every Indian was a hero. But the fur traders' attitudes towards the Indians were not entirely negative. While the book contains some invective, there are also many complimentary remarks.[23] Company traders, in contrast to the typical settler, were prepared, or perhaps had, to make allowances for the Indians.

Customs that outraged other Europeans were often described dispassionately by fur traders, and comparisons were sometimes made with corresponding western practices. The "indomitable passion" for gambling among some Indian groups was said, when carried to excess, to result in misery and degradation. Later, gaming was to be the subject of much anguished comment by missionaries and philanthropically-minded government officials. The "Fur Trader" observed the custom and momentarily lamented the Indians' "want of the civilised education of Europe." Yet, in the next instant, he was "humiliated by the remembrance of similar scenes in the most refined society." On observing mourners grieving at a Carrier funeral, the "Fur Trader" experienced a "gratification deep beyond measure to witness among rude beings such as these, the excitement of those pure feelings of our nature which remind us of our common origin."[24] Even the head flattening custom of the Indians of southern British Columbia that so shocked many Europeans was compared by Alexander Ross to the English women's habit of compressing their waists. "All nations, civilised as well as savage, have their peculiar prejudices," he remarked.[25] Traits that other Europeans were to find disgusting, the fur traders often recorded without judgment, although, as Lewis Saum has pointed out, the traders' tolerance was selective. Generally, "the excusable flaws in Indian nature were those that had little or no impact on the economics of trader–Indian relations."[26]

Another measure of the traders' familiarity with the Indians was that they tended to generalize less than other Europeans. While settlers were inclined to make racial generalizations about all the Indians of British Columbia, the fur traders had some awareness of individual differences[27] and an even greater consciousness of tribal differences. Not all the Indians were equally admired or disliked: therefore, many of the fur traders' judgments were not simply racist but rather the result of comparing one group of Indians with another.

The various tribes were classified according to a definite hierarchy of merit. If the southern tip of Vancouver Island is taken as a starting point, the Indians became more attractive in the eyes of the fur traders as one travelled northward along the coast or eastward into the interior. The Indians of the northern coast were thought to be superior to those of the south, and the coastal Indians generally were regarded as inferior to those who lived inland.

The notion that the Indians of the northern coast (the Haida particularly, but also the Tsimshian) were superior was based on observable physical differences, on the opinion that they were less degraded by western contact, and on the fact that they posed a greater military threat. Traders revealed their bias by describing the northern Indians as cleaner, fairer, taller, and better built than those to the south: in short, the Haida and Tsimshian were more attractive because they were seen to be more like Europeans. Perhaps the classic exposition of this point was written by Dr. John Scouler in a communication to the Royal Geographical Society of London.

> This northern family, if we select the Queen Charlotte's Islanders as specimens, are by far the best looking, most intelligent and energetic people on the N.W. coast, and in every respect contrast favourably with the Southern Tribes of Nootka Sound and the Columbia. They are taller and stronger than the Nootkans, their limbs are better formed, and their carriage is much bolder. They permit the hair of the upper lip to grow, and their mustachios are often as strong as those of Europeans. Their complexion, when they are washed and free from paint, is as white as that of the people of the S. of Europe.[28]

These comments were not penned by a fur trader, but Scouler gleaned much of his information from conversations with traders, many of whom would have agreed with his remarks.[29] Because they were thought to be more attractive physically, the Indians of the northern coast were more often taken as wives by fur traders than Salish women.

But the perceived superiority of the Haida and Tsimshian was not just a matter of physique; they were also seen to be morally and intellectually superior. The Haida particularly were thought to be adaptable and industrious and for this reason better able to withstand the degrading influences of western civilization. But they were also more warlike. Simpson once noted that the further north one goes on the coast the more formidable the Indians become.[30] It was a maxim that most company men agreed with, and they therefore anticipated hostility when they established forts in the area. "In the north," wrote Tolmie, expecting to be posted at Fort McLoughlin, one "must be continually armed to the teeth as the Indians are dangerous."[31]

The coastal Indians, then, were not equally esteemed by the fur traders. But the Indians of the coast were definitely considered to be inferior to those of the interior. This judgment was based on observable differences in ways of life. At its most simple level the view was that hunters were superior to fishermen. It was as if the method by which an Indian tribe gathered its livelihood imprinted a certain set of traits on its nature. "Fishing" Indians lived in a different environment and had a different way of life from "hunting" Indians, and fur traders claimed that these factors largely accounted for variations between tribes. The fishermen not only lived differently, but also looked, acted, and thought differently from the hunters. The idea that there was a close correlation between

environment and culture was common in the eighteenth and early nineteenth centuries, and observers of the coastal northwest saw something
akin to the "tropical exuberance" that Philip Curtin has described in
West Africa.[32] The coast was thought to be a luxuriant environment
that yielded a livelihood with little effort on the part of the Indians. Such
an environment made its inhabitants not only lazy, but also "gross,
sensual, and for the most part cowardly." By contrast "those tribes, who,
with nerves and sinews braced by exercise, and minds comparatively
ennobled by frequent excitement live constantly amid war and the chase"
were in every way more attractive.[33]

This view pervades the writings of the fur traders. Ogden, or the "Fur
Trader," wrote of the "stately independence" which distinguished "the
native hunter of the wilds of North America, from the more ignoble
fisher of its waters."[34] Douglas noted that few of the Indians of the
Cowlitz River area evinced "a desire to become hunters by courting the
nobler, elevating and more arduous exercise of the chase," while Tod
catalogued the differences between the two types of Indians. To him,
the fishers were mean, sneaking, thieving, and deceiving, whereas the
hunters were noble and generous.[35] It was almost as if by mounting a
horse the Indian transformed his whole character. In fact, Commander
Charles Wilkes of the United States exploring expedition asserted in
1841 that the Indians should never be seen except on horseback.
Mounted, he said, the Indians were "really men" and inspired a certain
amount of respect but dismounted they became "lazy lounging creatures,
insensible to any excitement but his [sic] low gambling propensities."[36]
It was this dichotomy between hunter and fisher that accounted for the
decreasing respect for the Indians as fur traders travelled westward from
the mountains to the sea. By the time they had reached the mouth of
the Columbia the Indians seemed quite detestable. They were, wrote
Dugald MacTavish, "the most miserable and wretched" of the Indians
that he had seen.[37]

This feeling among fur traders that the Indians of the interior were
superior to those of the coast was not entirely unrelated to some Indians'
view of themselves. The upper Thompson, for instance, looked down
on their lower Thompson neighbours and on the Salish, while the Indians
closer to the coast feared the more warlike up-river Indians.[38]

Economic considerations played a large part in the fur traders' assessment of the various Indian tribes. To the extent that the coastal Indians
were dealers rather than hunters they were not appreciated by the traders.
Company men preferred Indians who captured and brought pelts directly
to a fort to the apparently idle "home guards" who acted as middlemen
and forced up prices. Confident of the profits to be made as middlemen,
many fort Indians did not see any need to hunt for furs themselves, a
conclusion that did not particularly endear them to the traders. With
the arrival of settlers the economic basis for the notion that the interior

Indians were superior began to disappear, and yet the attitude persisted.

Writers who described Vancouver Island and British Columbia during the settlement period constantly reiterated the point that the inland hunter was a more admirable kind of Indian. Their preference was described in much the same terms as the fur traders'. One traveller was agreeably surprised at the physique of the Indians when he reached the Thompson River, and even went as far as to speculate that the interior Indians were European and the coastal Indians mongoloid in origin.[39] Their physical superiority was the visible evidence of less tangible characteristics that distinguished the interior tribes from those of the coast. In short, the inland Indians were "in every way a nobler race."[40] Even Franz Boas had to wait for his second period of field work in British Columbia and a trip to the Kootenays before he saw his "first real Indians."[41] This kind of opinion was both widely held and widely publicized among settlers.[42] Colonists also saw the interior Indians as a greater potential threat than the coastal tribes. Readers of the *British Colonist* were told that "it is not from the miserable, fish-eating tribes on the seaboard, but from the more noble and war-like redman of the interior, who live by the chase, that real danger is to be apprehended."[43]

The feeling that interior people, who had fewer contacts with Europeans than coastal people, were therefore less degraded, was common in other British colonies.[44] Yet, in some ways, the view is a curious one in the British Columbian context. Those settlers who thought at all about the future of the Indians usually saw it in terms of a settled agricultural existence. Presumably the coastal Indians, who already had fixed village sites, conformed more closely to this ideal than the more nomadic Indians of the interior.[45] There is an ambivalence about the settlers' disrespect for those Indians who most closely approached their supposed future status, although it is an ambivalence that ran deep in British thought about aborigines. Colonists were aware that western contact was as likely to be degrading as elevating to the Indians, and they despised those Indians who succumbed. The lingering hangover of the noble savage idea meant that the settlers still had a surreptitious regard for the Indians who still roamed wild and free.

Settlers also inherited and perpetuated the fur traders' image of the Indians of the northern coast. One visitor went so far as to say that "The Hydah Indian is probably the finest savage I have ever had the pleasure of meeting."[46] Because the northern tribes seemed a much greater military threat than the Salish, some considered that no colony could be established on Vancouver Island without being rendered safe against them by a strong detachment of troops. As in other parts of the British Empire the colonists at once feared and respected aborigines who were a potential danger.[47] So the northern Indians commanded some admiration from many of the settlers, while the Songhees were despised.[48] The mixed feelings with which the northern Indians were regarded were perhaps best expressed by a resident of Puget Sound, James G. Swan, writing in the *San Francisco Evening Bulletin* in 1860. The "very intelligence" of the Indians along with their courage and determination, made them a "terror and a dread" in the United States and Victoria; they were "the only real foe we have to look out for on this frontier." And yet, at the same time, Swan believed that "if it were possible to effect an exchange and substitute the northern Indians for the lazy, 'cultus' and trifling tribes of Flatheads, the Territory would be benefited."[49]

While fur traders and settlers shared some impressions of the Indians, the differences in their attitudes were much more marked. Settlers held many opinions about the Indians that the fur traders had not adhered to, and after settlement began the general tendency was for the image of the Indian to become more disparaging and more subjective. Their writings indicate that many settlers had little or nothing to say in favour of the Indian way of life. Many came to British Columbia with preconceptions, and few altered their views on the basis of experience.

The 1850s and 1860s were a period when racial attitudes were hardening in Britain, the birthplace of many of the first settlers of Vancouver Island and British Columbia. It has been argued that the changes in attitudes to other races were related to changes in the social structure of Britain,[50] but there were also other, more overt, indices of the development in thinking. The heady days of the abolition of slavery and of the Select Committee on Aborigines in the 1830s had passed. Both the movement for the abolition of slavery and the Aborigines Protection Society had lost much of their earlier singlemindedness and direction. The humanitarian movement enjoyed a resurgence of official influence while Earl Grey was at the Colonial Office, but this was its last fling, and it declined after 1852. By that time permanent under-secretary James Stephen, whose connections with "Exeter Hall" had always been strong, had retired to a chair of history at Oxford. A sign of the changing times was the establishment of the colony of Vancouver Island not in a hot flash of humanitarian zeal as New Zealand had been nine years earlier, but for the more prosaic reasons of imperial strategy. Events on the fringes of the empire also had their influence on metropolitan racial attitudes. The Indian Mutiny followed by the wars in South Africa in the 1850s, the Maori–European land wars in New Zealand, and the rebellion in Jamaica in the 1860s all shocked and horrified Englishmen. These conflicts seemed to corroborate negative views of aborigines and forced racial undercurrents closer to the surface.

Events such as these were both a cause and a result of racial thought. During the 1850s the scholarly debate between the advocates of monogenesis and polygenesis, having been largely resolved in favour of the former, was dropped as attention turned to evolutionary ideas. Evolutionary theories of race were being aired before the publication of *The*

Origin of Species in 1859 and seemed to be confirmed by the fate of aborigines in areas already settled by Europeans. None of the three theories on race—monogenesis, polygenesis, or evolution—changed the general British view that the races of the world were arranged in a hierarchy with themselves at the top. But in the late 1850s the notion of British superiority and aboriginal inferiority was being solidified from a generally held hypothesis into an empirically proven doctrine by the work of scientists and pseudo-scientists.[51] The general result of this trend was to confirm the racist error that race was the principal determinant of culture.

Settlers coming to Vancouver Island and British Columbia out of such a climate of opinion often held such fixed ideas about the inferiority of the Indian that contact modified them little. Immigrants with more refined sensibilities than most — or perhaps with greater pretensions — often found their first contact with the Indians shocking. Helmcken thought the first Indians he saw on nearing Victoria to be "dirty greasy nasty-smelling creatures," while another new arrival thought they were "the most hideous beings . . . imaginable." One young lady coming into Victoria on the *Tory* found her first sight of a naked Indian so upsetting that she burst into tears.[52] Those settlers whose first and most frequent contacts were with the Indians of the Victoria area based their stereotype on what were generally agreed to be the most "degraded" Indians of the colonies. A resident of Vancouver Island once noted that his contemporaries were far too apt to judge the whole race by those Indians they saw "lounging about the town," who were at once the most civilized and most debased of the Indians.[53]

The proposition that civilization would bring not only degeneration but also annihilation to the Indians was one that was much more frequently expounded by settlers than it had been by fur traders. Some recognized that their impact on the Indians was different from that of the traders. Captain Grant told the Royal Geographical Society in 1857 that hitherto the Indians' relations with white men had been mostly commercial ones that had not interfered with their "ordinary pursuits." But now settlement would mean both displacement and death for the Indians.[54] In further contrast to the fur traders, many settlers, including Grant, thought that the Indian and the European could not assimilate. The reason, in the words of one of the colonists, was that "their habits and natures" were "in direct opposition."[55] So the disappearance of the Indians was regarded as being as inevitable as the influx of European settlers. It was widely held, both in Britain and North America, that colonization by definition involved the extermination of the "inferior" indigenous peoples. The inevitability of the Indians' doom was said by some to be a law of nature.[56] At least one visitor to the Pacific northwest was prompted to ponder the question of why the Indians had been placed on the earth at all. Perhaps, he concluded, they were only meant to live a life in the wilds until "races of greater capacity were ready to occupy the soil. A succession of races, like a rotation of crops, may be necessary to turn the earth to the best possible account."[57] But whatever the reason given, many settlers looked forward to a not too distant future when the Indians would have disappeared.

Aware that their presence was tending to destroy the Indian and his way of life and sometimes even feeling guilty about it, the settlers were unlikely to see much value in the culture that they were eliminating. By disparaging Indian culture Europeans could convince themselves that little of worth would be lost if the Indian way of life was brought to an end. At the same time they reminded themselves, by comparison, of the excellence of their own institutions. With some exceptions, pioneer accounts of the Indians contained much that was contemptuous, and they were suffused with ignorance.

The tone of many reports of the Indians can be gathered from the chapter headings of books describing British Columbia. In his *British Columbia and Vancouver Island*, Duncan George Forbes MacDonald described the following as "Prominent Features in the Life and Character of the Indians—Slaves Horribly Abused—The 'Medicine Man' and the Dead — Mode of Scalping — Young Indians more Savage than Old — Horrible Modes of Torture — Barbarous Conduct of an Old Squaw — Shocking Cruelties to an Old Man and Instance of Cannibalism — Horrible Massacre of Emigrants—Cruel Custom of getting rid of Aged—." The picture is admittedly ameliorated by one account of a "Touching Instance of Parental Affection — ."[58] MacDonald wrote a good deal of drivel about the Indians, as he did about most topics that he tackled in his book, and his is an extreme example of the tendency to disparage the Indians. Nevertheless, MacDonald's caricature of Indian life demonstrated to the settler that there was little to be valued or preserved. Like many accounts, it also succeeded in treating all Indians as if they were the same and ignored the differences between the various Indian cultures of British Columbia. The fantastic and the bizarre were emphasized to make all Indians seem the same at least insofar as they were all so different from Europeans.

The image of the Indian certainly became less positive with the transition from fur trade to settlement. Some colonists, like the journalist Donald Fraser, may have found that they had "taken rather a fancy to these Indians"; but more would have agreed with John Coles, a rancher, who wrote that jailing an Indian for being a vagabond was absurd since they were "all vagabonds with a *very very few* exceptions."[59] For the prejudiced individual among the colonists every aspect of the Indians and their society seemed to confirm their inferiority. The Indian physique was described in disparaging terms.[60] "Phrenologically speaking," wrote one visitor, adding a dash of bogus science, "the development of the North American Indian is of a low order, the animal propensities preponderating greatly over the intellectual faculties."[61] Both the persons and the habitations of the Indians were said to be exceedingly filthy. Writers dismissed Indian ceremonies as "disgusting" or as "grotesque antics," accounts of which would only tax the patience of their readers.[62] The Indian mind was thought to be "full of weird strange fancies and imaginations," and the Indian to be "strangely superstitious."[63] Apart from a "few miserable superstitions, and a childish belief in omens," the Indians were believed to have no religious concepts and were regarded as "incapable of retaining any fixed idea." According to settler reports they acted more from instinct than from reason and were nearly destitute of any sense of right and wrong.[64] They were warlike, but treacherous and cunning rather than courageous. "In British Columbia," it was asserted, "the new arrival is waited for by the crafty bloodthirsty and implacable savage, who never throws away a chance, never exposes himself to the weapon of an enemy, nor misses an opportunity of slaughter and revenge."[65] The Indians were also said to be dishonest and deceitful as well as lazy and unsuited to manual labour. Perhaps one of the most revealing comments about the Indian was that he "exhibits very little deferential respect for his superiors."[66] The picture of prejudice was summed by Grant when he concluded that "the nature of the red man is savage and perverse. He prefers war to peace, noise to quiet, dirt to cleanliness, and jugglery to religion."[67]

Like most stereotypes, the settlers' view of the Indians was nurtured by ignorance. As long as they knew little about Indian society, the settlers had no reason to doubt their assumed superiority. When he was Indian reserve commissioner in the late 1870s, Gilbert Malcolm Sproat wrote that one of the most singular experiences that he had was the impossibility of getting accurate information about the Indians from people who lived in their midst. He was amazed that Europeans who had lived among the Indians for years had such a superficial knowledge of them. For instance, Sproat was told on occasion that the Indians were incapable of building irrigation ditches "when ingeniously constructed ditches several miles in length were almost visible."[68] Sproat's difficulty in gathering reliable information is indicative of the tendency of the colonists to filter out data that did not confirm their opinions of the Indians.

One might expect that the artistry of the north coast Indians would be a point in their favour in the minds of the settlers, a sign that the Indian possessed something that might be called a culture. A few admired Indian art and some were impressed with Indian "ingenuity" and "faculty for contrivance,"[69] but for others Indian art merely provided confirmation of the depravity of Indian nature. Their carving was dismissed as "hideous" or "grossly obscene."[70] Certainly Sproat believed that many settlers were steeped in an intolerance that prevented them from having any sympathy for the people among whom they were living. Nor was Sproat alone in this opinion. Robert Brown, the leader of the Vancouver

Island exploring expedition of 1864, wrote that few of the white settlers took the trouble to learn about the Indians, and even fewer really knew anything nefarious about them, although they were loud in their dogmatic denunciations.[71]

Of course, racial prejudice was not confined to the European settlers. The Indians themselves were not immune. While he was gold commissioner at Lytton, Henry Maynard Ball claimed that the Indians of the area treated the Chinese as lesser beings and that they did not miss any opportunity to commit outrages against them.[72] There is also evidence that the Cowichan considered themselves superior to the blacks who came to settle on southern Vancouver Island and Saltspring Island in 1858.[73]

Although vestiges of the concept remained, settlers, like fur traders, tended to reject the noble savage idea. A few individuals remarked that they had never seen a "Fenimore Cooper" Indian.[74] But, unlike the fur traders, the colonists were too often unprepared to make allowances for the cultural differences between themselves and the Indians. Some of their aspersions were probably justified from a relative point of view — Indians' houses may well have been dirtier than European ones — but many were merely examples of cultural differences. The Indians did not have European attitudes towards work, for example: they went through periods of relative inactivity, but they also worked extremely hard when necessary. But the settlers, viewing the Indians from the vantage point of their own values and ignoring the seasonal variations in the Indians' work patterns, simply generalized that they were lazy.

In many ways this oversimplified assessment of the Indian was self-perpetuating. Settlers repeated each others' published remarks about the Indians, with or without acknowledgement.[75] Nor were the Indians unaware of the attitude of many settlers towards their cultures, and their awareness only increased their reluctance to discuss their society. When Boas came to the coast, he found that some Indians were very suspicious of his information gathering. A Cowichan Indian responded to his requests by pointing out that the "whites look upon the Indians not as humans but as dogs, and he did not wish anyone to laugh at things that were their laws, such as painted houses and articles used for celebrating their festivals."[76] Observers in the early 1860s had noticed a similar response on the part of the Indians. Sproat found it difficult to obtain knowledge of Indian religious ideas because they commonly assumed that no white man was capable of understanding such mysteries. In Sproat's case they were correct. He went on to say that little reliance could be placed on Indian explanations of religious matters because in nine out of ten cases they were full of "lies and misstatements," either aimed at mystifying the inquirer "or owing to the mental weakness of the savage on religious subjects."[77] In the absence of authentic interpretations of customs, settlers substituted their own. Carrier ceremonies associated with the cremation of the dead were the subject of much jaundiced comment by Europeans. The artist Paul Kane, for example, being unable to learn of any motive or explanation for the customs, could "only account for them in the natural selfishness, laziness and cruelty of the Indians."[78] Undoubtedly settler opinion of the Indians often operated as a self-fulfilling prophecy. It has been argued that, in a situation where one group sees another as inferior, the subordinate group will tend to act in accordance with the role allotted to it, thus confirming the opinion of the dominant group.[79]

The missionaries, as a group, exhibited much more sympathy for the plight of the Indians than did the settlers, and yet missionary publications did little to ameliorate the image of the Indian. By the middle of the nineteenth century missions were less popular in Britain than they had been in the earlier decades, but missionary publications still reached a wide audience. Indeed, since missions relied on voluntary contributions, publications were essential to their existence. Missionary magazines were intended to whip up enthusiasm for missionary work, and one of the techniques they used was to show how the unredeemed aborigine was doomed to a life of barbarism. The darker the picture of Indian savagery, the greater the need for missionaries and the more God could be glorified by the Indians' conversion. In his first report from Fort Simpson in February 1858, William Duncan describes in graphic terms the cruel murder of a slave by a Tsimshian chief.[80] His account of this event turns up again and again both in missionary publications and in secular accounts of the Indians of British Columbia,[81] and the description is often used to demonstrate that such behaviour typified the Indian character.

The missionary could never deny the humanity of the Indians, for that would be to deny their capacity for salvation. Nevertheless, in their descriptions of the Indians as "miserable specimens of humanity" requiring to be rescued from a "state of heathen darkness and complete barbarism,"[82] missionary publications distorted Indian culture as much as works written by laymen.

In recent publications various scholars have examined and attempted to explain the causes of racial prejudice of the kind that existed in Vancouver Island and British Columbia. Roy Harvey Pearce in his study *The Savages of America* was one of the first to recognize the complexities of Indian–white relations. He argued that for the settler concerned to establish and defend a beachhead of civilization in the wilderness the Indian was the symbol of something that he must not allow himself to become.[83] The British colonist established a line of cleavage based on race and could not permit any crossing of that barrier by admitting that the Indian was in any way comparable to western man. So in their accounts of the Indians the settlers tended to stress those aspects of Indian life that were repellent to Europeans and thus denied their common humanity with the Indians. In Vancouver Island and British Columbia settlers were particularly uneasy about the presence of half-breeds because they blurred the racially determined distinction between "savage" and "civilized." While the children of mixed marriages played an important role on the fur-trading frontier, with the advent of settlement attitudes to both the marriages and the children became much less positive. This change in attitude was undoubtedly due, at least in part, to the arrival of European women in appreciable numbers. The fact that the governor's wife was part Indian was difficult for many of the colonists to cope with. Some found it necessary to explain Lady Douglas on the grounds that she was "not a woman of much colour."[84] Even worse than the half-breeds in the mind of the settler was the European who voluntarily assumed the way of life of the Indians. These men were a living denial of the absolute separateness of the two cultures.

In his book *Patterns of Dominance*, Philip Mason has noted that psychological research has generally confirmed the hypothesis that there is a strong correlation between racial intolerance and insecurity.[85] Certainly the Europeans felt insecure in relation to the Indians in the early years of settlement on the northwest coast. The colonists were overwhelmingly outnumbered, and some of them at least had been told fearful stories about the Indians before they left home.[86] Mason has also observed, more specifically, that an individual who has recently risen or fallen sharply in the social scale is likely to exhibit racial intolerance.[87] The point has particular pertinence in a colonial situation. In a population where the majority have recently left the homeland in order to better themselves and are therefore experiencing a period of dislocation, the need to reassure themselves of their own "civilization" can be satisfied by emphasizing the "savagery" of the aborigines. This tendency would be further strengthened to the extent that there was a heightened consensus in the colonial society.[88] There were, therefore, numerous pressures within the settler society for the perpetuation of prejudice.

At the beginning of this chapter the assumption was made that there was a relationship between the Europeans' image of the Indians and their behaviour towards them. This relationship is a complex one. Attitudes were both a cause and a result of action. The differences between the attitudes of fur traders and settlers coincided with their intentions. When trade was the Europeans' object the Indian was seen as primitive but responsive to the advantages of co-operation rather than hostile. When permanent settlement was the intention of the Europeans and they coveted Indian land, the Indian became a hostile savage, a hindrance rather than a help to the new arrival. The things written and said about the Indians became more and more abusive. But behaviour towards the Indians also arose out of the opinions that were held about them. Therefore one might expect that if the settlers' image was largely based on prejudice and ignorance there would be little in their behaviour and policies to benefit the Indian and that, as attitudes became more abusive, so would the treatment of the Indians.

Notes

1. James Robert Anderson, "Notes and Comments on Early Days and Events in British Columbia, Washington and Oregon . . . ," Provincial Archives of British Columbia (hereafter PABC), 170.

2. H.G. Barnett, *Innovation: The Basis of Cultural Change* (New York: McGraw-Hill, 1953), 399.

3. James Strange, "Journal," 6 July 1786, *James Strange's Journal and Narrative of the Commercial Expedition from Bombay to the North-West Coast of America* . . . (Madras: Government Press, 1929), 22.

4. John Meares, *Voyages Made in the Years 1788 and 1789, from China to the North West Coast of America* . . . (London: Logographic Press, 1790), 257; Peter Puget, "A Log of the Proceedings of His Majesty's Armed Tender *Chatham* Lieutenant Peter Puget Acting Commander Commencing 12 Day of January 1793," 4 May 1793, 45 (microfilm, University of British Columbia Library (hereafter UBCL)). I am not particularly concerned here with the debate about whether or not the northwest coast Indians ate human flesh. Warren Cook, in *Floodtide of Empire: Spain and the Pacific Northwest, 1543-1819* (New Haven: Yale University Press, 1973), 190, n. 107, has listed a number of contemporary sources in support of the contention that the Nootka, at least, were probably cannibals, although on investigation some of the references turn out to be somewhat inconclusive. It is also interesting that the Cook expedition, after a month at Nootka, could find "no certain proof" that Indians were cannibals: Samwell, "Journal," 3 April 1778, in *The Journals of Captain James Cook on his Voyages of Discovery; the Voyage of the "Resolution" and "Discovery," 1776–1780*, ed. J.C. Beaglehole, Parts 1 and 2 (Cambridge: Hakluyt Society, 1967), part 2, 1092. However, the essential point here is not whether cannibalism actually existed, but the ease with which many Europeans assumed that it did.

5. King, "Journal," [April 1778], in *Journals*, ed. Beaglehole, part 2, 1406–7.

6. C.P. Claret Fleurieu, *A Voyage Round the World, Performed during the Years 1790, 1791, and 1792, by Etienne Marchand* . . . , 2 vols. (London: T.N. Longman and O. Rees, 1801), 1: 477.

7. George Vancouver, *A Voyage of Discovery to the North Pacific Ocean, and Round the World; . . . Performed in the Years 1790, 1791, 1792, 1793, 1794, and 1795, in the "Discovery" Sloop of War, and Armed Tender "Chatham," under the Command of Captain George Vancouver*, 3 vols. (London: G.G. and J. Robinson, 1798), 2: 280.

8. Thomas Manby, Journal, 24 April 1792, "A Journal of Vancouver's Voyage, 1790–93," UBCL.

9. Bishop, "Journal," 11 September 1795, in *The Journal and Letters of Captain Charles Bishop on the North-West Coast of America, in the Pacific and in New South Wales 1794–1799*, ed. Michael Roe (Cambridge: Hakluyt Society, 1967), 97-98; Samwell, "Journal," 31 March 1778, part 2, 1090.

10. Vancouver, *A Voyage*, 1: 269.

11. See, for example, Cook, "Journal," 26 April 1778, in *Journals*, ed. Beaglehole, part 1, 322; Manby, "Journal," 24 July 1792, UBCL.

12. Cook, "Journal," 26 April 1778, part 1, 322; Alessandro Malaspina, "Politico-Scientific Voyages Around the World . . . from 1789–1784," translated

by Carl Robinson, UBCL, 2: 222; Fleurieu, *A Voyage*, 1: 403.

13. Jose Mariño Moziño, *Noticias de Nutka: An Account of Nootka Sound in 1792* (Toronto: McClelland and Stewart, 1970), 60.

14. "Haswell's Log of the First Voyage," [June 1789], "Hoskins' Narrative," [July and August 1791], and "Boit's Log," 8 July 1791, in *Voyages of the "Columbia" to the Northwest Coast 1787–1790 and 1790–1793*, ed. F.W. Howay (Boston: Massachusetts Historical Society, 1941), 96, 325, 372; Jacinto Caamaño, "The Journal of Jacinto Caamaño," *British Columbia Historical Quarterly* 2 (1938): 205; "Journal Kept on Board the Armed Tender *Chatham*," June and September 1793, PABC; Vancouver, *A Voyage*, 2: 343; Bishop, "Journal," 16 June 1795, 63.

15. Cook, *Flood Tide of Empire*, 60; George Dixon, *A Voyage Round the World; but more Particularly to the North-West Coast of America; Performed in 1785, 1786, 1787 and 1788 in the "King George" and the "Queen Charlotte," Captains Portlock and Dixon* (London: G. Goulding, 1789), 206.

16. "Haswell's Log of the First Voyage," 16 March 1789, 59.

17. Richard J. Cleveland, *Voyages and Commercial Enterprises of the Sons of New England* (New York: Leavitt and Allan, 1855), 108.

18. Charles Ross to Governor George Simpson, 1 October 1842, Hudson's Bay Company Archives (hereafter HBCA), D-5/7, Governor George Simpson, Correspondence Inward, 1821–1860.

19. W. Kaye Lamb, ed. *The Journals and Letters of Sir Alexander Mackenzie* (Cambridge: Hakluyt Society, 1970), 65.

20. W.F. Tolmie, *The Journals of William Fraser Tolmie: Physician and Fur Trader* (Vancouver: Mitchell Press, 1963), 10 December 1834, 297; see also William Tod to Edward Ermatinger, 29 June 1836, Ermatinger Papers, UBCL; John McLean, *Notes of a Twenty-Five Years' Service in the Hudson's Bay Territory*, 2 vols. (London: R. Bentley, 1849), 2: 261; and Lewis O. Saum, *The Fur Trader and the Indian* (Seattle: University of Washington Press, 1965), 5.

21. The conclusion was also reached by Saum, *The Fur Trader*, 11.

22. Alexander C. Anderson, "Notes on the Indian Tribes of British North America, and the Northwest Coast," *Historical Magazine* 7 (1863): 80.

23. [Peter Skene Ogden?], *Traits of American-Indian Life and Character, by a Fur Trader* (London: Smith, Elder, 1853), 5–6, 21, 188, and passim. In an article on the problem of the authorship of this book, F.W. Howay argues convincingly, although not with absolute finality, that the "Fur Trader" of the title page was Peter Skene Ogden ("Authorship of Traits of Indian Life," *Oregon Historical Quarterly* 35 (1934): 42–49). For other examples of the rejection of the concept of the noble savage see Fleurieu, *Voyage*, 1: 479; Ross Cox, *Adventures on the Columbia River . . .* (New York: J. & J. Harper. 1832), v.

24. [Ogden?], *Traits*, 152-53, 160.

25. Alexander Ross, *Adventures of the First Settlers on the Oregon or Columbia River . . .* (London: Smith, Elder, 1849), 99–100.

26. Saum, *The Fur Trader*, 176.

27. Ibid., 59.

28. John Scouler, "Observations of the Indigenous Tribes of the N. W. Coast of America," *Journal of the Royal Geographical Society of London* 11 (1841): 218.

29. See, for example, John Dunn, *History of the Oregon Territory and British North American Fur Trade . . .* (London: Edwards and Hughes, 1844), 283; Charles Ross to Simpson, 10 January 1844, in "Five Letters of Charles Ross, 1842–1844," ed. W. Kaye Lamb, *British Columbia Historical Quarterly* 7 (1943): 115; and Saum, *The Fur Trader*, 118.

30. Simpson to Smith, 17 November 1828, in *Fur Trade and Empire, George Simpson's Journal, Remarks Connected with the Fur Trade in the Course of a Voyage from York Factory to Fort George and back to York 1824–1825* . . . , ed. Frederick Merk (Cambridge, Mass.: Harvard University Press, 1931), 300.

31. Tolmie, *Journals*, 9 May 1833, 175.

32. Philip D. Curtin, *The Image of Africa: British Ideas and Action, 1780–1850* (Madison: University of Wisconsin Press, 1964), 61ff.

33. Anderson, "Notes on the Indian Tribes," 80.

34. [Ogden?], *Traits*, 79.

35. Douglas, Diary, 3 April 1840, James Douglas, "Diary of a Trip to the Northwest Coast," 22 April–2 October 1840," PABC; John Tod, "History of New Caledonia and the Northwest Coast," PABC, 63.

36. Charles Wilkes, *Narrative of the United States Exploring Expedition, During the Years 1838, 1839, 1840, 1841, 1842* (London: Whittaker, 1845), 4: 311.

37. Dugald MacTavish to Mrs. MacTavish, 19 October 1839, in *The Hargrave Correspondence 1821–1843*, ed. G.P. de T. Glazebrook (Toronto: Champlain Society, 1938), 307; Saum, *The Fur Trader*, 37, 115.

38. James Teit, *The Thompson Indians of British Columbia*, Memoirs of the American Museum of Natural History, Franz Boas, general ed. (n.p., 1900), 269–70; Wilson Duff, *The Upper Stalo Indians of the Fraser Valley, British Columbia*, Anthropology in British Columbia Memoir no. 1 (Victoria: Provincial Museum, 1952), 96.

39. R. Byron Johnson, *Very Far West Indeed: A Few Rough Experiences on the North-West Pacific Coast* (London: S. Low, Marston, Low and Searle, 1872), 85–86.

40. Anderson, "Notes and Comments on Early Days and Events in British Columbia," 112.

41. Boas, "Diary," 18 July 1888, *The Ethnography of Franz Boas: Letters and Diaries of Franz Boas Written on the Northwest Coast from 1886 to 1931*, ed. Ronald P. Rohner (Chicago: University of Chicago Press, 1969), 102.

42. See Blanshard's testimony, Great Britain, House of Commons, *Report from the Select Committee on the Hudson's Bay Company; together with the Proceedings of the Committee, Minutes of Evidence, Appendix and Evidence* (London, 1857), 286, 292; Alexander Caulfield Anderson, *The Dominion at the West: A Brief Description of the Province of British Columbia, its Climate and Resources* (Victoria: R. Wolfenden, 1872), 80, 98, 100; C.W. Barrett-Lennard, *Travels in British Columbia, with the Narrative of a Yacht Voyage Round Vancouver's Island* (London: Hurst and Blackett, 1862), 40; Robert Brown, Journal, 23 March 1866, "The Land of the Hydahs, a Spring Journey Due North . . . Spring of 1866," PABC; John Keast Lord, *The Naturalist in Vancouver Island and British Columbia* (London: R. Bentley, 1866), 2: 226ff; Matthew Macfie, *Vancouver Island and British Columbia: Their History, Resources and Prospects* (London: Longman, Green, Longman, Roberts and Green, 1865), 428; R.C. Mayne, *Four Years in British Columbia and Vancouver Island* . . . (London: J. Murray, 1862), 242.

43. *British Colonist*, 30 November 1869. Similar feelings were widely held in North America. A contributor to *Atlantic Monthly* claimed that the widespread idea that Indian management in Canada was superior to that in the United States could be explained by the fact that the American Indians were "bold and fierce hunters of the buffalo" and therefore difficult to deal with in comparison with the "quiet and gentle savages of a cold climate and a fish diet" (*Atlantic Monthly* 41 (1878): 385–86).

44. See H. Alan C. Cairnes, *Prelude to Imperialism: British Reactions to Central African Society 1840–1890* (London: Routledge and Kegan Paul, 1965), 17; and Curtin, *The Image of Africa*, 408–9. At least one writer on British Columbia during

the settlement period was aware of this comparison (see Macfie, *Vancouver Island*, 428).

45. The fur traders also saw these least admirable Indians as the most likely candidates for civilization (see Saum, *The Fur Trader*, 228).

46. William Downie, *Hunting for Gold: Reminiscences of Personal Experience and Research in the Early Days of the Pacific Coast* . . . (San Francisco: Press of the California Publishing Co., 1893), 216.

47. Rear-Admiral Phipps Hornby to J. Parker (Admiralty), 29 August 1849, HBCA, A-8/6. This attitude is clearly seen in the settlers' differing attitudes and behaviour towards the Maoris in New Zealand and the Aborigines of Australia, and T.O. Ranger has pointed out similar differences in settler opinion about the Shona and Ndebele prior to the revolts of 1896–97 in Southern Rhodesia (T.O. Ranger, *Revolt in Southern Rhodesia 1896-1897: A Study in African Resistance* (Evanston, Ill.: Northwestern University Press, 1967), ch. 1, particularly 36). See also Cairns, *Prelude to Imperialism*, 114.

48. Robert M. Ballantyne, *Handbook to the New Gold Fields:* . . . (Edinburgh: A. Strahan, 1858), 78; George Duncan Forbes MacDonald, *British Columbia and Vancouver's Island* . . . (London: Longman, Green, Longman, Roberts and Green, 1862), 128–29; Mayne, *Four Years in British Columbia*, 73; Charles Frederic Morison, "Reminiscences of the Early Days in British Columbia 1862–1876 by a Pioneer of the North West Coast," PABC, 78; Doyce B. Nunis, Jr., ed., *The Golden Frontier: The Recollections of Herman Francis Reinhart, 1851–1869* (Austin: University of Texas Press, 1962), 143; Gilbert Malcolm Sproat, *Scenes and Studies of Savage Life* (London: Smith, Elder, 1968), 23, 99; Charles Wilson, Journal, 23 March 1859, in *Mapping the Frontier: Charles Wilson's Diary of the Survey of the 49th Parallel, 1858–1862, while Secretary of the British Boundary Commission*, ed. George F.G. Stanley (Toronto: Macmillan, 1970), 46; Kuper to Moresby, 26 July 1852, Great Britain, Original Correspondence, Vancouver Island, 1846–1867, CO.305/3, microfilm, UBCL.

49. James G. Swan, *Almost out of the World: Scenes from Washington Territory the Strait of Juan de Fuca 1859–1861*, ed. William A. Katz (Tacoma: Washington State Historical Society, 1971), 97–98.

50. Douglas Alexander Lorimer, "British Attitudes to the Negro, 1830–1870" (Ph.D. dissertation, University of British Columbia, 1972), 146–47 and passim; Philip Mason, *Patterns of Dominance* (London: Oxford University Press, 1970), 22.

51. Curtin, *The Image of Africa*, 29, describes pseudo-scientists as those who are "misled by a little learning into wild speculations which the best science, even in their time, would not sustain on the basis of reason and evidence."

52. Dorothy Blakey Smith, ed. *The Reminiscences of Doctor John Sebastian Helmcken*, (Vancouver: University of British Columbia Press, 1975), 80; Charles Alfred Bayley, "Early Life on Vancouver Island," PABC, 2.

53. Robert Brown, Journal, 19 August 1864, "Journal of the V[ancouver] I[sland] Exploring Expedition vols. 1 to 5, 7 June to 14 September 1864," PABC.

54. W. Colquhoun Grant, "Description of Vancouver Island, by its First Colonist," *Journals of the Royal Geographical Society* 27 (1857): 303–4.

55. MacDonald, *British Columbia*, 160.

56. See, for example, Sproat, *Scenes and Studies*, 272; MacDonald, *British Columbia*, 132, *British Columbian*, 2 December 1865.

57. J.W. Boddam-Wetham, *Western Wanderings: A Record of Travel in the Evening Land* (London: R. Bentley and Son, 1874), 287.

58. MacDonald, *British Columbia*, 125.

59. *The Times*, 5 August 1858; *British Colonist*, 3 June 1859.

60. See, for example, John Domer, *New British Gold Fields: A Guide to British Columbia and Vancouver Island* . . . (London: W.H. Angel, n.d.), 24.

61. John Emmerson, *British Columbia and Vancouver Island: Voyages, Travels and Adventures* (Durham: W. Ainsley, 1865), 51–52.

62. Macfie, *Vancouver Island*, 431; Mayne, *Four Years in British Columbia*, 258–60; MacDonald, *British Columbia*, 156.

63. Newton H. Chittenden, *Official Report of the Queen Charlotte Islands for the Government of British Columbia* (Victoria: Printed by Authority of the Government, 1884), 19; Mayne, *Four Years in British Columbia*, 259.

64. Grant, "Description," 296, 308–10; Chittenden, *Official Report*, 18.

65. MacDonald, *British Columbia*, 70; Grant, "Description," 296; Barrett-Lennard, *Travels*, 41.

66. Chittenden, *Official Report*, 14.

67. W.C. Grant, "Remarks on Vancouver Island, Principally Concerning Townsites and Native Population," *Journal of the Royal Geographical Society* 31 (1861): 211.

68. Sproat to Philip Vankoughnet, deputy superintendent general of Indian affairs, 26 November 1879, and Sproat to superintendent general of Indian Affairs, 9 January 1878, Department of Indian Affairs, Black Series, Western Canada, RG 10, vol. 3612, file 3756, and vol. 3657, file 9193, Public Archives of Canada.

69. Macfie, *Vancouver Island*, 484–85.

70. William Henry Hills, Journal, 7 May 1853, "Journal on Board H.M.S. *Portland* and *Virago* 8 August 1852–8 July 1853," UBCL.

71. Brown, "Journal of the V[ancouver] I[sland] Exploring Expedition," 10 June 1864.

72. Ball to colonial secretary, 2 May 1860, British Columbia, Gold Commissioner, Lytton, Correspondence Outward, 1859–1870, PABC; see also The Bishop of Columbia, *A Tour of British Columbia* (London: Clay Printers, 1861), 18.

73. Richard Charles Mayne, Journal, 5 April 1860, "Journal of Admiral Richard Charles Mayne, 1857–1860," PABC; Robin W. Winks, *The Blacks in Canada: A History* (Montreal: Yale University Press, 1971), 278.

74. Barrett-Lennard, *Travels*, 44-45; Morison, "Reminiscences," 58.

75. John Domer, *New British Gold Fields: A Guide to British Columbia and Vancouver Island* . . . (London: W.H. Angel, n.d.), 24; William Carewe Hazlitt, *British Columbia and Vancouver Island* . . . (London: G. Routledge and Co., 1858), 187; Grant, "Description," 301; and MacDonald, *British Columbia*, 153. Grant claimed that the Indians "pass the greater portion of their time in a sort of torpid state, lying beside their fires," and the assertion was repeated by MacDonald in almost identical words.

76. Boas, "Diary," 6 September 1866, 54.

77. Gilbert Malcolm Sproat, "The West Coast Indians in Vancouver Island," *Transactions of the Ethnological Society of London* n.s. 5 (1867): 253; see also H. Spencer Palmer, *Report of a Journey from Victoria to Fort Alexandria via Bentinck Arm* (New Westminister: Royal Engineer Press, 1863), 7.

78. J. Russell Harper, *Paul Kane's Frontier Including "Wanderings of an Artist among the Indians of North America" by Paul Kane* (Austin: University of Texas Press, 1971), 108.

79. See Mason, *Patterns of Dominance*, 199; Peter Loewenberg, "The Psychology of Racism," in *The Great Fear: Race in the Mind of America*, ed. Gary B. Nash and Richard Weiss (New York: Holt, Rinehart and Winston, 1970), 187.

80. Duncan, Journal, 17 February 1858, William Duncan Papers, C.2154, UBCL.

81. See, for example [Church Missionary Society], *Metlahkatla: Ten Years' Work Among the Tsimsheean Indians* (London: Church Missionary Society, 1869), 16–17; [Eugene Stock], *Metlakahtla and the North Pacific Mission of the Church Missionary Society* (London: Church Missionary House, 1881), 19; and Mayne, *Four Years in British Columbia*, 285.

82. *Christian Guardian*, 6 April 1859; *Church Missionary Intelligencer*, July 1856, 167.

83. Roy Harvey Pearce, *The Savages of America: A Study of the Indian and the Idea of Civilization* (Baltimore: Johns Hopkins Press, 1965), 4–6, 48–49.

84. Emmerson, *British Columbia*, 35.

85. Mason, *Patterns of Dominance*, 35.

86. N. de Bertrand Lugrin, *The Pioneer Women of Vancouver Island 1843–1866* (Victoria: Women's Canadian Club, 1928), 77.

87. Mason, *Patterns of Dominance*, 35.

88. Louis Hartz has argued that fragment cultures "heighten consensus by shrinking the European social universe" (Hartz, "A Comparative Study of Fragment Cultures," in *Violence in America: Historical and Comparative Perspectives*, ed. Hugh Davis Graham and Ted Robert Gurr (New York: Bantam Books, 1969), 107). In Vancouver Island and British Columbia humanitarianism, which tended to militate against overt racism, was not as well developed as it was in the parent society; there was therefore a greater proportion of people of like mind in relation to the Indians than there was in Britain.

CANADA'S SUBJUGATION OF THE PLAINS CREE, 1879–1885†

JOHN L. TOBIAS

One of the most persistent myths that Canadian historians perpetuate is that of the honourable and just policy Canada followed in dealing with the Plains Indians. First enunciated in the Canadian expansionist literature of the 1870s as a means to emphasize the distinctive Canadian approach to and the unique character of the Canadian West,[1] it has been given credence by G.F.G. Stanley in his classic *The Birth of Western Canada*,[2] and by all those who use Stanley's work as the standard interpretation of Canada's relationship with the Plains Indians in the period 1870–85. Thus students are taught that the Canadian government was paternalistic and far-sighted in offering the Indians a means to become civilized and assimilated into white society by the reserve system, and honest and fair-minded in honouring legal commitments made in the treaties.[3] The Plains Indians, and particularly the Plains Cree, are said to be a primitive people adhering to an inflexible system of tradition and custom, seeking to protect themselves against the advance of civilization, and taking up arms in rejection of the reserve system and an agricultural way of life.[4] This traditional interpretation distorts the roles of both the Cree and the Canadian government, for the Cree were both flexible and active in promoting their own interests, and willing to accommodate themselves to a new way of life, while the Canadian government was neither as far-sighted nor as just as tradition maintains. Canada's principal concern in its relationship with the Plains Cree was to establish control over them, and Canadian authorities were willing to and did wage war upon the Cree in order to achieve this control.

Those who propagate the myth would have us believe that Canada began to negotiate treaties with the Indians of the West in 1871 as part of an overall plan to develop the agricultural potential of the West, open the land for railway construction, and bind the prairies to Canada in a network of commercial and economic ties. Although there is an element of truth to these statements, the fact remains that in 1871 Canada had no plan on how to deal with the Indians and the negotiation of treaties was not at the initiative of the Canadian government, but at the insistence of the Ojibwa Indians of the North-West Angle and the Saulteaux of the tiny province of Manitoba. What is ignored by the traditional interpretation is that the treaty process only started after Yellow Quill's band of Saulteaux turned back settlers who tried to go west of Portage la Prairie, and after other Saulteaux leaders insisted upon enforcement of the Selkirk Treaty or, more often, insisted upon making a new treaty. Also ignored is the fact that the Ojibwa of the North-West Angle demanded rents, and created the fear of violence against prospective settlers who crossed their land or made use of their territory, if Ojibwa rights to their lands were not recognized. This pressure and fear of resulting violence is what motivated the government to begin the treaty-making process.[5]

Canada's initial offer to the Saulteaux and Ojibwa Indians consisted only of reserves and a small cash annuity. This proposal was rejected by the Ojibwa in 1871 and again in 1872, while the Saulteaux demanded, much to Treaty Commissioner Wemyss Simpson's chagrin, farm animals, horses, wagons, and farm tools and equipment. Simpson did not include these demands in the written treaty, for he had no authority to do so, but he wrote them down in the form of a memorandum that he entitled "outside promises" and which he failed to send to Ottawa. Thus, the original Treaties 1 and 2 did not include those items the Saulteaux said had to be part of a treaty before they would agree to surrender their lands. Only in 1874, after the Indian leaders of Manitoba became irate over non-receipt of the goods that Simpson had promised them, was an inquiry launched, and Simpson's list of "outside promises" discovered and incorporated in renegotiated treaties in 1875.[6] It was only in 1873, after the Ojibwa of the North-West Angle had twice refused treaties that only included reserves and annuities, that the government agreed to include the domestic animals, farm tools, and equipment that the Ojibwa demanded. After this experience Canada made such goods a standard part of later treaties.[7]

Just as it was pressure from the Indians of Manitoba that forced the government of Canada to initiate the treaty process, it was pressure from the Plains Cree in the period 1872–75 that compelled the government of Canada to continue the process with the Indians of the Qu'Appelle and Saskatchewan districts. The Plains Cree had interfered with the geological survey and prevented the construction of telegraph lines through their territory to emphasize that Canada had to deal with the Cree for Cree lands.[8] The Cree had learned in 1870 about Canada's claim to their lands, and not wanting to experience what had happened to the Indians in the United States when those people were faced with an expansionist government, the Cree made clear that they would not allow settlement or use of their lands until Cree rights had been clearly recognized. They also made clear that part of any arrangement for Cree lands had to involve assistance to the Cree in developing a new agricultural way of life.[9]

In adopting this position, the Cree were simply demonstrating a skill that they had shown since their initial contact with Europeans in 1670. On numerous occasions during the fur trade era, they had adapted to changed environmental and economic circumstances, beginning first as hunters, then as provisioners and middlemen in the Hudson's Bay Company trading system, and finally adapting from a woodland to parkland–prairie buffalo hunting culture to retain their independence and their desired ties with the fur trade.[10] Having accommodated themselves to the Plains Indian culture after 1800, they expanded into territory formerly controlled by the Atsina, and as the buffalo herds began to decline after 1850, the Cree expanded into Blackfoot territory.[11] Expansion was one response to the threat posed by declining buffalo herds; another was that some Plains Cree bands began to turn to agriculture.[12] Thus, when the Cree learned that Canada claimed their lands, part of the arrangement they were determined to make and succeeded in making was to receive assistance in adapting to an agricultural way of life. So successful were they in negotiating such assistance that when the Mackenzie government received a copy of Treaty 6 in 1876 it accepted the treaty only after expressing a protest concerning the too-generous terms granted to the Cree.[13]

While willing to explore the alternative of agriculture, three Cree leaders in the 1870s sought means to guarantee preservation of the buffalo-hunting culture as long as possible. Piapot (leader of the Cree-Assiniboine of the region south of the Qu'Appelle River), and Big Bear and Little Pine (leaders of two of the largest Cree bands from the Saskatchewan River district) led what has been called an armed migration of the Cree into the Cypress Hills in the latter 1860s. All three men were noted warriors and Big Bear and Piapot were noted religious leaders, but their prowess was not enough to prevent a Cree defeat at the Battle of the Belly River in 1870,[14] and as a result they explored the alternative of dealing with the government of Canada, but in a manner to extract guarantees for the preservation of Cree autonomy. They were determined to get the government to promise to limit the buffalo hunt to the Indians—a goal that Cree leaders had been advocating since the 1850s.[15] When Big Bear met with Treaty Commissioner Alexander Morris at Fort Pitt in September 1876, he extracted a promise from Morris that non-Indian hunting of the buffalo would be regulated.[16]

Big Bear refused to take treaty in 1876, despite receiving Morris's assurances about the regulation of the hunt. Little Pine and Piapot also did not take treaty when the treaty commissions first came to deal with the Cree. Oral tradition among the Cree maintains that all three leaders wished to see how faithful the government would be in honouring the treaties,[17] but equally important for all three leaders was their belief that the treaties were inadequate and that revisions were necessary. Piapot thought Treaty 4 (the Qu'Appelle Treaty) needed to be expanded to include increased farm equipment and tools, and to stipulate that the government had to provide mills, blacksmith and carpentry shops and tools, and instructors in farming and the trades. Only after receiving assurances that Ottawa would consider these requests did Piapot take treaty in 1875.[18] Big Bear and Little Pine objected to Treaty 6 (Fort Pitt and Carlton) because Commissioner Morris had made clear that in taking treaty the Cree would be bound by Canadian law. To accept the treaties would mean being subject to an external authority of which the Crees had little knowledge and upon which they had little influence. Neither Big Bear nor Little Pine would countenance such a loss of autonomy.

Big Bear had raised the matter of Cree autonomy at Fort Pitt in 1876 when he met Commissioner Morris. At that time Big Bear said: "I will make a request that he [Morris] save me from what I most dread, that is the rope about my neck. . . . It was not given to us to have the rope about our neck."[19] Morris and most subsequent historians have interpreted Big Bear's statements to be a specific reference to hanging, but such an interpretation ignores the fact that Big Bear, like most Indian leaders, often used a metaphor to emphasize a point. In 1875, he had made the same point by using a different metaphor when he spoke to messengers informing him that a treaty commission was to meet with the Cree in 1876. At that time Big Bear said: "We want none of the Queen's presents: when we set a foxtrap we scatter pieces of meat all around, but when the fox gets into the trap we knock him on the head; we want no bait. . . . "[20] A more accurate interpretation of Big Bear's words to Morris in 1876 is that he feared being controlled or "enslaved," just as an animal is controlled when it has a rope around its neck.[21] In 1877, when meeting with Lieutenant-Governor David Laird, Little Pine also stated that he would not take treaty because he saw the treaties as a means by which the government could "enslave" his people.[22]

The importance of these three leaders cannot be underestimated, for they had with them in the Cypress Hills more than 50 percent of the total Indian population of the Treaty 4 and 6 areas. By concentrating in such numbers in the last buffalo ranges in Canadian territory, the Cree were free from all external interference, whether by other Indian nations or by the agents of the Canadian government — the North-West Mounted Police.[23] Recognizing that these men were bargaining from a position of strength, Laird recommended in 1878 that the government act quickly to establish reserves and honour the treaties. He was aware that the Cypress Hills leaders had the support of many of the Cree in treaty, and that many of the Cree leaders were complaining that the government was not providing the farming assistance promised. As the number of these complaints increased, so did Cree support for Big Bear and Little Pine.[24]

The Cree were concerned not only about the lack of assistance to farm, but when Canadian officials were slow to take action to regulate the buffalo hunt, Big Bear, Piapot, and Little Pine met with Blackfoot leaders and with Sitting Bull of the Teton Sioux in an attempt to reach agreement among the Indian nations on the need to regulate buffalo hunting.[25] These councils were also the forum where Indian leaders discussed the need to revise the treaties. On learning about the Indian council, the non-Indian populace of the West grew anxious, fearing establishment of an Indian confederacy which would wage war if Indian demands were rejected.[26] However, an Indian confederacy did not result from these meetings, nor was agreement reached on how the buffalo were to be preserved, because the Cree, Sioux, and Blackfoot could not overcome their old animosities towards one another.[27]

When in 1879 the buffalo disappeared from the Canadian prairies and Big Bear and Little Pine took their bands south to the buffalo ranges on the Milk and Missouri rivers, most of the other Cree and Assiniboine bands also went with them. The Cree who remained in Canada faced starvation while awaiting the survey of their reserves and the farming equipment that had been promised. Realizing that many of the Cree were dying, the government decided that those who had taken treaty should be given rations. As well, the government appointed Edgar Dewdney to the newly-created position of Commissioner of Indian Affairs for the North-West Territory; a farming policy for the western reserves was introduced; a survey of Cree reserves was begun; and twelve farming instructors were appointed to teach the Indians of the North-West.[28]

The new Indian Commissioner quickly sought to use rations as a means of getting control over the Cree. In the fall of 1879 he announced that rations were to be provided only to Indians who had taken treaty. To get the Cree into treaty more easily and to reduce the influence of recalcitrant leaders, Dewdney announced that he would adopt an old Hudson's Bay Company practice of recognizing any adult male Cree as chief of a new band if he could induce one hundred or more persons to recognize him as leader. He expected that the starving Cypress Hills Cree would desert their old leaders to get rations. As a means of demonstrating Canada's control over the Cree, Dewdney ordered that only the sick, aged, and orphans should receive rations without providing some service to one of the government agencies in the West.[29]

Dewdney's policies seemed to work, for when the Cree and Assiniboine who had gone to hunt in Montana returned starving, their resolve weakened. Little Pine's people convinced their chief to take treaty in 1879, but when Big Bear refused to do the same, almost half of his following joined Lucky Man or Thunderchild to form new bands in order to receive rations.[30]

Taking treaty to avoid starvation did not mean that the Cree had come to accept the treaties as written; rather they altered their tactics in seeking revisions. Believing that small reserves were more susceptible to the control of the Canadian government and its officials, Big Bear, Piapot, and Little Pine sought to effect a concentration of the Cree people in an Indian territory similar to the reservation system in the United States. In such a territory the Cree would be able to preserve their autonomy, or at least limit the ability of others to control them; they would be better able to take concerted action on matters of importance to them.[31]

Soon after taking treaty Little Pine applied for a reserve in the Cypress Hills, twenty-seven miles north-east of the North-West Mounted Police post of Fort Walsh. Piapot requested a reserve next to Little Pine's, while ten other bands, including most of the Assiniboine nations, selected reserve sites contiguous to either Little Pine's or Piapot's and to one another.[32] If all these reserve sites were granted, and if Big Bear were to take treaty and settle in the Cypress Hills, the result would be the concentration of much of the Cree nation and the creation of an Indian territory that would comprise most of what is now south-western Saskatchewan.

Unaware of the intention of the Cree and Assiniboine leaders, Canadian officials in the spring of 1880 agreed to the establishment of a reserve for all the Canadian Assiniboine and reserves in the Cypress Hills for each of the Cree bands that wished them. In 1880, the Assiniboine reserve was surveyed, but the other Indian leaders were told that their reserves would not be surveyed until the following year.[33] In the interim, most of the Cree went to the buffalo ranges in Montana.

The Cree effort to exploit the remaining American buffalo ranges caused them much trouble. The Crow, the Peigan, and other Indian nations with reservations in Montana were upset by competition for the scarce food resource, and these people threatened to break the treaties they had made with the American government and to wage war on the Cree if the American authorities did not protect the Indian hunting ranges. These threats were renewed when the Cree began to steal horses from the Crow and Peigan. To add to their difficulties, American ranchers accused the Cree of killing range cattle. American officials, not wishing trouble with their Indians and wishing to placate the ranchers, informed the Cree that they would have to return to Canada. Most Cree bands, aware that if they did not leave voluntarily the American government would use troops to force them to move north, returned to the Cypress Hills.[34]

They returned to find that Canadian officials were now aware of the dangers to their authority posed by a concentration of the Cree. A riot at Fort Walsh in 1880, which the police were powerless to prevent or control, assaults on farming instructors who refused to provide rations to starving Indians, and rumours that the Cree were planning a grand Indian council to discuss treaty revisions in 1881 all caused the Indian Commissioner much concern.[35] To avoid further difficulties over rations, in late 1880 Dewdney ordered that all Indians requesting rations be given them, regardless of whether the supplicant was in treaty.[36] There was little that the government could do at this time about the proposed Indian council or the concentration of Cree in the Cypress Hills.

In the spring of 1881, Cree bands from all regions of the Canadian prairies left their reserves to go south to meet with Little Pine and Big Bear. Even the new bands Dewdney had created were going to the council in American territory. What was also disconcerting to Canadian officials were the reports that Big Bear and Little Pine, who had gone to Montana to prepare for the council, had reached an accommodation with the Blackfoot and had participated in a joint raid on the Crow. To all appearances the Blackfoot, the Indian confederacy the Canadian government most feared, would be part of the Indian council.[37]

The Indian council was not held because the raid on the Crow led American officials to intervene militarily to force the Cree to return to Canada. With Montana stockmen acting as militia units, the American army prevented most Cree and Assiniboine bands from entering the United States. As well, the American forces seized horses, guns, and carts, and escorted the Cree to Canada.[38] The Cree–Blackfoot alliance did not materialize, for soon after the raid on the Crow, young Cree warriors stole horses from the Blackfoot and thereby destroyed the accord that Little Pine and Big Bear were attempting to create.[39]

The actions of the American military in 1881 were extremely beneficial to Canada. Not only did the Americans prevent the holding of the Indian council, but by confiscating the guns and horses of the Cree, the Americans had dispossessed the Cree of the ability to resist whatever measures the Canadian authorities wished to take against them. The Canadian authorities also benefited from Governor-General Lorne's tour of the West in 1881, for many of the Cree bands that had gone to the Cypress Hills in the spring went north in late summer to meet Lorne to impress upon him the inadequacy of the treaties and the need to revise them.[40] Thus, Lorne's tour prevented the concentration of most of the Cree nation in the Cypress Hills.

The threat posed to Canadian authority in the North-West by concentration of the Cree was clearly recognized by Dewdney and other Canadian officials in late 1881. They saw how the Cree had forced officials to placate them and to ignore their orders in 1880 and 1881. This convinced both Dewdney and Ottawa that the Cree request for contiguous reserves in the Cypress Hills could not be granted. Dewdney recognized that to grant the Cree requests would be to create an Indian territory, for most of the Cree who had reserves further north would come to the Cypress Hills and request reserves contiguous to those of the Cypress Hills Cree. This would result in so large a concentration of Cree that the only way Canada could enforce its laws on them would be via a military campaign. To prevent this, Dewdney recommended a sizeable expansion of the Mounted Police force and the closure of Fort Walsh and all government facilities in the Cypress Hills. This action would remove all sources of sustenance from the Cree in the Cypress Hills. Dewdney hoped that starvation would drive them from the Fort Walsh area and thus end the concentration of their force.[41]

Dewdney decided to take these steps fully aware that what he was doing was a violation not only of the promises made to the Cypress Hills Indians in 1880 and 1881, but also that by refusing to grant reserves on the sites the Indians had selected, he was violating the promises made to the Cree by the Treaty Commissions in 1874 and 1876, and in the written treaties. Nevertheless, Dewdney believed that to accede to the Cree requests would be to grant the Cree de facto autonomy from Canadian control, which would result in the perpetuation and heightening of the 1880–81 crisis. Rather than see that situation continue, Dewdney wanted to exploit the opportunity presented to him by the hunger crisis and disarmament of the Cree to bring them under the government's control, even if it meant violating the treaties.[42]

In the spring of 1882 the Cree and Assiniboine were told that no further rations would be issued to them while they remained in the Cypress Hills. Only if the Indians moved north to Qu'Appelle, Battleford, and Fort Pitt were they to be given assistance, and at those locations only treaty Indians were to be aided. The Mounted Police were ordered to stop issuing rations at Fort Walsh and the Indian Department farm that had been located near Fort Walsh was closed. Faced with the prospect of starvation, without weapons or transport to get to the Montana buffalo ranges, and knowing that if they were to try to go south the Mounted Police would inform the American military authorities, many Cree and all the Assiniboine decided to go north.[43] Even Big Bear discovered that his people wanted him to take treaty and move north. In 1882, after taking treaty, he, along with Piapot and Little Pine, promised to leave the Cypress Hills.[44]

Only Piapot kept his promise and even he did not remain long at Fort Qu'Appelle. By late summer of 1882, Piapot was back in the Cypress Hills complaining about how he had been mistreated at Qu'Appelle, and making the Cree aware of how they could lose their autonomy if the government could deal with them as individual bands.[45] On hearing this report, the other Cree leaders refused to leave the Fort Walsh region and insisted upon receiving the reserves promised them in 1880 and 1881. North-West Mounted Police Commissioner Irvine feared a repetition of the incidents of 1880 if he refused to feed the Cree and believed that the hungry Cree would harass the construction crews of the Canadian Pacific Railway for food, which would lead to confrontation between whites and Indians which the police would be unable to handle and which in turn might lead to an Indian war. Therefore Irvine decided to feed the Cree.[46]

Dewdney and Ottawa were upset by Irvine's actions. Ottawa gave specific instructions to close Fort Walsh in the spring of 1883. When Irvine closed the fort, the Cree faced starvation. As it was quite evident that they could not go to the United States, and as they would not receive reserves in the Cypress Hills, the Cree moved north. Piapot moved to Indian Head and selected a reserve site next to the huge reserve set aside for the Assiniboine. Little Pine and Lucky Man moved to Battleford and selected reserve sites next to Poundmaker's reserve. Big Bear went to Fort Pitt.

The move to the north was not a sign of the Cree acceptance of the treaties as written, nor of their acceptance of the authority of the Canadian government. Big Bear, Little Pine, and Piapot were aware that the other Cree chiefs were dissatisfied with the treaties, and were also aware that if they could effect concentration of the Cree in the north they would be able to preserve their autonomy, just as they had done in the Cypress Hills in the 1879–81 period. Therefore, the move to the north was simply a tactical move, for no sooner were these chiefs in the north than they once again sought to effect a concentration of their people.

By moving to Indian Head, Piapot had effected a concentration of more than 2 000 Indians. This number threatened to grow larger if the council he planned to hold with all the Treaty 4 bands to discuss treaty revisions were successful. Commissioner Dewdney, fearing the results of such a meeting in 1883, was able to thwart Piapot by threatening to cut off rations to any Indians attending Piapot's council and by threatening to arrest Piapot and depose any chiefs who did meet with him. Although Dewdney, in 1883, prevented Piapot holding a large council by such actions, Piapot was able to get the Treaty 4 chiefs to agree to meet in the late spring of 1884 for a thirst dance and council on Pasquah's Reserve, near Fort Qu'Appelle.[47]

While Piapot was organizing an Indian council in the Treaty 4 area, Big Bear and Little Pine were doing the same for the Treaty 6 region. Little Pine and Lucky Man attempted to effect a concentration of more than 2 000 Cree on contiguous reserves in the Battleford district, by requesting reserves next to Poundmaker, whose reserve was next to three other Cree reserves, which in turn were only a short distance from three Assiniboine reserves. Another 500 Cree would have been located in the Battleford area if Big Bear's request for a reserve next to Little Pine's site had been granted. Only with difficulty was Dewdney able to get Big Bear to move to Fort Pitt.[48] However, he was unable to prevent Big Bear and Little Pine from sending messengers to the Cree leaders of the

Edmonton, Carlton, and Duck Lake districts to enlist their support for the movement to concentrate the Cree.[49]

Dewdney was convinced that the activities of Big Bear, Piapot, and Little Pine were a prelude to a major project the Cree planned for the following year, 1884. He was also aware that his ability to deal with the impending problem was severely limited by decisions taken in Ottawa. The Deputy Superintendent-General of Indian Affairs, Lawrence Vankoughnet, was concerned about the cost of administering Dewdney's policies, and he ordered reductions in the level of assistance provided to the Cree and in the number of employees working with the Cree.[50] In making these decisions, Ottawa effectively deprived Dewdney of his major sources of intelligence about the Cree and their plans. It also deprived Dewdney of a major instrument in placating the Cree — the distribution of rations to those bands which co-operated.

Vankoughnet's economy measures led to further alienation of the Cree. In some areas, notably in the Fort Pitt, Edmonton, and Crooked Lakes regions, farming instructors were assaulted and government storehouses broken into when Indians were denied rations. The incident on the Sakemay Reserve in the Crooked Lakes area was quite serious, for when the police were called upon to arrest those guilty of the assault, they were surrounded and threatened with death if they carried out their orders. Only after Assistant Indian Commissioner Hayter Reed had agreed to restore assistance to the Sakemay band to the 1883 level and had promised not to imprison the accused were the police allowed to leave with their prisoners.[51]

The violence that followed the reductions in rations convinced Dewdney that starving the Cree into submission was not the means to control them. He wanted to use coercion, but this required an expansion of the number of police in the West. Therefore, he recommended that more men be recruited for the Mounted Police. In addition, Dewdney wanted to ensure that jail sentences were given to arrested Indians so that they would cause no further problems. Having seen the effects of incarceration on Indians, Dewdney was convinced that this was the means to bring the Cree leaders under control. However, what was needed in his opinion were trial judges who "understood" Indian nature at first hand and who would take effective action to keep the Indians under control. Therefore, Dewdney wanted all Indian Department officials in the West to be appointed stipendiary magistrates in order that all Indian troublemakers could be brought to "justice" quickly. As Dewdney stated in his letter to Prime Minister John A. Macdonald: "The only effective course with the great proportion [of Indian bands] to adopt is one of sheer compulsion. . . ."[52]

Dewdney used the policy of "sheer compulsion" for only a few months in 1884. He found that his efforts to use the Mounted Police to break up the Indian councils and to arrest Indian leaders only led to confrontations between the Cree and the police. In these confrontations the police were shown to be ineffectual because they were placed in situations in which, if the Cree had been desirous of initiating hostilities, large numbers of Mounted Police would have been massacred.

The first incident which called the policy of compulsion into question was the attempt to prevent Piapot from holding his thirst dance and council in May 1884. Assistant Commissioner Hayter Reed, fearing that the council would result in a concentration of all the Treaty 4 bands, ordered Police Commissioner Irvine to prevent Piapot from attending the council. Irvine was to arrest the chief at the first sign of any violation of even the most minor law. To be certain that Piapot broke a law, Reed promised to have an individual from Pasquah's reserve object to the council being held on that reserve in order that the accusation of trespass could be used to break up the meeting, which all the bands from Treaty 4 were attending.[53]

With a force of fifty-six men and a seven-pounder gun, Irvine caught up with Piapot shortly before the chief reached Pasquah's reserve. Irvine and the police entered the Indian camp at 2 A.M., hoping to arrest Piapot and remove him from the camp before his band was aware of what happened. However, when they entered the camp, the police found themselves surrounded by armed warriors. Realizing that any attempt to arrest the chief would result in a battle, Irvine decided to hold his own council with Piapot and Reed. This impromptu council agreed that Piapot should receive a new reserve next to Pasquah, in return for which Piapot would return to Indian Head temporarily.[54]

The agreement reached between Piapot and Irvine and Reed was a victory for Piapot. By getting a reserve at Qu'Appelle again, Piapot had approximately 2 000 Cree concentrated on the Qu'Appelle River, and he was able to hold his council and thirst dance, for after going to Indian Head, he immediately turned around and went to Pasquah's. Reed and Irvine were aware of Piapot's ruse, but did nothing to prevent his holding the council, for they were aware that the Cree at Qu'Appelle were prepared to protect Piapot from what the Indians regarded as an attack on their leader. Realizing the effect that an Indian war would have on possible settlement, and that the police were inadequate for such a clash, the Canadian officials wished to avoid giving cause for violent reaction by the Cree.[55] Piapot acted as he did because he realized that if any blood were shed the Cree would experience a fate similar to that of the Nez Percés, Blackfoot, and Dakota Sioux in those peoples' conflicts with the United States.

Dewdney and the police were to have a similar experience when they attempted to prevent Big Bear from holding a thirst dance and council at Poundmaker's reserve in June 1884. Dewdney feared that Big Bear's council, to which the old chief had invited the Blackfoot and all the Indians from Treaty 6, would result in a larger concentration of Cree than Little Pine had already effected at Battleford. Dewdney also believed that he had to undo what Little Pine had accomplished, and refused to grant Little Pine and Lucky Man the reserve sites they had requested next to Poundmaker. Big Bear was again told that he would not be granted a reserve in the Battleford district. Dewdney believed that the Cree chiefs would ignore his order to select reserve sites at some distance from Battleford, and that this could be used as a reason for arresting them. To legitimize such actions on his part, Dewdney asked the government to pass an order-in-council to make it a criminal offence for a band to refuse to move to a reserve site the Commissioner suggested.[56] In order to avoid violence when he attempted to prevent Big Bear's council and ordered the arrests of Lucky Man and Little Pine, Dewdney instructed the Indian agents at Battleford and Fort Pitt to purchase all the horses, guns, and cartridges the Cree possessed. He increased the size of the police garrison at Battleford and ordered the police to prevent Big Bear from reaching Battleford.[57]

All Dewdney's efforts had little effect, for Big Bear and his band eluded the police, reached Battleford, and held their thirst dance. The Cree refused to sell their arms, and even the effort to break up the gathering by refusing to provide rations had no result other than to provoke another assault on a farm instructor on 17 June 1884. When the police sought to arrest the farm instructor's assailant, they were intimidated into leaving without a prisoner. When a larger police detachment went to the reserve on 18 June, the police were still unable to make an arrest for fear of provoking armed hostilities. Only on 20 June, when the thirst dance had concluded, were the police able to arrest the accused and only then by forcibly removing him from the Cree camp. This was done with the greatest difficulty for the police were jostled and provoked in an effort to get them to fire on the Cree. That no violence occurred, Superintendent Crozier, in charge of the police detachment, attributed to the discipline of his men and to the actions of Little Pine and Big Bear, who did all that was humanly possible to discourage any attack on the police.[58]

The events at Battleford frightened all parties involved in the confrontation. Big Bear was very much disturbed by them, for he did not want war, as he had made abundantly clear to Dewdney in March 1884, and again to the Indian agent at Battleford, J.A. Rae, in June. However, he did want the treaties revised and establishment of an Indian territory.[59] Agent Rae was thoroughly frightened and wanted Dewdney and Ottawa to adopt a more coercive policy designed to subjugate the Cree. Superintendent Crozier argued for a less coercive policy, for unless some accommodation were reached with the Cree, Crozier believed that out of desperation they would resort to violence.[60]

On hearing of the events of May and June 1884, Ottawa decided that Dewdney, who was now Lieutenant-Governor in addition to being

Indian Commissioner, was to have complete control over Indian affairs in the North-West Territories. As well, the Prime Minister informed Dewdney that more police were being recruited for duty in the West and that the Indian Act was being amended to permit Dewdney to arrest any Indian who was on another band's reserve without the permission of the local Indian Department official.[61] Dewdney was thus being given the instruments to make his policy of compulsion effective.

Dewdney did not, however, immediately make use of his new powers. He still intended to prevent concentration of the Cree, and rejected the requests Big Bear, Poundmaker, Lucky Man, and others made for a reserve at Buffalo Lake, and later rejected Big Bear's, Little Pine's, and Lucky Man's renewed requests for reserves next to Poundmaker's.[62] However, rather than following a purely coercive policy, Dewdney adopted a policy of rewards and punishments. He provided more rations, farming equipment, oxen, ammunition, and twine, and arranged for selected Cree chiefs to visit Winnipeg and other large centres of Canadian settlement. If the Cree were not satisfied with his new approach, he would use force against them. To implement this new policy, Dewdney increased the number of Indian Department employees working on the Cree reserves, for he wanted to monitor closely the behaviour of the Indians, and, if necessary, to arrest troublesome leaders.[63]

While Dewdney was implementing his new policy, the Cree leaders continued their efforts to concentrate the Cree in an exclusively Indian territory. Little Pine went south to seek Blackfoot support for the movement.[64] Big Bear, Lucky Man, and Poundmaker went to Duck Lake for a council with the Cree leaders of the Lower Saskatchewan district. The Duck Lake council, attended by twelve bands, was initiated by Beardy and the chiefs of the Carlton District. Beardy, who acted as spokesman for the Carlton chiefs, had been relatively inactive in the Cree movements in the 1881–83 period. He, however, had been the most vehement critic of the government's failure to deliver the farm materials promised by the treaty commissioners. In the 1877–81 period, Beardy was a man of little influence in the Carlton area, but when Mistawasis and Ahtahka-koop, the principal Cree chiefs of the Carlton District came to share his views, Beardy's standing among the Carlton Cree rose dramatically.[65]

The Duck Lake Council, called by Cree leaders whom Dewdney thought were loyal and docile, and of which the Commissioner had no foreknowledge, was a cause of much concern. Especially vexing was the detailed list of violations of the treaty for which the Cree demanded redress from the government. The Cree charged that the treaty commissioners lied to them when they said that the Cree would be able to make a living from agriculture with the equipment provided for in the treaties. However, rather than provide all the farming goods, what the government did, according to the Cree, was to withhold many of the cattle and oxen; send inferior quality wagons, farm tools, and equipment;

and provide insufficient rations and clothes, and no medicine chest. The petition closed with the statement expressing the Cree sentiment that they had been deceived by "sweet promises" designed to cheat them of their heritage, and that unless their grievances were remedied by the summer of 1885, they would take whatever measures necessary, short of war, to get redress.[66]

Dewdney originally assumed, as did some newspapers across the West, that the Duck Lake Council was part of a plot by Louis Riel to foment an Indian and Metis rebellion. Dewdney's assumption was based on the fact that the Duck Lake Council was held a short time after Riel had returned to Canada. It was also known that Riel had attended it, and that he had advocated such an alliance and a resort to violence when he had met with the Cree in Montana in 1880.[67] Further investigation, however, made quite clear that Riel had little influence on the Cree. To allay the growing concern about the possibility of an Indian war, Dewdney had Hayter Reed issue a statement that nothing untoward was happening and that there was less danger of an Indian war in 1884 than there had been in 1881. Privately Dewdney admitted to Ottawa and his subordinates in the West that the situation was very serious.[68] After both he and Dewdney had met with Cree leaders throughout the West and after carefully assessing the situation, Hayter Reed stated that the government had nothing to fear from the Cree until the summer of 1885. What Reed and Dewdney expected at that time was a united Cree demand to renegotiate treaties.[69]

What Reed and Dewdney had learned on their tours of the Battleford, Edmonton, Carlton, and Qu'Appelle districts in the fall of 1884 was that Big Bear, Piapot, and Little Pine were on the verge of uniting the Cree to call for new treaties in which an Indian territory and greater autonomy for the Cree would be major provisions. In fact, throughout the summer and fall of 1884 Little Pine attempted, with limited success, to interest the leaders of the Blackfoot in joining the Cree movement for treaty revision. Little Pine had invited the Blackfoot to a joint council with the Cree leaders on Little Pine's reserve scheduled for the spring of 1885.[70] If the Blackfoot joined the Cree, Ottawa's ability to govern the Indians and control the West would be seriously jeopardized.

At the moment that the Cree movement seemed on the verge of success, Big Bear was losing control of his band. As he told the assembled chiefs at Duck Lake in the summer of 1884, his young men were listening to the warrior chief, Little Poplar, who was advocating killing government officials and Indian agents as a means of restoring Cree independence. Big Bear feared that if Little Poplar's course of action were adopted the Cree would fight an Indian war that they were certain to lose.[71]

Dewdney was aware of Little Poplar's growing influence on the young men of Big Bear's and the Battleford Assiniboine bands; however, he wished to wait until after January 1885 before taking any action, because after that date the new amendments to the Indian Act would be in effect. These amendments could be used to arrest and imprison Little Pine, Little Poplar, Big Bear, and Piapot, and thereby, Dewdney hoped, destroy the movements these chiefs led.[72] In anticipation of confrontations in 1885, Dewdney ordered that the guns and ammunition normally allotted to the Cree so they could hunt for food be withheld. In addition, Indian councils were prohibited, including the one scheduled for Duck Lake in the summer of 1885, to which all the Cree in Treaty 6 had been invited. Arrangements were made to place the Mounted Police at Battleford under Dewdney's command, and serious consideration was given to placing an artillery unit there also.[73]

To get improved intelligence, Dewdney hired more men to work as Indian agents with the Cree. These men were given broad discretionary powers and were to keep the Commissioner informed on Cree activities. As well, English-speaking mixed-bloods, many of whom had worked for the Hudson's Bay Company and had the confidence of the Cree, were hired as farm instructors. There would now be a farm instructor on each Cree reserve, with explicit instructions to keep the Indian Agent informed of what was happening on his reserve. Staff who had personality conflicts with any of the Cree leaders were either transferred or fired. Only Thomas Quinn, Indian Agent at Fort Pitt and his farming instructor, John Delaney, were not removed before March 1885, although both were slated for transfer.[74]

Dewdney found that his most important staffing move was the employment of Peter Ballendine, a former Hudson's Bay Company trader much trusted by the principal Cree leaders. Ballendine's job was to ingratiate himself with Big Bear and report on that chief's comings and goings. Ballendine won the confidence of Big Bear and reported upon how wrong Dewdney's earlier efforts to break up Big Bear's band had been. Because so many of Big Bear's original followers joined either Lucky Man, Thunderchild, or Little Pine's bands, Big Bear by 1884 was left with only the most recalcitrant opponents of the treaty. These individuals were only lukewarm in support of their chief's non-violent efforts to get the treaty revised. They favoured instead the course of action advocated by Little Poplar. Ballendine believed that the government could expect trouble from the Big Bear and Little Poplar bands. However, Ballendine emphasized that there was little danger of a Cree-Metis alliance, for the Cree were refusing to meet with the Metis, and were rejecting all entreaties from the Metis suggesting the two should make common cause. Instead the Cree, under the leadership of Big Bear, Beardy, and Little Pine, were planning their own council for the summer of 1885.[75]

Ballendine also developed a new source of information in Poundmaker, who was also acting as a police informer. It was from Poundmaker that Dewdney and the police learned that Little Pine was attempting to involve the Blackfoot in the summer of 1884, and wanted to do so in

January 1885, but was prevented from doing so because of temporary blindness — a possible sign of malnutrition from the hunger that most Cree experienced in the extremely harsh winter of 1884–85. Little Pine had sought to get Poundmaker to encourage Crowfoot to join the Cree movement but Poundmaker refused to aid Little Pine, and when Little Pine recovered from his blindness, he went south to meet with Crowfoot.[76]

While Little Pine met with Crowfoot, Big Bear was being challenged for the leadership of his band by his son Imases, also called Curly, and by one of his headmen, Wandering Spirit. These two men were spokesmen for the younger men of Big Bear's Band, and wanted to work with Little Poplar. In the winter of 1885, Little Poplar was journeying constantly between Pitt and Battleford enlisting support for his plan of action. Although Ballendine could not get precise information on Little Poplar's plans, he did report that by March 1885 Big Bear had asserted himself and that the influence of Imases and Wandering Spirit had seemed to wane.[77]

On the basis of these and similar reports, Dewdney and the police were convinced that, although a number of councils were expected in 1885, no violence was to be anticipated from the Cree. Nevertheless, Dewdney wished to prevent the Cree from holding their councils. His strategy was to make the Cree satisfied with the treaties. He therefore admitted in February 1885 that the government had violated the treaties and ordered delivery to the Cree of all goods the treaties had stipulated. In addition, he ordered a dramatic increase in their rations. If this failed to placate them he planned to arrest their leaders, use the police to keep the Cree on their reserves, and to depose any chief who attempted to attend an Indian council.[78]

Dewdney had the full support of Ottawa for his policy of arresting Cree leaders. The only reservations the Prime Minister expressed were that Dewdney have sufficient forces to make the arrests and that he provide enough evidence to justify the charges of incitement to an insurrection. Macdonald also volunteered to communicate with the stipendiary magistrates to assure their co-operation in imposing long prison terms for any Cree leader convicted of incitement.[79] Macdonald was willing to provide this assistance because Dewdney had earlier complained that he could not use preventive detention of Indian leaders because the magistrates "only look at the evidence and the crime committed when giving out sentences," rather than taking into consideration the nature of the man and the harm that he might do if he were released at an inopportune time.[80] All these preparations were complete when word reached Dewdney of the Metis clash with the Mounted Police at Duck Lake in March 1885.

The Riel Rebellion of 1885 provided Dewdney with a new instrument to make his coercive policy effective. The troops sent into the North-

West to suppress the Rebellion could be used to destroy the Cree movement for an Indian territory. The Cree themselves would provide the excuse Dewdney needed virtually to declare war on the bands and leaders who had led the Cree movement for treaty revision. During March 1885, the Cree did engage in some acts of violence that Dewdney chose to label acts of rebellion.

These acts were unrelated to the Cree movement for treaty revision. In fact, these acts that led to the subjugation of the Cree were committed by persons not involved with the Cree movement for autonomy. It is one of the ironic quirks of history that the leaders of the Cree movement had little or nothing to do with the events which would destroy that movement to which they had devoted ten years of their lives. Nevertheless, they would be held responsible for the actions of their desperate and hungry people. To heighten the irony, it was the Metis movement, from which the Cree had held aloof, which would give Dewdney the excuse to use military force to subjugate the Cree.

The Duck Lake clash coincided with a Cree Council on Sweetgrass Reserve. The council of the Battleford area Cree had been called to consider how they could press for increased rations. When word reached the Cree at Sweetgrass of the clash at Duck Lake, they felt that circumstances would make Indian Agent Rae willing to grant them more rations. Thus the Cree, taking their women and children with them to demonstrate their peaceful intent, set out for Battleford. Fear and panic prevailed at Battleford, for on learning of the Crees' approach, the town's citizens assumed that the Cree had thrown in their lot with the Metis. The town was evacuated; most townspeople took refuge in the Mounted Police post.[81]

When the Cree arrived at Battleford they found the town abandoned. They sent word to the police post that they wished to speak to the Indian Agent, who refused to leave the safety of the post. The Cree women, seeing the abandoned stores and houses filled with food, began to help themselves. Then, fearing arrest by the police, the Cree left town. On the way back to their reserves, as well as on their way to town, the Cree assisted a number of Indian Department employees and settlers to cross the Battle River to get to the police post, thus demonstrating the pacific nature of their intentions.[82]

Rather than returning to their individual reserves, the Cree went to Poundmaker's, for as the leader in the Battleford district to whom the government had shown much favour in the past, Poundmaker was seen as the man best able to explain to the government what had happened at Battleford. A second significant reason was the deaths of two prominent Cree leaders: Red Pheasant, the night before the Cree left for Battleford, and Little Pine, the night they returned. As it was the practice of the Cree to leave the place where their leaders had expired, both bands left their reserves and went to Poundmaker's, who, given the fears the whites had concerning a Cree and Metis alliance, might possibly defuse any crisis. Thus, in March 1885, Poundmaker became the spokesman of the Battleford Cree.[83]

No sooner were the Cree at Poundmaker's than they were joined by the local Assiniboine, who insisted that a soldier's (war) tent be erected, for events at the Assiniboine reserves convinced them that an attack on the Indian camp was imminent. The Assiniboine explained that when word had reached them of the Duck Lake fight, a few of their young men sought revenge on farming instructor James Payne, who was blamed for the death of a girl. The girl's male relatives killed Payne and murdered farmer Barney Tremont. The Assiniboine now assumed that the Canadian authorities would behave in a similar manner to the Americans and blame all Indians for the actions of a few individuals.[84]

Erection of the soldier's tent meant that the warriors were in control of the camp and that Poundmaker and the civil authorities had to defer to them. It was at this time that the Metis appeal for aid was received. The Cree refused to assist the Metis, although they expected an attack on their camp. Watches were set on the roads, and protection was offered to the Metis at Bresaylor for the settlers there had earned the enmity of the Batoche Metis. As long as no military or police forces came towards the Cree camp, the Cree remained on their reserves and did not interfere with anyone going to or leaving Battleford. The Mounted Police detachment from Fort Pitt and Colonel Otter's military unit arrived in Battleford without encountering any Indians. Nevertheless, reports from the police and local officials maintained that the town was under siege.[85]

While the Battleford Cree were preparing their defences, Big Bear's band was making trouble for itself. Big Bear was absent from his camp when the members of his band heard about the fight at Duck Lake. Wandering Spirit and Imases sought to use the opportunity presented by the Metis uprising to seek revenge for the insults and abuses perpetrated against the Cree by Indian Agent Thomas Quinn and Farming Instructor Delaney. Quinn had physically abused some of the Indian men, while Delaney had cuckolded others before he brought a white bride to Frog Lake in late 1884. Big Bear's headmen demanded that the two officials open the storehouse to the Cree, and when they refused to do so, they were murdered. This set off further acts of violence that resulted in the murder of all the white men in the camp save one.[86]

On his return to camp Big Bear ended further acts of violence. Although unable to prevent a minor skirmish between his young men and a small police patrol, he convinced his warriors to allow the police detachment at Fort Pitt to withdraw from the post without being attacked and to guarantee safety to the civilian residents of the Frog Lake and Fort Pitt regions. Big Bear then led his people north, where he hoped they would be out of harm's way and not engage in further acts of violence.[87]

Beardy also lost control of his band. He and the neighbouring One Arrow band had reserves next to Batoche. Before the clash with the police, the Metis had come to the One Arrow Reserve, captured Farming Instructor Peter Thompkins, and threatened the Cree band with destruction unless the Cree aided the Metis. Some of the younger men of One Arrow's band agreed to do so.[88] The Metis made the same threat against Beardy and his band, and although a few of his young men joined the Metis, Beardy and most of his people remained neutral.[89] It is doubtful that the Cree would have aided the Metis without the threat of violence. Earlier, the Cree of the Duck Lake region had threatened hostilities against the Metis, for the Metis had settled on One Arrow's Reserve and demanded that the government turn over to them some of One Arrow's Reserve. Ottawa, fearing the Metis more than the Cree in 1880, acquiesced. Over the next four years, one task of the local Indian Agent and the police was to reconcile the Cree with the Metis of the Batoche region.[90]

The Cree acts of violence in March 1885 were the excuse Dewdney needed to justify the use of troops against them. He maintained that the Battleford, Fort Pitt, and Duck Lake Cree were part of the Riel Rebellion. Privately, Dewdney reported to Ottawa that he saw the events at Battleford and Frog Lake as the acts of a desperate, starving people and unrelated to what the Metis were doing.[91] In fact, Dewdney had sought in late March to open negotiations with the Battleford Cree, but Rae refused to meet the Cree leaders. Subsequent efforts to open negotiations ended in failure because there was no way to get a message to Poundmaker, and after Colonel Otter's attack on the Cree camp any thought of negotiations was dropped.[92]

Publicly Dewdney proclaimed that the Cree were part of the Metis uprising. He issued a proclamation that any Indian who left his reserve was to be regarded as a rebel.[93] As well, to intimidate Piapot and the Treaty 4 Cree, Dewdney stationed troops on their reserves. To prevent an alliance of Blackfoot and Cree, Dewdney announced that he was stationing troops at Swift Current and Medicine Hat. Dewdney took these steps, as he confided to Macdonald, because he feared that the Cree might still attempt to take action on their own cause, and he was concerned because in the previous year the Cree had attempted to enlist the Blackfoot in the movement to revise the treaties.[94]

The military commander in the North-West, General F.D. Middleton, was not as concerned about the problems with the Cree. He wanted to concentrate his attention on the Metis. Although he did send troops under Colonel William Otter to Swift Current, he refused to order them to Battleford to lift the alleged siege until he received word of the Frog Lake massacre. Otter was then ordered to lift the "siege" and protect Battleford from Indian attack, but he was not to take the offensive. At the same time General Thomas Strange was ordered to bring Big Bear under control.

Otter reached Battleford without seeing an Indian. He was upset that he and his troops would not see action. He therefore proposed that he attack the Indian camp at Poundmaker's Reserve. Middleton vetoed the plan, but Dewdney welcomed it as a means to bring the Cree under government control. Taking the Lieutenant-Governor's approval to be paramount to Middleton's veto, Otter launched his attack. The engagement, known as the Battle of Cut Knife Hill, almost ended in total disaster for Otter's force. Only the Cree fear that they would suffer the same fate as Sitting Bull after the Battle of the Little Big Horn saved Otter's troops from total annihilation.[95]

The tale of the subsequent military campaigns against the Cree by Strange and Middleton and the voluntary surrenders of Poundmaker and Big Bear is found in detail in Stanley's *Birth of Western Canada* and Desmond Morton's *The Last War Drum*. With Big Bear and Poundmaker in custody, Dewdney prepared to use the courts in the manner he had planned before the Riel Rebellion. Both Cree leaders were charged with treason-felony, despite Dewdney's knowledge that neither man had engaged in an act of rebellion. Eyewitnesses to the events at Fort Pitt, Frog Lake, and Battleford all made clear that neither chief was involved in the murders and looting that had occurred. In fact, many of these people served as defence witnesses.[96] As Dewdney informed the Prime Minister, the diaries and letters of the murdered officials at Frog Lake showed that until the day of the "massacre" there was "no reason to believe that our Indians were even dissatisfied much less contemplated violence."[97] Ballendine's reports indicated that there were no plans for violence, that the Cree were not involved with the Metis, and that they planned no rebellion. Dewdney believed that the Cree had not "even thought, intended or wished that the uprising would reach the proportion it has. . . . Things just got out of control."[98] As Dewdney related to the Prime Minister, had the people living in the region not been new settlers from the East, and had they not fled in panic, much of the "raiding" and looting would not have occurred. In regions where people had not abandoned their homes no raiding occurred.[99] Therefore, the charges against Big Bear and Poundmaker were designed to remove the leadership of the Cree movement for revision of the treaties. They were charged to elicit prison sentences that would have the effect of coercing the Cree to accept government control. The trials were conducted to have the desired result, and both Big Bear and Poundmaker were convicted and sentenced to three years in Stoney Mountain Penitentiary.[100] Neither man served his full term, and both died a short time after their release from prison.

By the end of 1885, Dewdney had succeeded in subjugating the Cree.

Big Bear was in prison, Little Pine was dead, and Piapot was intimidated by having troops stationed on his reserve. Dewdney had deprived the Cree of their principal leaders and of their autonomy. He used the military to disarm and impoverish the Cree by confiscating their horses and carts; he increased the size of the Mounted Police force, and used the police to arrest Cree leaders who protested against his policies; he broke up Cree Bands, deposed Cree leaders, and forbade any Indian to be off his reserve without permission from the Indian Agent.[101] By 1890, through vigorous implementation of the Indian Act, Dewdney and his successor, Hayter Reed, had begun the process of making the Cree an administered people.

The record of the Canadian government in dealing with the Cree is thus not one of honourable fair-mindedness and justice as the traditional interpretation portrays. As Dewdney admitted in 1885, the treaties' promises and provisions were not being fulfilled, and Dewdney himself had taken steps to assure Canadian control over the Cree, which were themselves violations of the treaties. Thus, he had refused to grant the Cree the reserve sites they selected; he had refused to distribute the ammunition and twine the treaties required. His plans for dealing with the Cree leaders were based on a political use of the legal and judicial system, and ultimately he made use of the military, the police, and the courts in a political manner to achieve his goal of subjugating the Cree. Only by ignoring these facts can one continue to perpetuate the myth of Canada's just and honourable Indian policy from 1870 to 1885.

Notes

1. Douglas Owram, *Promise of Eden: The Canadian Expansionist Movement and the Idea of the West, 1856–1900* (Toronto, 1980), 131–34.

2. G.F.G. Stanley, *The Birth of Western Canada: A History of the Riel Rebellions* (Toronto, 1960).

3. Ibid., 206–15.

4. Ibid., vii–viii, 196, 216–36. It should be noted that the traditional interpretation of a Cree rebellion in association with the Metis has been challenged by R. Allen, "Big Bear," *Saskatchewan History* 25 (1972); W.B. Fraser, "Big Bear, Indian Patriot," *Alberta Historical Review* 14 (1966): 1–13; Rudy Wiebe in his fictional biography, *The Temptations of Big Bear* (Toronto, 1973) and in his biography of Big Bear in the *Dictionary of Canadian Biography* (hereafter DCB), vol. 11, 1881–90 (Toronto, 1982), 597–601; and Norma Sluman, *Poundmaker* (Toronto, 1967). However, none of these authors deals with Canada's Indian policy, and none examines what the Cree were doing in the period 1876–85.

5. Alexander Morris, *The Treaties of Canada with the Indians of Manitoba and the North-West Territories* (Toronto, 1880), 37; Public Archives of Manitoba (hereafter PAM), Adams G. Archibald Papers.

6. Public Archives of Canada (hereafter PAC), Indian Affairs Files, RG 10, vol.

3571, file 124–2; also vol. 3603, file 2036. See also Morris, *Treaties of Canada*, 25–43 and 126–27, for a printed account of the negotiations and the texts of the original and renegotiated treaties, 313–20, 338–42. Two articles by John Taylor, "Canada's Northwest Indian Policy in the 1870's: Traditional Premises and Necessary Innovations" and "Two Views on the Meaning of Treaties Six and Seven" in *The Spirit of Alberta Indian Treaties*, ed. Richard E. Price (Montreal, 1980), 3–7 and 9–45 respectively, provide a good account of the Indian contribution and attitude towards the treaties.

7. Morris, *Treaties of Canada*, 44–76; on 120–23 Morris demonstrates how he had to make Treaty 3 the model for the Qu'Appelle Treaty to get the Saulteaux and Cree of the Qu'Appelle River region to accept what he originally offered them. Compare Treaties 1–6 to see what the government was forced to concede. Also see Taylor's "Traditional Premises" for Indian contributions to the negotiation process.

8. PAC, RG 10, vol. 3586, file 1137, Lieutenant-Governor Morris to Secretary of State for the provinces, 13 September 1872; vol. 3576, file 378, entire file; vol. 3609, file 3229; vol. 3604, file 2543; vol. 3636, 6694–1.

9. PAC, RG 10, vol. 3612, file 4012, entire file; PAM, Archibald Papers, W.J. Christie to George W. Hill, 26 April 1871; Archibald to Secretary of State for the Provinces, 5 January 1872; also letters in note 15; William Francis Butler, *The Great Lone Land* (Rutland, Vt., 1970), 360–62, 368; PAC, MG 26A, John A. Macdonald Papers, vol. 104, entire volume; PAM, Archibald Papers, Joseph Howe to Archibald, 30 June 1872; PAM, Alexander Morris Papers, Lt. Governor's Collection, Morris to Minister of the Interior, 7 July 1873; PAC, RG 10, vol. 3625, file 5366, Morris to Minister of the Interior, David Laird, 22 July and 4 August 1875; vol. 3624, file 5152, Colonel French, Commissioner of the NWMP to the Minister of Justice, 6 and 19 August 1875; Morris, *Treaties of Canada*, 170–71; PAC, RG 10, vol. 3612, file 4012, entire file; PAM, Adams G. Archibald Papers, Petition of James Seenum to Archibald, 9 January 1871, and attached letters of Kehewin, Little Hunter, and Kiskion; Archibald to Secretary of State for the provinces, 5 January 1872.

10. Two excellent studies of the Cree in the pre-1870 era are those by Arthur J. Ray, *Indians in the Fur Trade: Their Role as Hunters, Trappers, and Middlemen in the Lands Southwest of Hudson Bay 1660–1870* (Toronto, 1974), and David G. Mandelbaum, *The Plains Cree*, vol. 37, Anthropological Papers of the American Museum of Natural History, Part 2 (New York, 1940).

11. Ibid. An excellent study of the Cree expansion is the unpublished MA thesis by John S. Milloy, "The Plains Cree: A Preliminary Trade and Military Chronology, 1670–1870" (Carleton University, 1972); also Henry John Moberly and William B. Cameron, *When Fur Was King* (Toronto, 1929), 208–12, describes part of the last phase of this movement. The shrinking range of buffalo and how the Cree reacted are also discussed in Frank Gilbert Roe, *The North American Buffalo: A Critical Study of the Species in Its Wild State* (Toronto, 1951), 282–333.

12. Henry Youle Hind, *Narrative of the Canadian Red River Exploring Expedition of 1857 and of the Assiniboine and Saskatchewan Exploring Expedition of 1858* (Edmonton, 1971), 1: 334; Irene Spry, *The Palliser Expedition: An Account of John Palliser's British North American Expedition, 1857–1860* (London, 1964), 598–60; Viscount Milton and W.B. Cheadle, *The Northwest Passage by Land, Being the Narrative of an Expedition from the Atlantic to the Pacific* (Toronto, 1970), 66–67; Edwin Thompson Perry, *Five Indian Tribes of the Upper Missouri: Sioux, Arickaras, Assiniboine, Crees, Crow* (Norman, Ok., 1969), 99–137; J. Hines, *The Red Indians of the Plains; Thirty Years' Missionary Experience in Saskatchewan* (Toronto, 1916), 78–80, 88–91.

13. Morris, *Treaties of Canada*, 77–123 and 168–239, discusses the negotiations of

Treaties 4 and 6 with the Cree and how he was forced to modify his offer. Also described is the Cree concern about their land. The reaction of the Mackenzie government is detailed in PAC, RG 10, vol. 3636, file 6694-2 and in particular, Minister of the Interior Report to Privy Council, 31 January 1877 and order-in-council, 10 February 1877.

14. Milloy, "The Plains Cree," 250–62; Alexander Johnson, *The Battle at Belly River: Stories of the Last Great Indian Battle* (Lethbridge, 1966).

15. Hind, *Narrative*, 1: 334, 360–61, carries reports of Mistickoos or Short Stick's comments on a council of Cree leaders that resolved to limit white and Metis hunting privileges. Viscount Milton and W.B. Cheadle, *The Northwest Passage by Land*, 66, 67, contains comments on the Cree determination to limit non-Indian involvement in the hunt. PAM, Adams G. Archibald Papers, letter no. 200, Macdonald to Archibald, 14 February 1871; letter no. 170, English halfbreeds to Archibald, 10 January 1871, all stress that Cree were taking action to limit non-Indian involvement in the buffalo hunt.

16. Morris, *Treaties of Canada*, 241.

17. Interview with Walter Gordon, Director of the Indian Rights and Treaties Program, Federation of Saskatchewan Indians, March 1974. Poundmaker made a similar statement in an interview quoted in "Indian Affairs," *Saskatchewan Herald*, 2 August 1880. The importance of Big Bear, Piapot, and Little Pine cannot be underestimated, for of those Cree chiefs who took treaty only Sweetgrass had the standing of these men, and Sweetgrass died within a few months of taking treaty.

18. Morris, *Treaties of Canada*, 84–87. More detailed information on the adhesions of Piapot and Cheekuk is to be found in PAC, RG 10, vol. 3625, file 5489, W.J. Christie to Laird, 7 October 1875.

19. Morris, *Treaties of Canada*, 240 for the quotation. See 355 for the clauses in Treaty 6 respecting acceptance of Canadian laws.

20. Ibid., 174.

21. Fraser, "Big Bear, Indian Patriot," 76–77 agrees that Big Bear was not referring specifically to hanging but to the effect the treaty would have on the Cree.

22. PAC, RG 10, vol. 3656, file 9093, Agent Dickieson to Lt.-Gov. Laird, 14 September 1877.

23. PAC, RG 10, vol. 3648, file 8380; vol. 3655, file 9000, Laird to Minister of the Interior, 9 May 1878.

24. PAC, RG 10, vol. 3655, file 9000, Laird to Minister of the Interior, 9 May 1878; vol. 3636, file 9092, Laird to Superintendent-General, 19 November 1877; vol. 3670, file 10771, Laird to Minister of the Interior, 12 November 1878; vol. 3672, file 10853, Dickieson to Meredith, 2 April 1878; vol. 3656, file 9092, Inspector James Walker to Laird, 5 September 1877; Department of Indian Affairs and Northern Development (hereafter DIAND), Ottawa, file 1/1-11-3, Laird to Minister of the Interior, 30 December 1878; Dickieson to Laird, 9 October 1878; Walker to Laird, 4 and 26 February 1879.

25. PAC, RG 10, vol. 3655, file 1002, Laird to Minister of the Interior, 9 May 1878; vol. 3672, file 19853, Dickieson to Vankoughnet, 26 July 1878; PAC, MG 26A, E.D. Clark to Fred White, 16 July 1879.

26. "News from the Plains," *Saskatchewan Herald*, 18 November 1878; "From the Plains," *Saskatchewan Herald*, 5 May 1879; "Contradictory News from the West," *Fort Benton Record*, 31 January 1879.

27. PAC, RG 10, vol. 3672, file 10853, M.G. Dickieson to Vankoughnet, 26 July 1878; *Opening Up the West: Being the Official Reports to Parliament of the North-West Mounted Police from 1874–1881* (Toronto, 1973), Report for 1878, 21.

28. PAC, RG 10, vol. 3704, file 17858, entire file; vol. 3648, file 162-2, entire file; vol. 3699, file 16580, order-in-council, 9 October 1879; vol. 3766, file 22541; E.T. Galt to Superintendent-General of Indian Affairs, 27 July 1880; vol. 3730, file 26279, entire file; vol. 3757, file 21397, entire file.

29. House of Commons, *Sessional Papers*, 1885, vol. 17, report no. 3, 157; Edward Ahenakew, *Voices of the Plains Cree*, ed. Ruth Buck (Toronto, 1973), 26. Dewdney in adopting this tactic simply copied what the fur-trading companies had done in the past. The Cree tolerated such practices because they improved the opportunities to have better access to European goods. See Arthur J. Ray and Donald Freeman, *"Give Us Good Measure": An Economic Analysis of Relations between the Indians and the Hudson's Bay Company before 1763* (Toronto, 1978), passim. Ray, *Indians in the Fur Trade*, passim, deals with the same practice in the post-1763 period. Mandelbaum, *The Plains Cree*, 105–10 discusses the nature of Cree political organization and leadership that explains their acceptance of such practices.

30. Morris, *Treaties of Canada*, 366–67. DIAND, Treaty Annuity Pay Sheets for 1879. More than 1000 Plains Cree took treaty for the first time in 1879 under Little Pine, Thunderchild, and Lucky Man. Others from Little Pine's and Big Bear's bands had already taken treaty a year earlier as part of Thunder Companion's band, while others joined Poundmaker, and the three Cree bands settled in the Peace Hills. A portion of the Assiniboine also took treaty under Mosquito in 1878, while many of the northern Saulteaux who had followed Yellow Sky took treaty in 1878 under the leadership of Moosomin.

31. PAC, RG 10, vol. 3745, file 29506-4, vol. 2, Ray to Reed, 23 April 1883; vol. 3668, file 9644, Reed to Commissioner, 23 December 1883. Although these materials refer to events in the Battleford district, as will be demonstrated, the tactics in 1883–84 were similar, if not exactly the same as those used in the Cypress Hills between 1879 and 1882. That they were not better recorded for the earlier period is due to the fact that the government had fewer men working with the Indians, and did not have as effective supervision in the 1879–82 period as it did at Battleford. Also much of the police and Indian Affairs material relating to this region in the 1879–82 period has been lost or destroyed.

32. PAC, RG 10, vol. 3730, file 36279, entire file; vol. 3668, file 10440, Agent Allen to L. Vankoughnet, 11 November 1878; *Sessional Papers*, 1883, vol. 16, no. 5, 197; *Settlers and Rebels: Being the Reports to Parliament of the Activities of the Royal North-West Mounted Police Force from 1882–1885* (Toronto, 1973), Report for 1882, 4–6.

33. PAC, RG 10, vol. 3730, file 26219, Report of surveyor Patrick to Superintendent-General, 16 December 1880; vol. 3716, file 22546, Assistant Commissioner E.T. Galt to Superintendent-General, 27 July 1880; vol. 3757, files 31393 and 31333; vol. 3757, file 20034; PAC, MG 26A, vol. 210, Dewdney to Macdonald, 3 October 1880.

34. PAC, RG 10, vol. 3652, file 8589, parts 1 and 2, entire file; vol. 3691, file 13893, entire file. The *Benton Weekly Record* throughout the spring and summer of 1880 carried reports of Cree and Assinboine horse-stealing raids, and reports of what the Cree were doing in Montana. On 7 May 1880, the paper carried an article entitled "Starving Indians," which was a strong denunciation of Canada's Indian policy and the effect it had on the Cree.

35. PAC, MG 26A, vol. 210, Dewdney to Macdonald, 29 October 1880; *Saskatchewan Herald*, 14 February 1881.

36. PAC, MG 26A, vol. 210, Dewdney to Macdonald, 26 October 1880 and 23 April 1880; *Saskatchewan Herald*, 14, 28 February 1881.

37. PAC, MG 26A, vol. 210, Dewdney to MacPherson, 4 July 1881; vol. 247, Galt to MacPherson, 14 July 1881; "Edmonton," *Saskatchewan Herald*, 12 November 1881.

38. Ibid., also PAC, MG 26A, vol. 210, Dewdney to Macdonald, 19 June 1881; vol. 247, Galt to Vankoughnet, 16 July 1881; PAC, RG 10, vol. 3739, file 28748-1, Dewdney to Macdonald, 3 April 1882; Fred White to Minister of the Interior, 9 June 1882; Freylinghausen to Sackville-West, 9 June 1882. *Saskatchewan Herald*, 1 August 1881; "Starving Indians," *Benton Weekly Record*, 14 July 1881; 25 August, 1 September, and 13 October 1881.

39. PAC, RG 10, vol. 3739, file 28478-1, C.G. Denny to Commissioner, 24 October 1881; vol. 3768, file 33642; vol. 3603, file 20141, McIlree to Dewdney, 21 June 1882; Glenbow Institute, Calgary, Edgar Dewdney Papers, vol. 5, file 57, Irvine to Dewdney, 24 June 1882; *Saskatchewan Herald*, 24 June 1882; *Edmonton Bulletin*, 17 June 1882.

40. PAC, RG 10, vol. 3768, file 33642, entire file.

41. PAC, MG 26A, vol. 210, Dewdney to Macdonald, 19 June 1881; vol. 247, Galt to Vankoughnet, 16 July 1881. *Saskatchewan Herald*, 1 August 1881; "Starving Indians," *Benton Weekly Record*, 14 July 1881. See also *Benton Weekly Record*, 25 August, 1 September, and 13 October 1881.

42. Morris, *Treaties of Canada*, 205, 218, 352–53.

43. PAC, RG 10, vol. 3604, file 2589, entire file. See also *Settlers and Rebels*, 1882 Report. See also Glenbow, Dewdney Papers, vol 5, file 57, White to Irvine, 29 August 1882; RG 10, vol. 3604, file 2589; "The Repatriated Indians," *Saskatchewan Herald*, 5 August 1882; "From the South," *Saskatchewan Herald*, 21 May 1882; "Back on the Grub Pile," *Saskatchewan Herald*, 24 June 1882.

44. Glenbow, Dewdney Papers, vol. 5, file 57, Irvine to Dewdney, 24 June 1882 and 25 September 1882; *Settlers and Rebels*, 1882 Report, 4, 5; *Sessional Papers*, 1883, vol. 16, no. 5, 197; PAC, RG 10, vol. 3604, file 2589; "Repatriated Indians," *Saskatchewan Herald*, 5 August 1882.

45. "Repatriated Indians," *Saskatchewan Herald*, 5 August 1882; Glenbow, Dewdney Papers, vol. 4, file 45, White to Dewdney, 12 October 1882; *Saskatchewan Herald*, 14 October 1882; "Big Bear and Others," and the "I.D.," *Edmonton Bulletin*, 21 October 1882.

46. Glenbow, Dewdney Papers, vol. 4, file 45, White to Dewdney, 17 October 1882; PAC, MG 26A, vol. 289, Vankoughnet to Macdonald, 2 November 1882.

47. PAC, MG 26A, vol. 11, Dewdney to J.A. Macdonald, 2 September 1883; PAC, RG 10, vol. 3682, file 12667, Dewdney to Superintendent-General, 28 April 1884.

48. PAC, RG 10, vol. 3668, file 10644, Reed to Commissioner, 23 December 1883; Robert Jefferson, *Fifty Years on the Saskatchewan* (Battleford, 1929), 103.

49. PAC, RG 10, vol. 3668, file 10644, Reed to Commissioner, 23 December 1883; *Edmonton Bulletin*, 9 February 1884; *Saskatchewan Herald*, 24 November 1883.

50. PAC, MG 26A, vol. 289, Vankoughnet to Macdonald, 4, 10 December 1883; vol. 104, Deputy Superintendent-General to T. Quinn, 21 September 1883; Dewdney to Superintendent-General, 27 September 1883; Deputy Superintendent-General to Reed, 10 April 1884; vol. 212, Dewdney to Macdonald, 2 January 1883 [sic! Given the contents of the letter, it is obvious Dewdney forgot that a new year had begun the previous day]; vol. 91, Dewdney to Macdonald, 24 July 1884; another letter but without a date, which was probably written in the first week of August 1884; vol. 107, entire file; PAC, RG 10, vol. 3664, file 9843, entire file.

51. PAC, RG 10, vol. 3616, file 10181; Burton Deane, *Mounted Police Life in Canada: A Record of Thirty-One Years in Service, 1883–1914* (Toronto, 1973), 140–53; Isabell Andrews, "Indian Protest against Starvation: The Yellow Calf Incident of 1884," *Saskatchewan History* 28 (1975): 4–52; *Edmonton Bulletin* 7 January, 3 February, 7, 28 July and 4 August 1883.

52. Glenbow, Dewdney Papers, vol. 5, file 58, Dewdney to Superintendent-General, 29 February 1884; PAC, MG 26A, vol. 211, Dewdney to Macdonald, 6 October 1883; vol. 212, Reed to Dewdney, 15 February 1884; Dewdney to Macdonald, 16 February and 9 April 1884.

53. PAC, RG 10, vol. 3682, file 12667, Dewdney to Superintendent-General, 28 April 1884; vol. 3686, file 13168, entire file; vol. 3745, file 29506-4(2), Reed to Colonel Irvine, 18 May 1884.

54. PAC, RG 10, vol. 3745, file 29506-4(2), Reed to Irvine, 18 May 1884; Irvine to Comptroller Fred White, 27 May 1884; White to Vankoughnet, 19 May 1884.

55. PAC, RG 10, vol. 3745, file 29506-4(2), Agent Macdonald to Commissioner, 29 May 1884; vol. 3655, file 9026, Dewdney to Superintendent-General, 13 June 1884.

56. PAC, RG 10, vol. 3745, file 29506-4(2), Reed to Superintendent-General, 19 April 1884. Similar report in vol. 3576, file 309B. PAC, MG 26A, file 37, Dewdney to Macdonald, 3 May 1884. Dewdney's request and actions were contrary to what the Cree had been told about how reserve sites could be chosen, as were the government's actions in denying the Cree reserves in the Cypress Hills and forcing them to move north. See Morris, *Treaties of Canada*, passim; PAC, RG 10, vol. 3576, file 309B, Vankoughnet to Dewdney, 10 May 1884; MG 26A, vol. 104, Dewdney to Superintendent-General, 14 June 1884. Campbell Innes, "Fine Day Interview," *The Cree Rebellion of 1884: Sidelights of Indian Conditions Subsequent to 1876* (Battleford, 1926), 13–15; *Saskatchewan Herald*, 19 April and 17 May 1884.

57. PAC, RG 10, vol. 3576, file 309B, Reed to Superintendent-General, 19 April 1884; Reed to Vankoughnet, 19 April 1884; Ray to Commissioner, 23 April 1884; Reed to Superintendent-General, 20 May 1884; Glenbow, Dewdney Papers, vol. 3, file 36, Dewdney to Macdonald, 12 June 1884.

58. PAC, RG 10, vol. 3576, file 309B, Ray to Commissioner, 19, 21 June 1884; Crozier to Dewdney, 22 June 1884; Jefferson, *Fifty Years on the Saskatchewan*, 108–9; Innes, *The Cree Rebellion of 1884*, 13–17, 28.

59. PAC, RG 10, vol. 3576, file 309B, Ray to Commissioner, 28 June 1884; see also Rae to Dewdney, 9 June 1884; Innes, "McKay Interview," 44; PAC, RG 10, vol. 3576, file 309A, Dewdney to Ray, 5 July 1884.

60. PAC, RG 10, vol. 3576, file 309B, Ray to Dewdney, 23 June 1884; Crozier to Dewdney, 23 June 1884.

61. Glenbow, Dewdney Papers, vol. 3, file 37, Macdonald to Dewdney, 18 July 1884, 11 August 1884, and 2 September 1844; vol. 4, file 45, Macdonald to White, 15 September 1884; PAC, RG 10, vol. 3576, file 309A, Vankoughnet to Dewdney, 27 July 1884.

62. PAC, RG 10, vol. 3576, file 309B, Ray to Commissioner, 30 June 1884; file 309A, Ray to Commissioner, 24, 29 July 1884; PAC, MG 26A, vol. 212, Dewdney to Macdonald, 14 July 1884 and J.A. MacRae to Commissioner, 7 August 1884; vol. 107, Ray to Commissioner, 29 July 1884.

63. PAC, RG 10, vol. 3745, file 29506-4(2), Dewdney to Superintendent-General, 7 August 1884; vol. 3576, file 309A, Ray to Dewdney, 19 July 1884; PAC, MG 26A, vol. 104, Dewdney to Department, 19 July 1884.

64. PAC, RG 10, vol. 3576, file 309B, Ray to Commissioner, 30 June 1884; file 309A, Ray to Commissioner, 24, 29 July 1884; PAC, MG 26A, vol. 212, Dewdney to Macdonald, 14 July 1884; J.A. MacRae to Commissioner, 7 August 1884; vol. 107, Ray to Commissioner, 29 July 1884.

65. PAC, MG 26A, vol. 107, Ray to Commissioner, 29 July and 2 August 1884; J.A. MacRae to Commissioner, 29 July 1884.

66. PAC, RG 10, vol. 3697, file 15423, J.A. MacRae to Dewdney, 25 August 1884.

67. PAC, RG 10, vol. 3697, file 15423, Reed to Superintendent-General, 23 January 1885; Reed to Dewdney, 22, 25 August 1884; PAC, MG 26A, vol. 107, J.A. MacRae to Commissioner, 29 July 1884; J.M. Ray to Commissioner, 2 August 1884; MacRae to Commissioner, 5 August 1884; vol. 212, MacRae to Commissioner, 7 August 1884; PAC, RG 10, vol. 3756, file 309A, J.M. Ray to Commissioner, 24, 25 July 1884; "Big Bear Rises to Speak," *Saskatchewan Herald*, 5 August 1882; *Saskatchewan Herald*, 25 July and 9 August 1884.

68. PAC, RG 10, vol. 3576, file 309A, Commissioner to Ray, 7 August 1884; Ray to Commissioner, 29 July 1884; see also in PAC, MG 26A, vol. 107; Glenbow, Dewdney Papers, vol. 6, file 69, Crozier to Comptroller, NWMP, 27 July 1884; PAC, MG 26A, vol. 212, Dewdney to Macdonald, 8 August 1884.

69. PAC, MG 26A, vol. 107, Reed to Dewdney, 23, 24, 25 August, 4 September 1884; Dewdney to Macdonald, 5 September 1884.

70. PAC, RG 10, vol. 3576, file 309A, Begg to Commissioner, 20 February 1885; "Indian Affairs," *Saskatchewan Herald*, 31 October 1884.

71. Glenbow, Dewdney Papers, vol. 6, file 66, Reed to Dewdney, 4 September 1884.

72. Statutes of Canada, 43 Vict., 27, "An Act to Amend the Indian Act, 1880," 12 April 1884; PAC, MG 26A, vol. 107, Dewdney to Macdonald, 24 August 1884.

73. PAC, MG26A, vol. 212, Reed to Dewdney, 7 September 1884; vol. 107, Dewdney to Macdonald, 24 August 1884.

74. PAC, RG 10, vol. 3576, file 309A, Reed to Dewdney, 12 September 1884; vol. 3745, file 29506-4(2), Reed to Dewdney, 14 September 1884; vol. 3704, file 17799, entire file; vol. 3664, file 9834 and 9843; vol. 3761, file 30836, entire file; Glenbow, Dewdney Papers, vol. 4, file 45, Reed to Dewdney, 12 September 1884; vol. 4, file 47, Crozier to Comptroller, NWMP, 4 November 1884; vol. 5, file 57, Crozier to Dewdney, 30 January 1885.

75. PAC, RG 10, vol. 3582, file 749, Ballendine to Reed, 8 November and 26 December 1884.

76. PAC, RG 10, vol. 3582, file 949, P. Ballendine to Reed, 20 November, 26 December, 2 January 1885; J.M. Ray to Commissioner, 27 December 1884; Crozier to Commissioner, NWMP, 14 January 1885; vol. 3576, file 309A, Magnus Begg to Dewdney, 20 February 1885; PAC, MG 26A, extract of Ray to Dewdney, 24 January 1885. Ray, Ballendine, and Crozier when they reported on Little Pine mentioned that their principal source of information was Poundmaker, although Ballendine did get some of his information directly from Little Pine himself.

77. PAC, RG 10, vol. 3582, file 949, Ballendine to Reed, 10 October, and 26 December 1884, and 2 January and 16 March 1885; Ballendine to Dewdney, 19 March 1885; PAC, MG 26A, vol. 107, extract of Ray to Dewdney, 24 January 1885. PAC, MG 271C4, Edgar Dewdney Papers, vol. 2, Francis Dickens to Officer Commanding, Battleford, 27 October 1884.

78. PAC, MG 26A, vol. 117, Dewdney to Macdonald, 9 February 1885; PAC, RG 10, vol. 3676, file 309A, Dewdney to Vankoughnet, 12 February 1885.

79. PAC, RG 10, vol. 3705, file 17193, Vankoughnet to Dewdney, 5 February 1885; Vankoughnet to Macdonald, 31 January 1885; vol. 3582, file 949, Vankoughnet to Reed, 28 January 1885; Glenbow, Dewdney Papers, vol. 3, file 38, Macdonald to Dewdney, 23 February 1885.

80. PAC, RG 10, vol. 3576, file 309A, Dewdney to Vankoughnet, 12 February 1885.

81. Jefferson, *Fifty Years on the Saskatchewan*, 125.

82. Ibid., 126–28; PAC, MG 26A, deposition, William Lightfoot to J.A. MacKay, 31 May 1885.

83. Jefferson, *Fifty Years on the Saskatchewan*, 127, 130, 138.

84. Innes, "Fine Day Interview," 185; Sluman, *Poundmaker*, 199–200, 184–85; Jefferson, *Fifty Years on the Saskatchewan*, 130–38.

85. Desmond Morton, *The Last War Drum* (Toronto, 1972), 98–102; Jefferson, *Fifty Years on the Saskatchewan*, 125–40.

86. PAC, RG 10, vol. 3755, file 30973, Reed to Commissioner, 18 June 1881; see also material cited in note 72 above. William B. Cameron, *Blood Red the Sun* (Edmonton, 1977), 33–61, vividly describes the slaughter at Frog Lake.

87. Cameron, *Blood Red the Sun*, passim.

88. Charles Mulvaney, *The History of the North-West Rebellion of 1885* (Toronto, 1885), 212–16; *Settlers and Rebels*, 1882 Report, 22, 26–27; PAC, RG 10, vol. 3584, file 1130, 1, Superintendent Herchmer to Dewdney, 5 April 1885.

89. Ibid.

90. PAC, RG 10, vol. 3697, file 15446, entire file; vol. 3598, file 1411, entire file; vol. 7768, file 2109-2; vol. 3794, file 46584.

91. PAC, MG 271C4, vol. 7, letters, Dewdney to White, March–April 1885. This correspondence reveals that in early April Dewdney believed that he had to deal with an Indian uprising. However, he did admit that this impression was based on scanty and often faulty or false information. By mid-April, Dewdney makes clear to White, the NWMP Comptroller, that he did not believe that he was dealing with either an Indian uprising or a rebellion.

92. PAC, MG 271C4, vol. 1, Dewdney to Begg, 3 May 1885; vol. 4, Dewdney to Middleton, 30 March 1885; RG 10, vol. 3584, file 1130, Dewdney to Ray, 7 May 1885; Jefferson, *Fifty Years on the Saskatchewan*, 128–33.

93. PAC, RG 10, vol. 3584, file 1120, Proclamation of 6 May 1885.

94. PAC, MG 26A, vol. 107, Dewdney to Macdonald, 6 April 1885.

95. Morton, *The Last War Drum*, 96–110.

96. Cameron, *Blood Red the Sun*, 195–204. Sandra Estlin Bingman, "The Trials of Poundmaker and Big Bear," *Saskatchewan History* 28 (1975): 81–95, gives an account of the conduct of the trials and raises questions about their conduct, particularly the trial of Big Bear. However, Bingman apparently was unaware of Dewdney and Macdonald's efforts to use the courts and whatever other means possible to remove Cree leaders.

97. PAC, MG 26A, vol. 107, Dewdney to Macdonald, 3 June 1885.

98. Ibid.

99. Ibid.

100. Bingman, "The Trials of Poundmaker and Big Bear," 81–95.

101. A very good account of Dewdney's actions to bring the Cree under

government control after 1885 is to be found in Jean Lamour, "Edgar Dewdney and the Aftermath of the Rebellion," *Saskatchewan History* 23 (1970): 105–16. For a discussion of the use of the Indian Act as a means of destroying Indian cultural autonomy see John L. Tobias, "Protection, Civilization, Assimilation: An Outline History of Canada's Indian Policy," *The Western Canadian Journal of Anthropology* 6 (1976). For a discussion of specific use of this policy against the Cree, and how the Cree reacted see John L. Tobias, "Indian Reserves in Western Canada: Indian Homelands or Devices for Assimilation," in *Approaches to Native History in Canada: Papers of a Conference held at the National Museum of Man, October, 1975,* ed. D.A. Muise (Ottawa, 1977), 89–103.

THE CONVERSION OF THE PORT SIMPSON TSIMSHIAN: INDIAN CONTROL OR MISSIONARY MANIPULATION?†

CLARENCE R. BOLT

Recent historical and anthropological literature has tended to reject the view that the Indians were passive participants in the fur trade dominating the northwest coast at the end of the eighteenth and beginning of the nineteenth centuries. Rather, Indians are seen to have had a decisive role in determining the nature of their relations with the fur traders. Robin Fisher asserts that this element of control ended with the advent of European settlement and that, at this time, European ways were forced upon the Indians, particularly by missionaries and government officials. Missionaries, he notes, came to convert the Indians to Christianity and therefore demanded the repudiation not only of traditional religious practices but of the total cultural framework.[1] The rise of numerous mission villages, complete with churches, schools and hospitals, is offered as proof of the pervasiveness of mission work in determining cultural changes.

Changes in indigenous cultures accompanying the intensification of European contact are frequently seen as evidence of native people's inability to maintain or accommodate their traditional way of life in the face of European civilization. In the case of British Columbia's Indians, Fisher postulates that sometime at the end of the fur trading era and the beginning of the settlement period they became incapable of exercising a great deal of choice or control in their relations with Europeans. He claims that the fur traders did not attempt to "direct" change among Indian societies, whereas the dominant powers of the settlement period, namely the church and governments, did try to reshape Indian culture.[2] In this framework, therefore, missionary successes are seen as the result

† *BC Studies* no. 57 (Spring 1983): 38–56.

of Indian inability to cope with a massive intrusion of European mores.

There are two possible explanations for this interpretation. First of all, very little serious analysis has been undertaken describing Indian reaction to missionaries and their reasons for accepting such innovations as churches, schools, hospitals and European social and political institutions. The available sources describing the settlement period are predominantly missionary records and government documents. As these sources have a strong anti-native bias, the changes effected by both missionaries and governments are seen as proof of Indian inability to withstand settlement forces. Secondly, twentieth-century life among the Indian people of British Columbia is often depicted as that of a demoralized people, disillusioned with the values of both traditional culture and western civilization. This current loss of confidence and inability to cope is often transposed to the nineteenth century and, furthermore, is linked to the coming of European settlers to B.C. The assumption seems to be that only demoralized and disillusioned people, those who have lost faith in their traditional cultural values, will convert to Christianity.[3]

The experience of the Methodist missionary, Thomas Crosby, who lived at Fort Simpson from 1874 to 1897, suggests a more complex series of reasons for conversion. A group of Fort Simpson Tsimshian, led by the chief Alfred Dudoward and his wife Kate, converted to Methodism in 1873 while trading in Victoria, and upon their return to Fort Simpson a public meeting was held at which they decided to ask for a Methodist missionary. During his first years at Fort Simpson, Crosby was remarkably successful in transforming the village from an Indian settlement to a model Canadian town. The Indians offered little resistance to the dismantling of their way of life. Towards the end of Crosby's tenure at Fort Simpson, however, the Tsimshian virtually turned their backs on Crosby's leadership and pursued a more independent course of action. One of the main reasons that they had converted was their hope that by forsaking their past they would acquire full Canadian citizenship along with its material, political and social rights. The governments' handling of the land question was a decisive illustration that such hopes would never be realized. Crosby was powerless to change the governments' position and, as a result, powerless as well to rally the Tsimshian around the mission. At Fort Simpson, therefore, the Tsimshian had a decisive role in the conversion process and in determining the success of the mission. They were not, as proponents of Social Darwinism would argue, accepting Christianity because of an inherent incapability of resisting the onslaught of superior ways. Rather, Crosby depended on their agreement for the implementation of his policies.

This article examines Tsimshian society before and after the arrival of Thomas Crosby, considers the progress of the mission among the Fort Simpson (Port Simpson, after 1880) Tsimshian, seeks to explain the Tsimshian's conversion to Christianity as an action deliberately chosen by them as a means to attain wider goals, and concludes with some suggestions about future analysis of missionary–Indian relations.

When Thomas Crosby arrived at Fort Simpson in the spring of 1874, the Tsimshian had been in contact with European civilization for over eighty years. The fur trading era began at least as early as 1792 when the Spanish explorer Jacinto Caamaño spent a month among the Tsimshian studying their way of life.[4] In 1831 the Hudson's Bay Company established Fort Nass but replaced it with Fort Simpson in 1834. The fur trade introduced the Tsimshian to both new material goods and the European market economy. The Coast Tsimshian enhanced their reputation as traders, acting as middlemen between the Europeans and the inland groups of Indians. Those who were adept at dealing with the Europeans quickly rose to social prominence, a fact that led to a rearrangement of traditional social positions. Many of the Tsimshian came to place less emphasis on such traditional activities as fishing, hunting and gathering, and instead to spend more time trading with other Indians for fur, meat, fish and potatoes, which in turn they traded to the Hudson's Bay Company for whatever European goods they desired.

The fur traders made no effort to "direct" change in Indian society, a fact that has prompted Jean Usher to state that contact "enhanced the existing cultural framework." "The aboriginal culture was largely oriented to the acquisition and display of wealth, and the influx of prestige goods from the traders only gave vitality to already existing cultural institutions."[5] Few new skills were needed, and change proceeded in existing directions. Art, crafts, house building and ceremonial life flourished. Even when the Tsimshian gave up their largely nomadic existence and settled around Fort Simpson in 1834, Indian "laws still functioned, and by potlatching intensively, they were trying to adjust their real situation to their social ideals . . . this was still an Indian dominated society, and the Indian solutions for these problems could still be applied."[6] Fisher has suggested that the fur trade was a "mutually beneficial symbiosis in which neither gained from the hostility of the other."[7] While coming to a similar conclusion, Philip Drucker has pointed out that "it is not the mere listing of culture items added or subtracted that is significant but the cultural processes and psychological factors involved."[8]

Such factors are, however, harder to evaluate. The growing preoccupation with non-traditional activities has already been noted. By the late 1850s, the Tsimshian spent most of their traditional hunting summer trading in Victoria. Furthermore, the increase in wealth and depopulation by disease, especially smallpox, led to a dramatic increase in both the number and scale of potlatches and feasts. Rather than stabilizing the social structure in an orderly way, potlatches became occasions for bitter confrontation and rivalry.[9]

The attitude required for the fur trade was also at variance with the traditional relation to non-human "beings" and violated many of the traditonal taboos. The Fort Simpson Journal reported in 1843 that the Indians were not bringing in enough fish and added that, "the reason they assign for it, is their having brought them so early to the Fort, they superstitiously imagine our mode of cooking them is the cause of the falling off."[10] The traders were astonished that the Indians did not realize that the school of fish had simply passed, "they being so tenacious of their own superstitious beliefs."[11] Calvin Martin has argued that the close relationship between human and other "beings" was characteristic of all North American Indian hunter-gatherer societies. Reality other than human was not seen as an aggregate of exploitable resources but rather there was a "genuine kinship and often affection for wildlife and plant-life"; human and other beings were bound by a compact and fulfilled each other's needs.[12] Hunting required certain rites and taboos so that the spirit of the being giving its life would not be offended. Failure to follow these prescriptions could lead to the withdrawal of the offended spirit's species from the area, lack of success for the hunter and/or the onset of disease. The coming of the Europeans brought new material goods but also the punishments associated with improper dealing with non-human beings.

The crucial question concerning the fur trade is whether or not the changes it brought to Tsimshian culture had impaired their ability to exert some control over their way of life. The answer is perhaps not as clear-cut as implied by Fisher and Usher on the one hand and Martin on the other. Fisher is correct in pointing out that the Indians actively pursued the fur trade for its alleged benefits. He underplays some of the effects on Indian societies. Undoubtedly traditional assumptions and patterns were altered, but the Tsimshian had not become demoralized puppets, an easy prey for European treachery.

This fact is strikingly illustrated by the arrival of the Anglican missionary, William Duncan, at Fort Simpson in 1857. Duncan's objective in coming to Fort Simpson was to establish a model Christian, Victorian village. During the first three years, he had virtually no converts. Between July 1861 and July 1862, of Fort Simpson's 1 500 residents, he baptized fifty-eight Indians, of whom only nine were over the age of 30.[13] The Tsimshian quite clearly felt that the strength of their old ways did not warrant a conversion to Mr. Duncan's alternative. Usher notes that the Tsimshian were still confident in their traditional ways so that a move to Christianity was not attractive.

> Before 1857, contact with Whites was on a regular, ordered basis. The Tsimshian appeared to be in control of their own society, and were coping remarkably well with the effects of guns, liquor and

disease introduced by European civilization. Their reaction to a missionary who denied the bases of their society was not that of a disoriented people.[14]

The gold rush of 1858, she notes, changed all of this as more and more Tsimshian went to Victoria and fell victim to European vices and diseases. By 1860, she concludes, the Tsimshian were demoralized and had lost control over their society. Yet curiously, Duncan began his attempts at converting the Tsimshian in June of 1858, the time of Tsimshian demoralization. It is puzzling to understand how Usher can describe the Tsimshian as confident, curious people in their response to Duncan when she notes that demoralization and dissatisfaction with old ways occurred at the same time Duncan began his efforts at converting them. Indeed, Duncan's inability to convert a significant number of Tsimshian prompted him to move with his converts to Metlakatla. In 1862, this community was expanded when a smallpox epidemic led many to flee to Metlakatla for refuge. Only then was he able to establish his model community.

However, the population at Fort Simpson remained considerably larger than that of Metlakatla. Most Fort Simpson residents chose not to follow Duncan and continued to adhere to traditional values. While it is likely that a number of Duncan's followers were attracted to the beliefs of Christianity, many more came to find refuge from smallpox and another significant group came to escape potlatch obligations associated with status, feasting and property rights. This latter factor resulted in many hard feelings towards the Metlakatlans and perhaps is one reason why Fort Simpson still had a larger population than Metlakatla by the time of Crosby's arrival in 1874.

Duncan nevertheless maintained the hope that his model utopia would attract all of the Coast Tsimshian. This hope was dashed in 1873 when a small group of Fort Simpson Tsimshian was converted to Methodism in Victoria. Responding to the pressure to westernize, and to the conversion of some of their number, the majority of residents at Fort Simpson decided that they wanted the western way of life and religion rather than the Tsimshian way, and issued a call for a Methodist missionary. The reasons for requesting a missionary were varied, ranging from a desire for western material goods to the attraction of Christian beliefs, particularly as seen in the Methodist religious services which appealed to the Tsimshian love of celebration and music. In addition, some were confused about traditional assumptions, others desired immunity from disease (through Christianity's alleged magical powers) and still others hoped for new prestige in the larger world of which they were becoming a part. But the crucial element in this decision was a conscious choice on the part of Tsimshian to convert. They may not have been aware of all the factors involved in such a decision but then Crosby, like most other missionaries, was not either.

When Crosby arrived at Fort Simpson, therefore, he had a warm welcome, unlike Duncan, and was able quickly to establish a Methodist Victorian setting. His evangelical revivalism contrasted sharply with Duncan's sombre Anglicanism and thus appealed to the Tsimshian. Crosby was born in 1840 in the heart of Methodism, in Pickering, Yorkshire, had emigrated to Canada in the mid 1850s, but did not consider himself "saved" until 1858 during the Great Awakening that swept North America that year. Revival meetings — at which fire-and-brimstone sermons were delivered, rousing hymns were sung, emotional prayers were offered and dramatic conversions took place — became for Crosby the mode in which Christianity could best be presented. In 1861, Rev. William ("California") Taylor, a missionary who spent ten years among the gold miners of California, inspired Crosby to become a Methodist missionary. Crosby's lack of formal education, a result of his working-class background, prevented him from receiving endorsement from the ruling body of the Wesleyan Methodist Church. In 1861 he paid his own way to British Columbia, and in the frontier setting his lively enthusiasm was quickly utilized by the small group of Methodists in British Columbia. By 1864 he had been appointed as an assistant to Cornelius Bryant, a Methodist missionary at Nanaimo. In 1871 he received formal recognition for his efforts and was ordained as a Methodist missionary, and in 1874 he was appointed to Fort Simpson.

One of Crosby's first moves at Fort Simpson was to build a pretentious frame church. In addition to Sunday services, he provided Sunday school instruction and held weekly prayer meetings and special services. Using the example of his own conversion experience, Crosby attempted to implement the lively, spontaneous and emotional revival mode of religious expression. When he arrived, the musical Tsimshian eagerly participated in worship and prayer. He also established an itinerancy system that allowed him to follow his parishioners to their spring and summer fishing and berrying grounds. The itinerancy system was broadened to extend his ministry over most of the northwest coast of British Columbia, a fact that would have a significant influence on his effectiveness at Fort Simpson in later years.

As well as introducing the whole array of Methodist religious practices and institutions, Crosby was successful in altering the patterns of everyday life. Education was the most important arena for social change, and Crosby was convinced that the key to future alterations in Tsimshian life lay with teaching the children the proper way of "civilization." In 1879 he opened the Crosby Girls' Home to "rescue" orphan girls from liquor and prostitution and to provide a stable setting for girls whose parents could be convinced by Crosby that the girls would be better off in the Home. The Home taught such feminine occupations as cooking, embroidery, sewing, washing, mothering and serving. These girls, it was hoped, would provide the nucleus for future Christian, Indian homes. By 1890, a boys' home had also been established to provide Christian discipline and training. Medical aid was also provided, since Crosby believed that medicine and the gospel were inseparable. In medicine he felt that he had "one of the most effective agencies in spreading the glorious gospel of the blessed God."[15] In 1890 a hospital was opened, funded partially by the federal and provincial governments.

Religion, education and medical aid, therefore, became the core of Crosby's program. On this basis Tsimshian society could be transformed entirely. This transformation was seen as an integral part of the Christian message.

> The missionary who cannot teach the Indian or heathen how to build his home or cultivate his land, or is too lazy to do it, is not a practical or successful missionary. How can a man teach religion and not teach industry, cleanliness and thrift of all kinds, for the Bible is full of such lessons?[16]

The communal long-houses — "dens of iniquity" — had to be replaced with single-family dwellings if the principles taught in church and school were to succeed. By the late 1880s all the residents in Fort Simpson lived in single family dwellings, minus all the traditional totem markers. Orderly streets with lamps and houses with picket fences, gardens and shrubs testified to the radical change Crosby had effected.

Traditional practices such as dancing, conjuring, potlatching and gambling were eliminated. Ceremonial paraphernalia and totems were destroyed. The people were encouraged instead to adopt the Victorian virtues of thrift, hard work and self-reliance. The principle of private ownership and property replaced that of communal ownership. Traditional leadership was also replaced with a village council, led and controlled by Crosby, to regulate such matters as sanitation, road-working, street lighting and other public works.

Crosby thus appeared to be remarkably successful in the implementation of his mission program. Some native practices—such as the giving of hereditary names along with their property rights, the rules of exogamy and customs controlling marriage, and laws regulating funerals — remained operative beneath the veneer of western mores. Furthermore, the old tribal councils continued to meet to regulate native affairs not dealt with by the new village council.[17] But these practices were not retained to deliberately subvert Crosby's work. There is little reason to doubt that their conversion to Christianity was sincere, and despite the often unconscious retention of centuries-old customs they made every effort to adopt the trappings of western society. It was easier, in many instances, to accept these trappings than change those patterns of living which, to them, were very personal and were often seen as being ingrained in the natural order. It was one thing to build a new house, for example, but quite another to marry someone from one's own phratry.

On the surface, the radical change of Tsimshian life appeared to be the result of Crosby's energy and drive. He seemed to have convinced the Tsimshian to give up their traditional cultural framework for a western one. However, a closer look at the mission indicates that the changes were as much the result of the eagerness of the Tsimshian to westernize as of Crosby's leadership.

The original request for a Methodist missionary is the first clue to the importance of the role of the Tsimshian in the success of the mission.[18] A second is the response of the Tsimshian to Crosby's role as a religious leader. As early as 1876 Crosby reported that church attendance was down: "There was a falling off, which was very painful to us."[19] From this time on Crosby had great difficulty in inspiring the revivalist level of enthusiasm he saw as a necessary expression of a living faith. In 1890 Rev. A. E. Green reported that

> we have been very much grieved by some who years ago were leaders in the work of God but who, becoming cold, would lead the people back to the old customs that they gave up as bad, when they first received the gospel. Many have been drawn away during the past three or four years to take part in the old heathen practices.[20]

Lack of enthusiasm for the leadership of the missionaries was usually interpreted as heathenism.

A particularly vexing problem for the missionaries was the Tsimshian failure to maintain missionary expectations of the Christian life. The Port Simpson Register is full of examples of members who shifted from full membership to "on trial" and then back again to full membership over the twenty-three years that Crosby lived at Port Simpson. From 1887 to 1896, in particular, there was a constant juggling of leadership positions in the church (local preachers, class leaders, leaders and exhorters) as well as a constant movement of people between the "on trial" and full-member status. Few managed to remain consistently in good standing for the whole period of Crosby's tenure.

The instability, more severe in Crosby's later years, indicated that Indian expectations of Crosby were not being realized. By 1885 the Indians were expressing widespread disillusionment about the mission. One of the natives, David Swanson, complained that although it had been eleven years since "we gave up our old way . . . no one has visited us to help us in anything connected with the improvement of our village."[21] He pointed out how the people had spent all of their money improving their village and building new homes, a school and church. Money and work were now scarce. Others noted that Crosby's work load kept him away often and prevented the kind of training they felt was necessary. They noted: "You have opened up God's word to us . . . and our hearts are happy. We want you to lead us in other things. In old times we had a way of our own; but we have put that away, and want to follow in the way that is taught to us. . . ."[22] Chief Albert Nelson reported that although not all had gone as they expected, they were not sorry that they had followed the Methodists. However, expectations had not been fulfilled: "We would like a missionary who could teach our children all things (trades, etc.). Mr. Crosby does not stay at home; he goes to visit other places."[23]

The issue that most clearly demonstrated that Indian expectations would not be met was the federal and provincial governments' handling of the Tsimshian land question. In 1876 the two levels of government had reached an agreement, based on a suggestion by William Duncan, that a commission be appointed to allocate reserves on the basis of each tribe's particular situation rather than on a set acreage. The federal government gave up the idea of extinguishing land title because of the probable expense. As long as the Indians remained quiet, they would not be inclined to raise the issue.[24] The federal strategy also avoided confrontation with the provincial government, which had jurisdiction over the provincial crown lands. This position guaranteed that the two levels of government would throw the problem of Indian land title back and forth while the Indians waited without satisfaction.

The problem predated Crosby's arrival and as early as 1874 he reported that, "we need the land reserve question settled here, and hope that the Indian commission will visit us soon, and let us know where the Indian land is to be; then we hope the people will build a better class of house."[25] A year later he stated that the Indians expressed great fear because of rumours that they would be driven from their land.[26]

These fears were somewhat alleviated in 1876 when the Governor General, Lord Dufferin, visited Fort Simpson and stated that the government of Canada did not distinguish between citizens on the basis of race or colour but was determined to do justice for all. He pointed out that Canada was especially proud of the Indians as Canada's ancient inhabitants and saw them as equal beneficiaries of Canada's good government and of the opportunity for earning an "honest livelihood."[27] In 1879 Indian Superintendent Powell came to Fort Simpson and assured the Tsimshian that they would not be cheated about their rights, especially since the area had "long been their home."[28]

These assurances were undermined in 1881 when the Indian Reserve Commissioner, Peter O'Reilly, was sent without notification to the Indians, to lay out reserves for the Tsimshian. Few Indians were home at the time, and at a meeting on 5 October the Indians handed O'Reilly a written petition laying out what they saw as necessary land for their reserve. O'Reilly flatly rejected the petition yet later reported that he had made no reserve without consulting the Indians and had given them every fishing station and cultivation plot they had requested.[29]

During the next few years the Indians made little progress in getting either the federal or provincial governments to listen to their claims. The Canadian Pacific Railway was by this time planning to establish a west coast terminus at Port Simpson, and in 1883 a number of white land speculators were able to secretly pre-empt land around the proposed harbour — land that O'Reilly had excluded from the reserve two years earlier.[30] In 1883 as well, an Indian agent was appointed despite the fact the Tsimshian had clearly indicated that they neither wanted nor needed one.

In 1884 a government inquiry into the land problems of the Tsimshian, at Metlakatla as well as at Port Simpson, concluded that the basic problem was that the missionaries were giving the Indians bad advice. The missionaries were blamed for the fact that the Indians would not accept the surveys by O'Reilly or submit to the Indian Advancement Act by accepting an Indian agent. The inquiry report noted that the Indians had been told that "Indian agents are for the good of Indians, The Indian Agents tell us what the Indians want."[31] apparently it was insufficient for the Indians themselves to tell the government what they wanted.

Two years later the Indians managed to persuade a reluctant Crosby to accompany them to Victoria to plead their case. The substance of their demands was that their rights be guaranteed by treaty. They acknowledged that they lacked legal expertise or advice, so all they could do was appeal to the provincial government in the name of Canadian or British justice. Their demands were simply dismissed. They were told by the provincial authorities that the difference between them and whites, "is that being still Indian, or . . . in the position of children, you are not permitted, so far, to exercise the franchise. . . . You are like children. We don't give our children the right to vote until they have come to manhood — to be taught to read and think properly."[32] It was pointed out that all land belonged to the crown and that the crown only gave Indians land because "they do not know so well how to make their own living . . . and special indulgence is extended to them and special care shown."[33] White settlers received no such benefit. One of the natives, Charles Burton, pointed out that all they wanted was some land so they could be free and that their ultimate goal was to become good British subjects, like white people.[34] This desire lay at the bottom of their initial request for a missionary, their change of lifestyle, and their hope for a resolution of the land question.

The only positive result of the trip, as far as the Tsimshian were concerned, was the promise of a joint provincial and federal commission to examine the issue. However, good feelings disappeared when more surveys were done before the commission arrived in the middle of October 1887. Few Indians were home at the time and the commissioners had been instructed to "be careful to discountenance . . . any claim of Indian title to Provincial lands."[35] The few that were home complained bitterly that subjection to the Indian Advancement Act and acceptance of an Indian agent were actually reactionary steps because they had advanced beyond such tutelary devices. The commission merely concluded that Tsimshian demands demonstrated the need for stricter enforcement of legislation concerning Canada's native people, namely by means of the Indian Advancement Act.[36]

Increasingly, the governments blamed the missionaries for the problems, believing that the Indians were incapable of the sophistication required to make demands about such matters as land title and federal and provincial law about Indian affairs. In 1888 there was talk at the federal level of putting pressure on the Methodist Church to have Crosby removed from his post.[37] In 1889, in an attempt to clear his name and to make the federal government aware of the real problem, Crosby went to Ottawa, armed with affidavits and statements from white residents, traders and Indians, laying out clearly the nature of the Indian grievances. In their statements, several Indians intimated that they were considering following William Duncan to Alaska where they could get decent schooling and proper government support. As had been the case with the commissions earlier, Crosby's efforts were unsuccessful in resolving any of the issues.

Following Crosby's failure, the Tsimshian decided to take another approach. In January 1891 over two hundred residents — most of the adult male population — signed a letter addressed to the local Member of Parliament, Robert Hanley Hall, complaining that the land question had not yet been settled. They reviewed the whole history of the problem, from Powell's assurance in 1879 to the commission of 1887. They pointed out that government inaction seemed calculated to "provoke us to break the law."[38] They expressed the desire to be like Canada's other citizens, with a simple form of municipal government so that they could manage their own affairs. The Crosby-directed council was no longer seen as an effective instrument for directing their concerns. Hall requested the Department of Indian Affairs to change the provisions of the Indian Advancement Act for the sake of the Port Simpson people. The request was denied by Deputy Superintendent Vankoughnet because, as he pointed out, there was a prevailing sentiment among government officials that the Indians had received enough from Canada, "the sentiment being to curtail the privileges and concessions already granted rather than in any way to increase them."[39]

Meeting failure here as well, the Tsimshian decided at the end of 1893 to ask for "an elective Indian council under the provisions of the Indian Advancement Act" as "a large number believe that the time is come when we should have an organized council."[40] This council would be directed by an Indian agent rather than by Crosby. The request was made, however, not in acquiescence to the federal government and its Indian policy but as a means to bring their struggle to a new level. As soon as the council was established in 1894, they used it to press their demands on the Indian agent. Obtaining no success, and fed up with what they perceived to be their Indian agent's incompetence and patronizing attitude, the council petitioned Ottawa in 1896 for his removal.[41] Shortly afterwards, the council reopened the land question, asking the federal government to make a fair settlement of their requests.

While the Tsimshian failed to have their land problem resolved, the ways in which they sought to deal with the problem revealed much about their goals and aspirations between 1870 and 1900. They were not hankering for a return to traditional mores. By the mid-1890s they were employed in a wide range of activities: "Salmon canneries, procuring and rafting saw-logs, hunting, fishing, boat-building, trading, working at saw-mills and steamboats, cultivating patches of land, carrying freight and passengers from place to place, (etc.)."[42] Visitors and government officials reported that the Indians appeared to be wealthy, with good, well-furnished homes. James Woodsworth, Superintendent of Methodist missions in western Canada, visiting in 1896, pointed out how eager the Indians were to have their own canneries, steamboats and sawmills as well as control over their political, social and religious lives.[43] They wanted power over their own destinies and did not want to be dependent on others — either whites for employment or missionaries for religion. Their goal seemed to be assimilation into white society as quickly as possible. Port Simpson, already the projected terminus for the Canadian Pacific Railway, became the seat of the government and police for the region in the 1890s. The Port also became an important stop for steamers to Alaska and the Nass and Skeena Rivers' territories. The Indians wanted a larger role in the developments affecting their village and the region.

The role of Crosby in everyday affairs was thus diminished. The new village council, established under the Indian Advancement Act, meant an end to the council Crosby had established twenty years earlier. But his loss of control in everyday affairs was also paralleled by a decline in the religious aspects of the mission. The dissatisfaction expressed in 1885 about the poverty of the village and the lack of progress in the land question was accompanied by a desire for more control over the religious expressions of the people. In 1885, Thomas Wright pointed out to Alexander Sutherland, Secretary of the Methodist Missionary Society, that it was the Tsimshian and not the whites that had first brought the gospel to Port Simpson and that, therefore, the Society ought to train native teachers.[44]

In 1888, in response to the desire of the Tsimshian to have more power over their religious expression, Crosby permitted the formation of the Band of Christian Workers, whose primary purpose was evangelism. While Crosby at this time had great difficulty channelling native enthusiasm into revivals, the Band had little problem gathering enthusiastic support. The Band members preached in the streets and conducted open air services that were punctuated by prayers and shouts and accompanied by lively music complete with a band of drums, horns and tambourines. Banners and flags with various slogans and texts were displayed and band members wore showy uniforms. The Band engaged in Sunday services outside of the regular Sunday worship services and during the winter held services during the week as well. The Band embraced almost all males at Port Simpson and often seemed to be the only element of the mission still religiously alive. Band members were also given permission to accompany Crosby on his missionary tours. But Crosby made no attempt to begin a training program for native religious leaders, and the Indians began to realize that permission to form the Band had only been granted because the missionaries did not see it as a threat to their power.

Indeed, missionary response to the group indicates that they saw it as a harmless safety valve through which Tsimshian religious enthusiasm could be displayed, while church services were conducted according to the manner prescribed by the missionaries. In 1891 the Band of Christian Workers requested that Crosby's municipal council give them permission to build their own worship centre. The request was, of course, turned down, for Crosby continued to control the council. The Band also sought permission to send out missionaries and to use their musical instruments in regular church services. Permission was granted on condition that Crosby's approval be obtained in each specific case.

By the end of 1893 the Band of Christian Workers, ignoring Crosby's objection, had erected its own building. In 1894 the missionaries, responding to the growing assertiveness of the Tsimshian, stated: "We reaffirm the resolution of last year in regard to the use of musical instruments and recommend to each missionary the organization of [a] Band of Christian Workers to be *controlled* by the missionary in charge."[45] But at the end of 1894 Crosby conceded that for the previous three years the Band had not been under the control of the church. The Band members had been successful in obtaining control of their own affairs while still belonging to the Methodist Church.[46] It is most significant, moreover, that the request of the Port Simpson Tsimshian to have their own village council under the Indian Advancement Act came immediately after the old municipal council, controlled by Crosby, had turned down the Band of Christian Workers' request to have their own building. Just as the Band sought independence from Crosby in the affairs of the Methodist Church, so the Tsimshian sought independence from Crosby in the affairs of their village. Paternalism was no longer acceptable. The Port Simpson Tsimshian were now charting their own direction.

Nevertheless, rejection of missionary control was not rejection of the values the missionaries stood for. The issue in the 1890s was the matter of power and control. The Tsimshian frustrations revolved around the fact that they could not become full members of Canadian society. They had adopted the external features of western society such as clothing, shelter, food, social relations and even Christianity. But religious organizations and governments would not allow them to become part of western society. They could attempt to think, act and live like other Canadians and forsake their past, but white Canadians would not accept them as equal partners.

Traditional analysis of missionary activity, when assessing the success or failure of the missionaries' program of conversion, has tended to place its emphasis on either the role of the missionary or on native loss of faith in their own culture.[47] The situation at Port Simpson indicates that the key to understanding Crosby's transformation of Port Simpson lies in recognizing the willingness of the Tsimshian to westernize. Most evaluations of missions place very little or no emphasis on the active role of the natives in their own conversion.

It is unfortunate that the ethnocentrism of the missionaries, who treated the Indians as "children" who needed "nursing," the "care, kind, loving Christian hearts can give them,"[48] is also a part of the historical literature on missions. The nineteenth-century view of missionaries, of the belief in the superiority of their culture and way of life (including religion), is unwittingly adopted by students of missions and of Indian–European relations in general.[49] The inability of Indian societies to combat the destructive power of western technology, particularly with the onset of settlement, has tended to lead most students of this interaction to overlook the nature of Indian response to European mores. As Freerk Ch. Kamma has pointed out, there has been,

> a too facile tendency to suppose that so-called primitive peoples are not capable either of discursive thought and reflection about their own cultural heritage or of adopting a critical attitude towards the great problems of life that will always exist, even with a relatively high degree of integration. The assumption appears to be that it is only through contact with Europeans that these people become aware of their problems.[50]

Undoubtedly, contact with Europeans presented new problems but native peoples dealt with these using in large part their traditional cultural framework.

This European ethnocentrism has resulted in the lack of a clear definition of the conversion experience. There is often an emphasis on the reasons for conversion rather than an understanding of the "act" of conversion. Most analysis has been correct in noting that religion and western mores came as a unified package. However, conversion is frequently defined only in religious terms and understood as the acceptance of a new religious framework. But as K. E. Read has pointed out, religious beliefs are not simply a logical set of ideas but are integrated into the life, the practices and being of a people. They are more than a "logically inter-connected system of ideas about the supernatural."[51] They are part of a whole way of looking at the world and reflect an approach to life. While conversion is frequently seen as the replacement of one set of religious symbols by another, it is in fact the acceptance of a whole new cultural framework. If we define culture as "the framework of beliefs, expressive symbols, and values in terms of which individuals define their world, express their feelings, and make their judgments,"[52] then religion is the network of symbols which give tangible expression to the orientation to life rooted in the cultural context. Conversion involves the adoption of a new cultural basis and thus includes a changed social structure as well as new religious symbols and experience.

Many Indians were aware of this complexity and of the radical implications of their conversion. Marius Barbeau's *The Downfall of Temlaham*, a somewhat over-romanticized account of Indian life, illustrates some of the soul-searching and complexity involved in the decision to become Christian. The Indians faced a choice between the familiar security, tradition and wisdom of their old ways and the risk of a new way, one that brought new forms of wealth and prestige, new ideas about life, liquor, disease and a confusing morality.[53] The Tsimshian at Port Simpson were aware of many of these factors and over the years often made reference to the fact that in becoming Christian they had not only forsaken Tsimshian religious practices but also adopted new styles of living, clothing, education and work. They made a connection between God's "written word" and the white man's way of living as contrasted to their traditional religious practices and their way of living by hunting, gathering and fishing. Conversion was thus a radical new orientation to life rather than the mere acceptance of new religious symbols and expressions.

In making their decision to accept the western cultural heritage, therefore, the Tsimshian had turned their backs on a way of life in which their religion and social institutions had been integrated with underlying cultural values. In becoming western it became imperative for the Tsimshian that their cultural values and everyday lives reflect the fact that they had forsaken their old culture for that of white Canada. The land issue was the most dramatic, poignant and painful demonstration of the fact that the rights of full citizenship would not be theirs. Political and economic power, the measure of worth in Canadian society, was denied. The fragmentation of Indian lives in the twentieth century is largely due to the fact that they have forsaken an integrated cultural framework for one in which they could not be full participants.

While most analyses of missions have exhaustively studied the background, personalities, goals and programs of missionaries, too few have looked at the nature of Indian response and have instead stereotyped most groups of natives in the manner described above. The paucity of sources describing the Indian viewpoint is perhaps the main reason for this deficiency. What is needed in future studies is a sensitive awareness of the nature of *both* Indian and western cultures, taking great care to be aware of ethnocentric biases, and a close look at the motives and responses of *both* parties in their interaction with one another.

Notes

1. Robin Fisher, *Contact and Conflict: Indian–European Relations in British Columbia, 1774–1890* (Vancouver: University of British Columbia Press, 1977), 119–45.

2. Ibid., 47–48.

3. Jean Usher, *William Duncan of Metlakatla: A Victorian Missionary in British Columbia*, National Museum of Man Publication in History, no. 5 (Ottawa: National Museum of Canada, 1974). Usher contends that the Tsimshian of Fort Simpson were converted because of the persuasive personality of William Duncan. Nevertheless, she makes the assumption that the loss of faith in traditional values was instrumental in the Tsimshian decision to convert. See 50–58.

4. Jacinto Caamaño, "The Journal of Jacinto Caamaño," *British Columbia Historical Quarterly* 2 (1938): 201.

5. Usher, *William Duncan of Metlakatla*, 34.

6. Ibid., 38.

7. Fisher, *Contact and Conflict*, 47.

8. Philip Drucker, *Cultures of the North Pacific Coast* (San Francisco: Chandler, 1965), 190.

9. Ibid., 61–64.

10. Hudson's Bay Company, Fort Simpson, Journal, 12 May 1842–22 June 1843, kept by John Work and Roderick Finlayson, entry 23 March 1843.

11. Ibid.

12. Calvin Martin, *Keepers of the Game* (Berkeley and Los Angeles: University of California Press, 1978), 186–87.

13. Usher, *William Duncan of Metlakatla*, 50.

14. Ibid., 57–58.

15. Thomas Crosby, *Up and Down the North Pacific Coast by Canoe and Mission Ship* (Toronto: Missionary Society of the Methodist Church, 1914), 302.

16. Ibid., 80.

17. Clarence Bolt, "Thomas Crosby and the Tsimshian of Port Simpson, 1874–1897" (MA thesis, Simon Fraser University, 1981), 114–17.

18. Ibid., 64–69.

19. Crosby letter, 16 February 1876, *Missionary Notices* no. 8, 129.

20. Green letter, 5 April 1890, *Missionary Outlook* 10 (1890): 109.

21. A.E. Sutherland, "Notes of a Tour Among the Missions of British Columbia," *Missionary Outlook* 6 (1886):3.

22. Ibid., 22.

23. Ibid.

24. Fisher, *Contact and Conflict*, 188.

25. Crosby letter, 20 January 1875, *Missionary Notices* no. 2, 38.

26. Crosby letter, 16 February 1876, *Missionary Notices* no. 8, 130.

27. Molyneux St. John, *The Sea of Mountains, An Account of Lord Dufferin's Tour Through British Columbia in 1876* (London: Hurst and Blackett, 1877), 1: 321–22.

28. Canada, Department of Indian Affairs, *Annual Report*, 1879, Indian Superintendent I.W. Powell's report, 121.

29. Public Archives of Canada (hereafter PAC), O'Reilly to the Superintendent General of Indian Affairs, 25 October 1882, Department of Indian Affairs, Black Series, Western Canada, RG 10, vol. 3605, file 2806.

30. Bolt, "Thomas Crosby and the Tsimshian," 125–26.

31. British Columbia, Metlakatla Inquiry, 1884, *Report of the Commissioners Together with the Evidence* (Victoria: R. Wolfenden, 1885), iv, Evidence.

32. British Columbia, *Report of Conferences Between the Provincial Government and Indian Delegates from Fort Simpson and Naas River* (Victoria: R. Wolfenden, 1887), 255.

33. Ibid., 256.

34. Ibid., 260.

35. British Columbia, *Papers Relating to the Commission Appointed to Enquire into the State and Condition of the Indians of the North-West Coast of British Columbia* (Victoria: R. Wolfenden, 1888), 416.

36. Ibid., Special Appendix no. 2, cvii.

37. PAC, Todd to Powell, 12 June 1888, RG 10, vol. 3776, file 37373-2.

38. PAC, Residents of Port Simpson to Hall, 8 June 1891, RG 10, vol. 3852, file 76586.

39. PAC, Vankoughnet to Vowell, 28 April 1891, RG 10, vol. 3852, file 76586.

40. PAC, Chiefs of Port Simpson to Todd, November 1893, RG 10, vol. 3862, file 83121.

41. PAC, Chiefs and Council of Port Simpson to Vowell, 30 January 1897, RG 10, vol. 3853, file 78547.

42. Canada, Department of Indian Affairs, *Annual Report*, 1897, Todd Report, 87.

43. James Woodsworth, *Thirty Years in the Canadian Northwest* (Toronto: McClelland & Stewart, 1917), 192, 194.

44. Sutherland, "Notes of a Tour," 2.

45. Methodist Church of Canada, British Columbia Conference, Port Simpson District, Ministerial Sessions, 1894, 221.

46. Provincial Archives of British Columbia, Crosby to Raley, 29 November 1894, G.E. Raley, Correspondence Inward, Raley Collection.

47. See Bolt, "Thomas Crosby and the Tsimshian," 164–74, for a detailed discussion on these two positions.

48. Jennings Letter, 30 April 1889, *Missionary Outlook* 9 (1889): 128.

49. This view is reflected by Fisher, *Contact and Conflict*, in his conclusion that Indian societies were enhanced by the introduction of western technological innovations. He assumes that the introduction of new technology, even one with a radically different philosophical and religious basis, allowed for change in Indian societies along existing directions.

50. Freerk Ch. Kamma, *Koreri, Messianic Movements in the Biak-Numfor Culture Area* (The Hague: Martinus Nijhof, 1972), 243.

51. K. E. Read, "Missionary Activities and Social Change in the Central Highlands of Papua and New Guinea," *South Pacific* 5 (1952): 229–38.

52. Clifford Geertz, *The Interpretation of Cultures* (New York: Basic Books, 1973), 44.

53. C. Marius Barbeau, *The Downfall of Temlaham* (Edmonton: Hurtig, 1973), 6, 12–13, 68, 76–77.

BEST LEFT AS INDIANS: THE FEDERAL GOVERNMENT AND THE INDIANS OF THE YUKON, 1894–1950†

KENNETH COATES

Assessing the current state of historical writing on government–Indian relations in the United States of America, Francis Paul Prucha argued that too much attention has been paid to the origins of federal programming, and too little to the implementation of those policies in the field. While some studies illustrate the impact of prevailing public attitudes on government programming, most stop short of tracing national policy changes to the level of implementation, and as Prucha has pointed out, "a policy can be fully understood only by watching it unfold in practise."[1] Consequently, historians know comparatively little about the regional application of federal Indian policy.

Prucha's critique of American historiography applies equally to Canadian scholarship. Commentators on the administration of Indian policy in Canada have typically sketched the broad contours of federal legislation relating to Indians. The consistently superficial analysis employed in these studies, often laced with critical assessments of the paternalism and colonialism inherent in the Indian Act, has resulted in a general characterization of national Indian policy as unwavering, highly centralized and goal-oriented. Indian agents in the field, charged with administering federal programmes, are described by implication as adhering without question to Ottawa's policies.[2]

An explanation for the lack of systematic regional studies may be found in the apparent simplicity and rigidity of federal policy. In a survey of contemporary Indian affairs, Ponting and Gibbins argue that the central goals of federal policy over the last century have been to promote native self-sufficiency, protect the Indians from the evils of white society, encourage conversion to Christianity, and assimilate natives into Cana-

† Revised by the author from an article originally appearing in *Canadian Journal of Native Studies* 4, no. 2 (1984): 179–204.

dian society.³ Although these objectives, in their broad contours, remained intact into the 1970s, national directives did not necessarily translate into local initiatives. In southern Canada, reservations, agricultural training programmes, and church-administered boarding schools figured prominently in native–government relations and seemed to conform to the structures entrenched in the Indian Act. In the north, by contrast, scattered settlements and continued nomadism prevented consistent administration and interfered with the uniform application of national policy.⁴ The actions of federal civil servants, including those of the Department of Indian Affairs in the Yukon Territory between 1894 and 1950, illustrate the uneven implementation of national Indian policy and the limited application of assimilationist objectives. Equally, the Yukon example illustrates that native policy included far more than the provisions of the Indian Act. In the Yukon, as elsewhere, the government also provided a variety of medical and social programmes for the Indians. These initiatives, together with occasional considerations of the Indians' long-term prospects, constituted federal native programming for the Yukon Indians. The Yukon experience illustrates that, while the policy guidelines defined in the Indian Act remained intact, federal authorities in the field had considerable flexibility in administering native affairs. In the Yukon, and in many other northern and non-treaty areas across the country, the continuation of Indian nomadism and harvesting patterns prevented the systematic application of federal policies.

The federal government initially refused to acknowledge any responsibility for its northern territories, let alone for the native inhabitants. Government officials saw little need to extend the treaty system, hastily implemented to clear agricultural areas for settlement, into the north. This neglect of the north, first broken by the cursory examinations undertaken by the Geological Survey of Canada personnel in the 1880s, was further challenged by northern missionaries, particularly William Carpenter Bompas of the Church Missionary Society. The incursions of an allegedly rapacious mining population and the resulting threat to the Indian population upset the missionary, who repeatedly petitioned the government to send a detachment of the North West Mounted Police to supervise the American immigrants. The federal government finally relented in 1894, but even then only partially out of concern for the Indians of the Yukon.⁵

Inspector Charles Constantine of the North West Mounted Police, dispatched in 1894 to investigate conditions in the Yukon gold fields, carried precise instructions on his responsibilities toward the Indians. Although he was the official representative of the Department of Indian Affairs, Constantine was cautioned "not to give encouragement to the idea that they [the Yukon Indians] will be received into treaty, and taken under the care of the government."⁶ The government anticipated little development in the north, and therefore saw no need to alienate Indian lands through treaty. Basic relief measures were contemplated, but the government wanted it clearly understood that the Indians were to receive no better treatment than any other Canadian or immigrant.[7] This policy persisted for some time. Throughout the lands north of the settlement belt, the government negotiated treaties only when native lands were required for permanent development. When such pressures mounted, as in the Mackenzie River valley in 1899–1900, the government "negotiated" treaties, promising annuity payments, reserves and guaranteed access to game, in return for native land surrenders.[8] Before 1896 and the start of the Klondike gold rush, these concerns simply did not apply to the Yukon. Even after the discovery at Bonanza Creek, and the rapid influx of miners into the west-central Yukon, the government remained convinced that the territory could not sustain permanent development. There was, consequently, still no need for a treaty.[9]

The lack of federal interest in a negotiated treaty did not preclude discussion on the matter. In 1902, Jim Boss, self-styled "hereditary chief of the southern Yukon Indians," acting through a Whitehorse lawyer, demanded "compensation because of the taking possession of their [the Indians'] land and hunting grounds by the white people."[10] The government rejected the petition, arguing that federal relief grants provided ample compensation for the ills suffered by the Indians.[11] The native people did not pick up the treaty issue again for more than half a century, but the Anglican Church kept the matter alive. Reverend A.E. O'Meara, then financial secretary for the Diocese of the Yukon, prepared a reasonably comprehensive treaty claim on behalf of the Indians between 1907 and 1910. The claim reflected its missionary origins, focusing on a request for Anglican-administered schools, game preserves, and community improvement projects. The penultimate proposal also called for the appointment of a full-time Indian agent, as well as provision for better medical care and official recognition of native marriages.[12]

Before the church document reached Frank Oliver, Minister of the Interior, the request for treaty negotiations had been dropped.[13] The clergy had correctly read the government's continued opposition to a land settlement for the Yukon Indians. Responding to the request, Oliver reiterated well-known government policy: "The Government seeks to protect the interests of all, whether Indian or white, but is not responsible for specifically protecting those of the Indian." The Minister rejected the paternalism inherent in expanded government assistance, claiming that it "had been most harmful to the Indians by accentuating their original communism, that is to say, the natural dependence of the Indians upon others." Acceding to the treaty request would change native ways, and in Oliver's judgement, they would "if left as Indians earn a better living."[14] The government made it clear, first in 1894 and again in 1910, that there would be no treaty for the Yukon Indians, although the signing of Treaty 11 with the Dene of the upper Mackenzie River basin did bring a number of Yukon Indians under treaty.[15] The Anglican clergy continued their interventions on behalf of their native charges, but they had abandoned the idea of a treaty.[16]

Throughout these discussions, the Yukon Indians were almost silent, while the continued activism of the Anglican clergy ensured that they were never without an advocate. As Commissioner F. Congdon remarked in 1903, "[I]nstead of teaching the Indians self-reliance and independence, they [Anglican missionaries] aid most strongly in making them mendicants. I am daily in receipt of letters from Indians written by a missionary, asking for all sorts of favours."[17] When natives approached the government on their own, they did so with reference to specific tracts of land. In 1900, Jim Boss asked for a parcel of land on Lake Laberge, arguing that it "has been occupied by his people from time immemorial."[18] In 1933, Joe Squam, "chief" of the Teslin Indians, similarly claimed lands in the Wolf Lake region on the basis that he had "hunted and trapped over this ground since a child."[19] In both cases, the appeals represented a desire for personal gain, rather than an assertion of a broader native claim. Boss's representation was successful and the government allocated a small reserve, but Squam's claims were quickly rejected, largely because the federal agent believed that the individual claim conflicted with the band's needs in the area. In a general sense, the Indians did not hesitate to defend their interests, but they seldom based their appeals to government on inherent right of occupation. Protests against game laws or inappropriate government regulations were based on economic hardship, not aboriginal title to land or resources.[20] This approach reflected the fact that the Indians continued to move about seasonally as they had for generations and that they remained confident that their largely unchallenged occupation of the land would continue indefinitely.

The federal government's primary objective, illustrated in Oliver's comments, was to maintain the Indians in their now "traditional" role as harvesters and trappers. From 1894 to 1950, there was little effort to assimilate the natives. Instead, and in the interest of preserving the "Indian way," the government sought to segregate the Indians from an allegedly avaricious and destructive white population. In setting aside their oft-proclaimed interest in assimilation, federal civil servants emphasized the need to protect the Indians from destruction. These objectives, assimilation and protection, although both part of the same federal Indian policy were, as J. Chamberlain has argued, inherently contradictory.[21] In the Yukon, the government followed the preferred national option of protection. This decision was manifested in the federal government's two central policy initiatives for the Yukon Indians: residential reservations and the preservation of access to game.

The desire to isolate the Indians first surfaced with the commencement of the Klondike gold rush in 1896. William Bompas requested a small reserve near Dawson City to keep his native communicants away from the miners. Despite the contrary judgements of North West Mounted Police Inspector Charles Constantine and Territorial Commissioner William Ogilvie, the Department of Indian Affairs allocated a small plot of land. The 160-acre parcel was situated three miles downstream from Dawson City, not far enough away to satisfy Constantine and Ogilvie, but somewhat removed from white settlement.[22] Debate over this reserve resurfaced shortly thereafter. Ogilvie's argument that "discoveries of gold have been made in that vicinity, and before I recommend any extension of the 160 acres, I will await the development of this ground, as gold mining ground," made it clear that developmental priorities outweighed concern for Indian needs.[23]

Residential reserves were established whenever development seemed imminent or when Indians moved too close to white communities. The discovery of silver and lead ore near Mayo, for example, attracted a number of Indians to the vicinity of the new town. The federal government laid out a reserve in 1915, situating it two and a half miles downstream from Mayo, and on the opposite side of the river. The selection of this site, which kept the Indians away from white influence while preserving potentially valuable lands for further development, was applauded by the territorial Indian agent in subsequent years.[24] The establishment of such a reserve did not ensure permanence. If whites demanded access to lands granted to the Indians, the government readily considered a transfer of reserve lands. The Whitehorse reserve was relocated four times between 1915 and 1921.[25] Although the interests of the white community usually governed the location of reserves, federal authorities occasionally permitted native needs to determine the appropriate sites. In 1898 at Tagish,[26] and again at Little Salmon in 1915, the government protected Indian reservations from white encroachment. As the federal surveyor responsible for laying out the Little Salmon parcel noted, however, "It is a matter of record that the Indians have not made any request for this reserve."[27] White encroachment on reserves and relocation of Indians were not unique to the Yukon. The distinctiveness of the Yukon experience lay in the use of residential reserves, which were small parcels of land designed solely as a site for seasonal homes. In many southern districts, where government policy called for the Indians to be trained as agriculturalists, they received larger reserves.

Residential reserves, usually allotted according to the Mayo model, were surveyed throughout the territory. In addition to the small sites near Dawson, Mayo, Little Salmon and Whitehorse, the federal government established reserves at Carcross, Teslin, Selkirk, Carmacks and Old Crow. The encouragement of native habitation on lands separated from centres of white population was an integral part of a larger plan. By maintaining social distance between natives and whites, and by keeping the Indians on the fringes of the mining economy, the authorities sought to preserve the nomadic, harvesting Indians in their "natural" state.[28] Plans to restrict Indian involvement in white social and economic activities served little purpose without an alternative. The desired substitute for integration was the preservation of native access to wild game. Almost all missionaries, North West Mounted Police (later Royal Canadian Mounted Police), and government officials despaired of the Indians accepting "civilization." Most believed that the Indians had to continue to hunt, trap and fish in order to survive. It followed, therefore, that Indian access to game had to be preserved. Limited white competition for animals and fish made the attainment of this goal reasonably easy.

While most officials agreed on the need to preserve Indian access to game, accomplishing it proved more difficult. As with residential reserves, the possibility of conflict between future development and native requirements limited the civil servants' willingness to take strong action. In the short term, there seemed to be few problems. Limited white settlement and restricted mining activity left most Yukon Indians largely unchallenged in their harvesting pursuits. Officials advanced several proposals to entrench this native–land relationship, including Acting Commissioner Lithgow's 1907 suggestion that all the Indians in the territory be removed to the Peel-Porcupine district, an area believed to be barren of mineral riches.[29] Not until the 1930s, when increased hunting pressure threatened game resources on a broader basis, did suggestions for substantial native-only game preserves receive serious consideration. Such hunting reserves had been adopted, seemingly with some success, in the Mackenzie River valley. Again, however, the federal government hesitated to support such a proposal for the resource-rich Yukon.[30] Harper Reed, Indian Agent for the Stikine district in northern British Columbia, brought forward the first such proposal in 1935. Arguing, contrary to the claims of the Royal Canadian Mounted Police, that whites were overhunting in the southern Yukon, Reed suggested that a substantial block of land be placed off limits to white hunters and trappers.[31] His plan floundered on other grounds. Charles Camsell, noted northern surveyor and then Deputy Minister of the Department of Mines, made it clear that Indian concerns were not on the government's list of priorities: "If we are not going to reserve our northern regions exclusively for the use of the natives but are looking to encourage the opening up of these regions to the people of Canada generally, then I think we must limit the extent of the preserves to meet the pressing needs of the natives but no more."[32] Development, not native access to game, took precedence in the Yukon.

This did not mean that the federal government was not concerned about Indian hunting and fishing rights. Government agents often acted to restrict white activities in favour of native needs. In 1929, when white trappers exploited the Old Crow flats muskrat stocks, and in 1932 when native fishing and trapping in the Little Atlin area faced a substantial white challenge, the government stepped in to protect the Indians' interest.[33] But the limits of this intervention were quite clear, for the idea of entrenching these rights to game preserves in hunting regulations found little favour in official circles.

The government's ambivalence finally succumbed to changing conditions and attitudes. Continued white hunting pressure, particularly during the construction of the Alaska Highway in 1942–1943, increased concerns about the future of Indian hunting. In 1947, Indian Agent R.J. Meek requested the implementation of registered traplines, a programme used to good effect in northern British Columbia. Under Meek's plan, the natives had first claim to trapping territories, with half-breeds and "old-timers" making their selections before the general allocation of traplines.[34] The registration programme, established in 1950, coincided with a prolonged downturn in fur prices, which sapped the vitality from the regional fur trade. Trapline registration stopped substantially short of proposals for Indian-only game preserves, but prior to 1950 it represented the outer limits of federal munificence.[35] While federal authorities, seconded by the territorial administration, believed in leaving the Indians as hunters and trappers, the imperatives of northern development interfered with the logical application of the preferred programme. The Yukon, by official definition, served as a resource base for the rest of the country. The government could not entrench native access to game without harming the prospects for future development, so Indian interests were repeatedly subordinated to concerns about possible economic expansion.

Judging by the behaviour of the Yukon Indians, most of whom remained hunters and trappers to 1950, the government's effort at segregation had worked. In truth, limited mining development, restricted settlement, a strong fur market and a native preference for harvesting over industrial labour ensured that the Indians remained as Indians. Government initiatives succeeded, it seems, in spite of themselves. Residential reserves and economic segregation were more symbols than effective policies. On this level, therefore, government programming for the Yukon Indians extended little beyond an acceptance of the status quo and an attempt to entrench the existing social and economic balance in the territory through federal initiative.

Federal Indian policy in the Yukon Territory bore only marginal resemblance to the national imperatives spelled out in the Indian Act. There was, for instance, little commitment to assimilation, the alleged cornerstone of national Indian policy. In place of the cultural imperialism usually associated with federal Indian programming, the government followed a plan of "best left as Indians." This contradiction may have been inherent in the government's programme, as commitment to protection and self-sufficiency almost by definition interfered with attempts at assimilation. Federal Indian policy, however, proved to be surprisingly flexible, permitting government agents in the field and in Ottawa to adapt national policy directives to local conditions. Given the Yukon's limited settlement and the substantial socio-cultural barriers to Indian participation in the mining economy, the government's acceptance of Indians as hunters and trappers was both logical and cost-effective. There was no systematic plan for the Yukon Indians. Rather, programmes such as residential reserves and protection of harvesting rights evolved on an ad hoc basis in response to changing circumstances.

For the government agents charged with administrating territorial Indian matters, the lack of a coherent policy limited their activities to more mundane matters, such as providing emergency rations and medical care for those who slipped below the margin of subsistence or of basic good health. It was clear to civil servants that the arrival of the mining frontier had been at best a mixed blessing for the Indians. New diseases and resource competition had brought an array of social and economic ills. The government responded, carefully and parsimoniously, based on an unwritten but generally accepted commitment to care for Indians displaced or injured by white advancement. It is at this level that understanding of the administration of Indian affairs in Canada is most deficient. In a recent essay on the north, Peter Usher commented, "The government had sought to remove any encumbrance to land title and settlement and the police maintained law and order. Beyond these measures, however, the government failed to detect any responsibility on its part for those people over whose territories it had assumed control."[36] While the observation may accurately describe some northern districts, it does not apply to the Yukon.

Government involvement in Indian health and welfare commenced with the arrival of the North West Mounted Police in 1894. Although enjoined against encouraging treaty negotiations, Inspector Constantine, official representative of the Department of Indian Affairs, was authorized to provide relief and medical assistance. In 1898, the police passed fiscal responsibility for such activities to the Yukon Territorial government, but officers in the field continued to provide the actual aid.[37] The Anglican Church demanded greater attention to Indian affairs than was possible under this ad hoc arrangement. The government responded in 1914 by appointing former missionary John Hawksley to the newly created post of full-time Yukon Indian Agent.[38] Hawksley offered little direction on Indian matters: his proudest boast was that "The Indians feel they have a place to go when they are in trouble where they can be advised and helped: they appreciate it very much."[39] Hawksley remained in the post until 1933 when, anxious to save money, the federal government passed the duties back to the Royal Canadian Mounted Police, who delegated a single officer, on a part-time basis, to deal with matters as they arose.[40] Under both Hawksley and the RCMP, the office of territorial Indian Agent functioned primarily as an administrative centre, dispensing and authorizing relief payments, organizing medical care and educational programmes, and reporting routinely to the Ottawa office. The position took on greater importance when R.J. Meek was appointed full-time Indian Agent in 1946. Meek's initiative and deep interest in native matters revitalized the office.[41] From Constantine to Meek, however, individuals responsible for the administration of Indian matters seldom addressed the broader issues facing native society. Instead, they responded to the short-term needs of Indians affected by the expansion of the northern mining frontier.

Relief, or welfare, has long been the government programme most readily identified with Indians. It is often assumed that the Indians willingly surrendered to the convenience of government assistance, abandoning more rigorous pursuits in favour of supplication at the Indian agent's table. Those administering the Yukon relief system almost universally shared this belief, and their attitudes subsequently shaped the programme. But the Yukon experience demonstrates that this is a misleading view of native interest in government support.

Federal authorities were reluctant to make extensive commitments to the Indians.[42] Faced with the near starvation of a small band of Indians at Moosehide in 1900, officials grudgingly accepted the need to offer more extensive aid. North West Mounted Police Inspector Z. Wood of Dawson authorized immediate dispersal of food to alleviate the crisis, only applying for official permission after the fact. That approval came grudgingly. Wood was cautioned that "whenever possible the Indians should be required to perform labour or supply game, skins or other commodities in return for the provisions issued to them."[43] In the short term, however, police officers were to "provide against anything like destitution."[44]

From 1900 onward, the federal government provided basic relief for those truly in need, but few took up the offer and the welfare rolls were limited to a small number of widowed, aged or infirm natives.[45] Occasionally relief was required on a broader scale, as at McQuesten in 1905 and in the southern Yukon in 1912, when game supplies were insufficient to meet group needs.[46] Even though few actually applied for assistance, the police officers administering the aid before the appointment of Hawksley believed that the availability of relief rendered the Indians graceless supplicants. The Commanding Officer of the Whitehorse Detachment commented in 1908, "It is evident that the government assistance given to sick and destitute Indians at Whitehorse is most injurious to the well being and morale of the Indians." He then proceeded to ascribe alcohol abuse, prostitution and general laziness to the "pernicious effect of relief."[47] The police consequently sought means of controlling anticipated abuse. Inspector Horrigan noted in 1912 that "young husky Indians asking for provisions were asked to split some stove wood. Needless to say in every case they found that after all they did not require provisions.

This plan has worked admirably in weeding out undeserving cases."[48] The government provided relief for those truly in need but the police, convinced that the Indians were inveterate malingerers, closely regulated the disbursement.

The relief programme expanded considerably under John Hawksley. The new Indian agent often called on his former missionary colleagues to assist him, while also allowing police officers and fur traders to allocate supplies when necessary.[49] Even with the expanded availability, there is little evidence that the Indians found the relief system desirable. It appears, in fact, as though only the truly destitute applied for aid. In this, the Indians were hardly different from those few whites whose sustenance depended on wild game. When resources were played out or grubstakes dwindled, white trappers and prospectors also fell back on meagre government handouts. Sustained by a viable, remunerative harvesting economy and facing little pressure to abandon their nomadic pursuits, the Indians found little attraction in eking out a marginal existence on the social and physical fringes of white communities. The relief system provided an important safety net for times when other means of support failed. In offering such aid, and assisting Indians harmed by white expansion, government agents were responding to local exigencies, not following general national objectives. In this administrative area, as with broader policy concerns, regional realities conditioned the scope and the substance of federal Indian programming.

While few Indians suffered significant economic distress, many did feel the ravages of European diseases, and a majority of those on relief accepted aid because of illness. Recognizing the non-Indians' role in the spread of these diseases, the federal government made substantial provision for medical care. Initially, North West Mounted Police surgeons offered assistance to the Indians whenever required. By 1906, the ad hoc reliance on police personnel had been superseded by a more permanent system. The Department of Indian Affairs placed four doctors on permanent retainer who attended to the Indians as required. When permitted by an authorized official, natives could visit the doctor, receive free medication and other aid, and were even hospitalized without charge.[50]

The federal government's involvement with medical care became particularly evident during epidemics. The Yukon Indians had been struck by repeated virgin soil epidemics (illnesses to which the natives had no natural immunity)[51] since the 1840s. After the arrival of the NWMP in the mid-1890s, the government attempted to control the spread of diseases and to care for the afflicted. As with most federal programmes for the Indians, other considerations also conditioned government response. Diseases carried by the nomadic Indians threatened, albeit not as seriously, the white population, and it served everyone's interests to control the dispersal of illness. Containing the epidemics in the Indian camps was an important form of preventative medicine for the rest of the territory, so government agents responded quickly to news of a potential epidemic by rigidly enforcing quarantines. This system, imposed repeatedly throughout the territory, worked in combination with regular medical attendance to provide the Yukon Indians with a surprisingly comprehensive medical care system.[52] In providing relief and medical care, the federal government informally acknowledged its obligation to care for Indians harmed by the advance of the mining frontier. But the ad hoc, crisis-driven interventions did not spring from any consistent desire to "improve" or "civilize" the Yukon Indians.

Educational initiatives, by contrast, seemed deliberately aimed at reshaping and undermining native culture. Recent studies of native education in Canada and the United States have defined church and government schooling as mediums of "cultural imperialism." More than any other branch of government programming, education was designed to eliminate the remaining vestiges of tribalism, paganism and backwardness. It was through education that governments undertook to transform indigenous, colonized societies into coloured versions of the European model.[53] The appearance in southern Canada of industrial and boarding schools, plus a widespread network of reserve day schools, suggests that government accepted this potentially powerful institution as a tool of assimilation. The emphasis on Christianity, industrial skills, work discipline and basic citizenship, combined with a ready deprecation of native talents, sought to destroy Indian culture and replace it with Canadian values and attitudes.[54] While this characterization may reflect goals and conditions in southern districts, it does not adequately explain the evolution of Indian education in the Yukon.

The federal government placed surprisingly little value on the educational offerings of the churches, and provided enough money to mollify clerical, rather than Indian demands. The Anglican Church held primary responsibility for native education in the territory, operating several seasonal day schools and the residential facility at Carcross. The day schools, in particular, found little favour with government officials. The irregular programmes, offered only when the Indians resided near a mission, were taught by teachers with widely varying qualifications. Through the 1920s and 1930s, many of the teachers were students on summer leave from the Anglican School of Theology in Vancouver. Their unquestioned enthusiasm could not compensate for their lack of knowledge of local conditions and their inability to converse in native languages. Justifying the federal government's limited interest in day schools, Indian Agent John Hawksley commented in 1933:

> The Indians, owing to changed circumstances, cannot afford to
> stay around the villages or leave their families while the men go
> away to hunt and trap, they are compelled to separate into small

parties and live in the woods for the purpose of hunting and trapping in order to make a living. Opportunities of obtaining work from the white people are very much reduced. To insist upon the Indian families staying in the village (which has been suggested) would mean that some of them would have to receive help in the way of provisions. It appears to be a much wiser policy to keep them independent, earning their own living, and they are less liable to get into bad habits.[55]

Faced with a choice between improved education and continued native self-sufficiency, the government clearly favoured the latter. Not until after World War II did the federal government place any importance on the day school programme. The modest grants provided for these schools served ultimately more as an indirect subsidy to the Anglican missions than as support for a deliberate plan of assimilation.

The missionaries, but not necessarily the federal government, had higher hopes for the Carcross Residential School. Children were removed from their parents at a young age and separated through their formative years from the influence of their tribal culture. As a total institution, designed to recast all aspects of the young minds placed under the teachers' care, in other parts of Canada the boarding school served for church and government as the primary means of assimilation. The federal government clearly had such objectives in mind when the industrial–boarding school programme expanded westward in the late nineteenth century. By the time the government agreed in 1911 to fund the Carcross Residential School, however, both government and church attitudes had changed considerably. To many, the industrial school concept had failed, offering the students unusable skills, raising false expectations and inadequately preparing the children for life after school. As early as 1906, the Special Indian Committee of the Missionary Society of the Church of England in Canada recommended that education be limited to basic literacy, elementary arithmetic, and "such additional work as will fit the child to take his place as workman in the locality in which he is to live."[56] The federal government, especially Frank Pedley and his minister, Frank Oliver, shared these opinions. Both men encouraged a less structured boarding school curriculum, and Oliver went even further, wondering on several occasions whether the boarding school format was of any utility.[57]

Carcross school administrators attempted unsuccessfully to overcome the contradictions inherent in their programme. Education centred on vocational training that would "be useful and profitable to them in after life." The teachers taught the boys to hunt and fish and provided basic handyman skills; girls were encouraged to develop beadwork and other "profitable" skills, as well as domestic talents. While modifying their educational offerings in accordance with the limited prospects for industrial work for Indians, the Christian teachers refused to alter their religious mission. They systematically encouraged the moral and spiritual "improvement" of the native children, even if it meant the equally systematic depreciation of Indian values and beliefs. Special emphasis was placed on hygiene, work discipline, manners, and Christian morality. The school's legacy lay in one fundamental contradiction. In the occupational area, training focused on skills essential for survival in the hunting and fishing camps, while co-incidentally the moral and spiritual message taught the children to abhor the culture of their home villages. The students carried this burden with them when they left Carcross. Ironically, the programme designed with the limited goal of making them "better Indians" only served to turn them into marginal people, caught between a native lifestyle they had learned to disdain and a white society unwilling to accept them as equals.[58]

Even in the field of education, the centrepiece of attempts to assimilate the Indians, the federal government had developed a sharply modified programme for the Yukon Territory. Departmental officials placed little value on the Church's work, viewing federal monetary contributions as an unavoidable subsidy for Anglican efforts. The government remained reluctant to encourage, let alone force, the natives to abandon nomadic patterns, even if it meant that the children would not be available for schooling.

The federal government's objective for the Yukon Indians departed in several significant respects from declared national objectives in the period before 1945. Several of the elements contained in the Indian Act, including encouraging self-sufficiency, protection of natives from white society and support for their Christianization, found their way into Yukon practice, although seldom as a result of deliberate administrative decisions. There was, by contrast, no commitment to assimilation. The authorities, even though aware of their power to force change, remained convinced that the Yukon Indians should be left as Indians. While the government consequently supported the natives' desire to hunt and trap, the low priority assigned to Yukon Indian matters prevented the entrenchment of native access to game and other resources. While shying away from an assimilationist model, the government did provide medical care and welfare, aimed principally at helping natives deal with the dislocations attending white expansion. The authorities retained their determination to keep Indians as Indians, supporting their desire to hunt and trap and working to avoid their absorption into the unreliable mining economy.

After World War II, federal programming with regard to Yukon Indians made a dramatic shift, ushering in a new era of government–native programming. The striking increase in interventionism after 1945 represented the practical manifestation of new national imperatives. The post-war commitment of Mackenzie King's Liberal administration to a national social welfare system foreshadowed major new directions in government programming for all Canadians. Much of the new activity stemmed from policies affecting all Canadians, including the Mothers' Allowance introduced in 1944, but other programmes originated more directly from a recognition of changing conditions in the Yukon, caused in part by the construction of the Alaska Highway and Canol Pipeline during the war, and a precipitous decline in fur prices after 1947.

Several of the new policies represented expansions of existing initiatives. The post-war period saw the extension of medical care outside the Dawson–Whitehorse corridor, a tuberculosis survey, the addition of a special tuberculosis wing to the Whitehorse General Hospital, the hiring of a Public Health nurse to administer routine medical services and provide health education, an immunization programme and special dental clinics. The government also expanded relief measures, particularly following the collapse of the fur trade.[59] Indian Agent R.J. Meek tried to remove the native people from welfare rolls, by "assisting the Indians to be self-supporting and reliant." Whenever appropriate, Meek declared, financial aid was "given to Indians to assist them in possible worthwhile fields of endeavour, in preference to direct relief."[60] As before, the myriad medical and welfare programmes available to Indians far exceeded those provided to the white population.

The programme with the greatest impact in the 1945–1950 period was the Mothers' Allowance. To qualify for the monthly allotments, a woman had only to be a resident of Canada with children under the age of sixteen registered in an attending school. Given the inadequate day school system in the Yukon, plus the refusal of most territorial public schools to accept native students, the government decided to eliminate the educational requirement for the Indians. There were other controls, however. Afraid that the Indians' nomadic lifestyle would lead to profligate waste of the federal grant, the government insisted upon issuing the payments "in kind." By providing food and clothing instead of a cheque, the authorities could dictate native spending. Seeing little of value in native diet, government officials insisted that canned milk, tomatoes, and prepared baby foods be included in individual allotments.[61] The programme had other, even greater significance than the important alterations it dictated in diet and material culture. Beginning in the early 1950s, the government began to apply the regulations regarding school attendance with increasing vigour, forcing Indian parents into a difficult choice between seasonal mobility and a more sedentary existence calculated to ensure a continuity of payments. The government expanded the day school and residential school programmes in the same period, drawing more children into its educational network and more families into permanent settlement near the towns.[62]

The federal government's new direction in social programming after 1945 had important consequences for the Yukon Indians. Mothers'

Allowances, pensions for the aged, educational support, employment programmes, expanded medical care and welfare were all part of a greatly enhanced level of government support. Through the 1950s and following decades, government intervention increased, as the federal civil service sought new ways to "improve" the natives' condition. For the Yukon Indians, it was only after 1945 that the federal government's native policy approached the interventionist-assimilationist level long believed to typify government–Indian relations in Canada.[63]

The Yukon example illustrates how declared public policy goals can be transformed in the process of becoming administrative practice. The national commitment to protection and assimilation remained intact well past 1950, but civil servants and Indian agents aware of local conditions did not apply the imperatives of federal legislation with unwavering conviction. Paradoxically, federal involvement in the Yukon was both more active and less interventionist than is typically suggested. Accepting an unwritten obligation to assist Indians affected by white expansion, the government offered relief and medical care significantly in advance of that available to white residents. At the same time, the Department of Indian Affairs shied away from a policy of direct assimilation. The policy of "best left as Indians" dominated until the 1950s. Residential reserves and preferential game regulations represented a conscious attempt to encourage the social and economic segregation of native and white, and hence preserve the "Indian way."

The federal government's non-intervention does not, however, indicate an interest in the long-term viability of native society in the Yukon. Territorial realities simply interfered with the logical application of national objectives. The low priority assigned to Indian affairs ensured that the government did not entrench the policy of segregation through permanent game preserves. Potential development, and not native access to resources, remained the principal consideration of the government. Federal authorities repeatedly rejected requests for guarantees of Indian trapping and hunting rights, preferring instead to protect the territory for mining and tourist hunting. Self-interest also had a more immediate dimension. Retaining the Indians on reserves and providing for their advancement toward the norms of non-Indian Canadian society required money, as the administration of southern Indians demonstrated. Allowing the Indians to sustain themselves through harvesting was a cost-effective means of looking after their interests, even if it required the abrogation, or at best postponement, of the declared government policy of assimilation. Not until after 1945 was the national dedication to assimilation pursued in the Yukon with the same vigour as in other parts of Canada.

While the policy guidelines of the Indian Act provided a framework for government–Indian relations, regional and national administrators enjoyed the latitude to relate national imperatives to local conditions.

Encouraging self-sufficiency and protecting the Indians from the white population were the elements of national policy that dominated Yukon programming. Officials established residential reserves but refused to negotiate treaties, and they protected Indian access to resources without granting game preserves. Indian needs were constantly subordinated to the hope of development, but limited mining precluded conflict over land. Even education did not lead to assimilation because of the government's limited financial support for church schools. Accordingly, officials were still doggedly asserting as late as the 1950s that the hunting and trapping life offered the best prospect for the Indians. For their part, the native people agreed with this view and still preferred to hunt game than to rely on meagre government hand-outs. The Yukon example is indicative of government policy in many of the northern and non-agricultural parts of the country. Local Indian policy was not always dictated by national norms, and even federal programmes were not necessarily consistent with the general concepts embodied in the Indian Act.

Notes

1. Paul Prucha, *Indian Policy in the United States: Historical Essays* (Lincoln: University of Nebraska Press, 1981), 14.

2. For a review of this literature, see R. Surtees, *Canadian Indian Policy: A Critical Bibliography* (Bloomington: Indiana University Press, 1982). For the post-Confederation period, see J.R. Ponting and R. Gibbins, *Out of Irrelevance: A Socio-Political Introduction to Indian Affairs in Canada* (Toronto: Butterworths, 1980).

3. Ponting and Gibbins, *Out of Irrelevance*, 3–30.

4. This has not prevented commentators from assuming that federal Indian policy was one-directional. Hugh Brody, *Maps and Dreams: Indians and the British Columbia Frontier* (Vancouver: Douglas and McIntyre, 1981); Louis-Edmond Hamelin, *Canadian Nordicity: It's Your North Too* (Montreal: Harvest House, 1979), 198–200; Paul Tennant, "Native Political Organization in British Columbia, 1900–1969: A Response to Internal Colonialism," *BC Studies* no. 55 (Autumn 1982): 3–49.

5. Morris Zaslow, *The Opening of the Canadian North, 1870–1914* (Toronto: McClelland and Stewart, 1971), 77–100.

6. Hayter Reed to Charles Constantine, 29 May 1894, Department of Indian Affairs (hereafter DIA), vol. 1115, Deputy Superintendent's Letterbook, 27 April 1894–16 November 1894, Public Archives of Canada (hereafter PAC).

7. Memorandum, 2 December 1897, DIA, vol. 1121, Letterbook 10, August 1897–9 June 1898, PAC; Hayter Reed to Bishop of Selkirk, 19 March 1897, Anglican Church Records, New Series, file 4, Yukon Territorial Archives (hereafter YTA); Canada, House of Commons, *Debates*, vol. 46 (1898): 814.

8. René Fumoleau, *As Long as This Land Shall Last: A History of Treaty 8 and Treaty 11, 1870–1939* (Toronto: McClelland and Stewart, 1973), 30–39.

9. David Hall, *Clifford Sifton: The Young Napoleon* (Vancouver: UBC Press, 1982).

10. Jackson to Supt. General of Indian Affairs, 31 June 1902, DIA, vol. 4037, file 317 050, PAC.

11. J.D. McLean to Jackson, 28 January 1902, DIA, vol. 4037, file 317 050, PAC; Congdon to Sifton, 10 September 1904, ibid.; Asst. Secretary—Memorandum to Mr. Pedley, 19 October 1904, ibid.

12. Memo for the Minister re: Yukon Indians, c. 1907, Anglican Church Records, New Series, file 2, YTA; Pedley to Oliver, 23 January 1908, Anglican Church Records, Carcross Property file; Notes made from interview with Reverend A.M. O'Meara re: Indians in the Yukon, 1908, Carcross Property file; Indian Matters: Recommendations of Messrs. Hawksley and O'Meara, 1908, ibid; Memo for Archbishop regarding Yukon Indian work, 1908, ibid.

13. Requests regarding Yukon Indians, 1908, Anglican Church Records, New Series, file 3, YTA.

14. Notes of interview with Mr. Pedley and Mr. Oliver, 26 February 1909, Anglican Church Records, New Series, file 2, YTA.

15. The inclusion of the Liard Indians, due solely to the configuration of the Mackenzie drainage basin, hardly constituted a deliberate recognition of aboriginal title in the territory or a significant deviation from previous policy. See Fumoleau, *As Long as This Land Shall Last*, 150–215. For a brief statement on the treaty issue in the Yukon, see "Land Entitlement of Indians of the Yukon and N.W.T." by Col. H.M. Jones, Director, Indian Affairs Branch, Active Files, file 801/30-0-1, Indian Affairs and Northern Development, Hull, Quebec (hereafter IAND).

16. On Anglican activities, see Roberts to Stringer, 7 January 1910, Anglican Church Records, New Series, file 2, YTA. That interest has been maintained to the present. Hugh McCullum and K. McCullum, *This Land is Not For Sale: Canada's Original People and Their Land* (Toronto: Anglican Book Centre, 1975). Native interest in land entitlements in the Yukon, as it did in the rest of Canada, took on new life in the 1960s, culminating in the 1973 release of a comprehensive land claim by the Yukon Indians. See Yukon Native Brotherhood, *Together Today For Our Children Tomorrow* (Whitehorse: YNB, 1973).

17. Congdon to Pedley, 28 May 1903, DIA, vol. 4001, file 207 418, PAC.

18. Miller to Ogilvie, 10 April 1900, RG91, vol. 7, file 1331, PAC; Commissioner to Deputy Minister of the Interior, 1 May 1900, ibid.

19. Squam to Indian Department, 22 August 1922, DIA, vol. 6761, file 420–21, PAC.

20. When trapline registration was introduced in 1950, for example, the main native protest was over the annual $10 fee. Meek to Gibson, 27 September 1950, YRGI, Series 3, vol. 11, file 12–23B, YTA; Moses, Tizya and Netro to Meek, 24 July 1950, ibid.; Petition from Chief William Johnson et al., 7 July 1950, ibid.

21. J.E. Chamberlin, *The Harrowing of Eden* (Toronto: Fitzhenry and Whiteside, 1975), 90.

22. Constantine to Deputy Minister of the Interior, 19 November 1896, file 801/30-0-1, IAND; Extract from William Ogilvie's letter, 8 November 1896, ibid.; Constantine to Dear Sir, 13 November 1896, Constantine Letterbook, Charles Constantine Papers, MG30, E55, PAC; Smart to Bompas, 12 August 1897, Anglican Church Records, New Series, file 4, YTA; McLean Memorandum, 26 April 1897, file 801/30-0-1, IAND; McGee to Minister of the Interior, 27 March 1900, RG91, vol. 7, file 1187, PAC.

23. Ogilvie to Secretary, Department of the Interior, 11 December 1900, RG91, vol. 7, file 1187, PAC; Commissioner to Bompas, 27 September 1900, ibid.

24. Hawksley to McLean, 7 April 1915, DIA, vol. 4081, file 478 700, PAC; Moodie to Sir, 1 April 1915, ibid.; Brownlee to McLean, 19 October 1915, RG91, vol. 46, file 29 967, PAC.

25. Hawksley to McLean, 25 November 1915, file 801/30-0-1, IAND; Hawksley to McLean, 19 October 1917, file 801/30-18-8, IAND; Bethune to Superintendent of Trusts and Reserves, 14 May 1958, file 801/30-0-1, IAND; Meek to Indian Affairs Branch, 17 February 1948, file 801/30-18-8, IAND.

26. Strickland to Officer in Command, Upper Yukon, 16 August 1898, file 801/30-3-5, IAND; Pereira to White, 14 September 1898, ibid.

27. C. Swanson to Commissioner, 1 September 1915, RG91, vol. 46, file 29 995, PAC; Brownlee to Secretary, Department of Indian Affairs, 19 August 1916, file 801/30-4-10, IAND; Report of Survey of Little Salmon Indian Reserve, c. 1916, ibid.

28. W. Bompas to Commissioner, 29 November 1904, RG91, vol. 29, file 13 013, PAC; J.J. Wright to Supt. General of Indian Affairs, 4 February 1902, file 801/30-0-1, IAND.

29. Brusar to Deputy Superintendent General, 17 June 1907, DIA, vol. 6479, file 940-1, pt. 1, PAC; Congdon to F. Pedley, 28 April 1903, DIA, vol. 3962, file 147 654-1, pt. 1, PAC; Secretary, Dawson Board of Trade to Rt. Hon. Frank Oliver, 19 August 1911, DIA, vol. 4062, file 398 746-1, PAC.

30. Commissioner of Y.T. to J.B. Harken, 16 March 1922, YRG1, Series 3, vol. 2, file 12-14B, YTA; Report by A.W. Elling, 16 January 1923, ibid, file 12-13C.

31. Extract from a report by Harper Reed, 8 May 1935, YRG1, Series 3, vol. 8, file 12-15A, YTA.

32. Camsell to Gibson, 14 September 1935, YRG1, Series 3, vol. 8, file 12–15, YTA; Reed to Perry, 12 July 1935, ibid.; Binning to Jeckell, 18 October 1935, DIA, vol. 6761, file 420–12, PAC; Jeckell to Director, Lands, N.W.T. and Yukon Branch, 18 October 1935; ibid.; Summary: Proposed Yukon Preserved For Sole Use of Indians, 1938, ibid.

33. Hawksley to McLean, 23 August 1929, file 801/30-10-10, IAND; Patsy Henderson et al. to Mackenzie, 26 May 1932, RG91, vol. 9, file 1490, pt. J, PAC; Hawksley to Jeckell, 11 July 1932, YRG1, Series 3, vol. 6, file 12-22B, YTA; Jeckell to Chairman, Dominion Lands Board, 15 July 1932, YRG1, Series 3, vol. 6, file 12-11B, YTA.

34. Gibson to Gibben, 19 May 1947, YRG1, Series 3, vol. 11, file 12–22, YTA; Meek to Indian Affairs Branch, 3 July 1947, DIA, vol. 6761, file 420-12-2-2, PAC; Extract from Indian Agent Meek's Quarterly Report, 1 July 1947 to 30 September 1947, 10 October 1947, YRG1, Series 3, vol. 11, file 12–22, YTA.

35. Meek to Indian Affairs Branch, 27 November 1947, DIA, vol. 6761, file 420-12-2-RT-1, PAC; Conn to Meek, 4 December 1947, ibid; Gibson to Gibben, 17 December 1947, DIA, vol. 6742, file 420-6-1-1, PAC; Meek to Indian Affairs Branch, Attention Hugh Conn, 17 January 1950, DIA, vol. 6761, file 420, 12-2-RT-1, PAC.

36. Peter Usher, "The North: Metropolitan Frontier, Northern Homeland?" in *Heartland and Hinterland*, ed. L.D. McCann (Scarborough: Prentice-Hall, 1982).

37. Pedley to Oliver, 23 January 1908, General Synod Archives, Anglican Church of Canada (hereafter GSA), M74-3, file 1-A-2. As late as 1903, Sifton believed there to be only seven hundred natives in the Yukon. House of Commons, *Debates*, vol. 11 (1901): 5449-5450; *Debates*, vol. 3 (1903): 7270-7273.

38. J.D. McLean to John Hawksley, 4 March 1914, YRG1, Series 2, file 29, 299, YTA; Supt. General to Governor General in Council, 12 January 1914, DIA, vol. 1129, Deputy Superintendent's Letterbook, 4 February 1911–29 May 1914, PAC.

39. Hawksley to McLean, 17 April 1929, DIA, vol. 7155, file 801/3-10, pt. 1, PAC; Hawksley to McLean, 13 June 1919, ibid. See also Hawksley's reports in Department of Indian Affairs, *Annual Reports*, especially 1915-1916, 115–117 and 1917, 30.

40. Jeckell to Chairman, Dominion Lands Branch, 17 November 1933, YRG1, Series 2, file 29, 299, YTA; T.E.L. MacInnes to R.A. Gibson, 23 July 1938, RG91, vol. 9, file 1490, pt. 7, PAC.

41. Robert McCandless, *Yukon Wildlife: A Social History* (Edmonton: University of Alberta, 1985).

42. House of Commons, *Debates*, vol. 46 (1898): 824.

43. Bompas to Wood, 6 July 1900, Royal Canadian Mounted Police Records, RG18, vol. 247, file 92, PAC; White to Wood, 20 July 1900, ibid; Wood to Comptroller, 5 July 1900, ibid.

44. Smart to McLean, 30 April 1902, DIA, vol. 4001, file 207 418, PAC; White to Smart, 1 January 1901, ibid; Accountant to Secretary, 1 May 1902, ibid.

45. Hawksley to Wood, 24 June 1902, RG18, vol. 147, file 92, PAC; Snyder to Asst. Commissioner, 19 November 1902, DIA, vol. 4001, file 207 418, PAC; Report of Supt. Wood, 1 December 1901, NWMP, *Annual Report 1902*, pt. 3, 10; Wood to Supt. General of Indian Affairs, 22 March 1903, DIA, vol. 3962, file 147 654–1, pt. 2, PAC; Report of Asst. Commissioner Wood, 1 December 1904, NWMP, *Annual Report 1905*, 1905; Report of Asst. Commissioner Wood, 1 December 1903, NWMP, *Annual Report 1904*, 12; Cuthbert to Asst. Commissioner, 31 January 1905, RG18, vol. 295, file 173, PAC; Supt. "H" Division to Asst. Commissioner, 3 March 1908, 1 May 1908, RG18, vol. 352, file 128, PAC; Report of Asst. Commissioner Wood, 1 October 1909, RNWMP, *Annual Report 1910*, 217.

46. Cuthbert to Asst. Commissioner, 30 September 1905, RG18, vol. 195, file 273, PAC; RNWMP, *Annual Report 1912*, 222.

47. Supt. "H" Division to Asst. Commissioner, 1 June 1908, RG18, vol. 352, file 128, PAC. See also Report of Inspector Routledge, 1 December 1902, NWMP, *Annual Report 1902*, 89. Not all police officers shared this view. Several argued for greater government assistance. Supt. "B" Division to Asst. Commissioner, 31 January 1904, RG18, vol. 272, file 267, PAC.

48. Report of Inspector Horrigan, 30 September 1911, RNWMP, *Annual Report 1911*, 212.

49. Report of Supt. Moodie, 30 September 1913, RNWMP, *Annual Report 1914*, 274; McLean to Hawksley, 4 March 1914, YRG1, Series 2, file 29, 299, YTA; Stringer to Townsend, 9 February 1915, Anglican Church Records, Carcross file, YTA; Stringer to Martin, 13 November 1916, GSA, M74-3, file 1-A-5A; Report of Corporal Hocking, 6 March 1914, RNWMP, *Annual Report 1915*, 740; Stringer to Chambers, 17 May 1916, Anglican Church Records, Chambers file, YTA; Stringer to W.D. [Young], 25 April 1917, Anglican Church Records, Young file, YTA.

50. Auditor General of Canada, *Annual Report, 1902–1903*, J-78; Ibid., 1904–1905, J-62. The Indians obviously patronized the service. Doctors were paid $2 per authorized consultation. In 1901–1902, the two busiest doctors, NWMP assistant surgeon G. Madore and medical doctor L.S. Sugden received $1516 and $1113 respectively, thus accounting for close to 1300 visits between them.

51. Alfred Crosby, "Virgin Soil Epidemics as a Factor in the Aboriginal Depopulation in America," *William and Mary Quarterly*, 3rd series, 33 (April 1976): 289–99.

52. Bompas to Wood, 6 July 1900, RG18, vol. 247, file 91, PAC; Bell to C.O., "B" Division, 2 September 1916, RG8, vol. 514, file 530, PAC. The major instance of government action in the face of an epidemic involved a smallpox outbreak near Rampart House in 1911–1912. See Ken Coates, *Northern Yukon: A History*, Manuscript Report No. 403 (Parks Canada, 1979).

53. P.G. Albach and G.P. Kelley, eds. *Education and Colonialism* (New York: Longman, 1978).

54. J. Gresko, "White 'Rites' and Indian 'Rites:' Indian Education and Native Responses in the West, 1870–1910," in *Western Canada: Past and Present*, ed. A.W. Rasporich (Calgary, 1975).

55. John Hawksley to A.F. Mackenzie, 29 August 1933, RG91, vol. 9, file 1491, PAC.

56. *Memorandum on Indian Missions and Indian Schools*, submitted on behalf of the Special Indian Committee of the M.S.C.C., 14 March 1906, GSA75-103, Missionary Society of the Church of England in Canada.

57. Frank Oliver to A.C.C., 28 January 1908, GS75-103, Series 2–14, Missionary Society of the Church of England in Canada; Frank Pedley to Rev. Norman Tucker, 21 March 1908, ibid; Notes of an Interview with Frank Oliver, 26 February 1909, Anglican Church Records, New Series, file 2, YTA.

58. An on-site study of the Carcross Residential School in the 1960s offered a very critical appraisal of the facility and the educational offerings. See Richard King, *The School at Mopass* (Toronto: Holt, Rinehart and Winston, 1967).

59. Gibben to Keenleyside, 4 September 1947, RG91, vol. 65, file 813, PAC; Quarterly Report of R.J. Meek, 1 October to 31 December 1949, DIA, vol. 8762, file 906/25-1-005, pt. 1, PAC.

60. Canada, Department of Mines and Resources, Indian Affairs Branch (hereafter IAB), *Annual Report 1949*, 200; Meek to Kjar, 15 March 1950, DIA, vol. 6761, file 420-12-1-RT-1, PAC. Employment opportunities included work at the Haines Junction Experimental Farm and several native housing projects. Most of the Indians assisted by Meek found short-term work as dog-team drivers or wood-cutters.

61. IAB, *Annual Report 1946*, 211; Guest, *Social Security in Canada* (Vancouver: UBC Press, 1980).

62. IAB, *Annual Report 1946*, 212; *Annual Report 1948*; Rowat to Jeckell, 4 June 1945, YRG1, Series 4, vol. 33, file 689, YTA; R.J. Meek to Indian Affairs Branch, 8 February 1950, DIA, vol. 8762, file 906/25-1-005, pt. 1, PAC.

63. See Peter Usher, "The North: Metropolitan Frontier, Native Homeland?"

MAPS OF DREAMS†

HUGH BRODY

The rivers of northeast British Columbia are at their most splendid in the early fall. The northern tributaries of the Peace achieve an extraordinary beauty; they, and their small feeder creeks and streams, are cold yet warm—perfect reflections of autumn. The banks are multicoloured and finely textured; clear water runs in smooth, shallow channels. The low water of late summer reveals gravel and sand beaches, textures and colours that are at other times of the year concealed. Such low water levels mean that all these streams are easily crossed, and so become the throughways along the valleys that have always been at the heart of the Indians' use of the land. In October those who know these creeks can find corners, holes, back eddies where rainbow trout and Dolly Varden abound.

The hunter of moose, deer, caribou (and in historic times, buffalo) does not pursue these large animals without regard to more abundant and predictable, if less satisfying, sources of food. The man who tracks and snares game, and whose success depends on his constant movement, cannot afford to fail for much more than two days running. On the third day of hunger he will find it hard to walk far or fast enough: hunger reduces the efficiency of the hunt. Hunger is inimical to effective hunting on foot; yet continuance of the hunt was, not long ago, the only means to avoid hunger. This potential source of insecurity for a hunter is resolved by his ability to combine two kinds of hunting: he pursues large ungulates in areas and with movements that bring him close to locations where he knows rabbits, grouse, or fish are to be found. These are security, but not staples. Hunting for large animals is the most efficient, the most rational activity for anyone who lives in the boreal forest. But such a hunter would be foolhardy indeed to hunt for the larger animals without a careful and strategic eye on the availability of the smaller ones.

In October, only a month after Joseph Patsah and his family first spoke

---

† From *Maps and Dreams: Indians and the British Columbia Frontier* (Vancouver: Douglas and McIntyre, 1981), 34–48.

to us about their lives, they suggested that I go hunting with them — and, of course, fishing. By now the rainbow trout would surely be plentiful and fat. Joseph said that he also hoped we could go far enough to see the cross. One evening, then, he proposed that we should all set out the next day for Bluestone Creek.

Between a proposal to go hunting and actual departure there is a large and perplexing divide. In the white man's world, whether urban or rural, after such a proposal there would be plans and planning; conversation about timing and practical details would also help to build enthusiasm. In Joseph's household, in all the Indian households of northeast British Columbia, and perhaps among hunters generally, planning is so muted as to seem nonexistent. Maybe it is better understood by a very different name, which is still to suppose that planning of some kind does in fact take place.

Protests against the hunting way of life have often paid hostile attention to its seemingly haphazard, irrational, and improvident nature. Before the mind's eye of agricultural or industrial man loom the twin spectres of hunger and homelessness, whose fearsome imminence is escaped only in the bright sunlight of planning. Planners consider many possibilities, weigh methods, review timing, and at least seek to deduce what is best. To this end they advocate reason and temperance, and, most important, they are thrifty and save. These ideas and dispositions, elevated to an ideal in the economics of nineteenth-century and secular puritanism, live on in the reaction of industrial society to hunters — and in the average Canadian's reaction to Indians. And a reaction of this kind means that a person, even if inclined to be sympathetic to hunters and hunting, has immense difficulty in understanding what planning means for hunters of the North.

Joseph and his family float possibilities. "Maybe we should go to Copper Creek. Bet you lots of moose up there." Or, "Could be caribou right now near Black Flats." Or, "I bet you no deer this time down on the Reserve. . . . " Somehow a general area is selected from a gossamer of possibilities, and from an accumulation of remarks comes something rather like a consensus. No, that is not really it: rather, a sort of prediction, a combined sense of where we *might* go "tomorrow." Yet the hunt will not have been planned, nor any preparations started, and apparently no one is committed to going. Moreover, the floating conversation will have alighted on several irreconcilable possibilities, or have given rise to quasi-predictions. It is as if the predictions are about other people — or are not quite serious. Although the mood is still one of wait and see, at the end of the day, at the close of much slow and gentle talk about this and that, a strong feeling has arisen about the morning: we shall go to Bluestone, maybe as far as the cross. We shall look for trout as well as moose. A number of individuals agree that they will go. But come morning, nothing is ready. No one has made any practical, formal plans.

As often as not — indeed, more often than not — something quite new has drifted into conversations, other predictions have been tentatively reached, a new consensus appears to be forming. As it often seems, everyone has changed his mind.

The way to understand this kind of decision making, as also to live by and even share it, is to recognize that some of the most important variables are subtle, elusive, and extremely hard or impossible to assess with finality. The Athapaskan hunter will move in a direction and at a time that are determined by a sense of weather (to indicate a variable that is easily grasped if all too easily oversimplified by the one word) and by a sense of rightness. He will also have ideas about animal movement, his own and others' patterns of land use. . . . But already the nature of the hunter's decision making is being misrepresented by this kind of listing. To disconnect the variables, to compartmentalize the thinking, is to fail to acknowledge its sophistication and completeness. He considers variables as a composite, in parallel, and with the help of a blending of the metaphysical and the obviously pragmatic. To make a good, wise, sensible hunting choice is to accept the interconnection of all possible factors, and avoids the mistake of seeking rationally to focus on any one consideration that is held as primary. What is more, the decision is taken in the doing: there is no step or pause between theory and practice. As a consequence, the decision—like the action from which it is inseparable —is always alterable (and therefore may not properly even be termed a decision). The hunter moves in a chosen direction; but, highly sensitive to so many shifting considerations, he is always ready to change his directions.

Planning, as other cultures understand the notion, is at odds with this kind of sensitivity and would confound such flexibility. The hunter, alive to constant movements of nature, spirits, and human moods, maintains a way of doing things that repudiates a firm plan and any precise or specified understanding with others of what he is going to do. His course of action is not, must not be, a matter of predetermination. If a plan constitutes a decision about the right procedure or action, and the decision is congruent with the action, then there is no space left for a "plan," only for a bundle of open-ended and nonrational possibilities. Activity enters so far into this kind of planning as to undermine any so-called plans.

All this is by way of context or background for the seemingly straight-forward proposal that we should set out the next morning to hunt moose and fish for trout at Bluestone Creek. Since there are many such apparent decisions in the following chapters, it is important that they be understood for what they are: convenient—but often misleading—reductions to a narrative convention of intimate and unfamiliar patterns of hunters' thought and behaviour.

"The next morning" came several times before we set out in the direction of Bluestone. Several individuals said they would come, but did not; others said they would not come, but did. Eventually, we drove in my rented pickup to a stretch of rolling forests, where hillsides and valley were covered by dense blankets of poplar, aspen, birch, and occasional stands of pine or spruce. After studied consideration of three places, Joseph and Atsin chose a campsite a short walk from a spring that created a narrow pool of good water in a setting of damp and frosted leaves.

There we camped, in a complex of shelters and one tent around a long central fire. It was a place the hunters had often used, and it had probably been an Indian campsite off and on for centuries. It was a clearing among thin-stemmed pine, a woodland tangled and in places made dense by a great number of deadfalls lying at all heights and angles to the ground. Night fell as we completed the camp. The fire was lit and was darkly reflected by these dead trees that crisscrossed against the forest.

Long before dawn (it cannot have been later than five o'clock), the men awoke. The fire rekindled, they sat around it and began the enormous and protracted breakfast that precedes every day's hunting: rabbit stew, boiled eggs, bannock, toasted sliced white bread, barbecued moose meat, whatever happens to be on hand, and cup after cup of strong, sweet tea. A little later, women and children joined the men at the fire and at no less heartily.

As they ate, the light changed from a slight glimmer, the relief to predawn blackness, to the first brightness that falters without strength at the tops of the trees. As the light grew, the men speculated about where to go, sifting evidence they had accumulated from whatever nearby places they had visited since their arrival. Everyone had walked — to fetch water, cut wood, or simply to stretch the legs a little. Atsin, at the end of a short walk that morning, returned with a rabbit. He had taken it in a snare, evidently set as soon as we arrived the evening before. It was white already, its fur change a dangerously conspicuous anticipation of a winter yet to come. Conversation turned to rabbits. All the men had noticed a proliferation of runs and droppings. It was an excellent year for rabbit, the fifth or sixth in a cycle of seven improving years. It might be a good idea to hunt in some patches of young evergreens, along trails that led towards the river. There could be more rabbits there. Lots of rabbits. Always good to eat lots of rabbit stew. And there could be rainbow trout in that place, below the old cabin, and in other spots. Or maybe it would be good to go high up in the valley. . . . This exchange of details and ideas continued off and on throughout the meal. When it had finally ended and everyone had reflected a good deal on the day's possibilities, the men set off. Perhaps it was clear to them where and why, but which possibilities represented a starting point was not easily understood by an outsider.

Atsin's younger brother Sam set off alone, at right angles to a trail that led to the river by way of a place said to be particularly good for rabbits. Two others, Jimmy Wolf and Charlie Fellow — both relations of Joseph's wife Liza — also set off at an angle, but in the opposite direction. I followed Atsin along another, more winding trail. Liza and her oldest child, Tommy, together with two other women and their small children, made their own way behind the men on the main trail; Atsin's son David attached himself to Brian Akattah and his ten-year-old nephew Peter. The choice of partner and trail was, if possible, less obviously planned than direction or hunting objective. Everyone was plainly free to go where and with whom he or she liked. As I became more familiar with this kind of hunt, though, I found that some individuals nearly always hunted alone, whereas others liked a companion, at least at the outset. No one gives orders; everyone is, in some fundamental way, responsible to and for himself.

The distance between camp and the particular bend in the river that had been selected as the best possible fishing place was no more than a mile and a half. No time had been appointed for a rendezvous. Indeed clock time is of no significance here. (Only Joseph had a watch and it was never used for hunting purposes.) Everyone nonetheless appeared from the woods and converged on the fishing spot within minutes of one another. This co-ordination of activities is not easily understood, although it testified to the absence of big game, of moose, deer, or bear. If any of the hunters had located fresh tracks, he would have been long gone into the woods. Atsin, who seemed to be an expert at the job, appeared with two rabbits he had shot after glimpsing their helpless whiteness in the dun-coloured undergrowth. But fishing was going to supply the next meal.

The river at this place flows in a short curve around a wooded promontory that juts from the main forest. Both sides are deeply eroded banks, where sandy rubble is given some short-lived firmness by exposed tree roots. On the far side the landscape is barer, with meadowy, more open land for fifty yards before the forested slopes rise towards the mountains. Where the trail meets the creek (sometimes no wider than ten rushing yards), it deepens into a pool. There, the water is held back by a shallow rib of rock over which it quickens and races to the next pool.

The fishing spot itself turned out to be a platform of jumbled logs that must have been carried by the stream in flood, and then piled by currents until they reshaped the banks themselves. The sure-footed can find precarious walkways across this latticework platform. At their ends the logs offer a view down into the deepest part of the hole. Through the sharp clearness of this water rainbow trout could be seen, dark shadows, hovering or moving very slowly among long-sunken logs and roots.

Joseph studied the water and the fish, then produced a nylon line. It was wound tightly around a small piece of shaped wood, a spool that

he carried in his pocket, wrapped in cloth. Along with the line were
four or five hooks (size 6 or 8) and a chunk of old bacon. On his way
along the trail he had broken off a long thin branch, and by the time we
had arrived at the creek he had already stripped off its side twigs, peeled
away the bark, and broken it to the right length. He tied some line to
this homemade rod and handed other lengths to Brian and David. The
three of them then clambered along the log platform, found more or
less firm places at its edge, and began to fish.

The baited hooks were lowered straight down until they hung just
above the stream bed. They did not hover there for long. Almost immediately the fish were being caught. The men could watch a trout
swim towards a bait and, with one firm turn of its body, part suck and
part grab the hook. The fisherman, with a single upward swing of the
rod, would pull it straight out of the water and onto the logs. Then each
fish was grabbed at, and missed, fell off the hook among the logs, was
grabbed again. . . . The fish, and the fishermen, could easily slip between
the gaps of the platform. As the trout thrashed and leaped about there
were shouts of excitement, advice, and laughter.

The trout were plentiful, as Joseph had said they would be, and fat.
One after the other they came flying through the air into someone's
hands, then to shore, where Atsin and Liza gutted them. A dozen or
more, fish of one or two pounds each, every one of them with a brilliant
red patch on its gills and red stripe along its sides — rainbow trout at
their most spectacular. Then the fishing slowed down. Enough had been
caught. Joseph, Brian, and David climbed back to the bank. We sat
around the fires to eat rabbit stew and cook some of the fish.

By this time it was early afternoon, but the meal was unhurried.
Perhaps the success of the moose hunt was doubtful, while a good supply
of rabbit and fish had already been secured. Conversation turned again
to places where it might be worth hunting, directions in which we might
go; many possibilities were suggested, and no apparent decision was
made. But when the meal ended, the men began to prepare themselves
for another hunt. Having eaten and rested and stared into the fire, one
by one the hunters, unhurried and apparently indecisive, got up, strolled
a little way, and came back. Then each began to fix his clothes, check a
gun — began to get ready. By the time the last of the hunters was thus
occupied, some had begun to drift away in one direction or another.
After a last conversation, the rest of them left, except for Joseph, Brian's
wife Mary, Liza, and the children, who stayed by the fire. Perhaps the
afternoon was going to be long and hard.

This time a group of men walked in single file, Atsin in front. After a
short distance, one went his own way, then others did so, until each of
them had taken a separate direction. I again stayed close to Atsin, who
made his way, often pushing his way, through dense bushes and small
willows, along the river bank. He said once, when we paused to rest

and look around, and think, that it was disappointing to find so few signs of moose, but there might be more fishing.

It must have been an hour before the men regrouped, this time on a high and eroded sandbar. The beach here was strewn with well dried driftwood. Atsin and Robert Fellows began to gather enough of this wood to make a large fire. Brian fetched water for tea. Atsin's brother Sam, together with Jimmy Wolf, cut fishing poles, fixed up lines, went a short way upstream to a spot where the water turned and deepened against the bank, and began to fish. Their lines hung in the water, baits out of sight and judged to be close to the bottom. From time to time they changed the angle of their rods to adjust the depth at which they fished; and by taking advantage of the pole being longer than the line, they periodically pulled the bait clear of the water, checked that all was well in place, and then dropped it easily back to where the fish should be.

But the fish were not there, or not hungry, or not to be fooled. Sam and Jimmy waited. There were no sudden upward whips of the pole, no bites, no shouts, no laughter. The others sprawled around the fire, watching the two fishermen, drinking tea, limiting themselves to an occasional squinting look towards the river and remarks about the dearth of game. The afternoon was warm and still. There seemed to be no reason for any great activity. Soon Jimmy decided to abandon the river in favour of a rest beside the fire. Sam forded the stream, crossed the sandbar, and tried his luck on the other side. From where we sat and lay we could see his head and shoulders, and the lift and drop of his long rod. It was easy enough to tell whether or not he was catching anything; he was not.

Moments, minutes, even hours of complete stillness: this was not time that could be measured. Hunters at rest, at ease, in wait, are able to discover and enjoy a special form of relaxation. There is a minimum of movement — a hand reaches out for a mug, an adjustment is made to the fire — and whatever is said hardly interrupts the silence, as if words and thoughts can be harmonized without any of the tensions of dialogue. Yet the hunters are a long way from sleep; not even the atmosphere is soporific. They wait, watch, consider. Above all they are still and receptive, prepared for whatever insight or realization may come to them, and ready for whatever stimulus to action might arise. This state of attentive waiting is perhaps as close as people can come to the falcon's suspended flight, when the bird, seemingly motionless, is ready to plummet in decisive action. To the outsider, who has followed along and tried to join in, it looks for all the world as if the hunters have forgotten why they are there. In this restful way hunters can spend many hours, sometimes days, eating, waiting, thinking.

The quality of this resting by the fire can be seen and felt when it is very suddenly changed, just as the nature of the falcon's hover becomes clear when it dives. Among hunters the emergence from repose may be slow or abrupt. But in either case a particular state of mind, a special way of being, has come to an end. One or two individuals move faster and more purposively, someone begins to prepare meat to cook, someone fetches a gun to work on, and conversation resumes its ordinary mode. This transformation took place that afternoon around the fire on the pebbled beach at just the time Sam gave up his fishing and began to walk back towards us. Atsin, Jimmy, and Robert all moved to new positions. Robert stood with his back to us, watching Sam's approach, while Atsin and Jimmy squatted where they could look directly at me.

In retrospect it seems clear that they felt the right time had come for something. Everyone seemed to give the few moments it took for this change to occur some special importance. Plainly the men had something to say and, in their own time, in their own way, they were going to say it. Signs and movements suggested that the flow of events that had begun in Joseph's home and Atsin's cabin, and continued with the fishing at Bluestone Creek, was about to be augmented. Something of significance to the men here was going to happen. I suddenly realized that everyone was watching me. Sam joined the group, but said nothing. Perhaps he, as a younger man, was now leaving events to his elders, to Atsin, Jimmy, and Robert. There was a brief silence made awkward by expectancy, though an awkward pause is a very rare thing among people who accept that there is no need to escape from silence, no need to use words as a way to avoid one another, no need to obscure the real.

Atsin broke this silence. He spoke at first of the research: "I bet some guys make big maps. Lots of work, these maps. Joseph, he sure is happy to see maps."

Silence again. Then Robert continued: "Yeah, lots of maps. All over this country we hunt. Fish too. Trapping places. Nobody knows that. White men don't know that."

Then Jimmy spoke: "Indian guys, old-timers, they make maps too."

With these words, the men introduced their theme. The tone was friendly, but the words were spoken with intensity and firmness. The men seemed apprehensive, as if anxious to be very clearly understood — though nothing said so far required such concern. Once again, it is impossible to render verbatim all that they eventually said. I had no tape recorder and memory is imperfect. But even a verbatim account would fail to do justice to their meaning. Here, then, in summaries and glimpses, is what the men had in mind to say.

Some old-timers, men who became famous for their powers and skills, had been great dreamers. Hunters and dreamers. They did not hunt as most people now do. They did not seek uncertainly for the trails of animals whose movements we can only guess at. No, they located their prey in dreams, found their trails, and made dream-kills. Then, the next day, or a few days later, whenever it seemed auspicious to do so, they could go out, find the trail, re-encounter the animal, and collect the kill.

Maybe, said Atsin, you think this is all nonsense, just so much bullshit. Maybe you don't think this power is possible. Few people understand. The old-timers who were strong dreamers knew many things that are not easy to understand. People—white people, young people—yes, they laugh at such skills. But they do not know. The Indians around this country know a lot about power. In fact, everyone has had some experience of it. The fact that dream-hunting works has been proved many times.

A few years ago a hunter dreamed a cow moose kill. A fine, fat cow. He was so pleased with the animal, so delighted to make this dream-kill, that he marked the animal's hooves. Now he would be sure to recognize it when he went on the coming hunt. The next day, when he went out into the bush, he quickly found the dream-trail. He followed it, and came to a large cow moose. Sure enough, the hooves bore his marks. Everyone saw them. All the men around the fire had been told about the marks, and everyone on the Reserve had come to look at those hooves when the animal was butchered and brought into the people's homes.

And not only that fat cow moose — many such instances are known to the people, whose marks on the animal or other indications show that there was no mistaking, no doubts about the efficacy of such dreams. Do you think this is all lies? No, this is power they had, something they knew how to use. This was their way of doing things, the right way. They understood, those old-timers, just where all the animals came from. The trails converge, and if you were a very strong dreamer you could discover this, and see the source of trails, the origin of game. Dreaming revealed them. Good hunting depended upon such knowledge.

Today it is hard to find men who can dream this way. There are too many problems. Too much drinking. Too little respect. People are not good enough now. Maybe there will again be strong dreamers when these problems are overcome. Then more maps will be made. New maps.

Oh yes, Indians made maps. You would not take any notice of them. You might say such maps are crazy. But maybe the Indians would say that is what your maps are: the same thing. Different maps from different people — different *ways*. Old-timers made maps of trails, ornamented them with lots of fancy. The good people.

None of this is easy to understand. But good men, the really good men, could dream of more than animals. Sometimes they saw heaven and its trails. Those trails are hard to see, and few men have had such dreams. Even if they could see dream-trails to heaven, it is hard to explain them. You draw maps of the land, show everyone where to go. You explain the hills, the rivers, the trails from here to Hudson Hope, the roads. Maybe you make maps of where the hunters go and where the fish can be caught. That is not easy. But easier, for sure, than drawing out the trails to heaven. You may laugh at these maps of the trails to heaven, but they were done by the good men who had the heaven dream, who wanted to tell the truth. They worked hard on their truth.

Atsin had done most of the talking this far. The others interjected a few words and comments, agreeing or elaborating a little. Jimmy told about the cow moose with marked hooves. All of them offered some comparisons between their own and others' maps. And the men's eyes never ceased to remain fixed on me: were they being understood? Disregarded? Thought ridiculous? They had chosen this moment for these explanations, yet no one was entirely secure in it. Several times, Atsin paused and waited, perhaps to give himself a chance to sense or absorb the reaction to his words. These were intense but not tense hiatuses. Everyone was reassuring himself that his seriousness was being recognized. That was all they needed to continue.

The longest of these pauses might have lasted as much as five minutes. During it the fire was rebuilt. It seemed possible, for a few moments, that they had finished, and that their attention was now returning to trout, camp, and the hunt. But the atmosphere hardly altered, and Jimmy quite abruptly took over where Atsin had left off.

The few good men who had the heaven dream were like the Fathers, Catholic priests, men who devoted themselves to helping others with that essential knowledge to which ordinary men and women have limited access. (Roman Catholic priests have drifted in and out of the lives of all the region's Indians, leaving behind fragments of their knowledge and somewhat rarefied and idealized versions of what they had to preach.) Most important of all, a strong dreamer can tell others how to get to heaven. We all have need of the trail, or a complex of trails, but, unlike other important trails, the way to heaven will have been seen in dreams that only a few, special individuals have had. Maps of heaven are thus important. And they must be good, complete maps. Heaven is reached only by careful avoidance of the wrong trails. These must also be shown so that the traveller can recognize and avoid them.

How can we know the general direction we should follow? How can anyone who has not dreamed the whole route begin to locate himself on such a map? When Joseph, or any of the other men, began to draw a hunting map, he had first to find his way. He did this by recognizing features, by fixing points of reference, and then, once he was oriented to the familiar and to the scale or manner in which the familiar was reproduced, he could begin to add his own layers of detailed information. But how can anyone begin to find a way on a map of trails to heaven, across a terrain that ordinary hunters do not experience in everyday activities or even in their dream-hunts?

The route to heaven is not wholly unfamiliar, however. As it happens, heaven is to one side of, and at the same level as, the point where the trails to animals all meet. Many men know where this point is, or at least some of its approach trails, from their own hunting dreams. Hunters can in this way find a basic reference, and once they realize that heaven is in particular relation to this far more familiar centre, the map as a whole can be read. If this is not enough, a person can take a map with him; some old-timers who made or who were given maps of the trails to heaven choose to have a map buried with them. They can thus remind themselves which ways to travel if the actual experience of the trail proves to be too confusing. Others are given a corner of a map that will help reveal the trail to them. And even those who do not have any powerful dreams are shown the best maps of the route to heaven. The discoveries of the very few most powerful dreamers — and some of the dreamers have been women — are periodically made available to everyone.

The person who wishes to dream must take great care, even if he dreams only of the hunt. He must lie in the correct orientation, with his head towards the rising sun. There should be no ordinary trails, no human pathways, between his pillow and the bush. These would be confusing to the self that travels in dreams towards important and unfamiliar trails which can lead to a kill. Not much of this can be mapped — only the trail to heaven has been drawn up. There has been no equivalent need to make maps to share other important information.

Sometime, said Jimmy Wolf, you will see one of these maps. There are some of them around. Then the competence and strength of the old-timers who drew them will be unquestioned. Different trails can be explained, and heaven can be located on them. Yes, they were pretty smart, the men who drew them. Smarter than any white man in these parts and smarter than Indians of today. Perhaps, said Atsin, in the future there will be men good enough to make new maps of heaven — but not just now. There will be changes, he added, and the people will come once again to understand the things that Atsin's father had tried to teach him. In any case, he said, the older men are now trying to explain the powers and dreams of old-timers to the young, indeed to all those who have not been raised with these spiritual riches. For those who do not understand, hunting and life itself are restricted and difficult. So the people must be told everything, and taught all that they need, in order to withstand the incursions presently being made into their way of life, their land, and into their very dreams.

NEGOTIATING THE INDIAN "PROBLEM"†

NOEL DYCK

> The first step in liquidating a people . . . is to erase its memory. . . .
> Before long a nation will begin to forget what it is and what it was.
> The world around it will forget even faster.
>
> Milan Kundera, *The Book of*
> *Laughter and Forgetting*

Remembering can be an act with an ethical purpose as well as a communicative function. This essay is concerned with both dimensions of remembering and with the articulation of a public problem within the context of interethnic communication. Specifically, it considers the formulation of the so-called Indian "question" or "problem" as a significant element in interaction between Indians and non-Indians on the Canadian Prairies.

Having declared these analytical concerns, I must at the outset acknowledge their having been shown to me by John R. McLeod, a Cree friend who practised a rather different approach to penetrate and —as far as it is possible to do so—to resolve these matters. Only gradually have I come to recognize the depth of understanding that informed his public acts of remembering. I am unable to replicate his artistry, but as the essay proceeds I present and draw heavily upon his experiences and insight.

The distinctive character of public problems is central to this discussion. Although many issues generate deep concern and attract considerable attention, not all social problems become public ones. Social issues are

† *Culture* 6, no. 1 (1986): 31–41. The author wishes to thank Garnet, Joanne and Barbara McLeod as well as Regna Darnell, Gordon Inglish, Robert Paine, Basil Sansom, Sally Weaver and the members of the Graduate Seminar in Sociology and Anthropology at Simon Fraser University for their comments on earlier versions of this article.

transformed into public problems when they become "matters of conflict or controversy in the arenas of public life,"[1] which, further, initiate demands for public action to rectify that which is deemed unacceptable. A sociological examination of public problems, then, will entail several lines of questioning: for example, why "an issue or problem emerges as one with a public status, as something about which 'someone ought to do something.'"[2] A sociological examination will also specify the constituent elements of public problems qua ideas, and chart the relations between them. At this point I shall deal briefly with the latter, leaving the historical evolution of the Indian "problem" to the next section.

The attribution of responsibility is fundamental to the shaping of public problems as ideas and to their subsequent handling in public arenas. But first, there is a need to fix causal responsibility and thereby to suggest appropriate ways of viewing and understanding public problems. For instance, are automobile accidents and fatalities caused mainly by improper driving or by faultily designed vehicles?[3] It is also necessary to allocate political responsibility for public problems — to say who ought to resolve the situation. Should more stringent policing of drivers be enforced or should the automotive industry be required to manufacture safe vehicles? Different definitions of causal responsibility can lead to varying assignments of political responsibility and, ultimately, to quite different kinds of proposed "solutions."

Finally, it is important to recognize that ideas about the causes of public problems combine both cognitive and moral judgments: "The cognitive side consists in beliefs about the facticity of the situation and events comprising the problem — our theories and empirical beliefs. . . . The moral side is that which enables the situation to be viewed as painful, ignoble, immoral. It is what makes alteration or eradication desirable. . . ."[4] Without both a cognitive belief that a given situation can, in fact, be altered *and* a moral judgment that this ought to happen, a situation is not at issue and, hence, not a public problem. This linking of cognitive and moral judgments in the rendering of public problems is crucial to this examination of the Indian problem and its effect on interethnic communication.

Politicians, the news media and the public in Canada have taken an increasing interest in the Indian question during the past twenty years, particularly since the White Paper controversy of 1969–70, when the federal government sought unsuccessfully to terminate its administration of Indian affairs.[5] Before this time, it was unusual for Indians to receive public attention, except as costumed additions to the local colour at public receptions held for visiting dignitaries such as the governor-general.

Today, extensive coverage is given to Indian claims to aboriginal land rights and to actions such as the Indian associations' recent attempts to block patriation of the Canadian constitution. Indian demands have become prominent issues both in Parliament and in the Canadian press.

The claims being pressed by Indian leaders are based upon arguments and sources of legitimacy that are unusual in Canadian public life and unavailable to other Canadians. One set of arguments involves their status as an indigenous people with special rights to land and to traditional ways of life associated with hunting, trapping and fishing.[6] A second set of arguments is derived from registered Indians' special constitutional and administrative status and from their long experience as the involuntary clients of a paternalistic and stifling form of federal administration. In their statements, Indian leaders regularly compare the present-day actions of the federal government with a deservedly unsavoury image of the Department of Indian Affairs in the past. The use of this tactic, and of frequent references to the established legal basis of Indian rights, arm Indian representatives with a unique set of arguments with which to advance their claims.

But these claims are being pursued primarily within specialized legal, political and administrative channels, the workings of which are not well known to most Canadians. Canadians, therefore, are often confused, not only by the exotic nature of Indian claims, but also by the procedures with which they are put forth, heard and acted upon.[7] In short, although there has been a virtual quantum leap in the amount of media coverage and political attention given to Indian issues, public understanding of these developments has lagged far behind the amount of information being disseminated. This has had the paradoxical effect of making public involvement in this increasingly publicized field more and more indirect, just when appeals to, and manipulation of, public opinion have become part of the new politics of "special status." Indeed, a key aim of the strategy of representation adopted by Indian associations in western Canada during the 1970s was to bypass local authorities and prejudices and to appeal to more sympathetic national and international audiences and jurisdictions for support.[8]

Given that there are relatively few Indian representatives to deal with the many public bodies that exercise control over one or another aspect of Indians' lives, tremendous demands are made on their time and energy. Those who can survive the hectic pace, nonetheless, rapidly acquire first-hand experience of testifying before parliamentary committees, appearing on television newscasts and dealing on a high level with bureaucratic agencies. This wealth of experience increases the growing, but as yet little appreciated, gap in know-how and technical sophistication that separates Indian leaders (and a surprising number of reserve Indians) from most other Canadians.

Although a recent survey of public awareness and opinions of Indians and Indian issues indicated that they were by no means priorities with Canadians,[9] there has, nonetheless, been an increased demand among interested non-Indians for explanations of what it is that Indians want.

The marketing success of books by Indian spokesmen such as Harold Cardinal[10] and George Manuel,[11] whose writings have explicitly addressed these matters, provides one measure of this trend. Books and newscasts, however, only partially satisfy this demand. Indian representatives who become public figures are thus regularly invited to speak to church groups, service clubs, teachers' associations, and university classes, as well as being approached by individual non-Indians who want to talk directly to an Indian about these matters.

It is often difficult for Indian leaders to fit such speaking engagements into their schedules, since meetings with band councils and government officials take precedence. But it is also the case that leaders who have taken the time to address non-Indian groups have sometimes found them to be extremely frustrating occasions. Evenings spent trying to explain the intricacies of contemporary Indian claims to ill-informed, though sometimes painfully sympathetic gatherings or individuals who want to "help the Indian people" may seem almost as intolerable as the prospect of facing a crowd whose members openly dispute the legitimacy of Indian claims. Moreover, in the Prairie provinces traditional patterns of interethnic communication and interaction have scarcely prepared Indians and non-Indians to discuss these matters with ease.

Contact between non-Indians and Indians in western Canada has always varied in nature and extent.[12] In some parts of the Prairies it is still possible to meet born-and-bred westerners who have never even spoken to an Indian. In other areas, especially in the vicinity of Indian reserves, there are well-established, though far from straightforward, patterns of interaction and communication between Indians and non-Indians. Braroe's study of interethnic relations in a small ranching community illustrates the highly stylized form that these may take, and points out the startling and systematic "ignorance" about Indians that both accompanies and sustains these patterns.[13] The writings of W.P. Kinsella convey the humour that sometimes pervades interethnic situations, but they also draw the reader's attention to some of the less pleasant aspects of Indian/white relations at the local level.[14]

Generally, however, Indians and non-Indians in western Canada stand on the opposite sides of a history of interaction and tend to be divided further by an unequal knowledge of each other. Non-Indians are by and large unaware of just how little they know about Indians and of how sharply the individual and cumulative cultural experience of living on federally administered reserves departs from that of any other Prairie dwellers. Nevertheless, whites are, almost without exception, versed in the body of speculations and beliefs that are identified as the Indian "problem," for this is a cultural doctrine that is communicated freely, extensively and almost exclusively among non-Indians in western Canada. Interaction between Indians and non-Indians is, in consequence, informed not only by the special status and problems of Indians, but also by what non-Indians already "know" about Indians and the Indian problem.

As a genre of discourse among non-Indians, the Indian problem entails both a series of concerns usually introduced as questions and an accompanying repertoire of observations and beliefs proffered as responses. The questions are often, though not always, rhetorical in nature, and can be posed either with genuine curiosity or with obvious antagonism. What are Indians like? How do Indians live? Why are Indians different from whites? What should be done for Indians? What should Indians do? Such questions, in varying ways, are raised by those who seek to understand or simply to comment upon particular events or general situations that in some way involve Indians, either as individuals or as a category of persons.

The responses that these inquiries trigger vary widely, depending upon the identities, inclinations and "knowledge" of the discussants, the circumstances of the discussions and a range of other social, cultural and situational factors. As this is a cautiously correct, but not especially illuminating, way of characterizing the responses, let me go on to suggest that probably the most telling feature of non-Indians' acquaintance with the Indian problem is that it is usually shared and expressed only in the company of other non-Indians. As such, it is discourse about others, which, because it takes place within ethnically exclusive channels, cannot be readily subjected to open scrutiny and critical evaluation. Furthermore, since the very broaching of the subject of the Indian problem between non-Indians invokes a sense of "us" as distinguished from "them," it remains a field of discourse that easily accommodates invidious distinctions, rhetorical licence and, sometimes, outright racist sentiments. For the moment, suffice it to say that the above-cited survey of Canadian opinions toward Indians and Indian issues found that respondents from Saskatchewan and Alberta were, on average, much less sympathetic to Indian aims than were respondents in other parts of the country.[15]

Some elements of the overall bundle of beliefs held by non-Indians about the Indian problem predate both the political developments of the last twenty years and even the settlement of the Prairies; these ideas are as old as the original forging of the dichotomy between indigenous peoples and the Europeans who came to North America, the dichotomy between "savagism" and "civilization."[16] Recent events, however, have generated a new set of concerns which in turn have been incorporated into the local repertoire of discourse about Indians and the Indian problem. Suddenly, non-Indians are also asking *each other*: "What are Indians asking for? Why do they expect to receive special treatment from the government?" And, sometimes, "why can't they be like the rest of us?"

The gradually mounting urgency of these questions further serves to inflate the currency among non-Indians of traditional white folk wisdom about Indians — "knowledge" that was once largely confined to those who administered Indians and to non-Indians who lived near reserves. Today, after several decades of increased media coverage and of widespread urban migration by Indians, there is scarcely anyone in western Canada who has not had the situation of Indians brought to their notice in one way or another. In an attempt to comprehend what is, for many non-Indians, a relatively novel set of concerns, a veritable premium has been placed upon the insights and knowledge that some non-Indians claim to have about the Indian situation.

Both the content and the modes by which this body of non-Indian knowledge about Indians is circulated reflect, compared to other parts of Canada, a reasonably tightly knit, though seldom recognized, regional non-Indian culture.[17] Superficially, the population of western Canada appears to be ethnically and culturally heterogeneous in the extreme. Yet, although the children and grandchildren of Mennonite, Ukrainian, French, Scottish, and Scandinavian settlers may still refer to their own, and to others', ethnic origins in certain situations, and although some of them may go to extraordinary lengths to maintain and display their respective mother tongues and cultural practices, even the most fiercely "ethnic" individuals have learned English and subscribed to a set of public values typical of the region.[18]

Foremost among these values is a notion of egalitarianism, which, in its most common form, proclaims that people are different in all sorts of ways but that no one is intrinsically better than anyone else. This is an egalitarianism which permits one to look down on others, but not to look up. In extreme statements this sentiment can be marshalled to censure those who are judged to be trying to raise their own worth and thereby to be belittling others' intrinsic merit by aggressively doing or being something out of the ordinary. Individual proclivities and differences in achievement are, within certain bounds, compatible with such notions of egalitarianism. Nonconformity, which is seen to challenge the legitimacy of accepted modes of thought and public behaviour, is invariably controversial.

Another much-honoured value is that of personal independence, a principle that is reaffirmed constantly in the political rhetoric of the Prairies, having been firmly anchored in the historical myths which western Canadians have of themselves and their past, namely, that "all of our parents or grandparents arrived here with nothing," and worked hard to settle the country and build the communities and the way of life of which Prairie people are proud. The image of hard-working people who take care of themselves is a popular one.[19] Fervent free-enterprisers and dedicated members of the Prairie co-operative movement alike agree upon the importance, if not upon the most appropriate means, of people taking action and responsibility for deciding their own destiny.

Non-Indians take these principles for granted when they ponder the ways of Indians and the Indian problem with friends, relatives, neighbours, and workmates. More to the point, Indians are deemed problematic in the minds of many whites, precisely because they do not seem to measure up in terms of these values, or, perhaps, even to share these beliefs. Some non-Indians declare themselves to be deeply offended by what they take as incontrovertible evidence that Indians are lazy, shiftless and "coddled" by the government. Others recognize the discrimination and lack of acceptance that Indians experience in Canadian society but remain puzzled about why Indians would want to remain Indians rather than seize any opportunity to become "just like the rest of us." Regardless of whether they are sympathetic or negative toward Indians, Prairie people point more often to Indians' alleged personality deficiencies and lack of initiative than to any other factor when asked to identify the main differences between themselves and Indians.[20] Whereas they may disagree about the best form of action, they do agree that something needs to be done "to get Indians going," to solve the Indian problem.

These concerns form a more or less conspicuous backdrop for interaction between Indians and non-Indians on the Prairies. On those infrequent occasions when Indian speakers undertake to speak to non-Indian audiences about contemporary Indian issues, these concerns, more often than not, comprise the main items on the listeners' unspoken agenda.

As mentioned, I have learned much about interethnic communication from John R. McLeod, a Cree elder from Saskatchewan, who was unable to turn away many invitations to speak to non-Indian audiences, not because of personal vanity, but because he sincerely believed in the importance of creating a better understanding between his people and the non-Indians who also live on the Prairies. I cannot say that his way of dealing with the difficulties inherent in Indian/white communication was typical of how Indians manage these kinds of situations, for these are as yet far from being a common type of interethnic event. Nor can I restrict myself—given my anthropological bent—to following the Cree custom of leaving it to the reader-cum-listener to determine the meaning of what a speaker has said. But first I must introduce the speaker.

Unlike his grandfather and several of his own grandchildren, John R. McLeod lived most of his life on an Indian reserve. His grandfather had been of that generation of Plains Cree that negotiated treaties with Queen Victoria's commissioners during the 1870s and moved onto reserves in the early 1880s, in the wake of the disappearance of the buffalo from the Canadian Prairies. John was born into what was, by the 1920s, a well-established system of reserve administration, although his family remained as much as possible uninvolved in activities such as farming, which fell under the direct control of Indian agents and farming instructors. During the Second World War, John, along with many other young

Indians, enlisted in the Canadian army, in spite of the fact that as an Indian he was not a full-fledged citizen and could not be conscripted.

After the war, John and his wife Ida raised a family and established a farm that was quite successful, compared with others in the surrounding agricultural district, and outstanding in terms of the reserve. Over the years John came to act as a pace-setter for his band: his was the first farm on the reserve to be connected to the electrical power grid; his house had the first television set, and for some years served as an informal community centre, especially for viewing popular Saturday evening hockey games. Equally enterprising in his activities off the reserve, John became the first Indian member of the district co-operative association.

Education emerged as one of John's major and continuing concerns, even though his own schooling had not gone beyond the third grade. Well before the federal government adopted a general policy of encouraging bands to send their children to non-Indian schools, John and his wife experimented with enrolling their sons and daughters in an off-reserve country school, managing to overcome the school board's misgivings about the wisdom of permitting Indians to attend its school. When John and Ida determined that their children were not receiving a superior education, nor being treated fairly by the teacher and other pupils, they withdrew their children and, as part of a federally backed scheme to introduce integrated or "joint" schooling into the area, sent them to larger and, so they were told, "better" schools in a nearby town. John joined the band's school committee, serving as its chairman for a number of years, and went on to become a key figure in the provincial association of Indian school committees. In time, he was also appointed as an Indian representative to a number of advisory boards created by the federal and provincial governments.

Disappointed, however, by the poor results and unhappy experiences of Indian children in joint schools, John began to question the suitability of integrated schooling. Encountering disbelief from government officials and school authorities that the program could be deficient and then their assurance that matters would improve when Indian children were better prepared to take advantage of integrated schooling, John started to explore the possibilities of improving on-reserve educational facilities. When Department of Indian Affairs officials advised him that this would constitute a backward step and one that was administratively "impossible" because of existing federal–provincial agreements and regulations, John set out to read for himself the many different pieces of legislation and the joint-tuition agreements that pertained to various aspects of the education of Indian children. Gradually, he developed a detailed knowledge of the legal and administrative structure of Indian schooling in the province.

After being forced to give up farming because of ill health, John joined the first small group of regular employees to be hired by the provincial Indian association when it began to receive substantial government operating grants in 1969–70. He served as the chairman of a task force that investigated the state of Indian education in the province, and subsequently set up an educational liaison program that furnished band councils and reserve-school committees with information and advice to help parents play a larger part in the education of their children. As well as visiting every band in the province, John attended workshops, conferences and liaison meetings with government officials, school trustees, teachers, and other educational personnel. His grasp both of conditions on reserves and of the structure of educational programming, financing and administration enabled him to play a key role in the campaign mounted in the 1970s to establish "Indian control of Indian education" and, more specifically, to reopen schools for Indians on reserves.[21]

Through his work John received frequent invitations to speak to professional and other non-Indian groups about education and other issues of concern to Indians. Believing it important that those interested should be encouraged, John accepted as many invitations as he could fit into his already busy schedule. He worked hard to prepare for these occasions, striving to overcome deficiencies in his style of presentation. With experience, he developed a relaxed manner of speaking and became adept in using blackboards to illustrate his points. Yet, despite his increasing self-confidence and skills as a speaker, John was often frustrated by his inability to "get through" to audiences.

This frustration finally came to a head in an especially difficult session with university students, to whom John was explaining what it was that Indians wanted; in brief, the group turned painfully silent after John detailed the particularly complex legislative and administrative amendments that were required in order to permit Cree language programs in schools. In the days following this talk John told his friends that he was finished with speaking to groups that, as he put it, "expect me to tell them what Indians want, but don't even know how their own government works."

Eventually, he was once again compelled by the considerations that had moved him in the first place and by his own obliging nature to meet those groups that invited him to their meetings. Now, however, his presentations took a different tack: he began by telling his listeners that since he only had a grade-three education he could only speak about things that had happened to him, things that he knew about.

On several occasions after this I heard John start his talks with a story about one or another incident that had occurred in his life. I listened to his stories, was touched by them with each telling and noticed that others, hearing them for the first time, were usually similarly moved. Sadly, I had not the wit to record these stories; nor, I discover, did anyone else. I have found, however, that my recollections of John's stories, presented below, tally reasonably well with those held by his family and other friends.

I remember a winter day like this when I was a boy. It was late in the afternoon and snowing lightly. I was up on a platform built between some trees back in the bush. I was taking pieces of meat that my father handed up to me and turning them as they froze so that they wouldn't freeze together. I was up on the platform because I was the youngest and the smallest. I must have been only seven or eight.

My father had asked the farming instructor for permission to slaughter one of our steers, but the farming instructor turned him down. He told my father that he would have to keep the animal until the summer, when he would get a better price for it. My father didn't say anything; he just walked away.

Some time later my father, my uncle and I went far back into the bush on a part of the reserve where no one was living, and we slaughtered that steer. My father had been careful to watch that no one saw us leave with the steer. Since it was snowing our tracks were soon covered over. And that is why I was up on the platform that day.

For the rest of the winter my mother would send me out to the bush every now and then to bring back some meat. I would be careful about going out there and coming back so that no one would see me. When I got home my sister would stand at the window to see whether anybody was coming to our place. My mother would use birch wood in the stove to cook the beef so that there wouldn't be much smoke coming out of the chimney. After we were finished eating she would throw all of the bones into the stove. Later I would take the ashes and burnt bones and throw them down an old well shaft so that no one would find them around our place.

In the spring my father told the farming instructor that the steer must have got lost in the bush sometime during the winter.

I want to tell you about how I went to school when I was a boy. When I was about 13 or 14 I was at home on the reserve for the summer. When the fall came and they (the Indian agent and farm instructor) collected the other children to go back to the residential school, I was out fighting fires in the forest reserve across the river. I was old enough to fight fires. Anyway, by the time I got back to the reserve they seemed to have forgotten me, so I stayed at home with my father until Christmas.

After Christmas the Indian agent came to our place and told my father that I would have to go back to school again. I didn't want to go back, and my father said he wouldn't make me go. One of my sisters had died at residential school, and he was still sad about that. But the agent said that I would have to go back because my father had agreed when I first went to residential school that I would stay there until I finished.

In a couple of days the agent came back with an RCMP from Melfort. I was going to try running for the bush, but it was too late. My father was sick, but he took off his moccasins and gave them to me to wear because mine were in pretty rough shape. And the RCMP took me to Melfort to wait at the RCMP barracks for the train to Prince Albert. When the train arrived the policeman handed me over to the train conductor. When we got to Prince Albert another policeman met the train and took me down to the police station because the train to Saskatoon didn't leave until morning. I guess they didn't know what else to do with me, so they told me to sleep in a cell.

The next day I travelled to Saskatoon the same way, and another policeman met me there at the train station. I stayed overnight in the jail in Saskatoon. I was scared. I didn't get much sleep that night because the guy they put in the next cell was really drunk and rough.

The next day I caught the train to Punnichy, but no one was there to meet me at the station. So I had to walk all the way out to the residential school. It was several miles, and it was really cold. No one was up when I got there, so I went down to the kitchen to look for something to eat. I hadn't eaten all day, but everything was locked up there.

And that's how I went to school when I was a boy.

One time after the war when I was farming I went to the farming instructor and asked him for a permit to sell a couple of heifers. He told me that the prices were not good, so I should wait until later. I didn't say anything; I just walked away.

But I decided that I was going to sell those heifers anyway, so one morning another fellow and I got up before dawn and loaded the animals into the back of my truck. We drove off the reserve with the lights off, taking it real slow and quiet. When we were off the reserve I took back roads all the way to Prince Albert. It took about two hours longer to get there that way, but we didn't want to run into anyone we knew on the way.

When we got to Prince Albert the sun had been up for a couple of hours. I drove over towards the stockyards, but stopped the truck a couple of blocks away. I wanted to go into the stockyards first to see whether the coast was clear. And when I got up to the ring, who do you think I saw leaning on the rail, right at the front? It was the Indian agent. I saw him, but he didn't see me.

So I walked back to the truck and told the other fellow that we weren't going to sell any heifers that day. We got into the truck and drove back to the reserve and unloaded the heifers.

Another time after the war I was driving off the reserve one day in the winter when I came to a place where a farmer had run his truck off the road. He was stuck in the snow in the ditch and there was no way that he could get the truck out himself. I stopped and pulled him out. He was really happy. He said, "let's stop in town and I will buy you a beer." I didn't know what I should say, so I just said "O.K."

When we got into Birch Hills we parked our trucks on the side street near the hotel. This wasn't the town that I usually came to, so I thought it might be all right and that maybe no one would recognize me. You see, I could drink if I wanted when I was in the army during the war, but when I came home I was just another Indian. And Indians weren't allowed to drink back then.

When we went into the beer parlour I pulled my cap down over my eyes so that no one could see me, and I picked a table at the back of the room. We sat down, ordered a beer and were just starting to drink when an RCMP came in and looked around. I knew who he was looking for. I guess someone must have seen me come in and told the police. He came over to our table and asked me who I was and where I was from. I told him my name and said I was from Kinistino, but he said, "Oh, no you're not. You're not a halfbreed—you're from the reserve, aren't you?" He took me out to the police car and put me in the back.

A couple of minutes later another RCMP brought a white guy who was drunk out to the car and put him in the back beside me. The drunk told them he was going to throw up, so they let him out. He got out and was sick, and then he tried to make a run for it. When the policemen caught up with him down the alley, he tried to fight them.

After a while, when they still hadn't come back, I decided to run for it myself. I got back into the truck and drove to the reserve as fast as I could. I didn't get to finish my beer that day.

I remind the reader that the above are not verbatim accounts, but narrative summaries of stories that I and others heard John McLeod recount to non-Indian audiences in locales as diverse as the school gymnasium in a buck-toothed prairie town, a convention hall in an expensive urban hotel and around the table in the kitchen of his own home. As such, these summaries lack much of the rich detail that allowed John's listeners to form visual impressions of the places and events he described. Nor do the summaries convey the engaging style of performance and the masterful metacommunication he practised with gestures, facial expressions and laughter to direct listeners' attention to key parts of his stories. In addition, the telling of these stories sometimes prompted an immediate dialogue in which members of the audience asked John to say more about various points raised in his stories. Thus, a thorough analysis of one of John's performances would require recordings of all of these components as well as others.[22]

But enough of the shortcomings of the ethnography. Further consideration of what we do know about the content of John's stories and the manner in which he told them reveals not only his well developed rhetorical sense, but also a sophisticated understanding of the Indian "problem" and of how it could best be addressed and redefined in the company of non-Indians.

John's use of personal narratives in these situations contrasted sharply with the aggressive political oratory that became popular with some Indian spokesmen during the 1970s, especially in their dealings with government officials,[23] and also in appearances before non-Indian audiences which they tried to "shake up." Presentations of this sort commonly feature lengthy, often obscure, claims of treaty and aboriginal rights and of Canada's other obligations to Indians, seasoned according to an individual speaker's tastes with more or less strident and frequent charges of racial prejudice and moral dishonesty on the part of non-Indians in general, or of members of the audience in particular. John was by no means an interactional pacifist, but he was determined to "get through" to non-Indians rather than merely to shock them.

At the same time, his considerable experience of meeting and working with non-Indians left him with few illusions about the kinds of ideas about Indians that whites on the Prairies are familiar with, whether or not they personally subscribe to these. Hence, he also eschewed another type of performance favoured by some Indian speakers, namely proclaiming the beauty and value of traditional Cree culture and ways of life. Although his own involvement in religious ceremonials and knowledge of both traditional and everyday forms of Cree speech equipped him as well as any other leader to speak about these matters, John recognized the latent scepticism and lack of respect that such a claim could readily encounter among some non-Indians.[24]

Instead, John made use of a traditional Cree genre, the personal narrative,[25] albeit in English and with audiences who knew far less about Indians than he knew about whites. The particular stories that he selected to tell them showed a fine appreciation of the various ways that non-Indians tend to think and talk about Indians and to judge them deficient in one sense or another. His stories spoke directly to these concerns, but in a quite unexpected fashion. And, since so few non-Indians (whether in small towns or in university faculties) know much about the history of Indian administration in this country, his listeners were usually staggered to hear, and sometimes almost unwilling to believe, that Indian agents and farming instructors had so completely dominated their Indian charges as recently as the late 1950s by means of sales permits, travel passes[26] and a variety of other socio-control mechanisms commonly associated with the South African regime. Yet, there was John, standing in front of them and matter-of-factly telling them how these things had happened to him. What is more, the Indians presented in John's stories were never simply the helpless and confused victims of an obviously unjust system; they resented and resisted the institutionalized assaults on their personal autonomy whenever and however they could, although they were not always successful in their attempts.

As well as telling stories about events that were "remarkable," "culturally interesting" and, for these audiences, "highly narratable,"[27] John McLeod displayed a style of presentation that almost invariably captured his listeners' attention and prepared them to hear his later statements (often about controversial matters such as the failure of integrated schooling to meet the needs of Indian children) far more openly than would otherwise be the case. As mentioned, several of the techniques John employed were characteristic of traditional Cree narrative presentations: his initial denial of competence ("I have only a grade three education"); the emphasis placed upon his personal involvement in the events he recounted; and the relatively simple form of his accounts, combined with his painstaking concern to describe events accurately, thereby demonstrating his reliability and right to speak about these things.[28] Furthermore, he made excellent use of "negatives" to underline for his audiences what Labov has termed "the defeat of an expectation that something would happen"[29]; for example, "we weren't going to sell any heifers that day" and "I didn't get to finish my beer."

Indeed, it was precisely *his* refusal to draw conclusions from his stories that enabled John to offend his audiences minimally, while he quietly went about dismantling their previous conceptions of the Indian problem.[30] John never said what the point of his stories was; he forced his listeners to discover this for themselves. His efforts were confined to challenging the cognitive basis of their understanding of the Indian problem by establishing *with them* a new set of facts about Indians that are seldom considered, if known, by non-Indians. He then left them to decide the moral of his stories, although his selection of narrative accounts anticipated the values that they would be likely to use in rendering such judgments. The extent to which listeners were willing to play their part in his performances, by recognizing and further pursuing the brunt of his stories through comments, questions or simply nonverbal signs of interest, governed his decisions about how much longer and how patiently he would speak to them.

More often than not, however, John was met with statements of surprise and with questions that could not have been less like those that non-Indians usually ponder in their private speculations about Indians and the Indian "problem." How could government officials deny freedom to someone like John who had voluntarily served his country? Was it true that Indians in Saskatchewan didn't receive the right to vote in federal and provincial elections until 1960? Were Indian children actually taken away from their parents against their will and sent to residential schools? In responding to these and similar questions, John not only told them more than they had ever heard about Indian administration, but he also unobtrusively demonstrated that, contrary to popular Prairie sentiments, all Canadians are not equal because we did not all "start out the same way."

As he warmed to his audiences and proceeded to tell them more about things that had happened to him and to other Indians, his non-Indian listeners would sooner or later have to confess either to him or to themselves, "I didn't know that." When he reckoned that his transition point had been reached and that they were listening to what he had to say rather than expecting him to speak to their conceptions of the Indian questions, then John would turn to some of the contemporary issues that meant much to him, and would offer explanations of what Indians were asking for and why they wished to be treated differently in some respects than other Canadians. And, more often than not, his explanations of fairly complex proposals to achieve goals such as Indian control of Indian education generated serious discussion. It is impossible to say what proportion of his audiences was converted to his way of thinking, but I do know that John was never short of invitations and return invitations to speak.

For those of John's friends who occasionally wondered why he bothered to spend so much effort talking to groups of non-Indians who were not particularly well informed or politically significant, or even sympathetic, it took a bit of reflection to realize that John had done as much for these same friends at one time or another. With his non-Indian friends and colleagues, as in his public performances, John was prepared to discuss frankly matters which, though of increasing importance on the Prairies today, often seem to be too sensitive or complicated to be dealt with openly in interethnic communication. In speaking to non-Indians as he did, John R. McLeod offered them something like the following personal affirmation, although never in so many words:

> I am an Indian, and these are some of the things that being an Indian has entailed for me.
>
> What has happened to me as an Indian will never happen to you.
>
> I am still talking to you.

The public rememberings of John R. McLeod reveal not only an effective tactic for channelling an audience's attention but, indeed, a more general strategy for working to resolve the concerns that brought him and his listeners together in the first place. By attending first to the "facts" or the cognitive basis of non-Indians' understanding of the Indian problem, he forestalled some of the more strident moral judgments, judgments that severely constrain interethnic communication about Indian claims for special status and special legal and administrative arrangements within Canadian society. In offering non-Indians a different way of viewing the problems of Indians, he provided his audience with the means to begin to consider very different solutions than those that in the past have been unilaterally implemented with such sad results by the Canadian government.

Notes

1. J.R. Gusfield, *The Culture of Public Problems: Drinking–Driving and the Symbolic Order* (Chicago: University of Chicago Press, 1981), 5.

2. Ibid.

3. See Gusfield, *The Culture of Public Problems*.

4. Ibid., 9.

5. Noel Dyck, "The Politics of Special Status: Indian Associations and the Administration of Indian Affairs," in *Ethnicity, Power and Politics in Canada*, ed. J. Dahlie and T. Fernando (Toronto: Methuen, 1981), 279–91; S.M. Weaver, *Making Canadian Indian Policy: The Hidden Agenda, 1968–70* (Toronto: University of Toronto Press, 1981).

6. The degree of recognition of these rights registered during the past dozen years both in Canadian and in international law has surprised even lawyers who have long been sympathetic to Indian claims.

7. A minority decision of the Supreme Court, for example, might have signal importance in altering the federal government's stance on aboriginal land rights, and would be reported by the media at the time the decision was handed down. Still, it is unlikely that many of those Canadians who pay any attention to such reports, but who are not working in the field of Indian affairs, would fully appreciate the extent to which this marks a vital turning point in Indian/government relations, let alone understand why and how this has happened. A great many, if not all Indians on the Prairies have a remarkably detailed understanding of these and similar matters.

8. I have heard this tactic summarized as: using television and other media to go over the heads of local "red necks" to appeal directly to friendlier folks in Toronto or Amsterdam.

9. J.R. Ponting and R. Gibbins, *Out of Irrelevance: A Socio-Political Introduction to Indian Affairs in Canada* (Toronto: Butterworths, 1980), 92.

10. Harold Cardinal, *The Unjust Society: The Tragedy of Canadian Indians* (Edmonton: Hurtig, 1969).

11. George Manuel and Michael Posluns, *The Fourth World: An Indian Reality* (Don Mills, Ont.: Collier Macmillan, 1974).

12. A 1976 survey of prairie-Canadian attitudes toward Indians asked specifically about the extent of respondents' contact with Indians: 57 percent reported, "contact with Indians living in their neighbourhood, 55 percent reported contact at work, 40 percent cited a close friend who was an Indian, 24 percent reported contact in clubs or organizations, and 11 percent mentioned Indian relatives. On the average, Prairie respondents reported at least two of the five types of contact, compared to an average of only one for non-Prairie respondents" (R. Gibbins and J.R. Ponting, "Prairie Canadian's Orientations towards Indians," in *One Century Later: Western Canadian Reserve Indians Since Treaty 7*, ed. Ian A.L. Getty and D.B. Smith (Vancouver: University of British Columbia, 1978), 88). These results may reflect a higher proportion of Indians to non-Indians in western Canada, compared to the rest of the

country. The authors also feel that the survey represented a substantial "over-reporting" of contact, especially with respect to the number of respondents who claimed to have Indians as close friends or as neighbours.

13. N.W. Braroe, *Indian and White: Self-Image and Interaction in a Canadian Plains Community* (Stanford: Stanford University Press, 1975).

14. W.P. Kinsella, *Dance Me Outside* (Toronto: Oberon Press, 1977); *Scars* (Toronto: Oberon Press, 1978); and *Born Indian* (Toronto: Oberon Press, 1981).

15. Ponting and Gibbins, *Out of Irrelevance*, 87.

16. Cf. R.H. Pearce, *The Savages of America: A Study of the Indian and the Idea of Civilization*, rev. ed. (Baltimore: Johns Hopkins Press, 1965).

17. In contrast to other regions of Canada, such as the Lower Mainland of British Columbia or Southern Ontario, the Prairie region possesses a high degree of demographic stability and social and cultural conformity. The rapid settlement of the Prairies in the early 1900s brought thousands of immigrants from all parts of North America, Britain and Europe, but there has been relatively little in-migration into the region since the 1920s. Instead, a consistent pattern of out-migration, especially of the better educated, has been established during the past half-century.

18. Hutterites may be one exception to this general statement. For more on this theme, see D.E. Smith, "Political Culture in the West," in *Eastern and Western Perspectives: Papers from the Joint Atlantic Canada/Western Canada Studies Conference*, ed. D.J. Bercuson and P.A. Buckner (Toronto: University of Toronto Press, 1981), 169–82.

19. Interestingly, the phrase used to identify esteemed barroom fighters on the Prairies is, "a man who can take care of himself" (N. Dyck, "Booze, Barrooms and Scrapping: Masculinity and Violence in a Western Canadian Town," *Canadian Journal of Anthropology* 1, no. 2 (1980): 191–98). For more on the Prairie ethos of independence, see J.W. Bennett, *Northern Plainsmen* (Chicago: Aldine, 1969).

20. Gibbins and Ponting, "Prairie Canadians' Orientations towards Indians," 85.

21. H. Cardinal, *The Rebirth of Canada's Indians* (Edmonton: Hurtig, 1977), 84.

22. R. Bauman, "Verbal Art as Performance," *American Anthropologist* 77 (1975): 298–300; J.A. Robinson, "Personal Narratives Reconsidered," *Journal of American Folklore* 94 (1981): 58–59.

23. N. Dyck, "Representation and Leadership of a Provincial Indian Association," in *The Politics of Indianness: Case Studies of Native Ethnopolitics in Canada*, ed. A. Tanner (St. John's: Institute of Social and Economic Research, Memorial University, 1983).

24. As I. Rodger has put it in a rather different context, "rhetoric is not merely in the gift of the speaker. For him to declare what he regards as a known truth is not enough; he must know enough about his audience to avoid saying too much and thus earning the response that his rhetoric is false" (I. Rodger, "Rhetoric and Ritual Politics: The Durham Miners' Gala" in *Politically Speaking: Cross-Cultural Studies of Rhetoric*, ed. R. Paine (St. John's: Institute of Social and Economic Research, Memorial University; and Philadelphia: ISHI, 1981), 62).

25. R. Darnell, "Correlates of Cree Narrative Performance," in *Explorations in the Ethnography of Speaking*, ed. R. Bauman and J. Sherzer (Cambridge and New York: Cambridge University Press, 1974), 315–16; R.J. Preston, *Cree Narrative: Expressing the Personal Meanings of Events*, Canadian Ethnology Service Paper no. 30, Mercury Series (Ottawa: National Museums of Canada).

26. As late as the Second World War, Indians were not allowed to travel off the reserve on the Prairies without a pass signed by the Indian agent or farming instructor, specifying the destination, purpose and time of their travel.

27. Cf. L. Polanyi, "So What's the Point?" *Semiotica* 25, no. 3/4 (1979): 211; Robinson "Personal Narratives," 59–60.

28. R.J. Preston, in *Cree Narrative*, notes that members of small-scale societies such as the Cree are fundamentally concerned with honesty in most interpersonal relations and that this carries over into the telling of personal narratives where speakers are expected to demonstrate the accuracy and reliability of their accounts. See also Darnell, "Correlates of Cree Narrative Performance."

29. W. Labov, *Language in the Inner City: Studies in the Black English Vernacular* (Philadelphia: University of Pennsylvania Press, 1972), 380–81.

30. In doing this, he honoured Paine's dictum that, "we can expect a political speaker to 'phrase' himself in a way that minimally offends his 'target' audience. . . . We shall see that one way of doing this is for the speaker to leave either his premise(s) or conclusion unstated" (R. Paine, "When Saying is Doing," in *Politically Speaking*, ed. R. Paine, 15).

THE FOURTH WORLD†

GEORGE MANUEL and MICHAEL POSLUNS

The Fourth World has always been here in North America. Since the beginning of European domination its branches, one by one, have been denied the light of day. Its fruit has been withered and stunted. Yet the tree did not die. Our victory begins with the knowledge that we have survived.

The celebration of the Fourth World, its real test of strength, and its capacity to endure, lies more with our grandchildren than with our ancestors. It is they who must cultivate the tree as a whole and honour the unique qualities of each root and branch.

Our grandfathers faced and endured the physical violence of wars, famine, and disease. They survived. We endured the social violence of legal disabilities and administrative oppression. We survived. Now there is the possibility that our grandchildren may yet face the danger of material success. They shall survive. Our past history and our faith in the future are united. We are neither the beginning nor the end.

The hope that we who could not be starved into submission may yet be assimilated by drowning in a sea of plenty ignores not only our own history but the present condition of the very peoples whose leaders harbour such hopes. Today in North America so many young people, whose own ancestors fled the plagues, famines, and wars of other continents, are trying to forsake the world they are in and find a world that will fulfil the promise of peace that they inherited from their grandfathers. Those who believe our values and culture have been preserved only through their own oppression should stop and reconsider. Do they think that if they stop the oppression we will stop being our parents' children?

Every Englishman knowledgeable of his own history knows that his countrymen have made their constitution grow and adapt to changing needs while the institutions that were the parts of their body politic, and

† From *The Fourth World: An Indian Reality* (Don Mills, Ont.: Collier Macmillan, 1974), 214–22.

the values that were their lifeblood and common bonds, endured. Such ancient institutions as the monarchy and Parliament were given major surgery rather than be allowed to die as happened elsewhere. Every schoolboy in the English-speaking world is taught not only to observe this pattern of growth and change but to take such pride in it that if he is not an Englishman by birth he becomes one by adoption.

At first the schoolboy may be disturbed to learn that neither the constitution of Great Britain nor of Canada has ever been codified, written down in a single document, from which all the majestic powers of his nation flow. He finds, for instance, that there is nothing in the British North America Act to describe, or even require that there be, an office of the prime minister. He finds that the provisions describing the Canadian Parliament begin by saying, "Canada shall have a Parliament similar in form to that of Great Britain." Yet there is no single British charter to say just what that will be.

If he continues his studies, he finds that independence has brought some important differences in form. "Similar in form" is only a point of departure from which the new generation could grow and take its strength in new soil, a different climate, and a new population. If the schoolboy were asked to describe his country's manner of government to someone who had never heard of Canada before meeting him, "similar in form to that of Great Britain" would not be a very helpful way to begin. He knows that without being told.

If he has had a good teacher he has been helped to discover that the peculiar strength of his country's constitution is that it has not been frozen onto a single handy paper to which he might point and say, "This is us." He comes to believe that if it were set down so easily and simply it would no longer be capable of that growth and change that has kept it strong and allowed it to endure nine hundred years and more. Constitutions that are alive and well are a collection of customs and practices that are recorded in whatever way seems suitable at the time that the practice was found good to the people who lived under it. Yet however loosely recorded, however many sources must be consulted to put together all the pieces, that constitution does stand as a valid symbol of the hopes and aspirations, customs and beliefs, traditions and taboos of the people who live under it at the present moment. It is more than a symbol; it is the very substance of the nation and its culture.

Why then should it be so hard to understand the root and branch of the Indian nations? Our claim to a special place in the past and future history of North America? Our belief that if the Canadian mosaic arises sensibly out of the history and culture of Canada, the case for Indian nationhood arises at least as clearly out of the history and culture that the Indian nations of North America have shared?

Our hopes for the Fourth World are at least as credible as the belief in a Canadian nation with nearly autonomous provinces, a diversity of languages and cultures, and a mutual respect for one another's view of the world. Indian institutions are as capable of growth and adaptation as any others. When anthropologists, government officials, and churchmen have argued that our ways have been lost to us, they are fulfilling one of their own tribal rituals—wish fulfilment. More often, bureaucrats have argued that it is simply impractical to work within an Indian tradition in a modern technological society.

It is also impractical for civil servants to work within a framework of parliamentary government with a House of Commons, a Senate, their time-consuming and tiring questions and committees, a cabinet who might object to the most minor administrative decision, a Treasury Board that watches every penny while developing only an intuitive view of where the dollars have gone. Those institutions have endured because they have been found to be useful tools with which to bend and shape and mould the technological and administrative machinery to serve the values and meet the needs of Canadian society. After all, the most common public criticism of Parliament outside of Ottawa, is not that it is impractical but that it fails to be an effective voice of the people.

The criticism that Indian people make is that even if the federal and provincial parliaments do serve the wishes of the great majority of Canadian people they can never fully serve the needs of our people. We do not doubt that these institutions might serve the purposes for which they were intended. We are saying that our own needs can be fully served only through the development of our own institutions.

There will be no significant change in the condition of unilateral dependence that has characterized our history through the past century and more until Indian peoples are allowed to develop our own forms of responsible government. The route to be followed to the Fourth World will be as diverse and varied as are the Indian tribes.

The Fourth World is not, after all, a final solution. It is not even a destination. It is the right to travel freely, not only on our road but in our own vehicles. Unilateral dependence can never be ended by a forced integration. Real integration can only be achieved through a voluntary partnership, and a partnership cannot be based on a tenant–landlord relationship. The way to end the condition of unilateral dependence and begin the long march to the Fourth World is through home rule.

It was the demand for home rule and responsible government in Upper and Lower Canada that gave rise to an enduring partnership among the provinces of Canada and between the dominion and her mother country. When Quebec and Canada were united as one province for twenty-five years they discovered that responsible government without home rule is meaningless. Confederation guaranteed local autonomy, at least for the two major powers participating. The smaller and poorer Maritime provinces demanded grants that would provide them with the economic power to participate in Confederation and allow a financial base on which to enjoy their local autonomy. Prince Edward Island and New-foundland stayed out of Confederation until they achieved terms they considered favourable. The New Brunswick government, which agreed to terms its people found unfavourable, was defeated and a more respon-sible and representative government took its place. If the western prov-inces and British Columbia appear to have accepted whatever they could get at the different times they entered Confederation, they have never stopped pressing their demands since they have been allowed to sit at the negotiating table.

The demand of Indian people that we be allowed to sit at the table where our lives are being negotiated, where our resources are being carved up like a pie, is not really very different from the demand made by every non-Indian group in Canada who share both a common history and a common territory. The whole history of Canada has largely been one long negotiation about the distribution of economic and political power.

. . .

The way to end the custodian–child relationship for Indian people is not to abolish our status as Indians, but to allow us to take our place at the table with all the rest of the adults. Indian status has far too often been described as a special status by those who wanted to create an argument to get rid of it. Indian status is neither more nor less *special* than those special provisions that have been made for different provinces, at Confederation and since, in order to make it possible for them to work within the partnership of Canada. These provisions were also the recognition of the unique needs of different peoples and groups. The provisions have been preserved because the differences have been found real. Yet everyone insists that they do not confer *special status* because they only *create conditions for the different groups to become equal partners*.

Why should there be a different kind of equality for us as Indian people than for the other groups of Canadians who share both a common history and a common territory that distinguish them from other Cana-dians? Of course, it is true that not all Indian people share a common territory in the way that a province occupies a single territory. Yet I can only imagine that our relationship with this land and with one another is far deeper and more complex than the relationship between the people of any province and their land, their institutions, or one another.

Nor can the Indian peoples be brushed off with the multicultural broom to join the diverse ethnic groups that compose the third element of Canada, that is, those who are neither French nor English. When the Englishman speaks of "the Mother Country," the French Canadian can still reply "Maître Chez Nous," the Jew can build his freedom in North America with the faith that if it fails there is yet another Promised Land, and the Eastern European who becomes an ardent Canadian nationalist still believes himself to be in exile from his native land. It seems as if every element in the Canadian mosaic is carved from a split personality. This itself is enough to distinguish the Indian peoples from the multicultural society.

When we say, "The Earth is Our Mother," we are saying that Canada is our Promised Land. Where other people look "homeward" for the medicines to heal themselves, this is our home. If the exiled condition in which Eastern Europeans believe themselves can only be ended with a change in the relationship between their mother country and the neighbouring great powers, our exile can be ended only with a change in our relationship with Canada. We know that many of those people who have come to our shores to find freedom will not go home when their country is liberated. On that day their freedom will be the freedom to choose. This is the freedom of the Fourth World. We ask no more for ourselves than the many immigrant groups ask for themselves. We do expect the same freedom and autonomy in our mother country as they demand in theirs, and ours. This is equality.

Clearly, we are neither an ethnic group nor a province of Canada. Although there are elements in both models that are useful, neither one will really work very well. The imposition of models on those who did not have a hand in the design has been the problem throughout our history. Clearly, the right to design our own model is the first step toward the Fourth World. Home rule begins with the opportunity to build that model with all the ingredients that the tides of history have washed up on our shores.

What is useful in the provincial model is that it teaches us that constitutional provisions and agreements have commonly been used to guarantee local autonomy, the customs, traditions, and values of those people who have been able to make their political presence felt. The basic concept of making special provisions for special needs, far from being a strange anomaly as some contemporary political leaders have led us to believe, has been an accepted way of making room at the table for those whom the present partners were prepared to welcome.

The "ethnic model" teaches us that a Confederation founded on the belief in "two founding races" can broaden its perspective when it appears to be politically expedient to do so. That is a source of enormous hope and confidence. If the Confederation can endure past the racial myths that were the midwives at its birth, there can be no finer proof that institutions survive through the will of men as much as through their purely economic virtues.

If there is no single model on which to build either a route or a vehicle into the Fourth World there is both a common philosophy and a common fuel.

The philosophy has been born from the desire to resolve two dilemmas that have been imposed through the condition of unilateral dependence.

We know that no Canadian government will ever deal fairly with the Indian peoples until we can negotiate from a position of strength. We also know that the kind of integration based on mutal respect, and acceptance of each other's values *as valid for the other*, will never happen until Indian people achieve the same standard of living as that enjoyed by city-dwelling, middle-class, white Canadians. The political and social dilemmas meet every time the Canadian taxpayers are told of the vast sums spent by their Department of Indian Affairs. Led to believe that the spending of this money is somehow directed for our benefit, the taxpayer resents the expenditure and wonders how people can be so foolish that they fail to benefit when so many hundreds of millions of dollars are spent on their behalf.

The energy to move away from this situation comes from the realization that the way to remain Indian is to dispel the myths that have given rise to these false dilemmas in the first place. Most Indian people not only want to remain Indian but do not believe that there is any conflict between wanting to live decently, even comfortably, and wanting to maintain and develop our own way of life as Indian people. Remaining Indian does not mean wearing a breech-cloth or a buckskin jacket, any more than remaining English means wearing pantaloons, a sword, and a funny hat. Yet on ceremonial occasions all people dress in the manner of their forefathers to remind themselves where they came from and who they are.

"I don't need to wear an Indian costume. I am an Indian," was Buffy Ste. Marie's reply when someone at a concert asked her why she did not wear traditional clothing.

Remaining Indian means that Indian people gain control of the economic and social development of our own communities, within a framework of legal and constitutional guarantees for our land and our institutions. Without those guarantees, our people and our institutions remain in a defensive position, and our only weapon is passive resistance. With the constitutional and material support to carry on that development, there would be no dilemma. The racial myths that were created to justify the seizure of our land base will only be fully dispelled when we have received the legal recognition of our effective title to the lands that remain to us, and sufficient grants to compensate for what is lost that we can afford to develop what does remain. Only then will we be able to demonstrate that there is no conflict between wanting to live comfortably and wanting to develop within our own traditional framework.

The desire for legal recognition of our aboriginal and treaty rights has taken on a religious perspective. But, as in most natural or traditional religions, the spiritual has not been separated from the material world.

Recognition of our aboriginal rights can and must be the mainspring of our future economic and social independence. It is as much in the long-term interest of the non-Indian peoples of North America as in our own interest that we be allowed our birthright, rather than that governments and churches perpetuate the Christian conspiracy that renders us the objects of charity while others enjoy the wealth of our land.

Immigrants to North America have long been considered on the basis of their skills and their usefulness to the economic development of the country. Unfortunately for the gross national product, we did not apply at the Immigration Office. The skills that those immigrants brought with them were at least the portable portion of their birthright. We, the first people of the land, must recover our birthright so that we can choose whether to become part of the North American economy or to develop within our own value system.

FURTHER READING

Bibliographies and Historiographical Essays

The major monographs dealing with native history in Canada are identified in the footnotes to the introduction. Students interested in continuing their investigations should consult the bibliographies and historiographical essays listed below. Shepard Krech III's excellent bibliography is a good starting point for student research.

Abler, Thomas Struthers, Sally M. Weaver, et al. *A Canadian Indian Bibliography, 1960–1970*. Toronto: University of Toronto Press, 1974.

Annis, R.C., ed. *Abstracts in Native Studies*. Brandon: Abstracts of Native Studies Press, 1984.

Fisher, Robin, "Historical Writing on Native People in Canada." *History and Social Science Teacher* 17 (Winter 1982): 65-72.

Grumet, Robert Steven. *Native Americans of the Northwest Coast: A Critical Bibliography*. Bloomington: Indiana University Press, 1979.

Helm, June. *The Indians of the Subarctic: A Critical Bibliography*. Bloomington: Indiana University Press, 1976.

Krech, Shepard III. *Native Canadian Anthropology and History: A Selected Bibliography*. Winnipeg: Rupert's Land Research Centre, 1986.

McGee, Harold Franklin. "No Longer Neglected: A Decade of Writing Concerning the Native Peoples of the Maritimes." *Acadiensis* 10 (Autumn 1980): 135-42.

Peterson, Jacqueline, with John Anfinson. "The Indian and the Fur Trade: A Review of the Recent Literature." *Manitoba History* No. 10 (Autumn 1985): 10-18.

Smith, Dwight, ed. *Indians of the United States and Canada: A Bibliography*. Santa Barbara: American Bibliographical Center, 1974.

Surtees, Robert J. *Canadian Indian Policy: A Critical Bibliography*. Bloomington: Indiana University Press, 1982.

Swagerty, W.R., ed. *Scholars and the Indian Experience: Critical Reviews of Recent Writing in the Social Sciences*. Bloomington: Indiana University Press, 1984.

Tooker, Elisabeth. *The Indians of the Northeast: A Critical Bibliography*. Bloomington: Indiana University Press, 1978.

Van Kirk, Sylvia. "Fur Trade Social History: Some Recent Trends." In *Old Trails and New Directions: Papers of the Third North American Fur Trade Conference*, edited by Carol M. Judd and Arthur J. Ray, 160-73. Toronto: University of Toronto Press, 1980.

Walker, James W. St. G. "The Indian in Canadian Historical Writing." Canadian Historical Association, *Historical Papers* (1971): 21-51.

——————. "The Indian in Canadian Historical Writing, 1972–1982." In *As Long as the Sun Shines and Water Flows: A Reader in Canadian Native Studies*, edited by Ian A.L. Getty and Antoine S. Lussier, 340-57. Vancouver: University of British Columbia Press.

Journals

Below is a list of the journals devoted to native studies. Other national journals, such as the *Canadian Historical Review* and *Canadian Ethnic Studies* and regional journals, such as *Acadiensis, Ontario History*, and *BC Studies*, frequently contain articles on Indian history.

Arctic Anthropology
Canadian Journal of Anthropology
Canadian Journal of Native Studies
Ethnohistory
Études/Inuit/Studies
Native Studies Review
Recherches Amérindiennes au Québec

Collections of Essays

Much useful material on native history, which is all too often overlooked, is available in published collections of essays and periodicals, the most important of which are identified here.

Axtell, James, ed. *The European and the Indian: Essays in the Ethnohistory of Colonial North America*. New York: Oxford University Press, 1981.

Barman, Jean, Yvonne Hébert, and Don McCaskill, eds. *Indian Education in Canada*. Vol. 1, *The Legacy*. Vancouver: University of British Columbia Press, 1986.

——————. *Indian Education in Canada*. Vol. 2, *The Challenge*. Vancouver: University of British Columbia Press, 1987.

Barron, F. Laurie, and James B. Waldram, eds. *1885 and After: Native Society in Transition*. Regina: Canadian Plains Research Center, 1986.

Boldt, Menno, and J. Anthony Long, eds. *The Quest for Justice: Aboriginal Peoples and Aboriginal Rights*. Toronto: University of Toronto Press, 1985.

Bolus, Malvina, ed. *People and Pelts: Selected Papers of the Second North American Fur Trade Conference*. Winnipeg: Peguis Publishers, 1972.

Buckley, Thomas, ed. *Rendezvous: Selected Papers of the Fourth North American Fur Trade Conference, 1981*. St. Paul: Minnesota Historical Society, 1984.

Damas, David, ed. *Handbook of North American Indians*. Vol. 5, *Arctic*. Washington: Smithsonian Institution, 1984.

Fitzhugh, William W., ed. *Cultures in Contact: The European Impact on Native Cultural Institutions in Eastern North America, A.D. 100–1800*. Washington: Smithsonian Institution, 1985.

Getty, Ian A.L., and Antoine S. Lussier, eds. *As Long as the Sun Shines and the Water Flows: A Reader in Canadian Native Studies*. Vancouver: University of British Columbia Press, 1983.

Getty, Ian A.L., and Donald B. Smith, eds. *One Century Later: Western Canadian Reserve Indians Since Treaty 7*. Vancouver: University of British Columbia Press, 1978.

Helm, June, ed. *Handbook of North American Indians*. Vol. 6, *Subarctic*. Washington: Smithsonian Institution, 1981.

Judd, Carol M., and Arthur J. Ray, eds. *Old Trails and New Directions: Papers of the Third North American Fur Trade Conference*. Toronto: University of Toronto Press, 1980.

Krech, Shepard III, ed. *Indians, Animals, and the Fur Trade: A Critique of Keepers of the Game*. Athens: University of Georgia Press, 1981.

—————— . *The Subarctic Fur Trade: Native Social and Economic Adaptations*. Vancouver: University of British Columbia Press, 1984.

Lussier, Antoine S., and D. Bruce Sealey, eds. *The Other Natives: The-les Metis 1870–1885*. 3 vols. Winnipeg: Manitoba Metis Federation Press, 1978–1980.

McGee, Harold Franklin, ed. *The Native Peoples of Atlantic Canada: A History of Ethnic Interaction*. Toronto: McClelland and Stewart, 1974.

Martin, Calvin, ed. *The American Indian and the Problem of History*. New York: Oxford University Press, 1987.

Morrison, R. Bruce, and C. Roderick Wilson. *Native Peoples: The Canadian Experience*. Toronto: McClelland and Stewart, 1986.

Morse, Bradford W., ed. *Aboriginal Peoples and the Law: Indian, Metis and Inuit Rights in Canada*. Ottawa: Carleton University Press, 1985.

Muise, D.A., ed. *Approaches to Native History in Canada: Papers of a Conference Held at the National Museum of Man, October, 1975*. Ottawa: National Museum of Man, 1977.

Peterson, Jacqueline, and Jennifer S.H. Brown, eds. *The New Peoples: Being and Becoming Métis in North America*. Winnipeg: University of Manitoba Press, 1985.

Ponting, J. Rick, ed. *Arduous Journey: Canadian Indians and Decolonization*. Toronto: McClelland and Stewart, 1986.

Smith, Derek G., ed. *Canadian Indians and the Law: Selected Documents, 1663–1972*. Toronto: McClelland and Stewart, 1975.

Trigger, Bruce G., ed. *Handbook of North American Indians*. Vol. 15, *Northeast*. Washington: Smithsonian Institution, 1978.

Bruce G. Trigger, "The Historians' Indian: Native Americans in Canadian Historical Writing from Charlevoix to the Present," *Canadian Historical Review* 67, no. 3 (September 1986): 315–42; L.F.S. Upton, "The Extermination of the Beothucks of Newfoundland," *Canadian Historical Review* 58, no. 2 (June 1977): 133–53; Cornelius J. Jaenen, "Amerindian Views of French Culture in the Seventeenth Century," *Canadian Historical Review* 55, no. 3 (September 1974): 261–91; John L. Tobias, "Canada's Subjugation of the Plains Cree, 1879–1885," *Canadian Historical Review* 64, no. 4 (December 1983): 519–48. © University of Toronto Press. Reprinted by permission of the University of Toronto Press.

Calvin Martin, "The European Impact on the Culture of a Northeastern Algonquian Tribe: An Ecological Interpretation," *William and Mary Quarterly*, 3d ser., 31 (1974): 3–36. Reprinted by permission of the author.

Bruce G. Trigger, "The Road to Affluence: A Reassessment of Early Huron Responses to European Contact," in *Affluence and Cultural Survival: 1981 Proceedings of the American Ethnological Society*, ed. Richard F. Salisbury and Elisabeth Tooker, 12–25. Reprinted by permission of the American Anthropological Association from *1981 Proceedings of the American Ethnological Society*, 1984. Not for further reproduction.

Arthur J. Ray, "Indians as Consumers in the Eighteenth Century," in *Old Trails and New Directions: Papers of the Third North American Fur Trade Conference*, ed. Carol M. Judd and Arthur J. Ray (Toronto, 1980), 255–71. © University of Toronto Press, 1980. Reprinted by permission of University of Toronto Press.

Sylvia Van Kirk, " 'Women in Between': Indian Women in Fur Trade Society in Western Canada," Canadian Historical Association, *Historical Papers* (1977): 31–46. Reprinted by permission of the author and the Canadian Historical Association.

Robin Fisher, "The Image of the Indian," *Contact and Conflict: Indian–European Relations in British Columbia, 1774–1890* (Vancouver: University of British Columbia Press, 1977), 73–94. Reprinted by permission of the publisher.

Clarence R. Bolt, "The Conversion of the Port Simpson Tsimshian: Indian Control or Missionary Manipulation?" *BC Studies* no. 57 (Spring 1983): 38–56. Reprinted by permission of the journal.

Kenneth Coates, "Best Left as Indians: The Federal Government and the Indians of the Yukon, 1894–1950," *Canadian Journal of Native Studies* 4, no. 2 (1984): 179–204. Reprinted by permission of the journal.

Hugh Brody, "Maps of Dreams," *Maps and Dreams: Indians and the British Columbia Frontier* (Vancouver: Douglas and McIntyre, 1981), 34–48. Reprinted by permission of the publisher.

Noel Dyck, "Negotiating the Indian 'Problem,' " *Culture* 6, no. 1 (1986): 31–41. Reprinted by permission of the journal.

George Manuel and Michael Posluns, "The Fourth World," *The Fourth World: An Indian Reality* (Don Mills, Ont.: Collier Macmillan, 1974), 214–22. Reprinted by permission of the authors.

1 2 3 4 5   0-7730-4767-0   92 91 90 89 88